Peasant Consciousness and Guerrilla War in Zimbabwe

Peasant Consciousness and Guerrilla War in Zimbabwe

A comparative study

Terence Ranger

Professor of Modern History
University of Manchester

JAMES CURREY

LONDON

James Currey Ltd
54b Thornhill Square, Islington, London N1 1BE

First published 1985 in Great Britain by James Currey Ltd
and in the United States of America
by the University of California Press

British Library Cataloguing in Publication Data
Ranger, T.O.
Peasant consciousness and guerrilla war in
Zimbabwe: a comparative study
1. Peasantry–Zimbabwe–Political activity–
History   2. Revolutionists–Zimbabwe–History
I. Title
322.4′2′09689   HD1339.Z5

ISBN 0–85255–000–6 Cased
ISBN 0–85255–001–4 Pbk

Typeset in 10/11 pt Times by Inforum Ltd, Portsmouth
Printed in Great Britain

CONTENTS

PREFACE

In March 1983 I gave eight lectures in the University of Cambridge at the invitation of the Smuts Trustees who wished in this way to inaugurate an annual Smuts Commonwealth Lecture series. The text of this book, though considerably enlarged, retains the same argumentative sequence as the text of my eight Cambridge lectures. The comparative dimension derives from the terms of the Trustees' invitation. They asked me to draw upon the recent experience of Zimbabwe in order to predict what might happen in South Africa. Prudently I declined this proposal. But I thought that I had better suggest another comparative approach, though this time a comparison of what had already happened rather than of what might happen in the future. I had noticed from 1976 onwards an increasing number of articles which compared events and prospects in Zimbabwe with what had taken place in Kenya and Mozambique. It seemed to me that it would be interesting to set my own recent research on Zimbabwe into this kind of context; to ask how far Zimbabwean historiography could be illuminated by the insights of Kenyan and Mozambican historiography; and to ask how far happenings in Zimbabwe could be regarded as analogous to those in the other two countries.

What I chose to compare, however, derived from another influence. In September 1982 I attended a conference on the present and future of Zimbabwean historiography organized by the History Department at the University of Zimbabwe. This stimulated me to think about what kind of history was now most appropriate to Zimbabwe. Subsequently I wrote a review of the new history school books which had been published in Zimbabwe during 1982. It seemed to me that though political leaders and others called for a 'people's history' the new books did not really deliver it. Admirable as they were as a corrective to the old colonial history, they focused mostly on the states and aristocratic achievements of the past and on the continuities of the nationalist struggle in the twentieth century. The experience of workers and peasants was largely missing. It struck me that it would be useful to compare the modern history of Zimbabwe, Mozambique and Kenya at one level of 'people's history', namely at the level of the contrasting experience of the African peasantries of the three countries.[1]

After I had given the lectures Professor Ian Phimister sent me a copy of his own review of the Zimbabwean school books. In it he defined the elements of a Zimbabwean 'people's history' and in that part of his review which concerned the rural areas he provided me with a retrospective text for what I have tried to do in this book:

An historical account of the so-called reserves would not only point to the relationship between their unfavourable situation (poor soils, remoteness from markets, etc.) and the settler economy's need for labour, as well as the protection thereby afforded white farmers from peasant competition. It would also trace the degrees to which different categories and classes of people maintained economic or social and cultural autonomy in the face of capital's onslaught, and to what extent and in what circumstances this changed over time. Peasant consciousness and resistance to attempts by the settler state to direct their day-to-day existence through the enforcement of 'good farming practices', controlled agricultural prices and cattle culling are constant and vital themes informing Zimbabwe's history. It is a perspective, moreover, which fits neatly with the recent observation that:

'the story of the nationalist struggle in Zimbabwe is not just the tale of the African National Congress and the National Democratic Party, of the ZAPU-ZANU split, the detention and exile of leaders, the launching of guerrilla struggle, the African National Council of Bishop Muzorewa and then the United ANC, of detente in Lusaka, at the Victoria Falls Bridge, Geneva and Lancaster House. It was also a history of civil disobedience by peasants and the landless in the 1950s, of widespread opposition to the British proposals before the Pearce Commission, of peasants in the TTLs [Tribal Trust Lands] supporting the guerrillas, and of people's councils in the no-go areas. There was a popular, often spontaneous element to the struggle and in many instances the people took the organised leadership by surprise.[2]

In attempting to touch upon this range of topics within a single book I have often drawn upon my own field and archival work on one Zimbabwean rural district in particular – Makoni District, which lies some two-thirds of the way between Harare and Mutare. I worked on the history of Makoni for six months between September 1980 and April 1981 and subsequently made two briefer visits, later in 1981 and in 1982. Makoni District is no more 'typical' of the experience of the Zimbabwean peasantry than any other district; so far as peasant success goes it is probably quite atypical for reasons which will emerge in this book. Readers should be warned that this undoubtedly affects my findings on peasant consciousness and peasant activism as a whole; when other district studies have been carried out we shall have a much richer, and no doubt more complex and contradictory, picture. Still, 'consciousness' above all other topics requires some detailed illustration and I have drawn mainly on the experience of Makoni District to provide it. In doing so I hope I have not exhausted the interest of Makoni's history; readers who become intrigued by it in this book may like to know that I hope to publish a monograph on the twentieth-century history of Makoni District by itself.

I have incurred many debts of gratitude in researching and writing. The Social Science Research Council, the University of Manchester and Heinemann Educational Books made grants towards my research in Makoni; the University of Zimbabwe provided me with accommodation in Harare and the community of St Francis African Church gave me abundant hospitality and assistance in Makoni. I made much use in this book, as elsewhere, of the interviews carried out by my two Zimbabwean research assistants, Peter Moda Chakanyuka and Sister Emilia Chiteka. Maurice Nyagumbo and Eddison Zvogbo gave me letters of introduction which opened almost all doors in Makoni. Guy Clutton-Brock has allowed me to draw on his abundant corespondence files. To John Lonsdale I owe a great deal of intellectual stimulation over the years and in particular thanks for his hospitality during the period of the lectures in Cambridge. My undergraduate and graduate students in Manchester, who have had to suffer all too frequent reference to what they ironically call 'the world-famous Makoni District', have contributed a good deal to my thinking by means of their scepticism and occasional enthusiasm. Above all, the people of Makoni, who gave me so generous a welcome so soon after a devastating war, have inspired me to write this book as an inadequate testimony to them and to the Zimbabwean peasantry as a whole. It goes without saying that neither they nor any of the other people I have thanked can be blamed for its inadequancies.

Terence Ranger
Manchester

NOTES
1 Terence Ranger, 'Revolutions in the wheel of Zimbabwean history', *Moto Magazine*, vol. 1, no. 8 (December 1982).
2 Ian Phimister, 'Pasi ne class struggle? The new history for schools in Zimbabwe', *History in Africa* (forthcoming). In the passage cited here Phimister quotes from Colin Stoneman (ed.) *Zimbabwe's Inheritance* (London: 1981)

SELECT
CHRONOLOGY

Note. This book does not set out to be a narrative history of colonial and nationalist politics from the centre. It is, rather, an account of consciousness at the grass-roots so that national events and national associations enter the book as they entered the rural areas — intermittently and from outside. This chronological table is designed to assist the reader who is unfamiliar with Zimbabwe's public history to place grass-roots responses within the framework of national political and administrative developments.

1917 Report of the Reserves Commission, the recommendations of which after amendment and ratification defined the boundaries of the areas of African communal tenure.

1918 Emergence of the movement to restore the Ndebele monarchy and set up a 'national home', under the leadership of Lobengula's son, Nyamanda.

1920 Emergence of Rhodesia Native Association (RNA) and other elite African associations.

1923 Establishment of 'Responsible Government' and transfer of power from the British South Africa Company to settler parliamentary government.

1924 Beginnings of the scheme for 'improvement' of African farming by means of trained Agricultural Demonstrators.

1926 Appointment of E. D. Alvord as 'Agriculturalist for the Instruction of Natives'. Alvord subsequently develops the policy of 'centralisation' to distinguish arable from grazing land in the Reserves.

1927 Establishment of the Industrial and Commercial Workers Union (ICU) in Southern Rhodesia. The ICU flourished until the mid 1930s with S. Masoja Ndhlovu as the main leader in Bulawayo and Charles Mzingeli as the main leader in Salisbury.

1929 Emergence of the Matabele Home Society (MHS) to represent the interests of the Ndebele town-dweller and to take up the campaign for the restoration of the monarchy and the establishment of a 'national home'.

1930 Enactment of the Land Apportionment Act, which divided the territory into the Reserves, land exclusively for white occupation on which Africans could live only as employees, and a new category of Native Purchase Areas where African yeoman farmers could gain limited ownership of farms. The Act was not implemented on a large scale during the 1930s.

Early 1930s The economic depression intensifies. Legislation is passed to benefit white farming — Maize Control Acts in 1931 and 1934; Cattle Levy Acts in 1931 and 1934. Native Boards are set up in many Reserves in order to undercut the influence of African urban associations. In Matabeleland the

Industrial and Commercial Workers Union and the Matabele Home Society nevertheless penetrate into the Reserves.

1932 Beginning of the Vapostori (Apostolic) churches in the eastern districts.

1936 Passing of the Sedition Act to repress expressions of political and religious discontent. The Southern Rhodesian Bantu Congress formed in November.

1941 The Natural Resources Act gives expression to anxieties over conservation and powers to conservation officers.

1942 Natural Resources Board Native Enquiry investigates the conservation problem in the Reserves and favours compulsion. The Compulsory Labour Act provides for conscript African labour to be provided especially to European farmers.

1944 Report of the Native Production and Trade Commission savagely criticises African peasant production and recommends 'modernisation' through compulsion.

1945 Strike by African railway workers in October extracts concessions from goverment and stimulates worker organisation.

1946 In January Charles Mzingeli and others form the Reformed Industrial and Commercial Workers Union (RICU) in Salisbury. Subsequently there emerge in Bulawayo the Federation of African Workers' Unions led by Jasper Savanhu and the African Workers' Voice Association led by Benjamin Burombo.

1948 General strike of African workers in Bulawayo, Salisbury and other towns. Burombo is tried but acquitted on appeal for his role in the strike. Thereafter he moves out into the rural areas, especially of Matabeleland, to campaign against implemention of the Land Apportionment Act and mass evictions. Burombo's organisation is banned in 1952; he dies in 1958.

1951 Enactment of the Native Land Husbandry Act under which rights of ownership to small plots of land in the Reserves was to be allocated to registered residents and agricultural rules enforced. Implementation of the Act is greatly accelerated in 1955 and arouses great opposition between 1956 and 1961. The Act is finally suspended in 1964.

1953 Southern Rhodesia becomes part of the Federation of Rhodesia and Nyasaland.

1955 In August the City Youth League is formed in Salisbury led by James Robert Chikerema, George Nyandoro and Edson Sithole. The League campaigns against the influence of Mzingeli and is a forerunner of mass nationalism. Meanwhile in Bulawayo the old Congress still exists with Joshua Nkomo as the leading figure.

1957 In September the Youth League merges with the Bulawayo branch of the old Congress to form the Southern Rhodesia African National Congress

(SRANC) with Nkomo as President. Chikerema as Vice-President and Nyandoro as Secretary.

1959 In February the Prime Minister of Southern Rhodesia. Edgar White-head. declares a State of Emergency. Congress is banned and 300 members detained. including Chikerema. Nyandoro and Maurice Nyagumbo. Nkomo is out of the country at the time and remains outside.

1960 In January the National Democratic Party (NDP) is formed as a successor to Congress. Its first president is Michael Mawema but Nkomo becomes President in October. Thereafter Robert Mugabe becomes an office holder.

1961 The Tribal Trust Land Act is passed after which the Reserves become known as Tribal Trust Lands. In December 1961 the National Democratic Party is banned. Almost immediately the Zimbabwe African Peoples' Union (ZAPU) is formed. again with Nkomo as President.

1962 In September the Zimbabwe African People's Union is banned. Up to this point ZAPU has been the sole nationalist organisation. with very wide support. It is decided not to form another party but to carry on the struggle 'underground'. In December the Rhodesia Front wins the election and forms the government of Southern Rhodesia. The RF soon begins to develop the idea of 'Community Development' in the rural areas.

1963 In April Nkomo takes most of the executive of ZAPU to Tanzania where he plans to set up a Government in Exile. He is not allowed to do so and tensions rise within the executive. In June Nkomo returns home. forestalling an attempt to dismiss him as President. In August his opponents found the Zimbabwe African National Union (ZANU) with Ndabaningi Sithole as its President. Leopold Takawira as Vice-President and Robert Mugabe as Secretary-General. Fierce competition ensues between ZAPU and ZANU.

1964 Competition and violence between ZAPU and ZANU continue until the parties are banned in August. Nkomo. Sithole. Mugabe. Tekere. Nyagumbo and many others are detained. The parties continue to operate in exile. based in Zambia.

1965 In October Ian Smith. now Prime Minister. makes his Unilateral Declaration of Independence.

1966 The operation to 'de-lineate communities' is completed and chief-doms mapped. In April the 'battle of Sinoia' is the first large-scale combat between guerrillas of ZANU's Zimbabwe African National Liberation Army (ZANLA) and government forces. ZAPU's armed forces. ZIPRA. are also engaged in guerrilla infiltration.

1967 The Tribal Trust Land Authorities Act gives chiefs and their land authorities rights to allocate land and to supervise cultivation.

1969 The Tribal Courts Act takes a step further the policy of reviving 'traditional' authorities in the TTLs.

1971   Ian Smith and Lord Home agree on constitutional proposals in November. These are to be put to the Africans as a test of acceptability. In December the African National Council is founded, its name chosen deliberately to make the same acronym (ANC) as the old Congress. Bishop Abel Muzorewa is chosen to lead the Council, the rest of the leadership consisting of ZAPU and ZANU restrictees or of previously a-political churchmen.

1972   The African National Council organises a 'No' verdict on the constitutional proposals and transforms itself into a political party. Meanwhile since 1970 ZANLA guerrillas have been infiltrating the north-east out of Mozambique and in December fighting begins there.

1974   In March the Congress of the African National Council commits itself to majority rule. In April the coup d'etat in Lisbon spells the end for Portuguese rule in Mozambique. ZANLA guerrilla activity greatly expands. At the end of the year an attempt is made at 'detente'. Nkomo, Sithole, Mugabe and the rest are released from prison to take part in 'unity' talks in Lusaka. Sithole has been deposed as President of ZANU by his fellow detainees who have elected Mugabe. The Front Line states insist that Sithole be reinstated. On December 8th the various parties grudgingly agree to the formation of an umbrella body, to be called the African National Council, under Muzorewa's chairmanship.

1975   The assassination in March of ZANU's leader in exile, Herbert Chitepo, leads to the arrest of most leaders and members of ZANU in Zambia. Ndabaningi Sithole's support for Zambia's action undermines his position. In April Mugabe and Tekere leave Rhodesia for Mozambique where they establish relations with the guerrillas. Mugabe gradually emerges as their recognised leader and leader of ZANU, though his dominance is only finally assured in 1977. In November 1975 a united guerrilla army is formed in Mozambique — the Zimbabwe People's Army (ZIPA).

1976   ZIPA becomes in effect only the army of ZANU and the title is eventually dropped so that the guerrillas coming in from Mozambique are once again members of ZANLA. Meanwhile ZAPU is operating from Zambia. ZANLA and ZIPRA each begin to carve out their own zones of guerrilla operation. In October the two parties come together to form the Patriotic Front (PF), an alliance never effective on the battlefield itself.

1977   The political situation is now clarified. Nkomo and Mugabe alone have any guerrillas at their command. Muzorewa is back in Rhodesia reviving his old party structures, now known as the United African National Council (UANC) while Sithole still claims to lead an internal ZANU. Both men, lacking military power, seek an internal political settlement and commence negotiations with Smith.

1978   At the beginning of the year African 'militias' are established in some TTLS. In June these become the Auxiliaries, most of whom fall under the influence of the UANC. In March the Internal Settlement Agreement is announced. It provides for a transitional government, with Smith as Prime

Minister but with other portfolios shared between white and black ministers. The war intensifies.

1979 In January the new constitution for Zimbabwe/Rhodesia is promulgated. In April elections take place at which Muzorewa's UANC win 51 of the 72 African Seats. Muzorewa becomes Prime Minister in June. In September, however, the Lancaster House conference opens attended by the leaders of the UANC, Sithole-ZANU, Mugabe-ZANU, and ZAPU. In December agreement is reached.

1980 Mugabe decides that the Patriotic Front is not to contest the elections as an alliance. Therefore ZAPU under Nkomo and ZANU/PF under Mugabe compete in the elections, which are also contested by Muzorewa's UANC and Sithole's ZANU. Mugabe and ZANU/PF win a smashing victory and form the new government with the coming of independence on 18th April.

Public events since April 1980 are sufficiently indicated in the last chapter of this book.

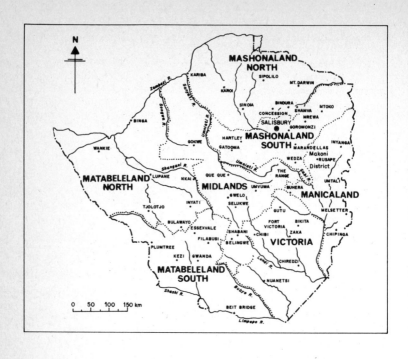

Map 1 *District Commissioners' stations in colonial Rhodesia*

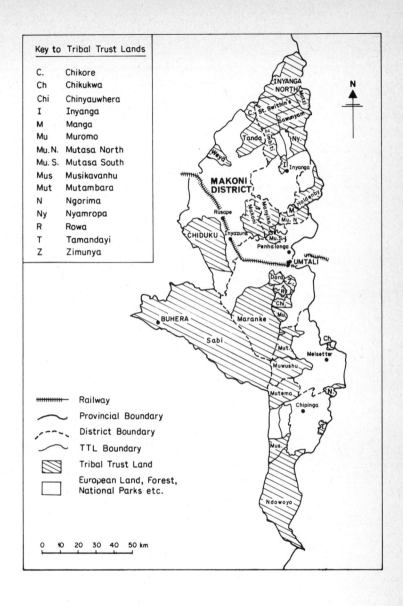

Key to Tribal Trust Lands

C.	Chikore
Ch	Chikukwa
Chi	Chinyauwhera
I	Inyanga
M	Manga
Mu	Muromo
Mu.N.	Mutasa North
Mu.S.	Mutasa South
Mus	Musikavanhu
Mut	Mutambara
N	Ngorima
Ny	Nyamropa
R	Rowa
T	Tamandayi
Z	Zimunya

Railway
Provincial Boundary
District Boundary
TTL Boundary
Tribal Trust Land
European Land, Forest,
National Parks etc.

0 10 20 30 40 50 km

Map 2 *Manicaland: Tribal Trust Lands*

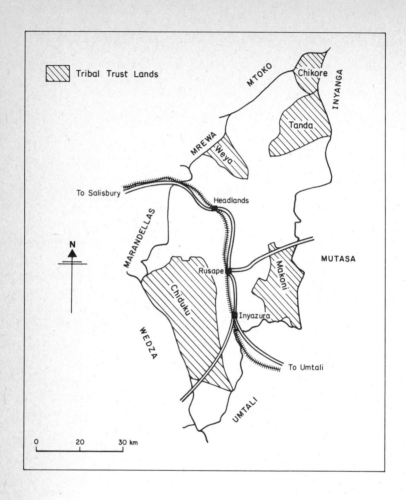

Map 3 *Makoni District*

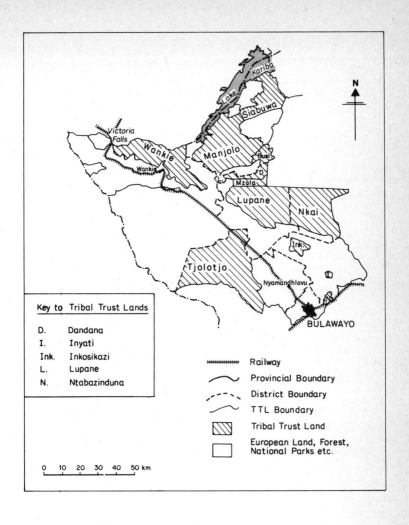

Key to Tribal Trust Lands

D.	Dandana
I.	Inyati
Ink.	Inkosikazi
L.	Lupane
N.	Ntabazinduna

Railway
Provincial Boundary
District Boundary
TTL Boundary
Tribal Trust Land
European Land, Forest,
National Parks etc.

0 10 20 30 40 50 km

Map 4   *Matabeleland North: Tribal Trust Lands*

xix

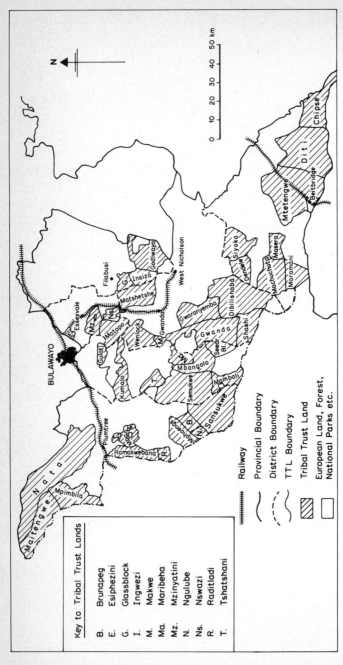

Key to Tribal Trust Lands

B.   Brunapeg
E.   Esiphezini
G.   Glassblock
I.   Ingwezi
M.   Makwe
Ma.   Maribeha
Mz.   Mzinyatini
N.   Ngulube
Ns.   Nswazi
R.   Raditladi
T.   Tshatshani

⊢⊢⊢⊢⊢   Railway
         Provincial Boundary
         District Boundary
         TTL Boundary
▨▨   Tribal Trust Land
☐   European Land, Forest,
         National Parks etc.

Map 5 *Matabeleland South: Tribal Trust Lands*

Plate 1   *The climax of peasant consciousness: Columbus Makoni campaigning for ZANU/PF in eastern Makoni Tribal Trust Land in March 1980. (Columbus Makoni on the far right.)*

Plate 2   *Columbus Makoni in the village, eastern Makoni, March 1980*

Plate 3   *News of ZANU/PF's election victory, eastern Makoni, March 1980*

INTRODUCTION

Laying the comparative foundations

Anyone seeking to make a comparative study of Zimbabwean agrarian history has no shortage of existing and already advanced comparisons to serve as a starting point. Some of these comparisons have covered a good deal of ground. Thus Gavin Williams has described the Riddell Commission's proposals for rural development in independent Zimbabwe as combining 'the worst aspects of the agricultural policies of Kenya (dependence on large-scale maize farming), Nigeria (settlement and irrigation schemes), Tanzania (villagization) and South Africa (betterment schemes). Thus far Zimbabwean peasants have resisted them, both under white rule and since independence.'[1] But most of the comparisons have been made with two African countries particularly in mind – Kenya and Mozambique. I have come across at least a score of academic articles comparing Zimbabwe and Kenya; at least half a dozen comparing Zimbabwe and Mozambique.

The reasons for the dominance of these two comparisons above all others are clearly set out by two of the writers concerned. In his 'Structural transformation in Zimbabwe: some comparative notes from the neo-colonization of Kenya', Michael Bratton remarks that:

Comparison between Kenya and Rhodesia is tempting on a number of scores. First, historical parallels in the development trajectories and economic structures of the two countries appear evident. Until 1945 each had a peripheral capitalist economy of the colonial type. Each specialized in the export of primary commodites – coffee and tea in Kenya and gold and tobacco in Rhodesia – and depended on the import of manufactured goods in return. When a domestic industrial and manufacturing base was established it was in both cases as a consequence of rapid and massive infusions of international capital creating conditions of economic boom.

Second, Kenya and Rhodesia are distinguishable from other colonial social structures by the presence of a relatively large class of settlers, a white national bourgeoisie. The dominance of this class was based upon pri-

vileged access to and exploitation of resources of land and labour. Over the
long run and despite periodic disagreements the interests of settlers were
roughly compatible with the interests of transnational capital. The political
demise of white settlers was a consequence in both cases of a protracted
military struggle against a nationalist guerrilla force enjoying considerable
support among underprivileged African strata.

Third, Kenya and Rhodesia constitute 'periphery centres' through
which the penetration of colonial administrative control and of international capital into a wider region has occurred . . . Choices of national
development strategy made within Kenya and Rhodesia therefore diffuse
and have impact far beyond national boundaries . . .

The Kenyan situation . . . does identify key ways in which structures of
colonial production undergo adaptation. One implication is that the owners
of domestic and transnational capital in Rhodesia can, if forced, relinquish
political control without fully sacrificing economic control.[2]

If the Kenyan comparison is thus perceived in terms of a similarity of *white* structures and interests, the Mozambique parallel is
perceived in terms of a potential similarity of *black* consciousness
and organization. Lional Cliffe, in his attempt to set up criteria for
an evaluation of the Zimbabwean nationalist movements, reminds
us that:

Several writers have made the distinction between those nationalist movements that were, typically, granted power in most of independent Africa
and in other ex-colonial regions, and some of the national liberation
movements that have not only engaged in some kind of armed struggle but,
in the process, have undertaken a social as well as a national revolution.
Davidson . . . and other writers like Saul, point to the . . . process that
occurred . . . in Mozambique. There is agreement that essential features of
this type of struggle, and of the movements that make possible this 'dual'
revolution, include first a variety of initiatives which 'close the gap between
the leadership . . . and the mass of the peasantry' (Saul), the leaders 'go to
the people' (Davidson): the leaders live with the people, have to win them
over so as not to be betrayed, and mobilise their energies for the struggle in
a variety of ways. In the liberated areas, new institutions and programmes
in health, education, agriculture and trade have to be undertaken, and in
such a way that popular commitment is maintained. In this way, the leaders
'acquire a clearer understanding of the economic realities of their country,
as well as of the problems, hopes, and suffering of the masses of people . . .'
A second essential is the 'deepening of national consciousness', the streng-
thening of a national unity that can overcome ethnic and other factionalism
. . .

In short, then, this model is of a nationalism which fuses what Fanon
described as the 'separate dialectic' of mass (mainly rural) protest and of
urban-based elite political organisation.[3]

Cliffe thereafter at once begins to turn 'to see how far the Zimbabwe movement approached this pattern.'

At first sight it looks as if these two comparisons situate the recent history of Zimbabwe in a very fruitful way. On the one side Bratton's Kenyan comparison highlights white dominance of land and the key role played by land resettlement in the 'neo-colonization' process. On the other side Cliffe's Mozambican comparison highlights the role of a mobilized peasantry in resisting such dominance and such neo-colonial adaptation. One ought to be able to discuss rural transformation and peasant war in Zimbabwe within these parameters.

Yet as I read across the whole body of this comparative work – much of it less subtle and sober than that of Bratton or Cliffe – I came to feel that it offered unreliable and even dangerous intellectual tools. I found the comparisons *as a whole* to suffer from three great weaknesses. To begin with, they served in all too many cases as moral propositions rather than as intellectual ones – the potential Kenyan comparison being offered rather in the spirit of an old-time preacher threatening his congregation with hellfire, or at the best limbo, while the Mozambican comparison was offered as a glimpse of an often all-too unobtainable paradise. Secondly, the comparisons were sometimes made by people who did not know both of the societies compared: as a result, the hypothesized 'Kenyan model' or 'Mozambican model' was frequently a crude parody of reality. Also as a result, thirdly, it too often seemed possible to the writers concerned that one or other of these models might be imposed in Zimbabwe, with scant regard for Zimbabwe's own historical specificity. If so-and-so won the war or the election or the rat race, it was said, things would go the Kenyan way; if someone else won, things would go the Mozambican way – as if these alternatives were fully and freely available to be chosen and applied. In short, the comparisons have mostly not been used so as to illuminate Zimbabwe's particular experience, structures and potentialities of change by means of a rigorous set of contrasts and parallels. They have been used instead to propose and predict alternative destinations or to pass judgement on Zimbabwe's African leaders and militants according to which point they registered on the Kenya/Mozambique scale.

Certainly, all those who make the Kenyan comparison do so in order to warn against Kenya's example. (It was rumoured during the government of Bishop Abel Muzorewa that Muzorewa was employing academic experts on Kenyan decolonization to advise him how best to achieve the same admirable results in Zimbabwe: if so I have not myself seen their reports). The warning is delivered

most explicity in a ZANU policy discussion document of 1977
prepared by A.K.H. Weinrich entitled 'Agricultural reconstruction in Zimbabwe':

During colonial days there have been many similarities between agricultural policies in Kenya and Rhodesia, and it seems that there are powerful
interests in Rhodesia today who aim at modelling the agricultural sector of
a free Zimbabwe on that of independent Kenya. This is a great danger and
it is essential that all efforts in this direction be stifled from the beginning.
To understand the negative forces of Kenyan development, the following
facts must be studied:
   During the colonial phase white farmers, who occupied the most fertile
land in Kenya, had seen to it that legislation was passed which eliminated
African peasant producers as competitors in the agricultural market, and
so, by barring African peasants from earning cash through crop sales, and
also by reducing the land available to Africans, the colonial system turned
African areas into cheap labour reserves from which white farmers could
draw workers for their farms.
   When it was realised that independence was imminent, white interests
did all in their power to assure that the monopolies they had built up should
be kept intact, even if individual farms were to change hands and blacks
took over property formerly held by whites. . .
   The key concerns of the planners of the new agricultural economy were
that private property be safeguarded and held sacred. . . The issuing of title
deeds, therefore, gave rise to two classes of peasants in the tribal areas: the
larger scale land owners who employed paid labourers and the struggling,
impoverished majority. The former paid their labourers very low wages, far
lower than white farm owners had done in the past . . . Such abuse could
not have arisen under a system of communal land tenure. This shows that
Kenyan policy fostered a new black elite whose interests are identical
with those of western capitalism. It did not improve the lot of the rural
masses . . . To carry out a true land reform in the future and to dislodge the
present black land owning class will be much more difficult than it was in
the early 1960s to replace white by black farmers . . . The ordinary peasants in Kenya are as poor as they were in colonial times.[4]

   As we shall see, this account underestimated both the resilience
and significance of Kenyan African peasant production and the
inegalitarian potentialities of communal tenure, but it sounded a
warning plainly enough. Most of the other articles which made the
Kenya comparison devoted themselves to giving this warning
more specificity. They focused on how such a Kenyan solution
might be imposed in Zimbabwe; on what interests or classes might
take the lead in seeking to achieve it.
   Sometimes they identified the western brokers of *détente* in
Southern Africa as the major agents of 'Kenyaization'. As Bratton
writes:

Introduction

When the details of the 'Kissinger proposals' for the transition to majority rule in Zimbabwe were made public in October 1976, containing generous proposals for the compensation of white Rhodesian settlers, a chord was struck among observers of African politics that the history of decolonization in Kenya was about to repeat itself. . . Western financial assistance in Kenya ensured a smooth transition from a colonial to neocolonial economy in which international capital was permitted expanded access to the resources and markets of Kenya and the East African region. Similarly the sudden concern of the Western bloc for majority rule in Zimbabwe and for the establishment of a 'Zimbabwe Development Fund' has been motivated by the prospect of the removal of the rich resources and markets of the Southern African sub-continent from the Western sphere of economic control.

The key element in this strategy in Kenya, as now in Zimbabwe, was massive loans from 'international monetary agencies to the new African government to compensate white settlers for the expropriation of farms.'[5]

Sometimes the comparisons focused more on Zimbabwe's African petty bourgeoisie as the instrument of the 'Kenya solution'. In 1980, William Duggan argued that:

In a Rhodesia where the end of settler rule is now at last forseeable . . . the birth of an African rural bourgeoisie evokes the Kenyan experience, in which independence was preceded by the enfranchisement of a rural elite loyal to the prevailing economic order . . . Decolonization on the Kenyan model is . . . not an impossible scenario for Rhodesia . . . in Kenya, for a rural elite to be given adequate land, the position of poorer families [had to] be so eroded as to make it possible to implement the plan rapidly only by military force. In Kenya this was done in the context of a civil war. In Rhodesia . . . there may be enough armable Africans willing to fight for the . . . entrenchment of their own economic privilege to turn the current nationalist war into a bloody civil war . . . A Swynnerton Plan in the countryside is therefore at least a possible option in Zimbabwe Rhodesia.[6]

Even when Zimbabwe's majority rule had in fact been attained in rather a different manner, the question of how Kenyaization might come to pass remained central to such essays in comparison. Now they focused, however, not so much on the 'lords of decolonization', nor on an existing rural petty bourgeoisie which might take arms in defence of economic privilege, but on the possible emergence of a genuine African bourgeoisie. In 1980, for example, Barry Munslow wrote that:

Zimbabwe is the largest industrial power in Africa after South Africa and possibly Nigeria, and it clearly has the potential at least for indigenous capitalist development. Recent studies of Kenya have chartered [sic] the early origins of an emergent African bourgeoisie there. Their findings are pertinent to our own investigation. . .

Through the judicious use of the state a *settler* bourgeoisie grew in power – and in the post-colonial Kenyan situation an *African* bourgeoisie is also growing, made possible (again) by control of the state apparatus. There is presently a fierce struggle going on for control of the Zimbabwe state: between settler interests and the two major nationalist movements, a struggle between both these movements and a struggle within each (which remain national *fronts* of various classes). In the Kenyan case . . . the indigenous bourgeoisie was able to use the state to promote its own growth. It achieved this politically by asserting its hegemony over the other classes in KANU, and by using state mechanisms for giving preference to local capitalists. . . Faced with enormous popular pressures for Zimbabweaniza-tion on the one hand and the constraint (stressed on virtually all sides) not to rock the economic system on the other, relatively favourable conditions for the growth of an African bourgeoisie may exist – the socialist commit-ment of the government notwithstanding. . .

With independence, there is the potential more than ever before for the rapid growth of an African agrarian bourgeoisie. They have an organisa-tion, the African Farmers Union, which proposed almost immediately after independence that its members should be the first to be moved onto the white farming areas, as they were the ones with the knowledge and capacity to use the land productively. . . Broadly the strategy put forward by these groups is based in the assumptions that there must be continuity and that any change must be predicated on individual tenure. . . The plan for the TTLS is essentially one of creating individual land tenure throughout . . . The obvious problems associated with these proposals mirror those found in the Kenyan case – although many of the resettled farmers may benefit, the majority do not and there is the serious possiblity of the growth of an indigenous agrarian bourgeoisie . . .

A Kenyan solution is certainly not inevitable, but the new government will have to pay close attention to the de facto developments taking place on the ground.[7]

By contrast with these Kenyan comparisons, the Mozambique example is always presented as an ideal. FRELIMO is seen as having become the ideal movement of 'people's war' and national liberation and ZANU and ZAPU are then measured against it. Writing in 1978, Basil Davidson described the Zimbabwean move-ments, in contrast to FRELIMO, as 'opportunist, confusedly demagogic, and given to rivalries and splits.'[8] In 1981, in his *The People's Cause*, Davidson argued that the liberation movement in Mozambique, and in Lusophone Africa in general, represented a coming to 'maturity' of the whole tradition of violent resistance to colonialism:

Each of the movements was able to develop a political and social maturity, and therefore unity, that could lay foundations for a new culture: indigenous and national, but also secular and modern. . . each combined a struggle against the colonial present with a struggle against all those aspects of the pre-colonial past which could no longer prove constructive. . . Each movement's strength therefore came and had to come from struggle 'at and from the grass roots of society, . . . [their] politics were . . . egalitarian, anti-elitist, insistently democratic . . . but what was developed by their practice was evidently more than 'politics'. Rather it was the political and moral consciousness of all who were involved or influenced, each person's attitude to his or her collective, each person's sense of self-identity and self-respect . . . With these movements and their development across the years, accordingly, there may be said to have opened a new phase in the history of Africa's confrontation with the world of the twentieth century.[9]

By contrast with this, Davidson's account of the Zimbabwean guerrilla movements, even in 1981 after majority rule had been achieved, was grudging in the extreme. In the 1960s 'there was no serious attempt to think through the actual problems'; when the parties *did* move to the concept of 'full-scale guerrilla war,' they 'jumped a stage in the process of successful insurrection. [They] supposed that military action would lead to political support, whereas, in every known example of success, the process was the other way round.' Thereafter, Davidson merely remarks that 'a new phase opened in 1972 as FRELIMO extended its operations . . . and opened new zones of contestation down the eastern border of Rhodesia,' and within a couple of paragraphs has arrived at the 1980 elections without any endorsement of the guerrilla strategies pursued in the 1970s.[10]

In an article published in 1977 and republished in 1979, John Saul took much the same view. Saul tells us that 'FRELIMO was prepared to help Zimbabwean militants learn the lessons Mozambicans had already learned – the necessity to clarify their goals and genuinely to mobilize their people – so that they could overcome their chronic disunity and toughen themselves for effective struggle.' But, Saul argues, the Zimbabweans possessed little capacity to learn the lesson:

the absence of that meaningful revolutionary practice which effective guerrilla struggle provides forestalled much real political growth for Zimbabwean nationalism. The dynamic process which had become a self-reinforcing pattern of development in the case of Mozambican revolutionary nationalism – political clarity facilitating guerrilla activity, this in turn encouraging greater clarity – remained for Zimbabweans a negative vicious circle out of which they found it difficult to break.

Saul discounts the ZANU offensives in the north-east in the early 1970s on the grounds that 'ZANU's incursions . . . were facilitated by FRELIMO' and that 'FRELIMO then entertained few illusions that ZANU had yet defined a political line capable of sustaining a genuinely transforming process of popular struggle.' According to Saul, FRELIMO thought that because they were 'too exclusively militarist in . . . orientation, ZANU's methods of work [were] still far removed from those which characterize a people's war.' Nor did FRELIMO think that out of the disputes within ZANU in 1975 and 1976 would emerge 'a genuinely revolutionary nationalism'. Rather, they 'smacked more of the . . . old wasting kind of petty-bourgeois political infighting . . .Small wonder that FRELIMO officials . . . in mid-1975 saw the military and political struggle in Zimbabwe at this time as more or less starting from scratch . . . In March 1976 . . . President Machel said: ". . . we would like the struggle to be a long one in order to liberate the mentality of Zimbabweans." Saul's one hope was the emergence of the 'third force', ZIPA, but this collapsed – as he noted in his 1978 postscript – in 'the vicious circle created by the pattern of petty-bourgeois politics in the Zimbabwean liberation camp.'[11]

As Cliffe notes, this analysis downplays 'the liberationary potential of the post-1976 struggle', and cites FRELIMO's asserted views 'in rather an ex cathedra tone'. Cliffe's own conclusion is that 'the history of the national movement, at least at the level of leadership, had not been markedly different from that of more illustrious movements like FRELIMO. The Zimbabwean movement has also experienced both the learning and liberating effect of popular-based armed struggle and also the leadership conflicts of an ideological character to which it also, typically, gives rise.' But Cliffe himself goes on to conclude that 'such struggles have been resolved in a counter-revolutionary manner' within the Zimbabwean movements, so that the 'elements that had advanced most in their political understanding . . .were removed from further influence on and by the continuing struggle.'[12]

The time has come for me to clarify my views on the totality of this comparative work. I do not deny, in the first place, that rhetorical use of the 'Kenyan model' and the 'Mozambican model' had a utility during the war itself as a way of dramatizing what was to be feared and what was to be desired. There is no doubt that such a rhetorical use of the concepts took place far outside the ranks of academic commentators. Thus in November 1980 'an irate and frustrated peasant' addressed the *Herald* on the land problem:

If reconciliation is to mean anything to the [peasant], land must be simply grabbed from the European farmer and redistributed to the [peasants] crowding in the tribal trust lands. Any student of the land question in this country will tell you that talk of compensation to white farmers is simply ridiculous if it means that our government should pay for such land to the dispossessed farmers. The total area of land allocated to one white family alone in 1892 was about 108,00 acres. Nothing was paid for those lands. Why then should the new ZANU (PF) Government be expected to pay a cent for these lands? In Kenya at independence, the British Government offered loans to Africans so that they could buy back European land from which they had been driven during colonial rule. The results were disastrous and humiliating to the African population. *We cannot respect that disaster here.*[13]

But I *am* concerned here with academic analysis and with whether the comparisons possess any rigorous explanatory value.

So far as academic analysis is concerned I am not hostile to comparison in itself. I am going to argue for the special character of the Zimbabwean experience and in particular for the special character of the Zimbabwean peasant experience. But this distinct Zimbabwean experience can only be established and illuminated and limited by comparison with the experiences of other African rural societies. In this way comparison can spring out of the historical reality of Zimbabwe. What I *am* hostile to is the free-floating use of comparisons unanchored in any historical reality.

An example of this is Gary Wasserman's article 'The economic transition to Zimbabwe', published in late 1978. Here Wasserman sketched three scenarios for the future of Zimbabwe – a Kenyan scenario as desired by international capital and Bishop Muzorewa; a Mozambican scenario as desired by Robert Mugabe; and a Zambian strategy as desired by Joshua Nkomo. Wasserman saw the Internal Settlement of 1978 as a Kenya-style attempt to 'give the settlers allies in their struggle to preserve their political grip on the economy', and to give African participants in the Settlement 'a long-range strategic [chance] to use positions of political authority to integrate themselves and their followers into the modern political economy.' As against this he described Mugabe's ZANU – though with scant respect for the reservations of the Davidson/Saul school of analysis – in the following terms:

Mugabe has attempted to mould the party into a revolutionary socialist movement modelled after Mozambique's ruling party, Frelimo. Throughout Mugabe's speeches run recurring themes. Armed struggle is the only route for the liberation of Zimbabwe. Liberation means not only toppling the settler regime and its allies, but also putting an end to an exploitative economic system set up in the interests of international capitalism. . . Compromises with present rulers will only result in neocolonialist solutions such as found in Kenya . . . Mugabe has been direct in his class analysis and insistent on the need to transform Rhodesia's political economy. . . he is not merely an agrarian reformer. . .

ZANU clearly wishes to seize and destroy the settler political structure in order to transform a capitalist economy into a socialist one along the lines of Mozambique. Foreign capital may be allowed, as it is in Mozambique, but its dominating presence would be reduced and it would not be allowed to align with domestic elite groups as found in Kenya. To accomplish this transformation, the strategy of armed struggle is necessary . . . to mobilize a traditional peasantry into a conscious political force able to seize and mould the political economy to their own ends. Having taken power through their armed strength, the rural masses will not willingly see their country's wealth channelled back into the hands of foreign or domestic elites.

As for Nkomo and ZAPU, to them 'the war is a tactical bargaining stance.' ZAPU's 'vague political platform' holds out hope to 'the businessmen and western policymakers supporting Nkomo' that they may achieve, if not a Kenyan solution, at least a Zambian one. Such a policy would, Wasserman argued, aim at:

Stability [for] the country by integrating Africans into the adaptive parts of the political economy, while transferring, with international funds, parts of the settler economy. The transfer of the bulk of settler-held farms and the placement of Africans into professional, small business and bureaucratic positions can be expected. The retention, though on new terms, of the large industrial and mining concerns and foreign investment, with the integration of a new indigenous elite into their domestic components, seems equally probable. If ZANU's model for Zimbabwe is Mozambique, ZAPU's is Zambia.[14]

This is an analysis which suffers both from taking too much at face value the rhetoric of African leadership and from assuming it possible for Zimbabwe to go along a Kenyan, Mozambican or Zambian path according to whichever leader wins out. It is clear that the rhetoric of Zimbabwean liberation movements was relatively easily adapted to the respective idioms of the front-line states in which they found themselves. ZAPU, proclaiming Kenneth Kaunda as the 'saviour' of Zimbabwe, did make some Zambian-sounding noises; ZANU, depending upon Mozambique for its access to the eastern frontier zones of Zimbabwe, certainly did develop a FRELIMO-style analysis. But the practicality of carrying out Zambian or Mozambican solutions *inside* Zimbabwe was and remains a quite different thing.

If I am not opposed to comparison in itself, neither am I opposed to the use of comparative historical and political analysis for immediate practical purposes. I see every reason for Saul in the 1970s to seek to advise North Atlantic radicals on which, if any, of the Zimbabwean nationalist movements to support and to seek to arrive at his conclusions by comparative analysis. I see every justification for Weinrich to draw upon a wide range of historical comparative material in her memorandum to ZANU on future agrarian policy. Indeed I very much hope that today the present Zimbabwean government keeps properly founded historical comparisons in mind. But the words 'properly founded' are crucial here.

To my mind the Saul/Davidson analysis of the Zimbabwean nationalist movements by means of a comparison with FRELIMO was faulty for two reasons. On the one hand its model of FRELI-MO, as an instance of what a liberation movement at its best *can* be, seems to me to have been nobly but impossibly utopian. On the other hand, its examination of the potential of the Zimbabwean liberation struggle focused too much on the level of leadership. Saul and Davidson had been able to enter 'liberated zones' in Mozambique and Angola and to witness FRELIMO and MPLA at work among the peasantry even while the guerrilla wars were going on. Neither Saul nor Davidson nor anyone else was able to enter guerrilla areas of Zimbabwe in the same way. While the war was on, no commentator knew what were the relations of guerrillas to peasants; nobody knew how far, to use Wasserman's terms, 'a traditional peasantry' had been mobilized into 'a conscious political force'; indeed, nobody knew whether the Zimbabwean peasantry *was* 'traditional' and needed to be moulded in this way. As Cliffe remarked in March 1980, with the advantage of the new perspective given by ZANU/PF's victory in the elections, the squabbles among the Zimbabwean leadership in exile seem in fact to have gone side by side with ' a relatively uninterrupted process of growing political consciousness, of mobilisation . . . among the guerrillas . . . and the people in the vast majority of the rural areas to which the struggle had spread'.[15] Judgements on the Zimbabwe liberation movements could not be soundly based without a knowledge of this 'grass-roots dialectic'.

As for Weinrich's work and the other work which deploys the Kenyan comparison, it seems to me that it does indeed raise a whole body of pertinent questions. Such comparisons focus attention upon rural differentiation amongst African peasantries and its historical roots; upon attempts by colonial or post-colonial governments to bring about 'land reform' in the interests of rural 'progressives'; upon the consequence of land resettlement schemes; upon the realities of rural immiseration. Together with the emphasis which emerges from the Mozambique work upon peasant consciousness and the relationship of peasants to the guerrilla war, these are precisely the questions I shall be discussing in this book. But it seems to me that the Kenyan comparative work, like the Mozambican, critically lacks one essential element: namely a historically based understanding of the Zimbabwean peasantry itself.

I intend in this book to attack the set of issues raised in the existing comparative work by adopting an explicitly historical approach to them. The whole body of comparative work, as we have seen, focuses intensely on the issues of the 1970s and on the prospects for the 1980s. These are in fact my own main interests also, and the second half of this book will be devoted to the last ten years of Zimbabwean history. But I believe that in order to understand that decade, and in particular in order to understand what has happened and may happen in the rural areas during the 1970s and 1980s, one has to start much earlier. It is necessary to begin with the making of the African peasantry in the first decades of the twentieth century, with their experience of the Depression in the 1930s, with the agrarian crisis of the 1940s – and then, from this foundation, go on to analyze their relationship to nationalism and liberation.

In taking this *historical* approach I intend to employ the comparative method in rather a different way. At the end of this book I shall return to the sorts of comparisons I have so far been citing in order to ask how far their propositions stand up to the historically grounded realities. But as I seek to establish these historically grounded realities, I shall draw heavily on studies by historians of African peasantries elsewhere in order to set up a range of illuminating comparisons and contrasts. In doing so I shall seek to preserve some continuity by drawing especially on recent historical work on agrarian Kenya and to a lesser extent on recent historical work on agrarian Mozambique. The point is that while more or less glib models of the 'Kenya way' have been formulated in the comparative literature I have been quoting, there has independently flowered a sophisticated historiography of Kenyan rural transformation which has a great deal to teach any Zimbabweanist. Similarly, while the Zimbabwean movements have been judged so severely in contrast to an idealized FRELIMO, a body of work on the experience of Mozambican peasantries under colonialism has grown up which raises many questions of interest to a historian of rural Zimbabwe. The historiography of Zimbabwe possesses a good many strengths but it has not so far explored some of the important themes which emerge from recent Kenyan and Mozambican agrarian historiography. So I hope that *this* rather humbling comparison will lead me to pose questions about the experience of the Zimbabwean peasantry in the past the answers to which can help us to arrive at a more secure comparison with rural Kenya and rural Mozambique in the present.

All these considerations have determined the sequence and shape of this book. Hence in Chapter 1 I propose to examine the formation of the Zimbabwean peasantry under early colonialism in order to arrive at some comparative idea of what sort of peasantry was being established and in particular of what kind of consciousness it displayed in the period before 1920. I shall argue that in this period, and hence also later on, the Zimbabwean peasantry differed from the various peasantries growing up in Mozambique and that such differences had significant implications for political and liberation history in the two countries. In Chapter 2 I shall turn rather to Kenyan comparative material in order to examine the effects of the Depression of the 1930s upon the Zimbabwean peasantry. I shall argue that Kenyan material on the absolute growth of peasant production in the 1930s and on the crucial process of differentiation which then took place among the Kenyan peasantry raises questions which, when pursued for Zimbabwe, destroy the conventional notion of the absolute decline and decay of Zimbabwean peasant agriculture in the 1930s. But I shall also argue that the outcome of the 1930s was nevertheless crucially different for the Zimbabwean as opposed to the Kenyan peasantry, especially so far as patterns of stratification were concerned.

In Chapter 3 I shall turn to the agrarian crisis in Zimbabwe in the period 1946 to 1953 – a period immediately recognizable to Kenyanists as that which climaxed in Kenya itself in the agrarian upheavals of Mau Mau. I shall seek to argue that the agrarian crisis in Zimbabwe displayed many of the features of that in Kenya. I shall seek to explain why what might have been the location of a Rhodesian Mau Mau – namely the areas of Ndebele 'squatter' settlement around Bulawayo – were in the end cleared of an African peasantry without violent confrontation. Then in a bridging passage to the later chapters I shall reflect on the implications of all this for the development of the Zimbabwean nationalist and liberation movements. I shall argue that if in Kenya the defeat of Mau Mau broke radical nationalism and allowed instead the development of a reformist nationalist front led by the educated and entrepreneurial elites of the other Kenyan regions, the opposite process took place in Zimbabwe. There was no outburst of radical armed resistance in Matabeland in the 1940s, but there was no crushing peasant defeat either. Meanwhile the events of the late 1940s and early 1950s intensified peasant consciousness even in those areas where there was little overt protest at the time. Peasant areas outside Matabeleland came to possess a sense of collective culture and a degree of radicalism which did *not* characterize the areas of Kenya outside Kikuyuland, and peasants in these other areas of Zimbabwe were able to link up with those in Matabeleland in the nationalist movements of the late 1950s. I shall argue that the existence, extent and intensity of this nationalist peasant consciousness produced a different balance between peasants, nationalist activists and ultimately guerrillas in Zimbabwe than that which developed in Lusophone Africa. Through all this I shall seek to discuss also the nature and significance of rural differentiation in Zimbabwe.

In the last four chapters I shall reach the 1970s and the set of issues which have concerned the recent comparative work on Zimbabwe. But in the fourth and fifth chapters I shall continue the confrontation with Kenyan historiography. No Mau Mau style movement took place in Zimbabwe in the early 1950s. But I shall compare Mau Mau itself with peasant experiences of the guerrilla war in Zimbabwe, as well as comparing these to guerrilla war in Mozambique. In Chapter 4 I shall examine the extent to which the theme of 'the lost lands' was dominant in the Zimbabwean guerrilla war at the district level and in the minds of peasants. In Chapter 5 I shall explore the role of 'cultural renewal' and of peasant religion in the Zimbabwean guerrilla war. These two chapters will suggest that the Zimbabwean guerrilla war in the the rural areas was rather more like peasant Mau Mau than any rigid evolutionary sequence of rural protest from the 'illusions' of Mau Mau to the effective rational ideology of FRELIMO would suggest. Like Kikuyu peasants the peasant participants in Zimbabwe's guerrilla war fought for their lost lands and they drew heavily upon symbols of their past and on rural religion to sustain them. But I do not wish any stress I lay on the role of cultural nationalism and religion to justify the censures of those who hold the Zimbabwean liberation movements to have failed to achieve a 'people's war'. I shall argue that in many very significant ways the Zimbabwean war was pre-eminently a people's war; that the balance of the equation of consciousness between peasants and guerrillas in Zimbabwe was very different from that in Mozambique, allowing for a more direct input by the peasantry into the ideology and programme of the war. In Zimbabwe, peasant demands for their lost lands were part and parcel of a developed consciousness of the mechanisms of their oppression; of an understanding of the ways in which the state had expropriated them to the direct advantage of settler farming. In Zimbabwe the development of rural cultural nationalism prevented the past from being expropriated in its turn by the belated 'traditionalism' of Rhodesia Front 'tribal politics'. In Zimbabwe rural religion served a number of practical and necessary ends.

In Chaper 6 I shall explore how far class differentiation among the Zimbabwean peasantry resulted in a virtual civil war in the Zimbabwean rural areas during 1970s, as is argued for Kikuyuland in the 1950s, or in the elimination of African entrepreneurs, as is argued for northern Mozambique. This question is obviously crucial to the possibility of either a Kenyan or a Mozambican solution in the Zimbabwean countryside – a Kenyan solution depending upon the existence of a strata of 'rich' peasants ('Kulaks'), able and willing to turn the military harassment and displacement of poor peasants to their own advantage, and a Mozambican solution depending upon the presumption of a poor peasantry united in its determination not to allow the re-emergence of local 'exploiters'. I shall argue that there *was* a significant element of class tension within the Zimbabwean guerrilla war but that the historical specifics of rural Zimbabwe had not produced either a Kenyan or a Mozambican situation. In Zimbabwe there was no possibility of kulaks taking over land in the communal areas; nor were peasants likely altogether to repudiate store-keepers and other local 'businessmen', with whom they had been jointly involved in nationalism and upon whom they depended to articulate peasant production to the market. Both the history of rural differentiation, and its limitations, in Zimbabwe, and the character of the combined peasant-guerrilla ideology which emerged from the rural war, militated against either an entrepreneurial triumph or the development of peasant collectivism.

In Chapter 7 I shall look at what has happened in the rural areas of Zimbabwe since the end of the war; at the unusual balance between a relatively strong peasantry and a relatively weak state; at the extent to which developments have been shaped either by peasant initiatives or by state intervention. I shall argue that in the Zimbabwean context the programme of land resettlement will not have the same consequences as Kenyan land resettlement schemes: I shall also argue that in the Zimbabwean context the interaction of party and peasantry is different from that in Mozambique. Finally, I shall seek to draw together my arguments in a brief conclusion. It will not surprise readers to know that this conclusion will set out a case for the importance of peasant agency in the twentieth-century history of Zimbabwe. Africans in the rural areas, I shall argue, strove to turn themselves into peasants in the early years of colonialism in preference to becoming labour migrants. Thereafter they defended the peasant option as best they could. Their resentment at the undermining of the peasant option powered the nationalist challenge to the Rhodesian administration and produced a strong

Introduction

peasant input into the ideology of the guerrilla war. Peasants in
Zimbabwe today believe that their support for the guerrillas was
responsible for the political transition to ZANU rule. They await
the fulfillment of their political programme.

But of course I do not suppose that peasant agency either has
been or will be the most powerful force in shaping the character of
Zimbabwe's political economy. And I am aware that although this
short book covers a great variety of issues it leaves out even more. It
does not deal directly with the involvement and influence of international capitalism in Zimbabwe and it deals only in passing with
the development of white agriculture and with the role of the state.
Moreover, while admitting that there is no way in which peasant
experience and peasant consciousness can be separated from worker experience and worker consciousness in a labour migrancy
system like that of Zimbabwe it has relatively little to say about
worker history. To this extent my focus perhaps remains too
restricted to the topics that have arisen out of my work in Makoni
District. I can justify myself partly on the grounds that while it is
more readily possible to find out about the operation of the Rhodesian state and the patterns of white farming from published sources,
it is very difficult indeed to find out much about the history of the
African peasantry, at any rate after the work of Robin Palmer runs
out in the early 1930s.[16] Perhaps a stronger and truer reason is that I
so greatly enjoyed my interactions with the peasantry of Makoni
and so much valued their readiness to entrust to me their sense of
the meaning of their experiences. Although I have complicated my
communication of their experience to others with all the elaborate
apparatus which a formal series of lectures in Cambridge requires, I
hope this book does not in any way distort their sense of their past
hardships or muffle their demands for future peasant prosperity.

Notes

1 Gavin Williams, 'Equity, growth and the state', in J.D.Y.Peel and
   T.O. Ranger (eds), *Past and Present in Zimbabwe* (Manchester:
   1983), p.119.
2 Michael Bratton, 'Structural transformation in Zimbabwe: some comparative notes from the neo-colonization of Kenya', in David Wiley
   and Allen Isaacman (eds.) *Southern Africa: Society, Economy and
   Liberation*, (Michigan State University: 1981), pp.84-5.
3 Lionel Cliffe, 'Towards an evaluation of the Zimbabwe national
   movement', unpublished paper presented to Political Studies Association of the United Kingdom conference, (Exeter, March/April 1980),
   pp. 1-2.

4 A.K.H. Weinrich, 'Agricultural reconstruction in Zimbabwe', unpublished *ms.*, 1977, pp. 9-12.
5 Bratton, 'Structural transformation', p.83.
6 William Duggan, 'The Native Land Husbandry Act of 1951 and the rural African middle class of Southern Rhodesia', *African Affairs*, vol. 79, no. 315 (April 1980), pp. 227-8, 238, 239.
7 Barry Munslow, 'Zimbabwe's emerging African bourgeoisie', *Review of African Political Economy*, no. 19 (1980), pp. 63, 64, 65-6, 69.
8 Basil Davidson, *Africa in Modern History. The Search for a New Society*. (London: 1978), p. 360.
9 Basil Davidson, *The People's Cause. A History of Guerrillas in Africa*, (London: 1981), pp.139-40.
10 ibid., pp. 142–5.
11 J.S.Saul, 'Transforming the struggle in Zimbabwe', *Southern Africa* (February 1977), republished in *The State and Revolution in Eastern Africa* (London: 1979), pp. 109, 112, 114, 115–16, 120–21.
12 Cliffe, 'Towards an evaluation', pp.5, 17.
13 Letter to the *Herald*, Harare, 14 November 1980, quoted in Peter Yates, 'The prospects for a socialist transition in Zimbabwe', *Review of African Political Economy*, no. 18 (1980), The letter is signed 'Rusunuguko Shungudzomwoyo', plainly a *Chimurenga*, or wartime, pseudonym. It seems more likely to have been written by an ex-guerrilla than by a peasant.
14 Gary Wasserman, 'The economic transition of Zimbabwe', *Africa Report* (November/December 1978), pp. 39-45.
15 Cliffe, 'Towards an evaluation', p. 17.
16 Robin Palmer, *Land and Racial Discrimination in Rhodesia* (London: 1977); idem, 'The agricultural history of Rhodesia', in Robin Palmer and Neil Parsons (eds), *The Roots of Rural Poverty in Central and Southern Africa* (London: 1977) pp. 221-54. See also the chapters by Ian Phimister and Barry Kosmin in the same volume. Ian Phimister's social and economic history of Zimbabwe, now in preparation, contains a great deal of material on Zimbabwe peasant history. Richard Mtetwa's unpublished doctoral dissertation, 'The political and economic history of the Duma people of south-eastern Rhodesia', University of Rhodesia, 1976, remains the fullest detailed study of a twentieth century peasant society. Until its publication its argument can most readily be consulted in summary form in T.O.Ranger, 'Growing from the roots: reflections on peasant research in Central and Southern Africa', *Journal of Southern African Studies*, vol. 5 no. 1 (1978), pp. 110-13.

Writing of the Irish under the Penal Code, Edmund Burke had the savvy to realize 'that the most poor, illiterate and uninformed creatures upon earth are judges of a *practical* oppression. It is a matter of feeling; and as such persons generally have felt the most of it . . . they are the best judges of it'. The point has local application.

The Catholic Commission for Justice and Peace, Salisbury, Rhodesia, 23 March 1973, file 'Counter-Terrorism', CCJP Archives, Harare.

Sir, as far as we are concerned we hate everything in force. We appreciate with pleasure everything free will.

The people of Wenlock Block, Gwanda District and Some People of the Matopo National Park to Chief Native Commissioner, 23 July 1949. File S.1542. C6, 1940–1952, National Archives of Zimbabwe, Harare.

1

The
Zimbabwean peasantry
under early colonialism
and the nature of
peasant consciousness

This chapter, devoted as it is to the African peasantry of Zimbabwe in the early colonial period, can nevertheless usefully begin with yet another citation from a paper focused upon present-day Zimbabwe. At the Leeds Conference on Zimbabwe in 1980, Vincent Tickner presented a paper entitled 'Class struggles and the food supply sector in Zimbabwe'. It was conceived as a 'pioneering effort to delineate a little more clearly some of the class forces operating' in the food producing sector of the Zimbabwean economy. Tickner characterized the 'peasantry in Zimbabwe' as follows:

[It] differs from the peasantry in some other countries in the comparative lack of importance attached to private ownership because of the African land tenure systems. Although some of these peasants are predominatly subsistence-oriented, many have been integrated with the market economy to the extent that they regularly sell surpluses to other consumers through different market channels, and some produce specifically for the market. The extent of their class consciousness appears fairly low . . .

It is difficult to assess the class consciousness of agricultural producers in TTLs (Tribal Trust Lands). It is clear that during the Liberation War . . . producers in areas of the country where the liberation forces were operating regularly and attempting to set up semi-liberated zones (particularly in zones controlled by ZANU) had their political consciousness raised regarding different modes of production and their place in class struggles, but it is difficult to assess the extent of this consciousness raising. Certainly, in the ZANU camps out of the country considerable efforts were made to develop collective agricultural production systems, and it is likely that these returning refugees will have an impact on the class consciousness of other producers within the country and more socialistic ways of organising . . . Still, it appears that ethnic and family considerations, and a desire for land are often more major considerations among TTL producers than market possibilities or communal organisation, or the relationship of the peasantry to wider class struggles, and their political activity reflects this.[1]

By contrast, Tickner thinks, there has 'been a long history of organised political activity among the agricultural work force' on white farms and ranches. The experience of this 'agricultural proletariat' as 'a large work force located together (particularly in large centralised compounds) has led to a greater worker political activity, and greater susceptibility to wider ideas of worker organisation.' Unlike the peasantry, this proletariat has developed ' a wider political consciousness that extends beyond purely economistic considerations.'

To my mind this analysis springs almost entirely from theoretical models of 'peasants' and 'proletarians', and from expectations about how each is likely to act politically, than from anything in the actual agrarian history of Zimbabwe. To my mind, indeed, Tickner's propositions exactly invert the respective militancy of peasants and agricultural labourers in Zimbabwe. Whatever notional advantages in terms of communication and solidarity might be offered by a farm compound were usually cancelled out by the repressive control mechanisms and the divided national and ethnic origins of the workers. On the other hand, peasant 'family considerations and a desire for land' have gradually led many peasants to an understanding of their 'relationship to wider class struggles', and provided, during the war, the bases of peasant radicalism.

What is involved here, obviously, is a notion of 'the peasantry' as a general category. At the back of Tickner's mind, no doubt, was the whole body of writing about the difficulty of mobilizing peasantries into collective resistance and about the necessity of creating peasant consciousness through 'people's war' and by means of the inspired leadership of revolutionary intellectuals. Now, I do not doubt that many African peasantries *have* been difficult to mobilize and have lacked a consciousness of the mechanisms of their exploitation. Plainly, many peasantries have existed and been expropriated in Africa without having to pay rents or to offer labour services to landlords; without having had their land seized for white commercial farming; without for much of the time encountering overt state violence or compulsion to grow cash crops; without being able to see with their own eyes the mechanisms of price fixing which have creamed off their surpluses. A particularly striking example, among many which might be given, are the Maka of south-eastern Cameroon, who offered much 'primary' resistance to colonial occupation and much 'secondary' resistance to colonial administration without ever being in a position to develop peasant consciousness despite their objective existence as a peasantry.[2] But the Zimbabwean peasantry were in a very different situation. They had had to struggle and to develop a certain level of consciousness in order to *become* peasants in the first place: thereafter they developed another level of consciousness as they saw only too clearly with their own eyes the expropriation of land, the use of state violence and the establishment by the state of discriminatory price mechanisms. The revolutionary potentiality of African peasants plainly depended upon what *kind* of peasants they were. The Maka were one kind: Zimbabwean peasants quite another.

Obviously this comparison with the Maka makes things too easy for me. What happens if I return to a comparison with Mozambique? An answer to this is made more difficult by the existence within Mozambican historiography of two quite different assessments of agrarian history and consciousness. An interpretation which was dominant until quite recently did indeed emphasize the lack of peasant consciousness in Mozambique, and especially in northern Mozambique where FRELIMO began its guerrilla war and where it established genuine 'liberated zones'. Thus Edward Alpers told us in 1978 that:

FRELIMO understood full well that the war being forced on them by the intransigence of Portuguese colonialism was a political as well as a military struggle. Victory depended as much on political mobilization as on military preparation, so that when the first cadres were sent abroad for military training, FRELIMO organizers were starting to work within northern Mozambique. As Barbara Cornwall, an American journalist who travelled with FRELIMO in northern Mozambique in 1968, puts it:

'The question was not only that of arming and supplying a guerrilla force, but equally important, how an ignorant and intimidated peasant mass, which had learned the hopelessness of earlier rebellions, had been persuaded to support at whatever personal sacrifice, the embryonic revolt then being organized by FRELIMO. The answer was careful and prolonged mobilization of the peasants long before the first shot was fired . . . '

This was not a simple task. According to Ali Thomas Chidudu, an original FRELIMO mobilizer among the Makonde: 'When I first began to organize, the people did not know about politics. They only knew that they had been miserable all of their lives'. Cornwall comments that 'The peasants had neither the time nor the background for theoretical argument and abstract thought. They were complete pragmatists and illiterate as well'.[3]

In my Cambridge lectures I took this characterization of the peasantry of northern Mozambique as accurate. I then tried to account for the contrast with a Zimbabwean peasantry which knew about politics as well as about being miserable. I argued that becoming a peasant in northern Mozambique had not been at all a matter of choice. The area had first related to the international economy as a zone of active slave-trading: often led by slaving chiefs, the population had put up a strong resistance to the establishment of formal colonial rule: when at last Portuguese control *was* established, exploitation took the form of forced production of cotton so that the population became peasants involuntarily. This was a situation which could produce both violent resistance and subsequent despair but could not easily produce a radical peasant consciousness.

Since then, however, I have encountered an alternative historiography of northern Mozambique, one which is simultaneously more plausible and at the same time more challenging to the analysis I wish to make. As I have quoted Alpers for the first interpretation of northern Mozambique's rural history, so I can now quote him for the clearest statement of a second view. In a paper delivered in May 1983, Alpers sought to explore the class base of the liberation movement in northern Mozambique. He began with a picture thoroughly familiar:

Northern Mozambique was the last region of Portuguese East Africa to be brought under effective colonial rule. Niassa Province remained in turmoil from 1890 to 1912 as a result of determined armed resistance to colonial penetration which was led by the principal Yao ivory and slave trading chiefs. The Maconde and Malemia plateaux of Cabo Delgado Province were completely ignored by colonial authorities until after the debris had settled from the inter-imperialist conflict of World War I.

But now Alpers made a very different point. He emphasized that in pre-colonial times 'the penetration of merchant capital and the circuit of commodity exchange' in the region had brought about a pre-Portuguese *peasantry*. 'Well before the imposition of meaningful colonial domination,' he argues 'virtually all of the peoples of northern Mozambique were already engaged in one or another form of commodity production for the expanding world market.'[4]

From this perspective the opposition of the peoples of northern Mozambique to Portuguese colonialism – which expressed itself in massive migrations out of Portuguese territory – was not so much an opposition of people forced to become cash-crop producing peasants against their will. It was instead an opposition from people who wanted to go on being peasants on their own terms. 'It seems probable,' Alpers continues:

that the people of northern Mozambique were willing to accept a certain degree of State economic intervention in their lives so long as they were free to meet those requirements by strategies that they regarded as determined by the more basic considerations of socially necessary labour time. Historically, this meant, in effect, a commitment to commodity production . . . So long as they were able to meet the requirements of the colonial State and their own extra-subsistence requirements in this way, there was no reason for them to emigrate. But when this option was assaulted by the State, as happened in 1922, and there were no other available options for producing surplus value on their own terms, many people packed up and moved to more congenial circumstances of colonial domination in Tanganyika Territory . . . Forced cotton production, which was inaugurated in 1926 in northern Mozambique but greatly intensified in 1938, came to dominate the political economy of the entire region. Together with corvée labor for the capitalist sisal plantations that were scattered near the coast, the restrictions placed on Africans to operate according to their own strategies within the sphere of commodity production were severe.

So far from any longer writing of an 'ignorant and intimidated peasant mass', Alpers now described northern Mozambican peasants as achieving 'an especially sophisticated response' to Portuguese colonialism. He also showed Maconde immigrants into Tanganyika settling down 'as producers of subsistence crops for which there was an expanded market': cassava and beeswax being especially in demand from the 1940s. As he summed up:

By the time of Tanzanian independence in 1961 (and six months before the formation of FRELIMO in Dar es Salaam) there were well established Mozambican communities in several different parts of Tanzania. Most, but by no means all, were Maconde. Some were workers on sisal estates who had settled down with their families at the physical periphery of the plantations . . .Some were subsistence farmers who earned the cash that they required through agricultural labor for Makonde cashew nut farmers. Some were peasants who produced surplus cassava for sale . . .Some were peasant-artisans who have made Maconde sculpture in ebony world famous. Finally, there continued to be a steady stream of short term oscillating migrants who annually crossed the Ruvuma to sell their labour or their commodities in Tanganyika. . .

The common concern of all these individuals was to improve their economic prospects within the constraints of colonial domination. . .While there may have been many who regarded Tanganyika as a refuge from Portuguese oppression, I am suggesting that their behavior needs also to be appreciated as a more positive assertion of their own class interests. I would go on to suggest further that these interests reflected an acceptance, rather than a rejection, of commodity production and a reasonable degree of wage labor within the immature capitalist mode of production that was characteristic of colonial Africa. What they absolutely rejected about Portuguese colonialism was the extreme degree of State intervention . . . In terms of their class interests, while these Mozambicans rejected Portuguese colonial rule, they did not necessarily reject the capitalist regime with which they had become familiar in Tanganyika. . . . It seems to me that Maconde immigrants in Tanganyika remained overwhelmingly a class of peasants with clearly defined peasant interests right into the early 1960s.[6]

All this is clearly very different from the earlier historiography which stressed the incapacity of cultivators in northern Mozambique to achieve any sort of class consciousness or to carry out any sort of class strategy. We can add to it the conclusions of the admirable account of peasant resistance to forced cotton production inside Mozambique produced by Allen Isaacman and his Mozambican collaborators:

Many of the peasants who fled to Tanzania and Niassaland [sic] became involved in the struggle for independence. . . Thousands of cotton producers who did not initially flee to Tanzania actively organised FRELIMO cells in those areas of Cape Delgado and Niassa where opposition to cotton had been particularly strong, such as the Makonde highlands in Cape Delgado and the Maniamba region in Niassa. Other peasants covertly provided food, shelter and strategic information to the liberation forces. Their support proved critical. As their homelands were liberated, the existing vestiges of the cotton regime and other colonial capitalist institutions were immediately dismantled. The central role of the cotton producers during this initial phase suggests that greater attention needs to to given to the peasant base of FRELIMO, which has been often overlooked.[7]

And yet there still *is* a contrast with the Zimbabwean case. Alpers still ends his lastest paper by putting much more stress on the necessity for political education than I shall do in my account of peasant participation in guerrilla war, arguing that the 'political implications of this analysis are that peasants could certainly be moblized against any colonial regime that sought to restrict their economic opportunities, but that they were not, therefore, likely to become a radical or a revolutionary force without considerable political education.' Without such politicization, 'the logic of their peasant aspirations' could carry the Maconde into attempts 'to transform themselves into small capitalist farmers and traders.' Those Maconde who succeeded in becoming entrepreneurs could then produce a 'populist' ideology which was designed to further their own interests and at the same time to mobilize the peasantry into a counter-revolutionary opposition to the radical leadership of FRELIMO. And Alpers concludes that 'when the earliest organizational manifestations' of populist politics 'emerged among the Maconde in Tanganyika, it was not difficult to appeal to Maconde peasants and workers there that this kind of politics was in their best interests.'[8]

I shall argue that the specific history of Zimbabwean peasants produced a different outcome. In Mozambique the northern third of the country had the experience under colonialism which we have been discussing. The other regions had different experiences. As David Wield points out, the 'agriculture of the centre was characterised principally as a plantation production area, with 72% of national production of sugar, 89% of copra, 100% of tea . . . In this area the peasantry constituted a rural semi-proletariat. The south, on the other hand, contained a reserve army of labour with little development of domestic productive forces.'[9] The experience of the Zimbabwean peasantry was different from any of this. The 'acceptance of commodity production', which I call the choice of the peasant option, took place on the Zimbabwean plateau rather than in a diaspora, and this meant a steady development of peasant consciousness on the spot. Peasants were engaged in direct competition with white farmers from the beginning of their experience with colonialism and their understanding of agrarian capitalism and of the ways in which the state supported it ultimately produced a consciousness which was highly conducive to mobilization for guerrilla war, though not particularly supportive of 'collective agricultural production systems.' 'The logic of peasant aspirations' generated several attempts at entrepreneurial farming within Zimbabwe but all were frustrated by colonial interventions so that a rural entrepreneurial leadership of 'populist' politics did not emerge. And very many Zimbabwean peasants had arrived at a radical political programme for themselves before guerrilla political educators arrived on the scene. The truth of these assertions I shall only begin to document in this chapter; their full demonstration is the business of this whole book.

In this first chapter I hardly need to document the extent to which peasant producers in Zimbabwe responded to the early colonial market or the extent to which Africans in early colonial Southern Rhodesia chose to relate to the new economy as peasants rather than as workers. That they did this, and how they did this, without the need for any state intervention in the organization or 'improvement' of African agricultural production, is admirably set out in the work of Giovanni Arrighi, Robin Palmer and Ian Phimister, the most accessible expression of which is to be found in Palmer and Parsons' *The Roots of Rural Poverty*.[10] Nor do I wish here to repeat my own criticisms of the position taken in that book, since they will be fully worked through in later chapters.[11] The only comment I wish to make at this point is that the body of work had remarkably little to say about peasant 'consciousness'. It was, indeed, at its weakest when it came to discussing the dynamics of self-peasantization: how it related to pre-colonial experience, what decisions were made by whom in order to accomplish it, what strategies had to be consciously pursued in order to maintain it.

This was all the more remarkable because alongside this body of work there exists for Zimbabwe an influential literature on the topic of 'worker consciousness'. In particular, Charles van Onselen has demonstrated the existence and operation among migrant labourers in the mining industry of strategies of self help and protest which document by implication their understanding of the system in which they were caught up. Van Onselen was not, of course, arguing for a fully developed proletarian class consciousness under early colonialism. Nevertheless, the demonstration of an early 'worker consciousness' without any parallel discussion of a peasant consciousness has had the effect of making all too many commentators on Zimbabwean history suppose that on the basis of a continuous development from such 'worker consciousness' there has emerged a proletarian activism in Zimbabwe, while the peasantry have remained 'un-modernized' and 'apolitical'.[12]

In fact, it seems clear that one cannot talk about 'worker consciousness' in a migrant labour system without also at the same time considering a parallel and connected 'peasant consciousness'. Here I can call to my aid my first comparison with recent Kenyan historiography, Sharon Stichter's *Capitalism and African Responses*. In her introduction to the book, Stichter writes:

Several strategies of adjustment and opposition developed, including avoidance of labour recruitment and active resistance to it, seasonal wage-earning, desertion from bad employers, work inefficiency, and small-scale strikes . . .In the peasant sector, where land, transport and marketing conditions were favourable, Africans responded by turning quickly to cash crop production, and tried to avoid the lower levels of the labour market. The existence of cash crop and subsistence options made resistance in the labour market possible. . .In different parts of Kenya, varying combinations of labour market, cash crop and subsistence strategies evolved.[13]

This notion of the combination and interconnection of peasant and migrant strategies enables Stichter to produce that rare thing, a study of worker history which at the same time continuously comments on peasants. In the course of what is a remarkably short book given its range of interests, she comments upon rather than explores 'the degree of class differentiation within both peasant and migrant labour sectors', and asserts the 'class dynamic' behind the apparent coalition of wage labourers and 'communal' cultivators in a populist nationalist movement. In her sixth chapter she turns to the specific topic of 'Migrants and class consciousness'. Almost at once she makes use of van Onselen's work on Southern Rhodesian mine workers to demonstrate 'a well-developed worker consciousness'. Going a little beyond van Onselen she claims that migrant workers 'were in fact a class, in the minimal sense of occupying a similar place in the structure of production', and also 'a class in the sense of engaging in individual and collective class-related action.' For my purposes, however, her most pertinent comment is that the 'worker consciousness' which van Onselen demonstrated was 'specifically a "migrant" one, requiring interpretation in the context of the changing structure of production in the Central African peasant sector as well as in the mines.' In Kenya, too, she writes, 'labour action took particular forms depending on the articulation of the peasant and estate sector in the migrant system. Class action, and by implication class consciousness, has passed through definite stages of development corresponding to changes in the degree of dependence on wage labour in comparison to peasant production.' Discussions of 'worker consciousness', then, would seem to imply discussions of 'peasant consciousness'.[14]

Stichter points out that so intimate were the connections between peasant and migrant strategies that the establishment of a successful system of peasant farming might depend upon the investment of capital obtained by labour migrancy, and that the continuation of successful peasant farming might depend upon exporting some of those resident upon the land in the form of migrant labour. But for the purposes of giving some sort of notion of what a 'peasant consciousness' consisted of in early colonial Zimbabwe, it seems most logical to consider those areas where an attempt was being made to resist demands for labour altogether and to opt for a full peasant solution.

In the first years of Rhodesian colonialism there were many such areas on the plateau. Many of the Native Commissioners in charge of districts reported African choice of the peasant solution and warned of the effect that this would have on labour supply. As the Native Commissioner at Mrewa's reported in March 1900:

Very high prices were paid to the Natives for grain; at some places as high as 15/- per bag . . . This was due to the competition caused by an influx of new traders into the district . . . Each year the Natives are increasing their lands so as to have a certain quantity of grain to trade and I expect they will go on doing this until they reach a certain limit. A store put down at a location makes its own trade. The purchase of grain from Natives by the Traders for cash ought to be restricted, as . . . it will have a very bad effect on the supply of labour.[15]

Some of them even offered rather simplistic accounts of the motives that lay behind early self-peasantization. Thus, in March 1899, W.E.Weale, Native Commissioner in Chilimanzi, reported that:

the trade they carry on with Europeans is mostly in grain for cash, clothes, blankets, beads, etc, also salt, of which they consume an enormous quantity. The natives of this district have not far to go to dispose of their grain, there being six general dealers . . . and every year they look forward to the trading season eagerly for the pleasure of disposing of their surplus grain and satisfying their different wants. This sort of feeling has naturally made them grow bigger crops as their wants grow, brass wire, cloths and beads are still just as eagerly bartered for grain by the women, whereas the men are going in more for clothing, hats, knives, pipes etc. During the trading season a great deal of grain was traded.[16]

But to get below this superficiality to the much less jolly reality that underlay self-peasantization we need to focus on the history of one particular district. The district I know best is Makoni.

Makoni District contains a good deal of fertile land and enjoys more regular rains than many other parts of the country. It was noted for its productivity in grain in pre-colonial times, before any very significant amount of male labour was invested in cultivation. It seems probable that grain from Makoni was traded to surrounding districts when they ran short of food, and that grain was among the commodities traded with Portuguese agents from Mozambique in exchange for guns. Nevertheless, in pre-colonial times men were much more concerned with contestations over other goods than they were in seeking to control productive land. Chiefs, headmen and their leading followers contested for women and cattle above all, and though the women obtained by raiding and in war were employed in cultivation, these contestations took up much male energy. This pre-colonial system overlapped with the new demands of European traders for grain and of European settlers for land in the 1890s – indeed the people of Makoni did very extensive trade with the Portuguese in exchange for guns in the rebellion years of 1896 and 1897, when most of them joined the risings against the Rhodesian whites, while others who stayed out of the risings could sell grain to the Europeans and their black troops at the greatly inflated 'rebellion prices'.

Despite this kind of trade in grain, however, the people of Makoni had not been 'virtually engaged in one or other form of commodity production for the expanding world market . . . well before the imposition of meaningful colonial domination'.[17] The people of Makoni were not already peasants nor striving to preserve peasant status against colonialism. For them the process of self-peasantization took place painfully in the aftermath of conquest and alienation of land. And it took place in defiance of the very different plans for the economic future of the district which were being adumbrated by the victorious whites.

The capture and summary execution of Chief Makoni, the flight of his people into the rocky highlands, the re-establishment of an authoritarian administration and the rapid alienation of great expanses of Makoni District to capitalist investment companies and to individual white farmers were all designed to break up the pre-colonial political and economic system. Under the new dispensation it was planned that grain surpluses would be produced by white commercial farming and Native Commissioners waxed lyrical over the agricultural potential of the district. The African men of Makoni were now to provide the labour force necessary for the development of white enterprise: the African women were to produce subsistence crops. Four Reserves were set up, smaller in extent than the Native Commissioner himself recommended, in which this subsistence economy was supposed to sustain the task of reproducing migrant labourers. And the line of rail from Beira through Umtali to Salisbury was rapidly built through Makoni District, running like a spinal cord through its agriculturally productive region. The railway was intended to knock the bottom out of 'rebellion prices' for African grain and to make possible in the longer term a viable white farming economy in Makoni, whose products could reach the markets of Salisbury and Umtali.

It seemed at first as if this new economy had been created at one blow. 'The present half year commences with the Mashona rising,' ran an administrative report in January 1897. 'As soon as Makoni's kraal was taken all the chiefs in this district were called upon to supply carriers to bring up food-stuffs from Chimoio. The number so supplied was far in excess of that ever supplied before in the same time . . . This office also sent down boys to work on the railway both on maintenance and construction.'[18] In Makoni itself the new 'loyalist' chief sent in large contingents of labour. And for the next two or three years administrative violence ensured that this labour flow was maintained. Messengers and African police combed the new Reserves searching for deserters from the railway work, 'thrashing' kraal heads and seizing cattle, fowls and property.[19] The violent atmosphere of the district was well caught in early 1899 by Native Commissioner Morris, temporarily in charge of Makoni

District while its own Comissioner was absent:

> I asked [chief Makoni] if he had any complaints to make and he complained of the treatment his people were subjected to by some of the Angoni police and native messengers . . . I found that the natives had very good reason for complaint. The messengers in some cases had taken their women and raped them and thrashed others with sjamboks . . .There was a very large demand for native labour . . . Makoni sent in over four hundred, of these about three hundred went to the Beira railway to work. He promised to send in two or three hundred more.[20]

Many other men were pressed into work, over and above the chief's consignment and since the Makoni District annual report of March 1899 estimated the total African adult male population as only some 5000 it is plain that a large proportion were being pressed into *chibaro* forced labour. The same annual report summed up the apparent achievements of the policy of administrative violence, being as enthusiastic about the propects of rapid growth for a white farming economy as about the potential of Makoni African men for industrial employment:

> Many [European] families that ran away during the rebellion are returning. I am certain that in a few years time Makoni will be one of if not the most thickly populated district in Mashonaland. The Mashona of this district I am sure is capable of being made a good workman. I have had ample proof of this here. I have supplied boys to bridge contractors and have heard these men say some of the young men in a few days were equal to any of the coast boys. I have seen Mashona boys myself using rivetting machines as well as any Colonial native. From what I have seen of raw natives coming to work in the Transvaal and in the Tati concession, I am of the opinion that boys from . . . Makoni's will compete with them.[21]

In fact things developed very differently. As open coercion of labour gave way to economic pressures Makoni became one of the districts notoriously least productive of migrant labourers. The experiences of forced *Komboni* (Company) labour were vividly remembered and resented, as they still are today. In 1981 the centenarian Manyukire Gorembeu recalled them for Peter Cha-kanyuka:

> Manyukire Gorembeu vividly remembers *Chibaro*, which the people called *Komboni*. He says Messengers were sent to every village to recruit labour-ers. 3 people were to be sent from every village. His father Kuchenga Gorembeu sent two sons from the family instead of one because he wanted his sons to look after each other. . . Manyukire took part in the *Komboni* which was the construction of the railway line between Salisbury and

Marandellas. He remembers that many people were disabled. . . The main job of Manyukire and his colleagues was wood cutting and carrying railway sleepers. He says most people preferred to be disabled because it meant relief from recruitment or duty.[22]

African men in Makoni similarly remembered their first traumatic experiences of working underground on the mines. And above all they disliked working for white farmers.

African labour resistance handicapped white commercial agriculture in Makoni District. So did competition from African-grown maize. In March 1900 Native Commissioner Ross wrote optimistically of white agricultural development in Makoni, noting that the 'white farmers in the District have also brought fresh land under irrigation with very good results. . . There is room for more white agricultural settlers; most of the vacant ground, amounting to hundreds of thousands of acres, is the property of certain pioneer syndicates, but they are one and all ready and willing to rent, sell or lease their lands on fairly favourable terms.'[23] Ross was over-optimistic. The investment companies of Makoni soon discovered that it was more profitable for them to raise rents from African 'squatters' or to trade in grain produced by the Africans living on their land than to sell or lease land to would-be white farmers. Makoni became for the next two decades the most developed of the African grain-marketing district economies of Southern Rhodesia and by far the largest marketer of African-grown maize.

This resistance to the planned colonial economy was made possible by the determined self-peasantization of most of the African population of the district. This was not an easy business, arrived at almost accidentally: not a question of marketing what had been produced before as a 'normal insurance' surplus against famine now that colonial relief measures brought relief from fear of starvation; nor a question of marketing a surplus which had hitherto been raided by the Ndebele – to cite two of the speculations which historians have advanced to account for early colonial peasant production in Zimbabwe. On the contrary, it involved the deliberate and painful adoption of a number of strategies designed to maximize the potentials of peasant production: strategies which meant important innovations in the division of labour, in staple crops, in location of residence, and subsequently in technology and ideology. These patterned changes testify to a 'peasant consciousness' in Makoni District just as clearly as the patterns of African migrant labour desertion confirmed 'worker consciousness' to van Onselen.

In order to become and remain a successful peasant it was

necessary first and foremost to have access to markets. In Makoni this involved a great and almost unperceived movement of population. Prior to the conquest, the African population had spread out over the whole district, clustered together in relatively few and widely dispersed fortified settlements, the largest of which were described by the whites as 'real towns'. As a result of the fighting of 1896 many people had fled from these settlements into the high lands of the north and east of the district. In the years after 1898, however, a great migration of people took place which was voluntary and willed but which was certainly not designed to reproduce the pre-colonial pattern. It was designed, rather, to produce a *peasant* pattern of settlement.

As early as August 1899, Native Commissioner Ross, back in his district after the curacy of the more tender-minded Morris, reported his struggle to control patterns of settlement:

During my absence from the District the last six months I find that a great many changes have taken place amongst the Natives, which, in my opinion, should not have been permitted, i.e. the large kraals which I located, have, to a great extent, been broken up, and small kraals dotted all over the District. . . The kraals I located consisted of from 30 to 150 huts, and I held the head of such kraals responsible, as far as possible, for any offence . . . by a Native under his control. Under the present circumstances it is impossible to cope satisfactorily with all the offences committed, as the heads of these small kraals have absolutely no control over the Natives.[24]

There thus began a process which was to lead to very dispersed peasant settlement, to the breakdown of all tributary payments of labour or crops to chiefs and headmen, and to the investment of all available labour in production for the market.

Soon the movement of families became more directed and systematic. It happened that the largest of the four demarcated Reserves, Chiduku, though allocated by the Native Commissioner in an area of land not applied for by whites, followed the line of the new railway, which ran only a few miles distant from its eastern border. The northern part of Chiduku Reserve was close to a network of farm roads which linked producing white farmers to the district centre and railhead at Rusape. Soon there began a movement of thousands of Africans into Chiduku. It was not at this stage that the whites were forcing them or even telling them to go into Chiduku. The huge land investment companies liked having African tenants on their lands to pay rents and dipping fees; producing white farmers liked having 'squatters' on their lands from whom they could buy grain cheap and levy labour.[25] Africans moved into Chiduku in order to be peasants, in an imperfectly documented

process which has tantalizingly similar patterns to the great movement of 'squatters' which has moved *out* of Chiduku and the other
Makoni Reserves on 'European' land since 1980. By 1907 there
were some 11 000 people in Chiduku Reserve cultivating an estimated 5250 ha: the other three Reserves together held only some
2700 people and 1450 ha of cultivated land.[26] In 1909 the clerk in
charge, Makoni, wrote of Chiduku as 'the largest and most suitable
for cultivation [which] carries considerably more natives than any of
the others, and latterly the number has greatly increased'.[27] By 1914
more than half of the total African population of Makoni was in
Chiduku, the rest being distributed among the other Reserves, the
investment estates and the farm. Instead of nucleated settlements
there was now a scatter of peasant family homesteads over the
whole productive area of Chiduku. At the end of the process, in
1926, the Assistant Native Commissioner, Makoni, summed it all
up. 'The natives of Makoni District,' he wrote, 'are wealthy as
regards stock and grain, it is therefore difficult to get them to turn
out and work . . . [they] move about selecting the best soil and then
making their kraals.'[28]

By 1926, as motor lorries began to penetrate the African Reserves, the improved communications meant that peasants could
afford to select the best soil even if it was located in previously
relatively inaccessible areas. In the founding years of the Makoni
peasant economy, however, they had to choose land close to the
town or the line of rail whether it was good land or not. Ironically,
the best testimony to peasant strategies of land settlement comes to
us from one of the greatest enemies of black farmers in Makoni, H.
Barnes Pope. Barnes Pope was spokesman for what he called the
'producing farmers' to the north of Chiduku; perennially short of
African farm labour, he had long lobbied for the Chiduku peasant
economy to be undercut by the removal of land close to communications from the Reserve. In 1914 he was cabled by the Lands
Department asking him to undertake 'immediate inspection certain
lands Makoni district'; he was to tour Chiduku and report on 'the
different classes and approximate extent of the soils encountered',
distinguishing between 'granite soil suitable for Native occupation'
and the richer soils that might be allocated to whites. 'The information,' he was told, 'is required with a view to the possible re-
adjustment of the boundaries.'[29] But Barnes Pope's report gave so
vivid a picture of an African peasant economy almost feverishly
focused on the grain trade that it was ultimately used by the High
Commissioner as an argument against the alienation of land which
was being so effectively used. As Pope reported:

The Reserve is heavily populated in all parts where it comes into contact with European occupation, the Natives having congregated in these parts on account of the facilities offered in trading their produce – in such localities practically the whole available land is under cultivation or lately abandoned. In other parts very few natives are found. The Natives grow large quantities of mealies, rapoko and munga for sale and may for the most part be considered farmers.

[In Tandi area, close to Rusape and the railway] a large number of kraals and practically every available portion of land is under cultivation . . . the whole population giving their time almost exclusively to the growing of crops for sale to the Indian traders.

[South of the Rusape river but along the eastern frontier of Chiduku, close to the line of rail] the whole of the available land on the railway borders is under cultivation by Natives and the population is very large for the class of country, the Natives having moved from the interior to be near Rusape and Inyazura for the trading of their produce.[30]

A later attempt to extract land from Chiduku – this time the part of the Reserve lying south of the Inyazura river – led to a tour of inspection by the Resident Commissioner. His findings revealed that the peasant economy flourished in this region of Chiduku also:

The Area south of the Inyazura River differed in character somewhat from the rest of the Reserve. The country was more open. . . From the time that the party entered this part of the Reserve until they left it, they were constantly passing through native gardens which were either being prepared for the coming season's crops, or had been under cultivation the previous season, or were old lands lying fallow. Native kraals were numerous, although none of them were large. . . The land is required for the accommodation of those natives at present residing upon it.[31]

Once in place, whether in Chiduku or on European-owned land close to markets, it was necessary to further the process of self-peasantization by making new allocations of labour time, by opening up greater areas of land to cultivation, and by growing new crops. Male labour now came to be invested in agriculture to a much greater extent than in the past. Men were heavily involved at the opening of the agricultural year. As early as November 1899 Native Commissioner Ross was reporting the end of the Makoni District's export of large numbers of male labourers. 'In many of the smaller kraal', he wrote, 'I find that they are now absolutely without food; living chiefly on monkey nuts, and occasionally being able to buy a little grain from the larger kraals . . . Labour is almost unobtainable at present, as the Natives are all busy preparing lands and sowing them, and cannot be tempted to go out to work, now that rain has fallen.'[32] The shortage of labour continued on into March 1900, all the men 'being busy with their lands.' 'A great deal of new land has been brought under cultivation this year and I anticipate that a larger quantity of mealies, etc will be traded in consequence.'[33]

By 1901 it had become clear that male labour was not only being invested in opening up and planting land. In April Ross reported that little labour was available because the men were all engaged in reaping.[34] In June he noted that 'labour has been very scarce during the last month, no boys whatever having been registered'; meanwhile men and women were carrying their grain into Rusape and the outlying stores and 'trading is being carried on to a great extent.'[35] From September, when the lands began to be opened up, through to June, when the crop was traded, Makoni men in the zones of peasant production put their labour into agriculture. By December 1909 a new Native Commissioner was coming to terms with the reality that Makoni District was just not going to provide labour to European farms or mines: 'The natives,' he noted, 'are fairly wealthy and very few of them are under any necessity of doing any work beyond their own farming operations.'[36] And in July 1910 the same Commissioner gave the most vivid picture available in the official reports of the male input to the Makoni peasant economy:

The natives in many parts of the District are still busy threshing their grain. While on patrol in the southern parts of the Makoni and Chiduku Reserves I saw splendid harvests . . . Labour supply has been very meagre, apparently owing to the natives being busy helping each other in their harvesting operations. At many kraals I visited I found gangs of young men engaged in threshing corn and in breaking up new lands for the coming season . . . I made further patrols during the month . . . and in all parts I found the natives civil and orderly and busy at their harvesting and conveying grain to trading centres for sale.[37]

These realities compelled a reluctant modification of administrative stereotypes. After the death of Ross Makoni District was briefly in the care of one Sweeney, whose annual report for 1908 somehow managed to combine a picture of the prosperity of Makoni peasant agriculture with the old allegation of male laziness. He estimated that at most one-third of Makoni men had worked for Europeans during the year:

This leaves a balance of very nearly two thirds of the able bodied men lolling about their kraals in idleness drinking beer. . . Tax money can be obtained quite easily by disposing of their surplus grain to European and Indian traders for cash. This system . . . not only has a bad effect on the labour supply . . . but induces the native . . . to spend his time at home in absolute idleness.[38]

But as the Chief Native Commissioner noted in 1909, 'the ordinarily accepted theory that the women do all the work in the fields is gradually being contradicted.'[39] Native Commissioner Meredith of Makoni had come to realize by the end of 1909 that his predecessor's picture of male idleness was very far from the truth. 'The natives,' he reported, 'appear to be increasing the acreage of their lands slightly every season as the demand for their produce increases . . . They are not averse to improvement in seed and would willingly experiment with a better class of mealies. They have no present desire to use European implements such as ploughs and harrows.' Meredith's account, indeed, describes the very height of intensive male labour input, when maize was largely grown by men as a cash crop and the hoe was being used to open up the land. Meredith noted that even fewer men were leaving Makoni for paid employment than before. 'The majority of them,' he wrote, 'prefer not to work at all. They are really competing farmers producing large quantities of grain which finds a ready sale.'[40]

A good deal of this male labour – and a good deal of female labour too – was put into an annual expansion of the family cultivated area. 'Each year the Natives are increasing their lands,' ran a report in 1900, 'and I expect they will go on doing this until they reach a certain limit. A store put down at a location makes its own trade . . . The purchase of grain from Natives by the Traders for cash ought to be restricted, as . . . it will have a very bad effect on the labour supply.'[41] In 1903, after yet further expansions of the cultivated area, Native Commissioner Ross of Makoni wrote to 'suggest the adoption of an Act similar to the Glen Grey Act . . . by which the native pays quit rent for the ground he cultivates; at present the paltry sum of 10 shillings per hut is so easily earned that it will never induce them to work.'[42]

Taxes were increased and grain prices fell; there were droughts and famines as well as good years – but the response of the Makoni peasants to every eventuality was always the same. They increased the cultivated area. By the end of the 1920s this process had almost reached its limit and it was reported that 'the number of cattle in the Reserve is becoming too large as so much of the ground is under cultivation.'[43] Nevertheless, Makoni peasants responded to the collapse of cereal prices in the depression year of 1930 by yet further extensions of their land. 'Natives have been warned,' it was reported, 'against increasing their acreage under mealies but pertinently point out that to secure an amount of money equal to preceding years they must dispose of a greater quantity of grain.'[44]

With increased labour input and on these extended cultivated areas, the aspirant peasantry of Makoni grew new crops. As early as

1898 the Native Commissioner, Umtali, writing of his whole region, remarked that:

We have an agricultural race superior to any that I know in South Africa with the single exception of the Basutos . . .The Natives of Mashonaland go in largely for manuring especially by phosphates . . .They seem eager to get the seed of any grain or vegetable which would find ready sale with the European . . . I have already seen potatoes, cabbage, cauliflowers, onions, cucumbers, beans, etc growing of which the Natives have had no previous knowledge.[45]

Peasants in Chiduku grew these crops for sale in Rusape and by the 1920s were growing them not only for sale to whites but 'for their own use'.[46]

But the key to successful self-peasantization in Makoni was the enormous extension of maize growing. Before 1900 maize had been little grown or used in Makoni. Old Manyukire Gorembeu remembers the days of his youth at the end of the nineteenth century as a period when farmers in Makoni 'grew their crops using hoes. They made small beds usually near mountains where there was fertile soil. They grew *rukweza*, pumpkins, *mhunga* and cowpeas especially. Maize came only in recent times.'[47] Similarly, Mapani Magadza recalls her girlhood in the early twentieth century when '*Njera* and *mhunga*, rice and cow-peas were chief crops. *Nzungu* and *Nyimo* were very important. Maize was rarely grown. If grown it was eaten when green. No meal was made out of maize. Dry maize was fried and pounded.'[48] But the younger Mbidzeni Luciah, who entered the same area of western Chiduku as a bride in the 1920s remembers that:

when she first came to Chakanyuka's the people grew crops by using hoes. . . Chief crops were *rukweza, mhunga* and *nzungu*. Maize was becoming important but was coloured maize . . . Maize was grown as a cash crop when whites bought it . . . People transported their crop products to Rusape. She took part in some of these trips. Often they slept at Utandi on their way to and fro. From their sales they bought a vest from a bucket of maize.[49]

All these three informants lived in the part of Chiduku furthest away from Rusape and the line of rail. In the northern and eastern areas of Chiduku the adoption of maize took place much more rapidly. As early as March 1900 Ross assumed that a large maize crop was being planned. 'A great deal of new land has been brought under cultivation this year,' he noted, 'and I anticipate that a larger quantity of mealies, etc will be traded in consquence.'[50] In May 1901 the Assistant Native Commissioner wrote of 'mealies being traded in large quantities'.[51] From then on Makoni became more and renowned as a maize producing district. Makoni first produced more maize; then sold more maize; then produced maize of better quality than any other district. We have already seen Native Commissioner Meredith in 1909 noting that Makoni peasants 'would willingly experiment with a better class of mealies.' By the end of the 1920s their experiments had been successful. As the District Annual Report noted, 'A very good stamp of mealies is grown by the Natives who are gradually improving in their methods of agriculture and monkeynuts are another staple crop for which a ready market is found. . . Market gardening is finding increasing favour.'[52] As this citation suggests, by the 1920s peasants in most parts of Makoni had long adopted maize as a staple food as well as growing it as a cash crop. 'It is a noteworthy fact,' a Commissioner noted in 1906, 'that the natives are taking more to mealies as the staple food. Rukweza is becoming neglected except for beer.'[53]

It was all very well to occupy land relatively close to markets or traders; to reallocate labour time; to open up more land; to adopt new staples and to grow new crops. In addition to all this, the Makoni peasantry also had to evade white attempts to subdue or to dominate their production. In particular they had to deal with traders who attempted to set up an effective monopoly so as to force down prices, or to pay in kind rather than in cash, or generally to exploit the peasant producer beyond what the new peasant moral economy thought acceptable.

Producers in Makoni were relatively well off in that the combination of large cereal surpluses and the railway attracted traders to the district and ensured sales even when producers in other districts could find no-one to buy. In Makoni white farmers themselves did an extensive trade in African-produced maize and cattle; Afrikaner *by-woners* trekked into the Reserves to buy African produce; Indian shopkeepers in Rusape tried to attract African grain producers to do business with them. But peasants were not satisfied. Often they protested to the administration. Thus in June 1916 producers in Weya Reserve, an area in north-west Makoni, remote from markets, 'asked to have a store established in their locality which will give *cash* for grain. . . There are four Reserves in this district,' wrote a Native Commissioner, 'and there is not a store in any of them. This is a growingly important consideration. . . . in view of the fact that every pound of grain sold has to be carried on the head.'[54] Peasants also protested vigorously when prices fell:

The natives have several times expressed their disgust at the low prices they are obtaining at present and regard the circumstances as a grievance against the traders, who they say will not give them more than a shilling for a large basket full of grain . . . Local labour does not appear to be plentiful. The natives have abundance of grain and are depending on raising all the money they want this season by selling it.[55]

Again, in June 1921, a month in which the Chief Native Commissioner reported for the territory as a whole that 'reports are practically unanimous on the complaints of natives with regard to the low price grain and stock command', the Makoni monthly report recorded that:

Financially the outlook is not good for natives – outside traders are paying much smaller prices for grain than last year and instead of the natives receiving between 7 and 8,000 pounds for their grain they will not get much more than half this amount this season. The natives find it difficult to understand that prices of clothing etc still keep up and prices for grain go down – this year two bags of grain will only purchase what one bag did last year.[56]

But peasants did not only complain against low prices. They also took action. Sometimes this was directed against individual traders whose prices were too low or who exploited the producer in other ways. Thus Takapera Moda Chakanyuka recalls how in the 1920s his family used to carry:

farm products like maize and groundnuts to 'Rangwani', a white farmer near Headlands. People were paid 5 shillings for one and a half bucketsfull of groundnuts and maize. 'Rangwani' used to make them fill the bucket to the brim saying it should look like Mount Wedza. Then he kicked it to spill the extra amount over the bucket edge and then asked them to refill to the brim so that it would look like Mount Chironga. Instead of receiving cash they were asked to buy from his store. Men got a vest for a bucket of maize and a pair of shorts for a bucket of groundnuts.
So they abandoned going to 'Rangwani', preferring Rusape. They spent a night in a cave in Utandi on their way to and from Rusape. Generally people carried their crops and later they used donkeys. Indian traders were far better than 'Rangwani' for they did not make them overfill buckets.[57]

On other occasions collective action would be taken against all traders. In August 1923 and again in October 1930 Makoni producers held back their grain from the market as a protest against low prices. In general we can credit the testimony of Harry Margolis, who became by far the largest grain trader in Makoni District, as to the shrewdness of his African peasant customers. In 1944 he argued that:

It can be shown that conditions of competition are more prevalent in the sphere of native trading than in any other sphere of commercial activity . . . Many of the traders are accustomed to low standards of living . . . Natives themselves are prepared to resort to any effort in order to obtain goods at the cheapest possible price, and it is well known that they will travel considerable distances in the hope of obtaining a particular article cheaper elsewhere . . . The natives knew (before 1939) exactly the price of the commodity they were buying from one store to another in any district . . .It would be useless for a trader to ask 1/6 for a kaffir hoe which the native knew was 1/- at other stores . . . The native knows the exact price of any commodity he wishes to purchase before he makes the deal. . . It may be true that traders resort to barter in the effort to augment their sales, but it is my considered opinion that their efforts are fruitless, as natives in general are well qualified to differentiate between a good and an inferior article. Long before it was compulsory, it was always my practice to insist on the native taking cash for his grain. The truth is that the native knows exactly what he is about, and if it suits him to accept conditions of barter nothing will move him otherwise, but if he desires to retain his money he will not hesitate to demand it.[58]

But perhaps the most striking demonstration of peasant consciousness – because of the degree of determination it required and because of the comprehension of the white system it displayed – was the refusal of African peasants in Makoni to accept famine relief from the administration or to buy back grain from the traders at famine prices. The peasants of Makoni understood very well that official famine relief had to be paid for in migrant labour which would take men out of the agricultural sector just when they were wanted for the still greater expansion of the cultivated area which was always the peasant response to drought and famine. They also understood very well that it would be fatal to fall into debt to traders. So they took what steps they could to avoid shortage. At a very early stage of self-peasantization they learnt to moderate their marketing of grain. 'The Natives,' reported the Native Commissioner, Makoni, in March 1901, 'were careful to retain sufficient grain for their own consumption; last year they traded all away and at one time of the year many kraals were in a starving condition.'[59] Thereafter an annual reserve was built up as an insurance. Thus in the 1913/14 season crops failed in Makoni after previous months of heavy grain trading. Yet the Native Commissioner was able to report in December 1913 that 'the natives have not shown a great amount of concern as they have plenty of grain in their stores.'[60] Still, whenever two bad years followed in succession these stores ran out and Makoni peasants had to cope for themselves with the threat of famine. Native Commissioners often recorded that in such situations those who had grain supplied the wants of those who had not. In fact the process of surviving drought without having to turn to the whites was much less collective and benevolent than that. Sometimes it could be achieved by individual initiative. Thus peasants close to the markets sold all the grain they produced in a drought year, even if it was inadequate for their subsistence needs; then with the high prices they got in a year of shortage they trekked into the interior, away from road and rail, and bought a greater quantity of grain with the money. But if no grain at all was raised by a peasant family, or if inadequate crops were harvested far from markets, more desperate measures had to be taken.

Oral informants in Makoni recall the last of the great pre-colonial famines:

Some of the great disasters Manyukire remembers are the great famine of the 19th century known as Masvaure or Gochenhere . . . He remembers hearing stories of some people who died on their way to seek relief from areas that had plenty. Those who died on the way back lost their parcels of food to others. Women left their areas of starvation to offer themselves as wives to men in the areas of plenty. . . These bands of wandering women often called at a village when there was beer.[61]

These extremities were supposed to have ended with the colonial pax, since wage labour and famine relief were now available. But still in 1903 a Native Commissioner could complain that even in the face of famine the men in his district would not go out to work but preferred more 'traditional' means of survival. 'If,' he noted, 'some more fortunate native guarantees to keep them in food, on promise of a sister or child as a wife at some future date, well and good.'[62] This was a costly, and soon an illegal, way of keeping male labour in the agricultural system. More frequently labour itself was pledged in return for food, or else family cattle were sold for grain. Thus Mbidzeni Luciah, who was born in 1909 in western Chiduku, remembers 'Chiguma's famine' in the early 1920s:

During this famine a good head of cattle was exchanged for a *dengu* (a basket that held 60 litres of grain) of *mhunga*. She heard stories of people who died of hunger on their way to areas of plenty. Some arrived and overfed and then died. She saw many people coming to Dewedzo for relief. The affected surrounding areas were Urozwi, Uhera, Makoni, Utandi and Wedza. Many people in Dewedzo made a fortune in the acquisition of cattle . . . Her father and brother both bought six cattle. Her mother bought one called *Chemhunga* because it had been bought with *mhunga* and was a very good breeder. When some found that no-one was prepared to offer grain for a whole beast they killed it and exchanged pieces of meat with grain.[63]

Those who had to dispose of cattle in this way tried to restock in a year of plenty. Thus in November 1923, after a much improved harvest, the Native Commissioner, Makoni, recorded that 'natives have been buying cattle to replace stock sold last year during the scarcity.'[64] But no doubt there were more permanent transfers of wealth in terms of cattle or the fruits of additional labour power. Some parts of Makoni seem to have escaped drought fairly regularly and thus to have been in a strong position relative to others. On the other hand, there is some reason to suppose that transfers of wealth during famines did something to balance the inequalities created in ordinary times by differential access to markets. The intensive maize producers of eastern and northern Chiduku, close to communications and regularly obtaining good prices, were particularly vulnerable to climatic conditions unfavourable to maize. They had to seek relief from those who lived further away from markets and who cultivated a much wider variety of crops. (Indeed Mbidzeni's story, cited above, documents precisely such a process.) In any case it is clear that coping with drought internally was a costly business and it is an indication of how determined peasants were not to become dependent upon the whites that they preferred it to administrative relief grain.

The result was that drought and famine did *not* break the Makoni peasant commitment to agricultural production and resistance to labour migration. Time and time again the Native Commissioner would predict that a year of dearth would result in abundant labour migration: time and time again this expectation was confounded. Time after time whites sought to offer relief maize in return for labour or for peasant acceptance of debt: time after time these offers were refused. Thus in 1911 white farmers in Makoni and elsewhere prevailed upon the administration to send Native Messengers to recruit labour forcibly for them in the Reserves: men were taken from planting their own fields and distributed to the whites: there ensued a season of drought and dearth.[65] In 1912 some of the white farmers who had enjoyed the fruits of this expropriation of labour offered maize to the hungry inhabitants of Chiduku. None of it was taken.[66] In July 1922, after another poor harvest, the Native Commissioner, Makoni, recorded that 'in the only applications I have had for famine relief I told the natives concerned I would supply whatever grain they required from local traders and guarantee the payment provided the natives would supply men in preparation for road work . . . So far not one native has turned out.'[67]

It seems to me that these aware, patterned and costly responses reveal an effective 'peasant consciousness' parallel to van Onselen's 'worker consciousness'. At this level, Makoni peasants were not 'intimidated'. Nor were they universally 'ignorant' and 'illiterate'. Makoni peasants took ideological initiatives which paralleled their productive responses. Makoni was one of the eastern districts which witnessed in the 1910s a grass-roots turning to Christian literacy, a movement which brought adult men and women into the village schools alongside their children. At first these peasant seekers after new skills did not discriminate between the three missionary societies which operated in Makoni: the grass-roots 'awakening' brought a flood of converts into the American Methodist, the Anglican and the Roman Catholic churches equally. But gradually there was a consolidation of particular zones of American Methodist, Anglican and Catholic folk Christianity as the varying churches offered significantly different models of rural society, each appropriate to one of the three levels of Makoni peasant consciousness.

The American Methodist Episcopal Church preached the gospel of the plough and aimed to turn out modern agricultural entrepreneurs. Their showpiece in Makoni District was Gandanzara village in Makoni Reserve, in an area favourably situated to supply the Umtali market. In 1923 the mission agriculturalist and overseer of the Gandanzara Circuit wrote:

The success of our native people in agriculture is really wonderful when you take into account that fifteen years ago this month I helped to start the first plow purchased . . .At present there are hundreds of plows owned by the natives and the crops grown are really wonderful. Some of our best stations like Gandanzara where the new methods have taken a firm grip are a wonderful demonstration. At this particular station every person who has any cattle has a plow, and there are forty-three plows owned by the people there. These people who own the plows are no longer poverty-stricken. They are the foundation of progress in the village whenever a forward move is to be made.[68]

'Many wagon loads of maize' poured out of Gandanzara in the 1920s. 'God's blessing truly rests upon the people of the Gandanzara circuit. They are a different people.'[69]

American Methodism, then, with its characteristic combination of revivalist enthusiasm under discipline, was the chosen church of the Makoni rural entrepreneurs. Anglicanism became the religion of the smaller-scale peasant producers of Chiduku: a network of Anglican villages rapidly grew up there, each focused upon the church and school and under the leadership of their evangelist. Canon Edgar Lloyd, for long the priest in charge of St Faith's Makoni, deliberately set out to create a peasant and a village church, 'traditional' in its use of totemic decorations, but 'modernizing' it its emancipation from the control of chief and headman and spirit medium over agrarian production. As for the Roman Catholics, their main station at Triashill lay cut off from communications and markets by a range of mountains. The full peasant option was not open to the men of Triashill, many of whom had to enter labour migration. But the Mariannhill fathers set out to recreate on their huge farm at Triashill a replica of pious nineteenth-century European Catholic peasant society. They introduced the rites of Ultramontane Catholicism – the Lourdes grottoes, the Fatima statues; they exorcised locusts and blessed seeds and prayed for rain. Pilgrimages to the sacred hills of Triashill farm brought back the migrant labourers and reconstituted the rural community. Folk Catholicism came to define the consciousness of a mixed subsistence-production and labour migration economy.

Nor was it only various forms of Christianity that gave content to peasant consciousness. In a recent paper I have argued that the Mwari High-God cult of western and southern Zimbabwe, which had been the major ideological support for the traditional tributary economy, came in the twentieth century to express instead the consciousness and interests of small-scale peasant producers.[70] A similar transition took place in the Makoni District. There the senior spirit mediums had validated the control by chiefs and headmen over the agricultural year and their right to tribute. In becoming peasants the people of Makoni had decisively broken away from the old tributary system and the rights of chiefs to tribute in produce and labour soon lapsed. But as the chiefs themselves became more and more dependent on colonial administrative patronage, a division of interest began to open up between them and the mediums. The chiefs were left oddly irrelevant to agricultural production. No chief in Makoni became an entrepreneur or a 'modernizing' farmer; nor could any chief any longer enforce the tributary system. Meanwhile, the ecological prescriptions of the mediums turned out to be quite consistent with one kind of peasant enterprise.

Men who farmed well within traditional ecological constraints enjoyed the favour and support of the mediums. Many peasants in Makoni, after all, were growing food crops, using hoes, employing traditional methods of enriching the soil. Mediums did *not* disapprove of such men marketing their surplus, though they *did* disapprove of the modernizing entrepreneurs of Gandanzara, with their ploughs and their refusal to observe the *chisi* rest days, proclaimed by the mediums in honour of the spirits. So mediums continued to command the loyalty of many peasants in Makoni. In 1981 Mapani Magadza described how her husband and his brother were evicted from white farmland in the 1910s and made their way to Nedewdzo in western Chiduku. Moving from land near markets to land more remote from them, the brothers found themselves in an area where productive farming went hand in hand with veneration of the spirits:

Zvitondi, the white farmer, was threatening them and demanding that they leave before reaping their crops. Chakanyuka and Mupfururi . . . were the two extended families to be adversely affected by this eviction. . . Mutakurwa Chakanyuka, head of the *guta*, stubbornly refused to evacuate before reaping his crops. *Zvitondi* was warning them that he would let his cattle feed upon their crops. However he did not. He let them harvest their crops . . . The people packed their crops into *makudza* (fibre baskets) loaded these on the backs of oxen . . . The journeys were made several times because they had plenty to carry to Dewedzo, their destination and to be their place of settlement . . . They were allowed to settle at an area of their choice. Chakanyuka chose to settle at Chipesa . . . Because Chakanyuka and Mupfururi were good at farming they were nicknamed *Ba Vana Banguranyika*, those who open an area to light. She first saw the use of *divisi* (fertility medicine) among the people they found living in Dewedzo. It was the spirit medium, Harudzingwi, who distributed *divisi* to the people. People were asked to gather together at this ceremony each family bringing their seed crops. Harudzingwi licked his fingers and dipped them into or touched the seed crops . . . This was done to keep away wild beasts and birds from destroying crops in the fields. They never went to drive birds from their *mhunga* and rice fields as people do now. She believes Harudzingwi was a great spirit medium . . . By the time they settled at Dewedzo churches had been established . . . The Roman Catholic Church was accepted by Mupfururi because it did not prohibit *mapira* sacrifices to the ancestors.[71]

Thus enterprising peasant agriculturalists at all levels of an increasingly differentiated peasant society adapted and developed ideologies in the first decades of colonialism.

I have been describing how men in Makoni chose the peasant option, stuck to it, and developed a set of strategies and a set of assumptions appropriate to the peasant role. Makoni was a particularly favoured area, both in terms of its natural fertility and in terms of communications. There were few other districts in which the peasant option could be so successfully developed, and some in which it could not be developed at all. But I am certain that the development of a peasant consciousness happened in many other parts of the territory. Recently Sarah Brown has examined African agriculture in Matabeleland during the first decade of the twentieth century. She has concluded that 'the Ndebele were able to make patterned responses similar to those of the Shona of Makoni district.' She shows that Ndebele cultivators opened up new lands; rapidly adopted the plough; grew new crops; and that 'the Ndebele peasants . . . were aware of their interests as a group and took action to protect these interests.'[72] Contrary to many preconceptions, the Ndebele were not only concerned with cattle raising: as one Matabeleland Native Commissioner remarked: 'the native realises where his market is and that the most easily disposed of grain is the mealie.' Indeed, Ndebele maize growers had a sophisticated appreciation of their role in the grain market. The Native Commissioner, Bulawayo, reported in 1914 that:

Early in August the reservation of goods and the enhancement of their price were evidence to the natives that the war was an event affecting all classes . . .A deputation of natives asked that the Government should intervene and prohibit the raising of the price of grain [by traders] 'because', they said, 'the grain is produced by us natives' . . .A number of natives had already formed a syndicate and bought a fairly large stock of mealies from a leading storekeeper.[73]

Brown remarks that the Matabeleland evidence 'does not reflect a radical form of militant consciousness since, after all, peasants chose to work within the new framework.' Nor would I wish to argue such a case for Makoni. There were several more stages to pass through before such a radical consciousness could emerge – stages which I hope to document in the chapters still to come. Plainly self-peasantization in Makoni, as elsewhere, was in many ways an adaptation to the colonial economy rather than a resistance to it. It is in fact notable that oral testimony concerning these decades in Makoni still refers to but does not passionately resent the loss of land to whites. The reason, I am sure, is that despite very extensive land alienation it was possible in this period to create a viable peasant economy. Many peasants were able to remain on 'white' land and to market their produce, while the Reserves still offered enough land to support peasant cultivation. As we shall see, the later evictions and alienations of the 1940s created a much more intense and bitter legacy of hatred and resentment because *these* evictions undercut and rendered impossible the peasant strategy.

Moreover, save at the level of the peasant strategy, Makoni peasants in the 1910s and 1920s chose to evade rather than to confront white power. When Native Messengers came into the Reserves in 1911 to press labour, and siezed women and stock in the course of doing so, the men made no resistance and no subsequent protest – they merely took to the hills, camping out there at night until the Messengers had left. It was left to Anglican teacher-catechists and to Anglican missionaries to make protest to the

Native Commissioner, carry the case to the Resident Commissioner and to give damning evidence at the subsequent Commission of Inquiry. In 1919 a police patrol, complete with Lewis gun, toured the Makoni Reserve. The peasants again resorted to evasion:

Though a large number of small kraals were passed and on every side were signs of a large native population, no more than twelve able-bodied natives were seen during the day . . . On the 23rd we left to patrol the northern and eastern portion of the reserve. We again passed numerous kraals, but saw scarcely any native. Those I saw, on both days, are a type entirely new to me, and though one cannot say they are insolent, they certainly appeared to be wanting in respect.[74]

The police commandant who led this patrol recorded some remarks which were to turn out to be very much to the point in the guerrilla war of the 1970s:

The country traversed was some of the most difficult I have seen in Rhodesia being extremely rugged . . . I am afraid should trouble ever occur in this Reserve that operations would have to be carried out either by European or Native infantry. The latter for preference as Europeans would experience considerable difficulty in climbing the hills, many of which would be almost impossible for men wearing boots.[75]

But in 1919 and for a many years thereafter there was no likelihood of trouble of this kind in Makoni. Given all this, my comparison with northern Mozambique might well seem to indicate the opposite of the case I have been arguing. After all, there was a good deal of resistance in northern Mozambique during precisely the decades in which the men of Makoni were turning themselves into peasants. And yet the point is that in becoming peasants they were not only relating directly to the colonial political economy; they were also engaging in something very like class contestation.

Certainly the white farmers in Makoni were in no doubt that they were engaged in a fierce struggle with black agriculture. They tried in every way they could to undermine black production and to shake labour for themselves out of the Reserves. Not content with the direct raid on labour in 1911 they tried twice to excise large portions out of the Chiduku Reserve and thus to drive black peasants away from markets and communications. These attempts were frustrated not by African peasant action but once again by the protestations of Anglian missionaries and the impressive industry of their converts. The Resident Commissioner, touring south Chiduku in 1920 to investigate whether the land should be handed over for white use, was impressed to discover a network of grain-producing Anglican kraals, each in 'charge of a native teacher . . . well educated and of more than usual intelligence . . . the native kraals clean and tidy, the men and women . . . better dressed than is usually the case.'[76] He recommended that the area be reserved for the use of these Anglican agriculturalists.

At this stage the majority of peasants had no way of frustrating white attacks upon them. But the knowledge that such attacks had been made and the knowledge of precisely which of their enemies had been behind them entered profoundly into peasant consciousness. In 1981 I collected oral traditions in Chiduku which still remembered Barnes Pope and the other white farmer agitators of the 1910s and 1920s and gloried in various improbable, though well-deserved, afflictions visited upon these enemies by the ancestral spirits.[77] Even at this stage of relative passivity Makoni peasants had an imaginative grasp of the realities of the Rhodesian political economy.

I find then that the Makoni case documents 'peasant consciousness' at an initial but significant level; I find that one can talk without too much rhetorical exaggeration about class contestation in the Makoni countryside; I find that an understanding of this consciousness and this contestation is essential to an understanding of later peasant nationalism and peasant war. In finding all this I am delighted to find myself fully in agreement with Phimister's latest analysis of the period I have been discussing. In a chapter of his eagerly awaited monograph on the twentieth-century social and economic history of Zimbabwe, Phimister documents 'rural struggle against capital and the state':

The attacks [on peasant farming] unleashed by the state and capital after 1907 were made on an increasingly uneven and broken social terrain. They did not simply roll across a smooth and featureless African landscape. On the contrary, their impact depended upon the shape assumed by two key features. One was the way in which each district was incorporated into the wider economy. The other, much more important, factor which itself crucially influenced the manner of regional incorporation, was the balance of class forces located in these same areas.[78]

Phimister goes on to work out these variables in relation to the two districts of Victoria and Belingwe. I have set out here some of the data available for a study of the 'balance of class forces' in Makoni. It was this balance of class forces – between black peasants and white farmers and between different layers of the black peasantry – which from district to district determined the shape of the rural societies upon which the impact of the Depression of the 1930s fell with such force. And it is to the impact of the Depression, the next stage in the evolution of Zimbabwean peasant consciousness, that I turn in Chapter 2.

NOTES

1 Vincent Tickner, 'Class struggles and the food supply sector in Zimbabwe', Leeds, 1980, pp. 9, 20.
2 Peter Geschiere, *Village Communities and the State. Changing Relations among the Maka of Southeastern Cameroon since the Colonial Conquest* (London: 1982).
3 E.A. Alpers, 'The struggle for socialism in Mozambique, 1960-1972', in Carl G. Rosberg and Thomas M. Callaghy (eds), *Socialism in Sub-Saharan Africa. A New Assessment* (Berkeley: 1978), pp. 276-77. The quotations are from Barbara Cornwall, *The Bush Rebels. A Personal Account of a Black Revolt* (New York: 1972), pp.30-4, 57.
4 E.A. Alpers, 'To seek a better life: the implications of migration from northern Mozambique to colonial and independent Tanzania for class formation and political behaviour in the struggle to liberate Mozambique', unpublished paper presented at Conference on 'The Class Base of Nationalist Movements in Angola, Guinea-Bissau and Mozambique', Minneapolis, May 1983, pp. 7,9.
5 ibid., pp. 11, 12-13.
6 ibid., pp. 20-23.
7 Allen Isaacman, Michael Stephen, Yussuf Adam, Maria João Homem, Eugenio Macamo and Augustine Pililão, ' "Cotton is the mother of poverty": peasant resistance to forced cotton production in Mozambique, 1938–1961', *International Journal of African Historical Studies*, Vol. 13, no. 4 (1980) pp. 614–15.
8 Alpers, 'The struggle for socialism' pp. 23-4, 25, 26.
9 David Wield, 'Mine labour and peasant production in southern Mozambique', in H. Dickinson (ed.) *Mozambique* (Edinburgh: Centre of African Studies, 1979), pp.79-80.
10 Robin Palmer and Neil Parson (eds.), *The Roots of Rural Poverty in Central and Southern Africa* (London: 1977).
11 T.O.Ranger, 'Growing from the roots: reflections on peasant research in Central and Southern Africa', *Journal of Southern African Studies*, vol. 5, no. 1 (1978) pp. 99-133.
12 Charles van Onselen, 'Worker consciousness in black miners: Southern Rhodesia, 1900-1920', *Journal of African History*, vol. 14, no. 2 (1973), pp. 237-55: idem, *Chibaro: African Mine Labour in Southern Rhodesia, 1900-1933* (London: 1976).
13 Sharon Stichter, *Migrant Labour in Kenya. Capitalism and African Response, 1895-1975* (London: 1982), p. xiii.
14 ibid., pp. 156-7.
15 Annual Report, Mrewa's, March 1900, file N 9/1/6, National Archives, Harare (NAH).
16 Annual Report, Chilimanzi, March 1899, file N 9/1/5, NAH. Weale

was not worried by the effect on labour recruitment, cheerfully suggesting the issue of 'good seed to the most intelligent natives'. The Native Commissioner in Hartley took a similar view: 'On every possible occasion I point out to them the profit that can be made from planting greater areas of ground, so as to reap a great deal more than they require for home consumption and thus be able to sell or barter the surplus. This is very desirable as the nearer to the mines kaffir grain can be brought the more cheaply can it be delivered there and the cheaper grain be bought so much the more easily can development be carried on.' Annual Report, Hartley, March 1899, file N 9/1/5, NAH.

17 Dr. H.H.K. Bhila has argued that in Manyika territory – to the east of Makoni and in more regular contact with the Portuguese over the centuries – a real degree of peasantization *had* taken place in pre-colonial times. H.H.K. Bhila, *Trade and Politics in a Shona Kingdom. The Manyika and their Portuguese and African Neighbours, 1575-1902* (London: 1982). Bhila writes:

The conventional view is that the peasantry came into being as a result of international capitalism . . . It should be noted however that production of surplus grain for purposes of selling was not anything new to the Manyika . . . There is ample evidence of this in local and inter-regional trade, long before the advent of colonialism . . . Viewed in this context, the emergence of the peasantry in a very embryonic form in Manyika and her neighbours south of the Zambezi dates . . . back to the thirteenth century and, in a much more recognisable form, to the sixteenth century. (p. 253)

Bhila's point is an important one, and one that helps to account for the responsiveness of Makoni African agriculture to market opportunity. Nevertheless, I do not think that cultivators in Makoni can be described as 'peasants' in pre-colonial times. There was relatively little male input into agricultural production and there was no *necessity* to produce annual surpluses.

18 Quarterly Report, Umtali, 11 January 1987, file NUA 2/1/1, NAH.
19 Nyakavina and Nyahangare versus Rudzidzo and others, 15 October 1901, file NUD 2/1/1, NAH. Rudzidzo and other Messengers were fined five shillings each for proved assault and theft.
20 E. Morris, monthly reports for May and June 1899, file N 9/4/3, NAH.
21 Annual Report, Makoni, 31 March 1899, file N 9/1/5, NAH.
22 Interview between P.M. Chakanyuka and Manyukire Gorembeu, Nedewedzo, Chiduku, 4 January 1981.
23 Monthly Report, Makoni, March 1900, file N 9/4/6, NAH. Ross also reported that 'a great deal of new land has been brought under cultivation this year and I anticipate that a larger quantity of mealies etc will be traded in consequence'; as a result he had not been able to supply much African labour, 'all being busy with their lands.'
24 Monthly Report, Makoni, August 1899, file N 9/4/4, NAH.
25 An example of the terms on which Africans lived on white-owned

farms is an 'Agreement entered into . . . between Hugh Williams of Laurencedale and Deda representing the Natives residing on the farm Laurencedale, in the Makoni District', 22 February 1902, file N 3/1/10, NAH. Williams guaranteed that 'he will not collect rent from the natives in kind or in other form' and that 'he will at no time take from the natives such land as they are cultivating without giving them land in return, such land to be sufficient to support them and their families.' In return each male African would 'work for three consecutive months at the option of the owner' though Williams undertook 'that he will not call out more than one fourth of the number of adult males at one time to work.' Plainly a peasant and a commercial farming economy both existed on Laurencedale. By contrast the local managers of the Bulawayo Estate and Trust Company which owned the Fairfield Estate carried out no farming operations of their own: they called out no labour but charged a rent of ten shillings a year per head. (A.R. Ross to Chief Native Commissioner, 16 August 1907, file N 3/1/10 NAH.

26 Clerk in charge, Rusape, to Acting Chief Native Commissioner, 16 August 1907, file L 2/2/117/31, NAH.

27 Clerk in Charge, Rusape to Superintendent of Natives, Umtali 8 April 1909, file L 2/2/117/31, NAH.

28 Assistant Native Commissioner, Makoni to Superintendent of Natives Umtali, 9 January 1926, file S.231, NAH.

29 F.W. Inskipp to H. Barnes Pope, Confidential cable, 24 March 1914, file NUA 3/2/1 NAH. The Anglican missionaries at St Faith's Makoni, protested against offical action being based on Barnes Pope's findings – 'evidence coming from such a source was likely to be be prejudiced, the anti-native policy of this gentlemen being well known in the district.' Petition of E.W. Lloyd, E.M. Lloyd and J. Hay Upcher to Resident Commissioner, 11 March 1918, file A 3/18/39/10, NAH.

30 Report on Chiduku, H. Barnes Pope, 28 April 1914, file ZAD 3/2/2, NAH.

31 High Commissioner to Administrator, 4 March 1920, file A 3/18/39/10, NAH. This letter reveals the highly conjectural basis of all population estimates for African areas at this time. The administration argued that there were only some 1543 Africans living in Chiduku south of the Inyazura river: the missionaries held that there were 5000: the Resident Commissioner arrived at an estimate of some 3900. Probably the figures for Chiduku population quoted earlier in this chapter are a serious underestimate.

32 Monthly Report, November 1899, file N 9/4/5, NAH.

33 Monthly Report, March 1900, file N 9/4/6, NAH.

34 Monthly Report, April 1901, file N 9/4/7, NAH.

35 Monthly Report, June 1901, file N 9/4/9, NAH.

36 Monthly Report, December 1909, file N 9/4/23. vol.3, NAH.

37 Monthly Report, July 1910, file NUA 6/2/1, NAH

38 Annual Report, Makoni, 1908, file N 9/1/11, NAH

39 Chief Native Commissioner's summary of 1909 Annual Reports, file

N 9/1/12, NAH. The CNC added his own sexist gloss: 'It is reported that in parts the women are becoming idle and useless, while native men from other parts are employed to do their work.'

40 Annual Report, Makoni, 1909, file N 9/1/12, NAH.
41 Annual Report, Mrewa's, 1900, file N 9/1/6, NAH.
42 Annual Report, Makoni, 1903, file N 9/1/8, NAH.
43 Monthly Report, March 1930, File S 235.524, 1930, NAH.
44 Monthly Report, December 1930, file S.235.524, 1930, NAH.
45 Native Commissioner, Umtali, 1 April 1898, file N 9/1/1, NAH.
46 Annual Report, Makoni, 1921, file N 9/1/24, NAH.
47 Interview between P.M. Chakanyuka and Manyukire Gorembeu, Nedewedzo, Chiduku, 4 January 1981.
48 Interview between P.M. Chakanyuka and Mapani Magadza, Nedewedzo, 9 Januray 1981.
49 Interview between P.M. Chakanyuka and Mbidzeni Luciah, Nedewedzo, 18 January 1981.
50 Monthly Report, March 1900, file N 9/4/6, NAH.
51 Monthly Report, May 1900, file N 9/4/8, NAH.
52 Annual Report, Makoni, 1929, file S.235/507, NAH.
53 Annual Report, Umtali, 1906, file N 9/1/9, NAH.
54 Monthly Report, June 1916, file N 9/4/30, vol.2, NAH.
55 Monthly Report, June 1909, file N 9/4/22, vol.2, NAH.
56 Monthly Report, June 1921, file N 9/4/40, vol.2, NAH.
57 Interview between P.M. Chakanyuka and Takapera Moda Chakanyuka, Nedewedzo, Chiduku, 16 January 1981.
58 Evidence of Harry Margolis to the Native Trade and Production Commissioners, 23 June 1944, file ZBJ 1/2/2, NAH.
59 Annual Report, Makoni, March 1901, file N 9/1/7, NAH.
60 Monthly Report, December 1913, file N 9/4/27, NAH.
61 Interview between P.M. Chakanyuka and Manyukire Gorembeu, Nedewedzo, Chiduku, 4 January 1981.
62 Annual Report, Mrewa's, March 1903, file N 9/1/8, NAH.
63 Interview between P.M. Chakanyuka and Mbidzeni Luciah, Nedewedzo, 18 January 1981.
64 Monthly Report, November 1923, file S.235.519, NAH
65 For a full account of the 1911 labour crisis see Terence Ranger, 'Literature and political economy: Arthur Shearly Cripps and the Makoni labour crisis of 1911', *Journal of Southern African Studies*, vol. 9, no. 1, (October 1982), pp.33-53.
66 Monthly Report, April 1912, file NUA 6/2/1, NAH. Native Commissioner Meredith wrote:

The mealie crops have been a failure but sundry natives have obtained sufficient mealies to enable them to sell the surplus to traders. The rukweza crops are not up to the average but the majority of natives will reap sufficient for their own consumption and to sell. There are many natives who have no crops but they will be able to purchase all the grain they want from the fortunate ones. Recently I informed the natives in the Chiduku Reserve that they could obtain mealies from Pope Brothers at 20/ per bag of 203 lbs . . . Natives say they do not need it.

67 Monthly Report, July 1922, file NUA 6/2/8, NAH.
68 Report by H.N. Howard, *Rhodesia Annual Conference*, 1923, pp.67-8. For a fuller account of the development of Makoni folk Christianity and its interaction with the peasant economy see: Terence Ranger, 'Poverty and prophetism: religious movements in the Makoni District', School of Oriental and African Studies seminar, October 1981; idem, 'Religions and rural protests: Makoni District, Zimbabwe, 1900 to 1980', in Janos Bak and Gerhard Benecke (eds), *Religion and Rural Revolt* (Manchester: 1984)
69 *Rhodesia Annual Conference*, 1923, p. 33; 1924, pp. 36-7; 1925, pp. 54-5.
70 Terence Ranger, 'Religious studies and political economy: the Mwari cult and the peasant experience in Southern Rhodesia', in Matthew Schoffeleers and Wim van Binsbergen (eds.) *The Social Science of African Religion* (London: forthcoming)
71 Interview between P.M.Chakanyuka and Mapani Magadza, Nedewedzo, 9 January 1981.
72 Sarah Brown 'The Ndebele, 1897–1912; aspects of religious, economic and political life in the early colonial era.' (Manchester University: BA Honours thesis, 1983), Chapter 2, 'Ndebele agriculture'.
73 ibid., p.29.
74 Commandant, British South African Police, Depot, Salisbury to Staff Officer, BSAP, Salisbury, 24 November 1919, file B 1/2/2, NAH.
75 ibid.
76 High Commissioner to Administrator, 4 March 1920, file A 3/18/39/10, NAH.
77 Ranger, 'Literature and political economy'.
78 Ian Phimister, 'Reconstruction and the rise of domestic capital, 1903–1922', unpublished ms.

2

The Great Depression and the Zimbabwean peasantry

In Chapter 1 I traced the experience of one Zimbabwean peasantry up to the end of the 1920s. Plainly that experience was not a 'typical' one. In the Makoni District there was relatively little sign even at the end of the 1920s of that slow but inevitable process of proletarianization which Ian Phimister detects as having taken place everywhere in rural Rhodesia. It is true that younger men had begun to go out for wage labour from the peasant zones of Makoni by the 1920s, but the continuing strength of their fathers' agriculture enabled them to be selective in the employment they took up, avoiding working for white farmers, and enabled their families to use wages to invest in ploughs and other equipment. Moreover, on the eve of the Depression, peasants in Makoni were responding to the collapse of maize prices partly by preparing to grow twice as much maize as before and partly by withholding grain from the traders. These strategies had served them well in the past; but could they possibly save them again? Or was even Makoni peasant success, and still more the peasant economy in less favoured areas, bound to be fatally undercut by the impact of the Depression? If so, what pertinence could the 'peasant consciousness' described in Chapter 1 have to the recent war and to the present rural situation?

There is one dominant account of the effect of the 1930s, seen as the climax of years of white pressure on African peasants, which insists upon the collapse of any such tradition of consciousness. The case is best stated by Robin Palmer:

by the end of the 1930s, the agricultural economy of the Shona and the Ndebele, like that of the Kikuyu and most South African peoples, had been destroyed. The struggle between 'the European farmer seeking to reduce the African to a proletarian and the African seeking to retain the maximum amount of economic independence' had been won conclusively by the Europeans . . . The reasons for the European triumph fall into three broad categories. In the first place, after 1908 European agriculture was heavily subsidized while African agriculture was utterly neglected . . . Secondly, the competitiveness of the African peasantry was reduced by increasingly forcing them off European land . . . Once settled in the reserves they could aspire to be little more than subsistence cultivators . . . Thirdly, as if the earlier financial discrimination were not enough, came the repressive legislation of the 1930s, born of a fear of competition. The Land Apportionment Act of 1930 . . . confined African purchasers to separate and largely non-productive areas, and endeavoured to pack as many Africans as possible into the reserves . . . The Maize Control Amendment Act of 1934 discriminated blatantly against African maize-growers . . . Thus the marked European prosperity of the post-1945 period was achieved, as in South Africa, as a direct result of African poverty.[1]

This analysis has seemed all too plausible for Southern Rhodesia. And yet if we look at the other cases to which the Southern Rhodesian case is here compared there must arise some doubts. Let us take in particular the two master comparisons of this book – the agrarian economies of northern Mozambique and Kenya. In northern Mozambique the 1930s did not see the *destruction* of peasant agriculture: rather they saw a re-peasantization. Recent writers have shown how the Salazar regime attempted through the 1930s to extract industrial raw materials and especially cotton from Mozambique. After years of relatively little success:

In 1938 the Salazar regime . . . initiated a far-reaching program designed to put teeth in the earlier legislation and insure [sic] a basic shift in rural production.
    At the heart of this policy was direct state control over all aspects of prouction and marketing. A State Cotton Board . . . was established to oversee the development of cotton production throughout the colonies . . . The [board] . . . fixed mandatory dates for planting the cotton, determined the type of seeds to be distributed, and defined the various qualities of cotton . . . At the district level, local Board representatives suggested to state officials the minimum acreage that each peasant had to cultivate . . . The revitalized cotton regime depended . . . on the effective mobilization of peasant labor.

The numbers of peasant producers within this highly coercive scheme rose rapidly. Allen Isáacman and his collaborators estimate that there were some 20 000 in 1935; 80 000 in 1937; 534 000 in 1939; and 791 000 in 1944, 'three fourths of whom were in the northern three provinces.'[2]
    Barry Munslow has remarked that this policy 'forcibly trans-

formed African cultivators into a cash-crop producing peasantry.'[3]
Edward Alpers, on the other hand, sees it as marking a high point in
a contestation over what *type* of peasantry should exist within the
colonial political economy:

Forced cotton production, which was inaugurated in 1926 in northern
Mozambique but greatly intensified in 1938, came to dominate the political
economy of the entire region. Together with corvée labor for the capitalist
sisal plantations that were scattered near the coast, the restrictions placed
on Africans to operate according to their own strategies within the sphere
of commodity circulation in northern Mozambique were severe. Thus . . .
after 1938 there was certainly an intensified participation in the twin
strategies of emigration and resettlement and oscillating labour migration.[4]

But in whichever way we see it, the forced cotton regime clearly
implied that the Portuguese state wished to foster a type of African
peasant production rather than to proletarianize rural cultivators.
   Still, it could be argued that the Mozambican colonial state was
too different from the Southern Rhodesian for this comparison to
do much to disturb Palmer's conclusions. After all, as Munslow
remarks, 'the political economy of Mozambique is rather unique in
that it was not the colonising bourgeoisie which was foremost to
profit from the exploitation of the country.'[5] There are plainly many
more similarities between the Rhodesian and the Kenyan states and
for this reason the Kenyan parallel is likely to be very instructive. In
fact Palmer makes his own comparison, maintaining that 'by the
end of the 1930s the agricultural economy of the Shona and the
Ndebele, like that of the Kikuyu . . . had been destroyed.' And yet
we know from the whole thrust of recent work on Kenya as a whole
and on the Kikuyu in particular that Palmer was quite wrong about
at least one half of this proposition.
   The crisis of the 1930s, such work tells us, meant that in Kenya the
colonial government came to realize the indispensable value of
African peasant production to the state. D.W. Throup, for example, writes that:

The economic depression of the 1930s had severely shaken the confidence
of the local European communities . . .In Kenya, the colonial government
had attempted to preserve the fiscal basis of the colonial state by encouraging Africans, for the first time since before 1914, to increase their production for the export market. With lower production costs, unfettered by
heavy mortgage debts to the commercial banks, for a short period in the
late 1930s African peasant production had appeared to be essential to the
economic survival of Kenya.[6]

John Lonsdale adds to this picture:

White maize farmers were allowed to go to the wall . . . while planters continued to buy African maize . . .There was no *general* solution to white producers' problems which the inner state could mediate. Still less was this the case when one considers that any extensive subsidy for European production out of African taxation would have endangered the state's *fiscal reproduction* – obliged as it was to pay up to 30% of its revenues in meeting metropolitan loan charges. With settlers slipping out of the indirect tax-payment net . . . these payments could be made only out of intensified African production. And this was possible only by encouraging merchant capital to get nearer to the point of production in the African areas – i.e. to invest in wattle-curing, tobacco-curing, cotton-ginning, even the beginnings of coffee-pulping for Africans.[7]

We are plainly a very long way away from a 'triumph' for European farmers. And Gavin Kitching's remarkable book shows how far we are away from the 'destruction' of African agriculture:

Despite the depression both the cultivated area and the total and marketed output increased in all the districts of Kikuyuland and central Nyanza during the decade 1930–40 . . .Moreover, the range of inedible and edible African 'cash' crops increased during this decade; there was the marked expansion of wattle acreage in Kikuyuland . . . The absence of any coherent sets . . . of statistics on cultivated area and output make it impossible to trace accurately the progress of agricultural production in Kikuyuland during this decade, but all the impressionistic evidence is of an expansion in production of all crops . . .The insistent direct evidence of the expansion of output and of the cultivated area is powerfully supported by evidence relating to an increase in the number of land disputes (resulting from land shortage), by the marked increase in outright sales of land to richer households . . . and by the abundant evidence of the decline of grazing land.

As is implied in this citation, Kitching also sees the 1930s in Kikuyuland as a key period for rural differentiation, with African commercially produced maize becoming concentrated in 'a few, less densely populated, lowland locations', while 'the more densely populated upper locations' came more and more to rely on wattle, and with a process of land-purchase which came to create relatively large landholders within the Kikuyu Reserve as well as numbers of landless.[8]

Now, if Palmer can have been so wrong about the Kikuyu half of his comparison, we must ask ourselves whether he can have been equally wrong about the Shona/Ndebele half. Was there *this* sort of

Kenyan development in the Rhodesian African peasant economies in the 1930s? Some of the points made by Paul Mosley, in the only rigorous and well-founded comparison to have been made of the two countries, suggests that this may indeed have been the case. Right up to the 1950s, Mosley writes, the land policies of Kenya and of Southern Rhodesia 'could be described, with differences of emphasis, as identical.' And he finds that the 'process of individualisation' which produced land sales in Kikuyuland in the 1930s was equally present in the African peasant economy of Southern Rhodesia in these years. It was not, in his view, until the 1950s that 'sharp differences emerged' in the character and trajectory of the peasant societies of Kenya and Rhodesia.[9]

I think that it *is* useful to make this Kenyan comparison. I believe that it throws up many more similarities between the two peasantries than a reading of Palmer on Southern Rhodesia would suggest to be possible. At the same time it also throws up many significant differences: so many and so significant that already in the 1930s peasant history in the two countries was sharply diverging.

Let us take the similarities first. It seems clear that in Rhodesia as in Kenya the events of the 1930s made the colonial government take the African peasant economy much more seriously: in Rhodesia, as in Kenya, administrative officers sought in that decade to variegate African production and to assist in marketing. Moreover, in some districts in Rhodesia peasant output and marketing not only recovered by the end of the 1930s but also achieved new levels. Finally in many districts there emerged more clearly than before an African entrepreneurial class, cultivating much more land and marketing a much greater surplus than the average peasant producer, and as in Kenya this entrepreneurial class was relatively advantaged by the Depression and by administrative responses to it.

Makoni District itself provides a pertinent example of the recovery and even expansion of peasant marketing. In 1929 some 31 500 bags of grain were sold; in 1930 only some 20 500 bags; sales hardly went above these figures in the first half of the 1930s and in 1935 only some 19 500 bags were marketed. But in 1937 and again in 1938 more than 88 000 bags were sold. At the same time the amount of groundnuts marketed in Makoni also increased considerably. And the evidence suggests that there was sustained improvement in the quality of peasant produce. Thus in his annual report for 1938 the Native Commissioner, Makoni, wrote of 'an abundant crop in all Native Reserves, covering all products. Traders comment on the improvement of products offered for purchase, the maize comparing very favourably with European grown crops. There is an increase in production compared with last year.'[10] By 1940 the

Commissioner was writing of a peasant economy apparently fully recovered, still based on the marketing of food crops but able to prosper in new areas of the district because of the transport revolution. He reported:

an abundant harvest of grain . . .Natives will not grow cotton . . . for ready markets for nuts, maize and beans exist near at hand . . . The improvement in quality as well as quantity of grain produced is outstanding . . .Marketing of the varied crops produced here offers no difficulty; the Reserves are not too distant from rail, and even the remoter kraals are served by visiting lorries from buyers.[11]

Makoni was once again atypical. Mosley's aggregate figures show a general decline in prosperity for Rhodesian peasant agriculture during the 1930s, though not a disastrous one. However, he suggests that thereafter there was a general recovery. So far from having been destroyed, he argues, 'the African agricultural economy of Southern Rhodesia appears about as prosperous' in the mid-1950s, both in terms of production per head and of real income, 'as it was in 1914', that is to say as it was during the last stages of Palmer's 'golden age'.[12] Some districts recovered within the 1930s; others took longer to recover; yet others broke into the grain market effectively for the first time during that period; and yet others took up the new crops introduced in the 1930s. Thus while Makoni rejected cotton and stuck with maize, Hartley District, 'by no means one of the most prosperous African farming districts in the inter-war period', had become 'emphatically the most prosperous in the early 1950s, having by far the greatest African cotton acreage.'[13]

These overall district fortunes conceal, however, the growing differentiation within districts which was especially marked, and remarked upon, during the 1930s. From the late 1920s there come a steady stream of reports from Native Commissioners in Mashonaland and Manicaland of the emergence of plough-using entrepreneurs within the reserves. From the late 1920s also, many Native Commissioners warned that these entrepreneurs would drive others into landlessness. In August 1927, for example, the Native Commissioner, Goromonzi, wrote that:

It appears to me that farming for the sale of crops in native reserves should be discouraged. Native reserves are limited in size and if the wholesale ploughing of unlimited areas is allowed, it is only a matter of time when they will cease to produce the food supply for the population. It will naturally follow that some natives will as a result of industry, good farming methods and intelligence gradually bring larger areas under the plough and the less intelligent will go to the wall . . . The natives in this district with the introduction of the plough and a market at their door are breaking up greater areas every year.[14]

In the same year E.G. Howman, Native Commissioner, Salisbury, wondered aloud whether 'intensive farming for profit on a progressively increasing area' was for the good of the African community. For, he noted, 'As men are not equal in energy or brain some will inevitably lag behind and this is the class which as a Native Commissioner I have to consider. The inevitable result of encouraging the natives to farm the reserves for profit will be that the energetic ones will bring under cultivation even larger extents of land.' Howman foresaw the emergence in the Reserve of two classes: 'the native who has raised himself in the world, built a house, planted trees, and cultivates 100 acres of land by modern methods', and the 'backward native with no land at all.' He predicted that 'in the not far distant future' the landless class would be demanding to be given land for subsistence production and that the government would have to cope with an internal class struggle in the African rural areas.[15]

So far from bringing such entrepreneurial activities to an end, the onset of the Depression further stimulated them. In Chindamora around the Domboshowa agricultural training school, it was reported, cultivators who had been working with official demonstrators on 'improved' farming methods were now responding to the fall of grain prices by means of extensive rather than intensive farming:

Those men who have received instruction are not attempting to carry out the new methods. Our [demonstration] plot system has resulted in these men having for three years had for sale a much larger surplus crop than ever before, they have become accustomed to a larger income . . . Now to continue that income they are breaking up more and more land which they are working almost entirely on the old methods . . . Really large acreages are being put under the plough by a few men . . . Timber is being ruthlessly destroyed . . . the amount of grazing is diminishing at an appalling rate. . . Swan . . . obtained much the same impression on his last extended trek from the other Reserves.[16]

Seeking to defend the official demonstration scheme, the Native Agriculturalist, E.D. Alvord, correctly pointed out that in the recent past such entrepreneurial activity had been admired and encouraged:

Most of these six men were progressive natives, with implements and wagons, etc before our demonstration work was started. . . One has fenced his lands and owns a mealie planter. These men live near the school and in proximity to the store whose owner has the supply of grain and meal to the school. They have had a ready sale for all they could grow and in various ways have been stimulated to produce as many bags of mealies as possible . . . Production rather than intensified farming has been given greater emphasis. These men have been encouraged to form a *Farmers* Association and to become farmers. They were praised for their decision to use the yields of the demonstration plots for the purpose of purchasing a measuring machine with which to measure their mealies.[17]

But both he and the Chief Native Commissioner were mistaken when they emphasized the exceptional nature of this Chindamora situation. The six men, wrote the Chief Native Commissioner were 'temporarily suffering from an over-dose of demonstration – from excessive stimulant . . . The problems and difficulties in the outside districts are quite different.'[18]

Such enterprising ploughmen were in fact increasingly to be found in districts remote from the 'excessive stimulant' of Domboshowa. Thus in April 1935 the Native Commissioner, Mtoko, in the remote north-east, detected signs even there of the emergence of plough entrepreneurs of the sort he had first encountered in Seke Reserve near Salisbury:

If the Natives find that there is a steady market for their crops the tendency will be to take up even more land in the Reserves. . .The advent of the plough brought about the large increase in the acreage, we must watch that the introduction of the present scheme [of officially assisted marketing] does not bring about a still larger acreage under the plough. . . [There was] a marked tendency among those Natives in the Seke Reserve of Goromonzi District who worked under the guidance of the Agricultural Demonstrator to grab an undue amount of land for the purpose of growing crops for sale. I have noticed the same tendencies among the few enlightened Natives of this district. . . Care must be taken that individuals do not plough up too large an area to the detriment of the less progressive Natives, and I think some guidance should be given district officials so that a uniform policy may be adopted throughout the country in restricting the acreage any one Native may cultivate in a Reserve.[19]

And in Makoni District in 1937 it was reported that it was 'notice-able how many natives are extending the area of tillage: observation is being kept on certain areas, for it appears that the more go-ahead native is adding to his lands, and when the lazy native awakens, or town-employed boys return home, necessity for demarcation of inidividual lands may arise.'[20] In February 1938 more detail was given. 'One native', it was reported, 'has 81 acres under cultivation in the Chiduku Reserve; a bank account of £300 (he says); and it is common report that this native sold nearly 1,000 bags of maize this year. Such large holdings are rare, admittedly, but there are many natives who hold an unfair proportion of the arable lands in reserves.'[21]

These entrepreneurial peasants were at a considerable competitive advantage under conditions of Depression. This was so not only because many of them were able to invest their savings from teachers' or Native Messengers' or police salaries at a moment when most other peasants had little or no access to cash, but also because they were advantaged by official intervention in Reserve agriculture. From the late 1920s African Agricultural Demonstrators were sent out into selected Reserves. Their method was to recruit so-called 'plot-holders' on an acre or so of whose land the Demonstrator would grow intensively. The crops when harvested were the property of the plot-holder and could be marketed by him. A number of men allowed the Demonstrator to work for them in this way while they themselves ploughed and cultivated very many more acres extensively. As late as 1944, when as we shall see there had been in most places a decisive move away from such a pattern, the Native Commissioner, Ndanga, complained that 'There have been two demonstrators stationed in this Reserve for some years and [they] have made no headway in producing 'master farmers'; their followers are still plot-holders, cultivating their one acre under improved methods and a large number of acres under the old destructive methods.'[22] Entrepreneurs also learnt from Demonstrators how to grow new cash crops – at the American Methodist Episcopal show-village of Gandanzara in Makoni Reserve, for example, the headmen established a successful cultivation of wheat by means of the aid of successive Demonstrators. Demonstrators themselves were selected for training from among the ranks of the mission-educated and naturally sought to work with similarly 'progressive' men. In its early years the Demonstration scheme worked very much in the interests of the entrepreneurial minority.

Moreover, when Maize Control was imposed in the 1930s, with all the harmful consequences for African peasants in general which I shall discuss in a moment, the steps taken by the Native Department to ease the general crisis of the African peasantry in fact only advantaged the same enterprising few. As Mosley tells us, 'The only African maize which actually obtained the full local price was a proportion of that delivered by them (or by their Native Commissioners) direct to the [Maize Control] Board.'[23] But nearly all the maize surrendered to Native Commissioners for delivery to the Board came from a small number of big growers. The pattern is very clear in Makoni. In August 1931, before the scheme of receiving maize in the Native Commissioner's office had been initiated, the Acting Native Commissioner, Makoni, stimulated the formation of a Hongwe Farmers Association in Makoni Reserve, consisting of 'about 50 of the more intelligent natives, including the three Demonstrators':

I explained the provisions of the Maize Control Act with it regulations and suggested that the Society might undertake the acceptance of small quantities of maize and operate it as a pool. To this they were in full agreement . . . It was decided that when funds permit, a wagon should be purchased and loaned to its members at a nominal charge for the transport of maize to the Rusapi Depot [of the Maize Control Board].[24]

The Acting Native Commissioner wanted the Farmers Association to include 'representatives of the whole of the Makoni Reserve and . . . it was important that Chief Makoni (although not quite up to the standard of those present) should be a member of the committee.' In this way it would represent the whole peasant community and not just the entrepreneurs. But things did not work out that way.

When the system of receiving grain at the Native Commissioner's office began, the Native Commissioner reported in August 1934 that so far 370 bags of maize had been surrendered at his office, all of them from only nine 'larger producers'; optimistically he added that 'the smaller growers are now beginning to surrender maize.'[25] But in September, when 681 bags had been surrendered, 533 of which had been awarded the top grade for quality, he was compelled to admit that 'the effect of these operations has only been to assist the larger growers.' Accordingly, he had set up a 'Bucket Pool' for smaller producers, offering an immediate payment of 9d a bucket, 'the maize to be bagged at this office.' But no small-producer maize came into this pool, small peasants preferring to deal with traders.[26] In March 1935 the Clerk, Makoni, summed up the 1934 experience, recording that 'Although 1,618 bags of maize were handled by the office on behalf of Natives, this figure only represents some 4% of the surplus maize disposed of . . . Only 24 Natives surrendered their maize through this office so it will be seen that our efforts only touched the fringe of the problem of assisting the Native to obtain an economic price for his maize.'[27] The largest of the Makoni entrepreneurs was one Sirewu, who in 1931/2 the deepest Depression harvest year, was paid out no less than £55 for maize surrendered to the Board.[28] The Makoni administrative staff, complaining that their work was not benefiting peasants as a whole, made further efforts to serve greater numbers of producers. In

March 1936 the Clerk of the Rusape office spelt out the division of producers into the overwhelming majority who had to sell their maize to farmer-producers for what they could get, and the small minority who could deliver to the Board:

I venture to comment as follows on the working of the Maize Control Act in this district. Returns show that approximately 56,180 bags of maize were sold to Europeans and to Asiatic traders in this district. Only 1,069 bags were surrendered to the Maize Control Board. . .There is one very notice-able drawback concerning trade between native and farmer-consumer or trader and that is that the native is often presumed upon to supply overweight. One trader informed me that he insists on a bag of 240 lbs weight. The native is handicapped in knowing what weight he supplies – he can only say whether he sells a large . . . or small sack of maize . . .The tendency is that the local price is controlled largely by what the native is offered for maize and not what he demands. In this respect the surrender of maize to the Control Board appears to be a useful safety valve.[29]

By the end of 1936 the safety valve had been made available to more people. The Native Commissioner's office was handling two or three times as much maize – but all this achieved was to bring into play a second rank of entrepreneurs who made use of the office to cut their costs. In October 1936, the Native Commissioner reported that:

Grain has poured into this office for disposal to the Maize Control Board. To date some 4,000 bags of maize and 240 bags of munga etc have been dealt with on behalf of the natives . . . Some other arrangements must be devised for next season . . . Most of the growers despatch their maize to the office expecting the staff to bag, weigh and send off their products. One crowd obtained a truck at Inyazura and addressed 150 bags of maize to me; this entailed convicts being sent to off-load the maize, a payment of £3 mileage in advance, cartage of the bags here for weighing and re-sewing. Generally, the natives think that all they have to do is to deposit their maize here, and then run off, to reappear for payment later.[30]

So far I have drawn heavily on official material to document the rise of the Reserves entrepreneurs in the 1930s. But it is possible to give at least one example of the process seen from the inside, and a significant example at that. In his autobiography, Bishop Abel Muzorewa describes the experiences of his father's family during the colonial land-rush in Makoni:

They were among the first to be evicted by the Europeans from their rich farmlands of the Headlands area, halfway between the present cities of Salisbury and Umtali. Today as one travels between those towns following the rail line across the high plateau, one passes for one hundred miles through the historic homeland of the Makoni people. Gradually family after family was evicted to make way for white farmers . . . My relatives chose to resettle at a place called Murango, about five miles from Inyazura. Today that place is also a European farm. In the 1920s a European farmer wanted that good land and they were evicted once again . . . This helps to explain my own father's drive in life to have land to call his own.

This man, Haadi Philemon Muzorewa, became an American Methodist convert and attended church at the main AME centre in Chiduku. He became a pastor-teacher at Old Umtali and at Chiremba. Then, early in the 1930s, he 'decided to try his hand at farming':

Finding the soils too poor at Muziti . . . he decided to seek a patch of fertile virgin soil. He found it at Chinyadza about ten miles away [but still in the Chiduku Reserve]. Visiting our village, one could see that this place was chosen carefully as a homestead. The house and granaries were in the middle of a pocket of rich brown and black soil . . . the envy of every farmer in the area . . . Near our village my father discovered some forty to fifty acres of relatively rich soil near the top of Mabvuwo Mountain. It was there that our family carried out a heroic struggle to wrest a good living from the land. First, my father made the herculean effort required to clear the land for ploughing. There were long days of felling trees, of cutting and digging and burning the stumps . . . Then the planting took place. Soon the top of the mountain was crowned with rich green fields of maize, groundnuts, *rapoko* (millet) and beans. The last was a valuable cash crop . . .Especially close was our friendship with two other Christian families who lived a short distance away – the Nyatangas and the Jijitas. . . All three had served as pastor/teachers. All had moved into the Chinyadza area with their wives and children hoping to build a good life as farmers and committed Christians . . . Living apart from their traditional family homes, our three families were released from those pressures to conform with past ways which make it so difficult for many of the Shona people to be progressive. Here at Chinyadza my parents were free to build a rectangular house instead of just round huts . . . It was a major expedition each year to transport our crops to the marketing depot in Rusape twelve miles away. First, the grains had to be packed into sacks and tied. Next, they were loaded on the ox-drawn carts, each with a capacity of about twenty-five bags. Each wagon was drawn by a team of as many as eighteen oxen . . . The journey to Rusape took almost two days.[31]

Fortunately there is in the American Methodist Archives at Old Umtali a manuscript life of another of these Chinyadza entrepreneurs, pastor-teacher Jim Nathaniel Jijta. It records that 'From 1920–1924 he resided at a place called Nyahwa where he did extensive farming but did not continue for a long time because that area was allocated as European Purchase Area. He moved to Chinyadza in the area of Chief Tandi under the paramount Chief Makoni. He laboured hard to establish a Methodist Church among the Anglican Church area.' Martin Meredith has described Muzorewa as coming from 'a simple peasant family'. Plainly in Makoni terms, neither the Muzorewa nor the Jijita families were all that 'simple'. And the two fathers, relatively prosperous themselves, 'managed to educate [their] children.' Jim Nathaniel Jijita's biography ends with a list of the eminent men and women produced by his Chinyadza village school – one bishop, Abel Muzorewa; one accountant, Basil Muzorewa; two ministers of religion, John and Elliott Jijita; seven nurses, two builders, one carpenter; two teachers, Laban and Denford Jijita; a church leader, Rodrek Jijita. Fittingly, the achievement of these Reserves entrepreneurs is commemorated where it took place: after Jim Nathaniel's death in 1942, his family and other American Methodists 'decided to build a permanent church building at Chinyadza in his memorial.'[32]

The atmosphere of these memoirs is certainly reminiscent of the biographies of Church of Scotland Kikuyu 'progressives'. But the time has come to turn from the similarities between Kenya and Rhodesia and to note the differences. In the light of these differences, indeed, a good deal of what I have said already has to be seen in quite another perspective.

The chief difference, of course, lay in the settler control of the Rhodesian state. Throup tells us that the 'depression caused the Kenya Goverment to question the unquestionable, and to ponder whether Kenya really was a "White Man's Country", as the settlers had so confidently proclaimed.'[33] In Southern Rhodesia, too, the Depression challenged white optimism. As J.A. Edwards has written in his unpublished doctoral thesis on Rhodesia between 1935 and 1939:

The pattern of settlement reached after nearly fifty years of rule carried the mark of disappointment . . .White Rhodesians had already abandoned much of the Colony by 1935, withdrawing to the less inhospitable highveld . . .They left the other two thirds of Southern Rhodesia largely to Africans or to nothing . . .By the middle thirties the settler knew without a shadow of doubt that his community would always remain small, a minority living among masses of Africans. It was this fearsome truth that gave the ideal of survival such desperate strength.[34]

The settler 'ideal of survival', however, was not going to produce state realization of its fiscal dependence on African production, or a state attempt to link that African production more intimately with mercantile capitalism. Nor was it going to produce a Mozambique-style attempt to export peasant-produced raw materials for metropolitan industries. In Rhodesia, too, the African peasantry had a crucial role, but a quite different one. Their production was to be taxed, by means of a variety of complex devices, in order to subsidize white survival.

Mosley has best described how this happened. Setting out the sequence of elaborate maize control legislation and practice in Southern Rhodesia in the 1930s, Mosley brings home what it meant for African producers:

Instead of being able to sell to the highest bidder amongst local European farmers, miners and traders . . . [peasants] were now the unwilling clients of a monopsonist, the Maize Control Board, which appointed traders who had formerly had to compete for African maize as their buying agents. This not only reduced the price they received but also increased their vulnerability to sharp commercial practices.[35]

Kitching has written of Kenya in the 1930s that 'in contrast to other writers . . . I do not believe that the maize regulations were efficacious in making Africans "pay" (either as producers of consumers) for the tribulations of European agriculture. It seems more likely that Africans continued to pay for it much as they had always done, through the tax system, with the maize regulations having an entirely marginal effect.'[36] In Rhodesia at the same period, however, there can be no doubt that most of the African maize surplus was expropriated in order to subsidize white production. As Mosley concludes, the 'existing channels of African maize supply thus came in the 1930s to be used to sustain a kind of outdoor relief service for the European primary producing community.'[37] In so far as the Rhodesian state was more concerned than before with the African peasant economy, it was not in order to stimulate it to greater and more varied market activity. The two main needs were to ensure law and order in the countryside at a time when thousands of unemployed young men were forced back into it from the towns and mines, and to ensure that the tattered goose that laid the golden egg of subsidy for white farming was not killed off in the process.

Thus the attempts by the Rhodesia adminstration to introduce new crops and to reduce dependence on maize were very half-hearted and limited in comparison with Kenyan innovation. And it was this whole atmosphere of constraint which ensured that if Mosley can write that 'the African agricultural economy of Southern Rhodesia appears about as prosperous in 1955 as it was in 1914', he can also add immediately that the Kenyan African agricultural economy appeared *twice* as prosperous in the later year than in the earlier.[38]

So one must conclude that the 1930s in Southern Rhodesia saw neither the 'destruction' which Palmer posits nor an expansion of black peasant production along the lines described by Kitching. Yet there is a good deal more to the contrast between Kenya and Rhodesia than this. An extremely important distinction arose in the relationship of the state in both territories to the emergent African entrepreneurial group in the African communal areas. In Kenya whatever reservations administrators had and expressed about the social undesirability of the developing differentiation, the sale of land, etc., no effective action was taken to prevent them. The new landowners within the Kenyan Reserves emerged as loyalist allies of the state in the emergency of the 1950s and their presence *in situ* in the Kikuyu Reserve was one of the factors that made it impossible for Mau Mau fighters to operate from *within* an African peasant society as guerrillas did in Zimbabwe in the 1970s. In Rhodesia, on the other hand, the state came by the end of the 1930s to define the kind of entrepreneurs which I have documented above as totally undesirable. It acted against them very effectively, more or less driving them out of the Reserves. Differentiation of a more restrained kind certainly did continue to exist in the Reserves, but there was to be no permanent large landholding class. The Rhodesian regime found no loyalist farmer allies within the Tribal Trust Lands during the guerrilla war.

There were several reasons for the growing administrative dislike of the entrepreneurs in the Reserves. One arose from the jealous watch that white farmers kept on black competition – it was not politically possible for any number of black producers actually to be seen as *benefiting* from Maize Control. Another arose from the vested interest which the administration came to have in the 1930s in maintaining customary 'organic' society and traditional law and order in the Reserves. This meant supporting the authority of the chiefs and headmen against the subversive prestige of 'new men' – in Rhodesia, unlike in Kenya, most African chiefs had clung to their 'traditional' prestations rather than themselves becoming the most vigorous of entrepreneurs. A third reason arose from the odd but pervasive ideology of paternalist egalitarianism among district administrators. Then there was the need to preserve land in the Reserves against the rapidly approaching day when the implementation of the Land Apportionment Act would mean the incursion into them of thousands of peasant families evicted from white land. And over and above all these reasons there was the growing ideology of 'conservation'.

As William Beinart has recently shown, there was a key transition throughout south-central Africa in the 1930s from a concern with *white* farming as a source of soil erosion to a concern with a *black* crisis of conservation. At the opening of the period it was possible for an administrator in Umtali District to dispute the settler opinion that 'the use of land in Native Reserves is inclined to be wasteful . . .This is far from being the case, and . . . native cultivation, particularly with the hoe rather than the plough, has always been on the lines of careful husbandry . . . Hitherto in the Reserves there is little, if any, erosion.'[39] By the end of the 1930s, however, it had come to be universal wisdom that the Reserves were in a full blown ecological crisis. Indeed, much of the tension between black peasants and white administrators in the 1930s and 1940s arose from their quite different perceptions of the nature of the crisis in African agriculture. Peasants saw it as a crisis brought about by low prices, government intervention in marketing, the increasing diversion of labour into conservation works, etc. Government saw the crisis in terms of bad African methods threatening a collapse of the productivity of the soil.

Now, in all this the entrepreneurial ploughmen were cast as the villains of the piece. Recently the heroes of progress, converts to the 'gospel of the plough', they now figured as destroyers of the environment. In 1929, the Native Commissioner, Mrewa wrote that:

It will be several years before the use of the plough by the native can be considered an improvement on their own method of preparation of the soil for crops; the ploughing is in most cases badly done . . . They very often select land to be turned over by the plough, just because there are no trees in it, that would have been considered a waste of time to be turned over with the hoe. To see two lands alongside each other, on the same granite soil, dotted with tree stumps, land being put into cultivation for the first time, the one turned up by the plough, and the other with the hoe, is an object lesson. In the one done with the hoe the contour of the ground has been studied, and the ridges made with a view to draining the lands from heavy flooding, but still to prevent erosion; the crop stands high and dry in the heaviest rains, and gets all the benefit of the humus turned between the sods which form the ridge. The other is a scarified piece of ground . . . no thought being given to flooding wash or anything else, patches of grass left where they could not get the plough to work, the crop existing where it can.[40]

As will have been noticed in my citations on the Reserve entrepreneurs, it was they above all others who relied on the plough to open up extensive lands. Indeed, they were in many ways different from *either* the type of individual landholders whom Mosley sees emerging in Kenya or those he sees emerging in Rhodesia. Mosley's Rhodesian entrepreneurs are farmers working in the Native Purchase Areas, the lands specially set aside for an African yeomanry under the Land Apportionment Act of 1930. But during the 1930s, as we shall see, very few Native Purchase farms were surveyed and allocated. The entrepreneurs about whom I have been writing were the entrepreneurs who still mattered by far the most in the 1930s and they were precisely what I have been calling them – *Reserves* entrepreneurs. They greatly preferred farming land in the Reserves and under 'communal tenure'. In the Reserves they could use all the land they could farm and then leave all of it lying fallow while they moved on to open up a similar amount; a Native Purchase farmer had to operate year after year on the same land. Some Reserves were closer to communications than most of the Purchase Areas; they also already possessed trading roads and schools and stores. And in the Reserves entrepreneurs could more easily call upon the communal work parties for assistance in harvesting. On the other hand these men were also unlike the landholders of the Kikuyu Reserve. They did not wish to *buy* land, even if they had been able to do so. They wished rather to take advantage of the operation of the system of communal tenure, which allocated land to those able to use it rather than to those who most needed it. In short, they were most like the men whom Kitching describes for the Kipsigis Reserve in Kenya, who in the 1930s took up 'land-extensive maize mono-cropping, using the plough.' Indeed, the District Commissioner, South Lumbwa, whom Kitching cites from 1934, might well have been writing about the Rhodesian Reserves:

A situation is arising in this district which may well prove a matter for anxiety in a year or two. A number of the more advanced Kipsigis are plough-owners, and as the tribe has no system of land tenure other than as a community, these plough-owners tend to cultivate very large areas indeed, thus reducing the available amount of grazing. If at any time the squatters are removed from the . . . farms, and have to return with their cattle to the Reserve, the overstocking question may arise here.[41]

It was because they operated within the Reserves that the Rhodesian entrepreneurs were vulnerable to administrative intervention. The administration now had a new model of the progressive hero – the intensive 'master-farmer', applying new methods to a small amount of land. The American ex-missionary, E.D. Alvord, who became the Rhodesian government's master-planner for the transformation of the Reserve, has given us a fascinating picture of *his* ideal African farmer:

the case of Vambe, who lived on Shiota Reserve, south of Salisbury. In 1928 he was a poor man, dressed in ragged clothes, and lived in a primitive pole and mud hut which he and his family shared with the goats and fowls . . .His one wife was dressed in a ragged, greasy goat-skin drape, naked from the waist up and his three little children ran about naked. When the Demonstrator was placed on the Reserve in 1928, Vambe became one of his first plot-holders. He had a plough and was tilling a total of 32 acres of old, worn out soil, almost pure sand. But, his cattle kraal was belly deep in years of accumulated, well rotted manure. In 1929 he harvested more bags of maize from his one-acre demonstration plot than from his other 31 acres combined. He realised immediately how foolish it was to waste his time, labour and seed in ineffective farming methods. In November 1929 he added 3 more acres to the original unit and started a systematic crop rotation on 4 acres with outstanding results . . .Maize stood about 12 feet high, rupoko 5 feet high and peanuts 2 feet high . . .He then added 4 more acres to the rotation and spent his full time on the 8 acre, 4 course rotation, abandoning all primitive methods. He also made his two wives submit their labours to a proper 4 course rotation on two acres each. By 1934, Vambe had three wives, each with crop rotations. He also had a farm cart, two ploughs, a harrow, a planter and a cultivator.[42]

But as we have seen the majority of the Reserves entrepreneurs did *not* draw these conclusions from the work of the Demonstrators, and instead added 'land-extensive maize mono-cropping' to their rotation plots.

Alvord, the Native Commissioners and finally the Rhodesian government as a whole came to see these men as the main obstacle to their plans for the Reserves. In September 1937 Alvord wrote to the Chief Native Commissioner complaining that 'certain more ambitious Natives are hogging large areas of the best land and producing crops for sale . . . many others cannot find suitable land on which to grow their food. We must enforce a redistribution of lands in the Reserves and these men who farm for profit should be requested to buy land in the Native Purchase Areas.' Those who chose to remain in the Reserves, he added, could cultivate no more than six acres.[43]

A week or so later, at a conference of white farmers, the Prime Minister, Godfrey Huggins, echoed Alvord's views, seeking to reassure his suspicious audience:

In spite of everything maize was still the most profitable crop that the native could produce, and the native had not land enough to be a very serious competitor . . .From a purely Native Affairs Department point of view, the problem was not so much possible competition, but how to keep the native living in his own areas. Undoubtedly in some areas in the Reserves there was a more intelligent type of native who was using far too

71

much land; in fact in some Reserves individual natives were using so much land that there was not enough to go round. For a period of years they had been surveying native Reserves and dividing them up if possible . . .The next step to be under-taken was to assist the Chiefs to apportion the land and to stop those natives who were growing big crops, to enable the other natives to have chance to make a living.[44]

As Huggins implied, the instrument chosen to undercut the Reserves entrepreneurs was survey and 'centralization' of the Reserves. Originally designed as a conservation measure pure and simple, by which a division was made between exclusively arable and exclusively grazing land, 'centralization' became a means of 'redistribution of lands in Reserves'. Thus in March 1938 the Assistant Agriculturalist wrote to Alvord about three Reserves which desperately needed centralization. In all three cases the reason advanced was the activity of the plough-owning maize growers. In Mondoro South 'non-indigenous natives have cleared acres and acres of the best soil . . . working it as though it was a private farm'; one of these men reaped 300 bags of maize which he sold to mining compounds; he used 'no rotation of crops and no manure . . . which means he will soon be looking for another 100 acres of good soil to ruin.' In Chiweshe Reserve there was 'private farming on large acreages . . . Some natives have the idea of being progressive farmers by ploughing these areas all up and down the slope, planting maize every year.' In Msane Reserve 'natives think that more maize means more money', so that large areas were being put to the plough. Under centralization 'everyone would be much happier because there would be sufficient land for all.'[45]

In Makoni District Native Commissioner Phayre advocated centralization in order to combat extensive farming and in order to make room for those who were due to be moved off European land into the Reserves with the implementation of Land Apportionment. In December 1937 he reported that:

Extensive patrols have been carried out: native lands are being extended indiscriminately; natives are becoming difficult to find owing to their making lands far from their kraals and centralisation is a matter which must be advocated for this district. I am certain that by centralisation we shall be able to accommodate some hundreds of natives in this district, particularly in Chiduku Reserve.[46]

By January 1938 he was able to report that:

With a view to settling many more natives in the Reserves, the Chiduku and Weya areas have been scrutinised: I am satisfied that we can absorb the 794 natives in private locations in the district in our Reserves by judicious location of kraal sites, and by stopping the growing practice among natives of each lad erecting his hut some distance from where the kraal site formerly was.[47]

In February he recorded that he had:

attended meetings of natives . . . in reserves; advice was repeated as to methods of cultivation, and the adoption of rotation plots was stressed. Natives were informed that eventually such methods must be forced upon them if they, themselves, will not think of their children's right to inherit un-impoverished land sites. . . Natives on unoccupied farms have been lectured as to the advisability of seeking new homes at once, and not to wait for the arrival of the last few months of that period when all must enter Reserves . . . [They ask] 'Where can we go? How can we leave land where we have always lived?' . . .In the Chiduku Native Reserve there is ample room, and this without having immediate recourse to centralisation of land. One native has 81 acres under cultivation . . . Such large holdings are rare admittedly; but there are many natives who hold an unfair proportion of the arable lands in reserves. And the crops reaped therefrom would not exceed the fruits of much smaller lands cultivated in the manner outlined and stressed daily by demonstrators.[48]

By September 1938 Phayre was able to report that 'the centralisation of the Makoni Reserve is almost complete'; Weya and Chiduku were to follow.[49] In his Annual Report for 1938 Phayre was able to present his achievement as an amiable mixture of persuasion and 'control':

There is an increase in production compared with last year in spite of judicious limiting of land. I mentioned last year that natives were unfairly extending their lands to a degree unfair to other kraal members: lectures have resulted in more attention being paid to present lands, and a fair attempt at more intensive cultivation and care of old land. . .Now that the Makoni and Weya Reserves are centralised I hope for better control of native education in agriculture'.[50]

To many people in the Makoni Reserves the process did not seem nearly so amiable. Chiefs and headmen resented the severe limitations on their power to allocate lands: 'all chiefs, heads of kraals and others [were] told that where natives remove to another kraal their vested lands must be reserved, and not absorbed by others without first referring to this office. Generally, natives of the Makoni Reserve welcomed this,' claimed Phayre, 'as, they allege, heads of kraals usually gain by the removal of natives from their land'.[51] Yet centralization was in fact unpopular with almost everybody and is today remembered as the end of the 'good old days' and the beginning of the era of government interference in every detail of peasant life. Centralization meant a great upheaval as the land was surveyed and divided, new 'lines' laid down for houses, and new sites for schools and churches chosen. 'Recently centralisation has been proceeding in the Makoni Reserve', wrote Alvord in October 1938, creating many problems for church adherents in that folk Christian area. 'Centralisation and the laying out of "lines", as the Natives term them, results in a migration of people.'[52] When surveyors arrived in Weya to commence centralization late in 1938 there was very general opposition: 'the local headmen have not been co-operating,' wrote the Land Inspector, adding that centralization was taking place there simultaneously with 'a large number of natives on the adjacent farms . . . being moved into the Reserve' and that in any case neither the original or the new occupants of Weya were going to be allowed to settle on the newly zoned arable land until soil erosion and conservation works were carried out there.[53] In Makoni and Chiduku the peasants obeyed the 'centralisation officer' and 'rebuilt their houses on the building sites indicated to them', but it was an expensive business. Many peasants sold their 'scrub and aged stock' in order to be able to 'feed and pay part of the wages of casual native employees assisting in the removal and ploughing.'[54] And once made, the centralization allocations could only be maintained by compulsion. As W.H. Stead noted in his 1941 annual report, 'Stern measures in the form of extensive prosecutions had to be taken at the commencement of the ploughing season to stop natives cultivating in the grazing area and doing damage to soil conservation works.'[55]

If the centralization was unpopular with chiefs, headmen and peasants in general it was especially unpopular with the Reserves entrepreneurs against whom it was in particular directed. As the arable was divided from the grazing and the 'lines' set up, an equalizing allocation of land was made as well. Native Commissioner Jowett, who arrived in Makoni at the end of the centralizing process, told the Native Trade and Production Commissioners in 1944 that the administration in Makoni had had 'to limit . . . the extent to which the individual can use communal land for profit . . . in fairness to the rest.'[56] It was true that at this stage the Native Department did not dispose of enough staff to monitor fresh land allocations continuously. 'I don't think yet that we can really tell people they have to live in one assigned place for ever,' Jowett told the Commissioners. 'It is not possible to organise production . . . without taking Native custom and the old system of land tenure into consideration.'[57] S.G. Gilmour, Land Inspector, told the Natural

Resources Board Native Enquiry Commissioners in 1942 that land was supposed to be allocated under centralization on the basis of four acres 'to a single man'; but that even after allocations had been made 'we have no record of what land those natives have . . .Some Native Commissioners choose all the village sites; other Native Commissioners give the natives about two years and then say "By next rains all villages are to be moved to the line" and other Native Commissioners don't worry much about the villages but say "All your lands in the grazing area are to be abandoned . . . " Some Native Commissioners believe in allowing natives to pick their own land and their own kraal sites: other Native Commissioners insist on picking the kraal sites themselves.'[58] A real degree of precision, and a breach with customary tenure, had to await the Land Husbandry Act of 1951, which should be seen as a measure aimed *against* entrepreneurial individualism, rather than as a measure introducing that concept. But even if some Reserves entrepreneurs in some places managed to hold on to larger lands despite centralization, there is no doubt that in general centralization was a heavy blow to the extensive plough-farmers of the Reserves.

In 1933, for example, an early battle was fought over centralization in Chindamora Reserve. Alvord hoped that centralization there would remedy a situation in which 'tribal and communal organisation has been completely broken down . . . and certain ambitious natives have claimed and are working lands scattered all over the area.'[59] Once the centralization was complete, however, the Assistant Native Commissioner, Goromonzi, took up the cudgels on behalf of the aggrieved entrepreneurs. 'The new lands allocated,' he wrote, 'are much smaller than those previously held . . .Past industry in developing large lands has proved to natives to have been a waste of labour,' and, he argued, the resulting discontent might be exploited by 'native political agitators'. 'Lenin may have looked upon Russia with a sense of gratification and self-congratulation', concluded this defender of private enterprise, 'because it conformed to his view of the ideal state but ideals differ.'[60] By the early 1940s, however, few Native Commissioners any longer defended the Reserves entrepreneurs. Most would have agreed with the memorandum submitted to the Native Trade and Production Commission by the Assistant Native Commissioner, Wedza, an area which had been well-known before centralization was effected there for its vigorous cluster of entrepreneurial farmers. 'The writer's views,' it noted; 'are purely communistic . . . the thought of creating a capitalist native class is too appalling to contemplate.'[61]

Now, it may be objected that in singling out a quotation like this, and in dramatizing the plight of the extensive plough-farmers of the Reserves, I am overemphasizing the egalitarian effect of government policies during the 1930s and early 1940s. This very period, after all, has been seen in quite a different way – as a decade in which there began to *emerge* an elite of master-farmers, Native Purchase Area yeomen and irrigation scheme settlers. In a very interesting preliminary study of the irrigation schemes in Melsetter and Chipinga districts, for example, Philip Robertshaw has argued that these schemes, which began in the early 1930s, constitute a striking example 'of the rather remarkable pattern of rural change which was emerging in most parts of Zimbabwe at the time . . . the transfer of local economic captaincy from one variety of agricultural entrepreneur to another qualitatively different one.'[62] If Robertshaw is right then the 1930s saw not so much the elimination of rural differentiation as its re-establishment on a new basis. The free-ranging extensive farming entrepreneurs, making their own decisions on crops and production techniques were to be replaced by holders of master-farmer certificates, who cultivated intensively under official supervision, and by the regimented settlers on irrigation schemes. At the same time there began to grow up outside the Reserves a new body of Native Purchase Area Farmers.

Oliver Pollak has described the original aspirations of the Native Purchase Area scheme, pointing out that 'this land was located next to the reserves, and it was hoped that the communal agriculturalists would learn from their more advanced neighbours . . . [The] purchase areas would establish a content peasant middle class, loyal to the colonial regime.' He has also described the development of one of these purchase areas:

Within three years of the inception of the purchase areas scheme a group of farmers in the most viable area, Marirangwe, about fifty miles south-west of Salisbury, banded together as a farmers' association to present their problems to government . . .Marirangwe was fully taken up by 1936 and its over thirty settlers constituted a stable if somewhat heterogenous community. In 1933 Aaron Jacha, Titus Hlazo, Paul Mandiki and Charles Ndawana were assembling regularly . . .These men were mission educated (most notably at Epworth) and had been associated with the Domboshowa Training School . . .They believed in self-help . . . as nascent capitalist farmers.[63]

This certainly sounds like the effective emergence of a new entrepreneurial class.

I do not dispute the significance of these developments and in a later chapter try to assess their overall effect in the period after the Second World War. But here I can make a range of points. The first is that, whatever the eventual success of the 'master-farmer' scheme in the Reserves, its implications were quite different from the potential consequences of an unchecked growth of the Reserves entrepreneurs. That might well have produced clear-cut divisions between large farmers and landless families; the master-farmers were always themselves going to be small peasants. The second is that the Native Purchase scheme got off to an absurdly half-hearted and slow start in the 1930s. As Pollak himself makes clear, Marirangwe was very much the exception. Roger Woods has summed up the history of the scheme in the 1930s:

The evidence is that 'progressive natives' (i.e. those with capital) met nothing but frustration in trying to acquire land. By tying the pace of settlement to the speed of surveying the areas the Land Board had actually settled only 893 farmers by the outbreak of World War 2 . . . It so happened that many of the successful applicants in the 1930s were retired BSA policemen, evangelists and teachers from Missions, and the odd 'boss-boys' from European farms and mines. Most of them were old and many had their origins in Nyasaland, Mozambique or South Africa . . .Many of these people had little or no recent experience of agriculture and the expectations of 'pockets of highly productive Native farms providing an example to the adjoining reserves' were not fulfilled.[64]

'The Native Purchase Areas,' concludes J.A. Edwards, 'were a remarkable exercise in self-deception,'[65]

And this leads me to the third point. If the old-style Reserves entrepreneurs had every reason for discontent by the end of the 1930s, the new Native Purchase Area farmers were also very disgruntled. When Jacha, Hlazo, Mandiki and Ndawana assembled together at Marirangwe they did so 'to air grievances over roads, water supply, schools, dip tanks and title deeds.' The Southern Rhodesia Bantu Farmers' Congress, which emerged in 1938 out of the initiatives of the Marirangwe settlers, was also a forum for the expression of grievance. As Pollak writes:

The Ministry of Native Affairs, while instrumental in creating a separate African freeholding class, continued to view rural Africans as an irresponsible and undifferentiated mass . . .During the first phase of dialogue a pattern of mutual recrimination had been established between the Farmers' Union and the government. The farmers claimed that as a developing sector they had the right to expect substantial government aid. Lack of purchase area profitability and other difficulties were due to the failure of the authorities to take this responsibility seriously. The government . . . could afford to disregard the politically insignificant black farmers and directed them to rely on their own resources and free enterprise. The farmers' problems, it was claimed, were due to their imprudent and inefficient methods.[66]

By the end of the 1930s, therefore, though African agriculture had survived everywhere, had recovered in some places, and actually expanded in others, both small peasant producers and larger entrepreneurs had good reason for grievance. The Reserves entrepreneurs were being undercut; the Native Purchase farmers felt neglected. Peasants in general had experienced a severe decline in crop prices; they had been placed much more at the mercy of the trader; their capacity to withstand drought without making fatal commitments to white labour demands had been greatly impaired; with centralization they had been compelled to abandon their homes, without compensation for 'improvements', so as to move into the 'lines'; they were beginning to hear their administrators talk of compulsory destocking and conservation; peasants living on European-owned or -designated land had begun to be moved into the Reserves and many more were under notice that they too must move by 1940; peasants living in the Reserves feared that their own land and cattle holdings would be reduced to accommodate the people and stock who were to be moved into the Reserves. The general uneasiness at the end of the 1930s comes out clearly in Native Commissioner Phayre's report on Makoni for February 1938:

These natives on [European] farms – formerly old tribal lands – present a new avenue of consideration: to these natives it was suggested that so many of them work away from their kraal, leaving their respective wives to till small lands, that it cannot be said the land holds attraction to a great degree to them . . . I met chiefs and headmen, and to them I appealed for collaboration in working out a scheme of gradual settlement in their respective areas: all pleaded their areas were full.[67]

It was clear that the peasant option had already become more difficult to maintain and was going to be yet more difficult in future. What, then, was the consequence of all this for peasant consciousness?

We know something of the peasant response to the developments of the 1930s in northern Mozambique and in Kenya. Isaacman and his collaborators have described reactions to forced cultivation of cotton in Mozambique:

The central arena of struggle focused on the appropriation of labor – there the peasants sought continually to minimize their involvement and, simultaneously, improve their working conditions . . .To avoid the tyranny of the cotton regime, many peasants deserted to neighboring countries . . . or fled to relatively uncontrolled areas in the backwater regions of the colony. . . Others who engaged in covert acts of sabotage, convinced state and concessionary company officials that their lands were unsuitable for cotton production . . . Several documented cases exist of cotton producers who created permanent refugee communities in remote zones beyond the effective control of the colonial regime.

And they tell us that 'there were somewhat greater opportunities to resist in the northern districts of Cabo Delgado and Niassa than probably anywhere else'.[68]

In Kenya, too, there were some striking protests. The most dramatic of these was the march on Nairobi by thousands of Kamba cattle-owners. J.R. Newman has described the character of the Kamba protest movement and assessed its consequences in ways which are very revealing for Zimbabwe. Newman sees the Kamba protest as a 'substantial populist movement' which mobilized in particular 'landless cattle owners . . . faced with the reduction of herds to an uneconomic size.' As Newman comments, the shortage of grazing for such men was at least in part a consequence of the activities of plough entrepreneurs in the Kamba Reserve:

The rich peasants or large farmers, individuals who had benefited from the opportunities for work and trade in the early colonial period, and had accumulated sufficient capital to establish themselves as producers of regular grain surpluses and as traders of that grain, had advanced themselves whilst others in the same area were in relative and absolute economic decline. The beginnings of capitalist farming had made land and labour valuable resources. More and more grazing land had been taken over for arable purposes, and investment in ploughs and harrows increased. The Kenya Land Commission estimated for Machakos in the early 1930s that plough owners cultivated twice the acreage of those without. . . Outright land sales and the increase of arable agriculture reduced the amount of communal grazing and contributed to a growing landlessness.

One might have expected there to have been a tension between the landless protestors and the larger plough entrepreneurs. But in fact Newman shows that the plough entrepreneurs provided the *leadership* of the whole protest movement:

The four principal leaders . . . all . . . attended the same school . . . Kioko has described this group as follows: 'Those of us at school then . . . are the ones who realised the value of change in life and who became the prominent farmers, teachers and clerks' . . . [They] obtained access to clerical and teaching jobs available at that time to only a small minority of Africans . . . Their work in Nairobi was the basis of their wealth as farmers and traders within Machakos District; they bought ploughs, cultivators and land, and they hired labour. By the 1930s they were well established as part of a class of rich peasants.

For such men 'any substantial reduction [of cattle] would have affected the work oxen and the supply of manure required to maintain the arable land.' So they put themselves at the head of the protest against destocking and used their organizational skills and Nairobi contacts to make that protest so effective.

As for the consequences, Newman sees them as far-reaching:

The defeat of compulsory destocking in Machakos forced the government to work with the economic trends within the African areas rather than to cut arbitrarily across them by force . . . A policy of land enclosure, government support for individual ownership, and concentration on capitalist farmers was direct recognition of, and support for, the increasing economic differentiation within rural society.[69]

Newman's analysis of Machakos can be generalized for Kenya as a whole in the 1930s. John Lonsdale writes that:

In the inter-war years elites bickered while classes began to form. Both chiefs and mission elites competed to articulate African grievances at the inequities of state policies which taxed resources to subsidise white settlers. . . But more and more, these conflicts revolved about the perquisites of privilege between elites whose intermediary position in the state enabled them jointly to exclude the majority of the population from the possibility of similar self improvement. . . Their ability to monopolise advantage was reinforced by the formal institution of Local Native Councils in the mid 1920s, by which the colonial government sought to reconcile chiefs and mission elites in joint projects for the improvement of their areas out of local taxation which fell equally on rich and poor alike, but from which the wealthy and influential could gain the largest unearned increment . . . And all this visible conflict about the inexorable concentration of privilege was played out against the silent gathering of difference between rich and poor peasants . . .This was the basis for the Mau Mau rebellion. Rural elites initiated a political organisation from which they soon recoiled when they realised that it was outrunning their control. Farm squatters and the labourers of Nairobi joined hands under the leadership of radical labour leaders to regain lost rights to land in a movement which turned as much against the Kikuyu landed gentry as against the white farmers and the colonial state.[70]

Now, all this was very different from developments in Zimbabwe in the 1930s. In the rural areas of Southern Rhodesia there were no fugitive maroon communities, no marches of peasants on the capital. Reserve entrepreneurs were unable to force the Rhodesian government to work with the economic trends which they represented rather than cutting 'arbitrarily across them by force'. On the face of things the Rhodesian *via media*, neither directly coercing peasant production, as in Mozambique, nor allowing the perpetuation within the Reserves of sharp differentiation as in Kenya, paid off in a much more placid countryside. General historians of Southern Rhodesia have tended to pass over the 1930s with hardly a word, as a time when nothing happened. Despite all the hardships of the early 1930s and the apprehensions of the later 1930s, the Native Commissioner, Makoni, could still write in his 1940 annual report, that 'the native has full faith in government methods even though he may find it difficult to understand them.'[71]

Indeed, a kind of myth of the 1930s can be found in both white and black autobiographies. In Hardwicke Holderness's forthcoming book, an affectionate account of his boyhood in the 1930s leads to an expression of his belief that up to the end of the Second World War there had been neither substantial injustice nor substantial sense of grievance in Southern Rhodesia. Lawrence Vambe, having offered us a volume-and-a-half of much less affectionate reminiscence of his own restricted and disadvantaged adolescence, oddly enough comes to much the same conclusions:

It is my firm conviction that the 1930s presented the Europeans with a perfect opportunity to win the trust and co-operation of their black fellow men. . . The majority of Africans, especially those in the rural areas, were still prepared to accept white leadership. The African chiefs had long been reduced to impotent nonentities . . .The growing political consciousness among the black populace was generally unorganised . . .Political militants were in fact a tiny minority and lived mainly in the towns, out of touch with the vast mass of the people in the country. It is tragic that the opportunity offered at that time for the beginnings of co-operation between the races was so resolutely squandered.[72]

There is some truth in all this. It is true that none of the existing political organizations succeeded in making any effective contact with rural grievances. It is also true that unlike Kenya there did not exist within the African rural areas a sufficiently secure, established and self-confident elite which could both provide local leadership and link up with urban politics.

In Makoni District in 1929 and 1930, for instance, returning migrants from the towns of Rhodesia and South Africa, embittered by the collapse of employment opportunity, brought with them the ideas of the South African National Congress and the Industrial and Commercial Workers Unions (ICU), and also of the Young Manyika Ethiopian Society, which some of them had formed in the towns to express regional aspirations and grievances. The missionaries were alarmed. As Father Jerome O'Hea wrote from Triashill in September 1930:

There is a certain amount of trouble, of a Bolshi sort, brewing and coming to the surface among the Manyikas . . .The Young Ethiopians, the ICU and a few local societies are talking a great deal of hot air in the Reserves and, especially when they are drunk, I have managed to pick up a certain amount of their plans . . .Boys back from Capetown and Johannesburg are particularly active and it is really astonishing to hear the clear echoes of Moscow out here in the wilds. The missionaries, of course, are merely for the sake of drugging the blacks to make them the slave of the whites . . .A fairly good grasp of the theory and practice of the 'class war' being in the hands of the black . . . it is easily to be understood how the slighest grievance is seized upon and ventilated to the full.[73]

The administration kept a close eye on returning migrants – in June 1930, for example, the Superintendent of Natives, Bulawayo, warned that one Mandichomira, who had addressed a Congress rally in Cape Town, was on his way home to Inyanga: 'He is probably an emissary of the ICU.'[74] But they were not too worried about the effect of such men on the peasantry. As the Native Commissioner, Inyanga reported in November 1930:

There are no signs of unrest in this district among the natives. The Young Manyika Society does not exist in the district. There are societies established in . . . Cape Town, Bulawayo and Salisbury, known as the Young Ethiopian Manica Society. The objects are political and many of the younger natives of the district belong to one or other of the branches in the towns. Endeavours have been made in the district to establish branches but without any success. The older men are not interested and the younger men are never long enough at the kraals to get going . . . I dare say there are a few extremists who come from the towns occasionally with something new which they like to parade before the others. Such persons are not taken seriously by the people as their foreign ideas do not fit with the present thoughts of the people.[75]

Nor was such peasant apathy surprising since the urban-based associations signally failed to make any connection with the rural grievances of Mashonaland or Manicaland. In 1931, for example, organizers of the Southern Rhodesian ICU 'which [sic] have hitherto confined their activities to Salisbury town . . . penetrated into the District. A meeting was held in Chikwakwa Reserve, at which Dzingene, the organising secretary, spoke. The usual grievances about having to take off hats and the inconsiderate behaviour of some employers were referred to, but the older natives were not interested.'[76] In the same report, the Native Commissioner noted that 'the price of maize [had] dropped heavily, and the ramification of the Maize Control Act made it more difficult than ever for the native to dispose of his grain.' Peasants had more to worry about than having to take off hats. Similarly, ICU representatives who entered the Umtali Reserves in 1931 spoke of the need 'to organise themselves for the improvement of industrial conditions', and not surprisingly made 'little or no progress'.[77]

As for more elite bodies, like the Southern Rhodesian Native Association (SRNA), whose Umtali branch contained many American Methodist Episcopal converts and might have made connection with the grievances of the Reserves entrepreneurs, their meetings focused on 'immorality in the municipal location, conditions at the native hospitals, postal facilities for natives, the delivery of parcels by the Railway . . . and the establishment of a Native Village Settlement.'[78] Just to be on the safe side, the Native Department refused an application from the SRNA to work in the Reserves, but it plainly would not have mobilized peasant discontent even had it done so. The bodies set up by the Native Purchase Farmers *were* concerned with rural issues, of course, but 'they shunned identification with the bulk of the African population and the Farmers' Union was only open to purchase farmers.'[79]

Most Native Commissioners believed that the politics of the young men were futile, those of the elite associations trifling, and those of the peasant masses non-existent. As the Native Commissioner, Melsetter wrote in 1930:

The Native Self-Constructing Society has continued its apparently moribund existence . . . Of alien communistic questioning, however, among the Natives who have returned from Johannesburg, one hears now and then; those questionings about liberty, equality and fraternity, old in Europe, but never bruited before in Africa. But apart from these occasional mutterings . . . the great bulk of the people remain silent, unquestioning, inert.[80]

Yet despite all this I believe myself that the more hesitant view of the Native Commissioner, Mazoe, was closer to the mark. 'It is usual to state,' he wrote in 1931, 'that the natives are peaceful and contented but I do not think the latter adjective can be truthfully applied . . .The effect of the Maize Control Act upon the sale of their mealies . . . did not improve matters and, in view of the fact that they see all the European mealies being sold as usual, it is very difficult to give them a satisfactory explanation.'[81]

In fact it was impossible to give them a satisfactory explanation. The peasants of Mashonaland and Manicaland had nowhere to run away to; nor could they help themselves by sabotaging production. They did not have clusters of self-confident entrepreneurs to offer political leadership; nor was the Rhodesian colonial state consciously dependent upon finding local African rural allies. So

Rhodesian peasants nursed their grievances and kept their developing understanding of their predicament pretty much to themselves. But it is clear, nevertheless, that peasant consciousness matured during the 1930s. In particular, peasants of all sorts became much more aware of the role of the *state*, where in the period before 1930 they had been more aware of the emnity of white farmers.

The effects of Maize Control were only too immediate and obvious to those trying to maintain a peasant strategy. As the Chief Native Commissioner predicted in April 1931:

the restrictions are bound to be unpopular with the Native Population. It will be impossible to explain the economic necessity for control in a way that they will understand. It will simply be regarded as a harsh measure, designed to embarass them and make it more difficult for them . . . Those who have been in the habit of selling to farmers, small mines, prospectors and others will be most indignant when they find they cannot do so.[82]

The prediction was soon justified. In September 1931, for example, the Assistant Native Commissioner, Amandas, reported on a meeting with local chiefs and others. Both chiefs were outspoken in articulating the grievances of the peasantry. Chief Chiweshe 'complained of traders only paying in goods or tickets for grain. They had bought ploughs and wagons but these implements were now useless, as there was no market for their produce . . . They were losing ground and becoming like animals or the backward people of the remote portions of Darwin District.' Chief Makope complained that his people 'used to sell their mealies at the farms and at Bindura and Shamva and elsewhere and could always get the cash they required, but today the traders were the only people who were allowed to deal with their maize.' And two Reserves entrepreneurs joined in the protest. One of them, Joseph Gusha, described the efforts made to improve the quality of maize produced; 'the Natives had obtained good seed from Europeans. Some have produced 200 to 300 bags.' He himself had produced 230 bags but could sell none of it. Bob Garanda complained that he had produced 400 bags but 'could sell none of it as he was unable to move it.' And he articulated the challenge that was being made all over rural Rhodesia at that time: 'They had been taught by the white people to grow food but now it rotted in the kraals.'[83]

These protests at the collapse of the market hardened into quite explicit indictments of discrimination against peasant producers by the state. 'At the meeting of the Native Board held in the Zvimba Native Reserve,' it was reported in June 1934, 'some plain speaking was heard. Members spoke on the subject of their maize and said that since control was introduced the price for their maize was lower than before and they were being barred from usual markets.'[84] From Amandas came a report of the increasingly bitter feelings of the Chiweshe people. 'At the Chiweshe Reserve Board Meeting,' the Assistant Native Commissioner reported, 'the Maize Control Bill met with a very adverse reception. Many of the members openly accused the Goverment of continually making laws for the benefit of the European farmer exclusively, detrimental in every way to Native interests.'[85] By September 1934 the Chief Native Commissioner was writing to the Prime Minister's office to warn that 'the good relationships existing between Europeans and Natives may possibly be placed in jeopardy' by the operation of the Act.[86]

Not only chiefs and commissioners and entrepreneurs but also even traders who were close to their African suppliers articulated peasant outrage. For example, Harry Margolis, the great grain trader of Makoni District, wrote in 1944 that:

It is regrettable that in the case of Maize, which is the native's bread and butter crop, an organisation should have been set in motion which places him at a disadvantage with the European farmer . . . In the days prior to the promulgation of the Maize Control Act, the native received a price for his maize, [which] although fluctuating, approximated its market value. Under present conditions he receives a price not only below that of the European but the high price which the European farmer receives is paid at the expense of the native grower . . . despite the fact that in 9 years out of 10 if it were not for the native crop the Colony would have had to import maize for local uses.[87]

Nor was this varied protest altogether ineffective. It could be used to demonstrate that peasants would not stand for *anything*; that it would be dangerous to push them too far. In October 1937, for example, the Secretary for Native Affairs produced a long critical memorandum on resolutions passed by white farmers' associations which demanded 'total exclusion from the local market of farm produce of the Black peasant which can be grown and profitably sold at an internal price level in that market by the white farmer or planter.' The Secretary pointed out that 'this internal price level is artificially raised in the case of wheat and maize' and that while the local market was often termed 'the European market', 'the real consumers in it were largely Natives, who had also played an important part in establishing it.' In the remainder of his memorandum the Secretary for Native Affairs argued two propositions – first that African peasant production remained fundamental to the country's economy, despite all its handicaps, and second that African peasants constituted a hidden political potential:

What is asked for is economic privilege on a colour basis. One result would be a retardation of the incentive to produce among the Black peasants, and the proposed monopoly could hardly fail to increase costs to other local industries, not only of food-stuffs for the labourers in mines, tobacco plantations, etc but of the supplementary feed necessary for animal production . . .

The direct or indirect repression of the production of wealth by the Natives . . . may precipitate the issue of Native representation . . .The effect might be to spread to this Colony the racial antagonism apparently growing in the Union. There is at present no cause for alarm, but I am informed that there are already slight signs of discontent in certain quarters of Matabeleland . . . [in] the dangerous international situation . . . we wish to give no cause for native unrest.

Native producers and consumers are part of our economic structure – a most important part, surely, for they constitute the most important factor in production – even in what is called European production. . . Markets are likely to be increased not by handicapping Black peasant production of primary products, but rather by gladly accepting the cheaper production, and using European ability to handle it, perhaps by converting the cereals into animals or secondary products giving a higher return and also meeting marketing requirements instead of attempting to force markets to over-pay a group of protected producers.[88]

Following up his attack on white farmers, the Secretary for Native Affairs turned to the question of soil conservation. What was needed was 'a generally applicable Land Management Act,' since 'European farmers will certainly not all voluntarily subject themselves to advice which may conflict with opportunist interests.' African peasant producers, on the other hand, presented no difficulty for conservationist measures which were easy to introduce 'in the present comparatively docile state of the Natives.'[89] Here he was certainly deceived by appearances. We have already seen how deeply centralization was disliked. When I interviewed the present Chief Makoni and his councillors in 1981 they told me of the late 1930s: 'Life began to be tough in those days. We couldn't produce food enough to last all year round. Centralization was to blame for this. The Chief was left with no land to distribute. The Europeans said "You plough here, between these ridges"; when the children grew up there was no more land. . . We were no freer than water in a bottle.'[90] As for contour ridging, Native Commissioner Phayre was under no illusions that it could be carried out voluntarily. In September 1937 he reported that he had 'attended a demonstration of contour ridging. I fear the labour involved will prevent operations by natives for a long time. . . There is immense scope for work in Reserves, but for a satisfactory outcome . . . the presence of a whole-time European is indicated. And force, in the main, will have to be applied.'[91] 'Contour ridging in Reserves meets with no degree of welcome', he wrote in 1939.[92]

By the end of the 1930s Native Commissioners were coming to contemplate a degree of compulsion which no-one would have thought it possible to apply to white farmers, however inefficient. In July 1944 there was an illuminating exchange between the Native Trade and Production Commissioners and Native Commissioner Jowett of Makoni:

Commissioners: What is the reaction of the Natives to this reduction in the size of plots owing to centralization?
Jowett: They dislike any restriction intensely.
Commissioners: You cannot blame them. Until they see that it is not as adverse as they thought it would be. Or do they still retain their resentment after they find they are getting a much better return?
Jowett: You see, the bulk of the population still doesn't cultivate reasonably well . . .They are going on wearing out their land.

For Jowett 'the only remedy' was 'compulsion'; peasants would have to be forced to adopt intensive methods and to build contours; if compulsion were to be applied, the peasant 'will dislike it, but he will say, "I am compelled to do it and I will have to do it!" '[93]

'He will not passively resist?' asked the Commissioners. 'Oh, yes,' replied Jowett, 'he would resist passively.' And it seems clear that peasant 'passivity' throughout the 1930s was the passivity of resistance rather than of docility. Peasants did not actively resist administrative orders that they should leave their land and move elsewhere. But they constantly frustrated all attempts to establish tidy dividing lines between black and white areas. In 1938, when Native Commissioner Phayre was preparing for the full implementation of Land Apportionment and drawing up his plans to move all Africans into the Reserves, he noted that 'Natives of this district still adhere to their roaming propensity, and do not hesitate to dispose themselves on any vacant lands, whether Crown property, or that of absentee owners.'[94] Sometimes force and the threat of force *were* used by peasants to defend lands, but in this period it was against other Africans. All over the country peasants clung on to land which had been set aside under the Land Apportionment Act for occupation by Native Purchase farmers. They sought to drive off any would-be African purchasers. Thus in November 1934 Land Inspector Craig reported to the Acting Assistant Director of Native Lands that in north Makoni 'natives at present living on Native Purchase Area are endeavouring to discourage land-holders from taking up land in the Division.' In December two peasants were convicted for assaulting one Mapenda 'for wishing to take up land in the Maparura Native Purchase Area'; the Native Commissioner, Makoni, called headman Maparura in and 'warned him that if there was any further molestation of intending purchasers I would have him and his people moved into a Reserve.' But no farms had been occupied in Maparura NPA by the end of the 1930s.[95]

Where they could, then, peasants in Mashonaland and Manicaland acted to protect their interests. But one of the reasons for the lack of dramatic events in the Rhodesian rural areas in the 1930s was that the peasants had little which they *could* directly attack. There was no destocking drama as among the Kamba of Kenya because the Native Affairs Department had not yet introduced compulsory destocking. The Chief Native Commissioner, under pressure from the Natural Resources Board Native Enquiry in 1942, expressed very considerable reluctance to confront the hitherto largely passive strength of the peasantry. 'It has been our policy to try and secure their co-operation rather than to do something which they will oppose.' The commissioners urged that destocking had become an immediate necessity:

Chief Native Commissioner: There is a time when de-stocking should be done, but that is not just at this time . . . [while] you might not get any serious opposition you would fail to get co-operation and that in my mind is essential.
Commissioners: But wouldn't it be better to face a little opposition than to put off the evil day until the land is ruined?
Chief Native Commissioner: I don't think it has got to that stage yet.
Commission member: I think de-stocking should go on right away.
Chief Native Commissioner: That is where we differ. I feel we have to keep the native contented.[96]

There certainly was not a golden age of good relations in the 1930s: rather there was a postponement of the question of compulsion. Peasants knew that the state had intervened; they knew they were poorer as a result; they waited the inevitable next stages.

Meanwhile below the level of explicit political ideas, there *was* an upheaval of consciousness in Makoni District in the 1930s, an upheaval which found its expression mostly in new religious ideas. The collapse of the market in the early 1930s; official interference with some of the essentials of the peasant strategy, so that it became more and more difficult to play off one trader against another or to move about in search of the best land; the increasing hostility of the administration towards the 'progressive heroes' of the previous decade – all served to call into question the continuing relevance of Makoni's mission-Christian peasant ideology. Even the core area of American Methodist enterprise, Gandanzara circuit, found it difficult to maintain its level of support for the church. One missionary wrote in 1931 that 'Practically the only means the people of this circuit have of raising money is through selling grain. This year the grain crop was cut short by drought. The price has gone lower and lower and is now selling at from three shillings to five shillings per bag for mealies. At most of the trading stores it is impossible to sell for cash, but only in exchange for goods.'[97] Christians had to give 'from two to three times as much' grain as they had in the past in order to keep open schools and churches. But even Gandanzara failed to keep this up. 'There is,' it was reported, 'relatively little cash in the hands of the native people. The Maize Control Act, the locusts, a poor mealie crop, low prices for all produce and the inability to obtain cash . . . all these together make it very difficult in some villages to maintain the Pastor-Teachers and Ministers.' By the end of 1934 'Gandanzara was so far behind in its 1934 collections that even the people themselves did not wish to have schools until the debts were paid.' The African ministers of the AMEC, meeting in their 'Native Christian Conference' in July 1935, deplored 'the hard task of the people in our out-stations', asked that the Mission funds be used to keep schools open, and debated the proposition that 'it is apparent that our Christian people are gradually withdrawing themselves from the Church and they regard it as an instrument of oppression.'[98]

Everywhere in Makoni peasants, and in particular adolescents of peasant families, were withdrawing from the churches. And there arose a prophet out of Makoni, Shoniwa Masedza Tandi Moyo of Gandanzara, later to be known as John the Baptist or Johana Masowe.[99] His Apostolic church preached a withdrawal of children from schools and the importance of a self-reliant life as artisan craftsmen or as co-operative farmers rather than as peasants or migrant workers. Amon Nengomasha tells us that:

Baba Johan had the conviction that one could not lead a proper and holy life unless he could fend for himself. That is the most important belief expressed by Baba Johan. If he satisfied his material needs, he would be able to satisfy his spiritual. It was very difficult at first because most of his converts lived in rural areas and knew only about agriculture. The first message to these people was 'first of all, all you people must learn to work together. Have a common field; you might have individual fields but at least you must have one field designed for the Church' . . . At Gandanzara there was one field, the other was at Dewedzo.[100]

Masowe's Apostles confronted the African agents of both the colonial administration and the mission churches – 'You are not true ministers of the word because you sell it for money. Our Lord did not do that nor His Apostles. But you do. Our Lord cast out devils and evil spirits, you cannot.'[101] Masowe criticized not only the worldliness of the missions, their corrupting participation in the colonial political economy, but also the superficiality of their faith. Obsessed with the gospel of the plough and with literacy, both now rendered useless by the Depression, the Missions had not sought to apply the power of Christ and of the Holy Spirit to the *real* problems of the rural areas. So the Masowe church exorcized evil spirits, healed witches, and prepared a cleansed flock for a spiritual existence in withdrawal from participation in the colonial economy either as peasants or workers.[102]

At the same time many other peasant families turned increasingly to the spirit mediums in another kind of critique of the mission entrepreneurial ethic and of government policies. Thus in 1931 many offerings were sent to a woman 'very intelligent, clear of speech and an expert at repartee . . . under the delusion that Chaminuka's spirit has entered her and her only desire is to assist and do good amongst her fellow beings.' She claimed to be 'the Government in charge of rain' and was said to have told peasants to pay tribute to her rather than to the administrators since 'Government is stealing the Natives' money.'[103] The Inyanga Native Board requested the Native Commissioner in early 1931 that all landowners, including missionaries, be instructed to allow rain ceremonies to be carried out at ancestral shrines on their land. The Catholic superior at Triashill, required by the Native Commissioner to allow Chief Mandeya to sacrifice at his 'sacred graves' replied with indignation:

That is what the hut is required for: Pagan superstition and witchcraft! You will understand that I, a minister of the Catholic Church, will not give any help nor permission to that . . . I am surprised that you, the representative of a Christian King and Government should ask me for it . . . So long as I am in this charge that hut shall not be built up . . . If I see it built up I shall burn it down.[104]

By the mid-1930s it seemed as if the mission churches were in a state of crisis. In the end mission folk Christianity survived. Masowe's teachings, though an effective and penetrating critique of colonial political economy and colonial ideology, could not in the long run offer a practical guide to living in the Reserves. The collective fields of his church, like the large acres of the Reserves entrepreneurs, fell victim to the reallocation of land during centralization. He and many of his followers left Makoni to begin their remarkable trek around the cities of Southern and East Africa, where they developed artisanal skills. In Makoni itself his church seemed relevant at the end of the 1930s only to those who had dropped out of the attempt to remain peasants and who had become dependent on male migrant labour. In other parts of the district the revival of the peasant option, attended as it was by so many difficulties, meant also a revival of mission folk Christianity. The 'progressive' converts of the mission churches saved the day by launching a series of Revival movements headed by associations of African churchmen, and particularly of devout African church-women. The wives of the American Methodist teachers and evangelists, through the *Rukwadzano* association, organized huge Revival meetings throughout the district which held much of Makoni for their powerful form of Christian ideology. But within these Revivals the balance of power and of interpretation shifted between black and white. By the end of the decade the religious ideologies of different types of rural consciousness and response were more clearly defined and more profoundly indigenized than ever before.[105]

I have been seeking to show, then, that the 1930s *was* a crucial decade for the peasantries of Mashonaland and Manicaland, though not in the same way, or with the same implications for consciousness as for the Kikuyu, the Kamba or the peasants of northern Mozambique. Consciousness *had* been further elaborated and differentiated within an overall resentment at what had been done to every type of Reserves producer by the state. Further stages were needed, of course, before Shona peasantries were ready to support a radical nationalism or the liberation struggle. The peasant option had to be not only restricted and impeded but really threatened with 'destruction'; government interventions in peasant cultivation had to reach a peak of coercive intensity which was still only foreshadowed by the developments of the 1930s; peasants had to encounter political movements which spoke directly to rural grievance and held out some sort of hope of alleviating it. All these things were to come to Mashonaland and Manicaland in the next decades.

What happened in *Matabeleland* in the 1930s and what was to happen there in the next decades was another story, however, and one to which I shall turn in the next chapter.

NOTES

1   Robin Palmer, 'The Agricultural History of Rhodesia', in Robin Palmer and Neil Parsons (eds.), *The Roots of Rural Poverty in Central and Southern Africa* (London: 1977), pp.243-4.
2   Allen Isaacman, Michael Stephen, Yussuf Adam, Maria João Homem, Eugenio Macamo and Augustine Pililão, ' "Cotton is the

mother of poverty": peasant resistance to forced cotton production in Mozambique, 1938–1961', *International Journal of African Historical Studies*, vol. 13, no. 4, (1980), pp. 585–6.

3 Barry Munslow, 'Peasants, politics and production. The case of Mozambique', unpublished paper presented to Political Studies Association of the United Kingdom conference, Exeter, 1980, p. 4.

4 E.A.Alpers, 'To seek a better life: the implications of migration from northern Mozambique to colonial and independent Tanzania for class formation and political behaviour in the struggle to liberate Mozambique', unpublished paper presented to Conference on 'The Class Base of Nationalist Movements in Angola, Guinea-Bissau and Mozambique', Minneapolis, May 1983, p. 13.

5 Munslow, 'Peasants, politics and production', p. 1

6 D.W.Throup, 'The origins of Mau Mau', Institute of Commonwealth Studies, London, October 1982, p. 1.

7 J.M.Lonsdale, 'Unhappy Valley: state and class formation in colonial Kenya', unpublished paper, February 1982, p. 8.

8 Gavin Kitching, *Class and Economic Change in Kenya. The Making of an African Petite Bourgeoisie* (New Haven and London: 1980), pp. 58, 73.

9 Paul Mosley, 'The settler economies: studies in the economic history of Kenya and Southern Rhodesia, 1900–1963 (University of Cambridge: PhD thesis, April 1980), pp. 33 and 34. It is important to realize that the whole process of self-peasantization involved 'individualisation' in the sense of families moving from the tributary economy. Thus the annual report for Makoni in 1921 remarked: 'What little power the Chiefs possess is becoming less . . . as the tribes become broken up and scattered it is necessary to deal with individuals and the work cannot be done through the Chiefs'. File N 9/1/24, National Archives, Harare (NAH). Mosley, however, is referring to a further stage of 'individualisation' in which entrepreneurial families set themselves consciously apart from the peasant community as land-owning 'progressives'. He remarks that 'individualisation' was in Southern Rhodesia 'channelled off into the Native Purchase Areas' while 'in Kenya it was perforce confined within reserves'.

10 Annual Report, Makoni, 1938, file S.1563, NAH. The remarkable status of Makoni as a maize marketing district is confirmed by comparison with other districts. In the 1938 report the total African population of Makoni is stated at 36 186 and 88 379 bags of maize were sold. In Charter District, with much the same African population at 36 926, it was estimated that 121 050 bags of grain had been produced but that only 5224 bags had been traded. In Salisbury District only 8000 bags had been sold; in Hartley only 6940 bags; in Mazoe only 50 992. Admittedly 1938 was a poor harvest but this only makes the Makoni figure the more remarkable.

11 Annual Report, Makoni, 1940, file S.1563, NAH. The report remarked that 'perhaps wisely, the natives of the Chiduku and

Makoni Reserves are concentrating on the improvement of grain quality rather than quantity at present.'

12 Mosley, 'The settler economies', p. 84. See also, idem, 'Agricultural development and government policy in settler economies: the case of Kenya and Southern Rhodesia, 1900–60', *Economic History Review*, vol. 35, no. 3 (August 1982), pp. 390–408.

13 Mosley, 'The settler economies', p. 108.

14 Native Commissioner, Goromonzi, to Chief Native Commissioner, 4 August 1927, file S.138.22. 1926/1927, NAH.

15 E.G. Howman to Chief Native Commissioner, 10 September 1927, file S.138.22.1926/1927, NAH.

16 G.E.P. Broderick, C.W. Swan and S. Haworth to Director of Native Education, 10 April 1929, file S. 138.72.1927/1930, NAH.

17 E.D. Alvord to Director of Native Education, 13 May 1929, file S.138.72.1927/1930, NAH.

18 Chief Native Commissioner to Director of Native Education, 30 April 1929, file S.138.72.1927/1930, NAH. These exchanges were part of a debate between Alvord and critics of his demonstration programme. The Native Commissioner, Goromonzi, spoke for many when he asserted in August 1927 that 'grain should be grown for food, not for sale'; such critics had in mind a vision of an egalitarian subsistence economy in the reserves. Alvord had a vision of an egalitarian marketing economy: 'No individual can be permitted to go into farming for himself on a large scale', he wrote in his draft annual report in January 1929. 'It is our aim to teach them how to grow on one acre the quantity of crops they now grow on ten . . . Our policy is one of conservation . . . and intensive farming on small areas.' (File S.138.72.1927/1930, NAH). But the Chief Native Commissioner's comments on the Chindamora entrepreneurs offer one good reason why they did not focus on improved intensive farming. 'Supplies of manure are not so inexhaustable as to allow for progressive fertilisation and so the Natives fly to the alternative of extensive cultivation.'

19 Native Commissioner, Mtoko to Chief Native Commissioner, 11 April 1935, file S.1542.S. 12. 1934/1936, NAH

20 Monthly Report, Makoni, October 1937, file S.1619, NAH.

21 Monthly Report, Makoni, February 1938, file S,1619, NAH.

22 Monthly Report, Ndanga, March 1944, file S.1619, NAH.

23 Mosley, 'The settler economies', p. 58.

24 Acting Native Commissioner, Makoni to Chief Native Commissioner, 18 August 1931, file S.138.22. 1931/1933, NAH.

25 Monthly Report, Makoni, August 1934, file S.235/527, NAH.

26 Monthly Report, Makoni, September 1934, S.235/527, NAH.

27 Clerk, Makoni to Chief Native Commissioner, enclosing memorandum to Native Commissioner, Makoni, 23 March 1935, S.1542.S.12. 1934/1936, NAH.

28 Native Commissioner, Makoni to Chief Native Commissioner, 25 September 1933, file S.1542.M2, NAH. In this letter the Native

Commissioner listed four names of Makoni producers who had been
issued 'participation certificates' by the Maize Control Board, but the
largest sum due to any of the others was £15. A rapid survey of
participation certificate-holders in other districts revealed that
outside Makoni the highest payment due was £15 5s to a producer at
the Range office. Sirewu was clearly an outstandingly large producer.

29 Memorandum, Clerk, Makoni, 10 March 1936, file S.1542.M2,
NAH.
30 Monthly Report, Makoni, October 1936, S.235.529, NAH.
31 Bishop Abel Muzorewa, *Rise up and Walk. An Autobiography*
(London: 1978), pp. 2-3, 8-9, 11, 14.
32 'The History of the Pastor-Teacher Jim Nathaniel Jijita', Reverend
Elliott Jijita, Family Secretary, file 'Persons', American Methodist
Archives, Old Umtali. It is interesting that both Jijita and
Muzorewa's father, Haadi Philemon Muzorewa, are listed among the
four producers with participation certificates for the 1931/2 harvest.
Haadi Muzorewa was paid out £15; Jijita £5.
33 Throup, 'The origins of Mau Mau', p. 1.
34 J.A.Edwards, 'Southern Rhodesia. The response to adversity,
1935–1939' (University of London: PhD thesis, 1978), pp. 9, 10-11,
21.
35 Mosley, 'The settler economies', p. 54. Mosley cites on p. 54 a cable
from the Native Commissioner, Mazoe, sent in July 1931: 'Traders in
reserve now in position of monopolists and dictate not only price, but
medium with which to buy grain, which medium is trade goods only.'
36 Kitching, *Class and Economic Change in Kenya*, p. 61.
37 Mosley, 'The settler economies', p. 56.
38 ibid., p. 84
39 W. Edwards to Chief Native Commissioner, 28 August 1931, file
S.138.21, vol. 4, NAH.
40 Annual Report, Mrewa, 1929, file S.235/507, NAH. Interestingly the
Native Commissioner, in a fit of male chauvinism, added:

> There is no question that the younger generation of native is being
> pushed by his womanfolk into the use of the plough, and the
> slovenly method of agriculture. The man with the plough and oxen
> has a better chance of a 'pick' in the marriage market than the one
> without, but I am not sure that the one without is not better off, as
> when he does take to himself a wife, she will be one of the old-
> fashioned kind; she may not be able to knit a jersey or crochet
> doily, and may not know a lot about hygiene, but she will always be
> ready to help him in his lands.

41 Kitching, *Class and Economic Change in Kenya*, p. 94
42 E.D. Alvord, 'Development of native agriculture and land tenure in
Southern Rhodesia', unpublished ms., 1958, pp. 25-6. In the light of
the data deployed in this and the previous chapter, Alvord's estimate
of the agrarian situation in 1927 is a very peculiar one:

In 1927 . . . the people in many parts of the country were . . . primitive and poverty-stricken . . . One could truthfully say they were a people just emerging for their prehistoric past. The men were largely hunters and pastoralists, leaving what little tillage that was done to the women . . . There was little inducement to produce grain for sale. The markets all belonged to the European farmers. Even in the near vicinity of Salisbury and other large towns there was no market for their crops . . . The total grain sold that year when compared to the population, averaged less than one-fourth of a bag per person.

43 E.D. Alvord to Chief Native Commissioner, 20 September 1937, file S.1542.A4, 1937/1939, NAH. Alvord added that the future limit should be four to six acres per family: 'tillage will have to be controlled and soil conservation and crop rotation systems enforced.'
44 Address by Godfrey Huggins to Joint Conference of the Rhodesian Agricultural Union and the Matabeleland Farmers Union, 28 September 1937, file S.1542.A6, 1936/1937, NAH.
45 Assistant Agriculturalist to Agriculturalist, 26 March 1938, file S.1542.A4, 1937/1939, NAH.
46 Monthly Report, Makoni, December 1937, file S.1619, NAH.
47 Monthly Report, Makoni, January 1938, file S.1619, NAH.
48 Monthly Report, Makoni, February 1938, file S.1619, NAH.
49 Monthly Report, Makoni, September 1938, file S.1619, NAH.
50 Annual Report, Makoni, 1938, file S.1563, NAH.
51 Monthly Report, Makoni, February 1938, file S.1619, NAH.
52 E.D. Alvord to Secretary, Native Affairs, 26 October 1938, file S.1542, A4, NAH.
53 Land Inspector, Salisbury to Chief Native Commissioner, 10 December 1938, file S.1542.A4, NAH.
54 Annual Report, Makoni, 1940, file S.1563, NAH.
55 Annual Report, Makoni, 1941, file S.1563, NAH.
56 Evidence of L.V. Jowett, 14 July 1944, file ZBJ 1/1/2, p. 1094, NAH.

Jowett had only recently arrived in Makoni District. The peasant farmers of that district would have been disturbed had they heard the following exchange:
Commissioners: If prices were controlled perhaps at a lower figure than they are today, the Natives would simply not bring in his grain. He would let it rot.
Jowett: I am not sure that under present conditions it is a good thing for the Native to produce too much grain for sale . . . Until the Native's methods of production improve I am not anxious to see a tremendous lot of grain marketed . . . Some districts are being saved by the mere fact that they are so far from rail that it is not profitable to produce.

57 ibid., p. 1089.

58 Evidence of S.G. Gilmour, 7 August 1942, Natural Resources Board Native Enquiry, file S.988, NAH.
59 E.D. Alvord to Director of Native Development, 15 October 1932, file S.138.72, 1930/1933, NAH.
60 Assistant Native Commissioner, Goromonzi to Native Commissioner, Salisbury, 16 December 1933, file S.138.72, 1930/1933, NAH.
61 Memorandum prepared by W.G. Swanson, Assistant Native Commissioner, Wedza sub-district, 31 May 1944, file ZBJ 1/2/2, NAH.
62 P. Robertshaw, 'Irrigation in Melsetter and Chipinga: a case study in the transfer of agricultural hegemony', Manchester, June 1983.
63 Oliver Pollak, 'Black farmers and white politics in Rhodesia', *African Affaris*, vol 74, no. 296 (July 1975) pp. 264–6.
64 Roger Woods, 'The dynamics of land settlement. Pointers from a Rhodesian land settlement scheme', Dar es Salaam, December 1966, p. 3.
65 Edwards, 'Southern Rhodesia. The response to adversity', p. 11.
66 Pollak, 'Black farmers and white politics', pp. 267, 269.
67 Monthly Report, Makoni, February 1938, file S.1619, NAH.
68 Isaacman, Stephen, Adam, Homen, Macamo and Pililão, ' "Cotton is the mother of poverty" ', pp.595, 598, 607.
69 J.R. Newman, *The Ukamba Members Association* (Nairobi: 1974), pp. 15-16, 3-4, 33-4.
70 J.M. Lonsdale, 'African elites and social classes in colonial Kenya', paper presented to Round Table on Elites and Colonisation, Paris, July 1982, pp. 11–13.
71 Annual Report, Makoni, 1940, file S.1563, NAH.
72 Lawrence Vambe, *From Rhodesia to Zimbabwe* (London: 1976), p. 106.
73 Jerome O'Hea to Monsignor Brown, 11 September 1930, Box 195, Jesuit Archives, Mount Pleasant, Harare.
74 Superintendent of Natives, Bulawayo to Chief Native Commissioner, 5 June 1930, file S.138.22. 1930/1931, NAH. Mandichomira's statement, enclosed, shows that he had been working in South Africa without returning home since 1924.
75 Native Commissioner, Inyanga to Chief Native Commissioner, 20 November 1930, file S.138.22. 1930/1931, NAH. The Catholic missionaries took their own steps against activists. In May 1932 they expelled three returned Congress members from Triashill farm. Provincial Secretary, ANC, Western Province, Cape Town to Resident Magistrate, Inyanga, 25 May 1932; Native Commissioner, Inyanga to Chief Native Commissioner, 6 June 1932, ibid.
76 Annual Report, Salisbury, 1931, file S.235.509, NAH. In the previous year's report the Native Commissioner, Salisbury, wrote:

> Certain wild statements are often made and it is the apparent aim of the speakers to awaken the native to class consciousness. I do not think that the extremists among the speakers and leaders meet with much sympathy . . . In this connection may I quote an extract of an

address read me in Seki Reserve . . . 'We must not forget that we are young children and must always try by all means to follow in father's footsteps. We must not treat the white man as an enemy of the black man as many others think. We must not at least treat them as having come to this country to rob us of our land.'

77 Annual Report, Umtali, 1931, file S.235.509, NAH.
78 Annual Reports, Umtali, 1928, 1930, 1931, file S.235/506, 508 and 509, NAH.
79 Pollack, 'Black farmers and white politics', p. 266.
80 Annual Report, Melsetter, 1930, file S.235.508, NAH.
81 Annual Report, Mazoe, 1931, file S.235.509, NAH.
82 Chief Native Commissioner to Secretary/Premier, 17 April 1931, file S.138.72, 1930/1933, NAH.
83 Assistant Native Commissioner, Amandas to Chief Native Commissioner, 8 September 1931, file S.138.22, 1931/1933, NAH.
84 Monthly Report, Lomagundi, June 1934, file S.235.527, NAH.
85 Assistant Native Commissioner, Amandas to Chief Native Commissioner, 21 June 1934, file S.1542.M2, NAH.
86 Chief Native Commissioner to Secretary, Premier, 27 June 1934, file S.1542.M2, NAH.
87 Evidence of Harry Margolis, 23 June 1944, file ZBJ 1/2/2, NAH.
88 Secretary for Native Affairs, Memorandum, 7 October 1937, file S.1542.A4, 1937/1939, NAH.
89 ibid.
90 Interview with Chief Muzanenamo Makoni and councillors, Makoni, 8 February 1981.
91 Monthly Report, Makoni, September 1937, file S.1619, NAH.
92 Annual Report, Makoni, 1938, file S.1563, NAH.
93 Evidence of L.V. Jowett, 14 July 1944, file ZBJ 1/1/2, NAH.
94 Annual Report, Makoni, 1938, file S.1563, NAH.
95 Acting Native Commissioner, Makoni to Chief Native Commissioner, 31 December 1934, file S.1542.L4, 1933/1935, NAH.
96 Examination of Chief Native Commissioner by Natural Resources Board Native Enquiry, 19 November 1942, file S.988, NAH.
97 *Rhodesia Annual Conference*, 1931, pp. 36–87.
98 Green file, 'Christian Conference, Agenda and Minutes, July 3 1935', American Methodist Archives, Old Umtali; *Rhodesia Annual Conference*, 1935, pp. 248, 253, 255.
99 C.M.Dillon-Malone, *The Korsten Basket Makers: A Study of the Masowe Apostles an Indigenous African Religious Movement*, (Manchester: 1978).
100 Interview with Amon Nengomasha, 17 February and 3 March 1977, National Archives Oral History Project, AOH/4, NAH.
101 Yakobo Mwela, 'The Mission of Renewal', 1934, USPG Archives, Westminster, Series E.
102 Terence Ranger, 'Poverty and prophetism. Religious movements in the Makoni District, 1929–1940', School of Oriental and African

Studies seminar, October 1981.

103 Assistant Native Commissioner, Buhera to Native Commissioner, The Range, 3 March 1931; Native Commissioner, The Range to Chief Native Commissioner, 28 July 1931, file S.138.22, 1930/1931, NAH.

104 Father Kaibach to Native Commissioner, Inyanga, 11 February 1931, file S.138.22, 1930/1931, NAH. 'Uncompromising harshness of this sort,' noted the Chief Native Commissioner, 'cannot but be detrimental to the good relations which it is our endeavour to maintain with the subject race.'

105 For a comparative account of the crisis for the church in the 1930s see Rosemary Lawson, 'Protest or participation? A study of Wesleyan Methodist African agents in Southern Rhodesia during the 1930s' (Manchester University: BA Honours thesis, 1982).

3

Kenya and Rhodesia,
1940 – 52:
Mau Mau
and Matabeleland

Because of the declaration of the Mau Mau emergency in 1952 historians of Kenya have paid particular attention to the agrarian developments of the preceding decade. There was no Mau Mau in Southern Rhodesia. Instead there was a general strike in 1948 which affected all the towns of the colony, and which some interpreters have seen as marking the beginning of a new era of proletarian consciousness. Thus, while analysis of Kenya's 'peasant war' has thrown much light on rural conditions, in Southern Rhodesian historiography increasing attention is being paid to the background to the 1948 strike, to urbanization and industrialization in the 1940s.

As Sharon Stichter reminds us, both events took place within interconnected peasant and migrant labour economies. Stichter indeed sets the uniqueness of Mau Mau in just such a comparative context:

It is often assumed that migrant labour economies are in themselves unstable. This view is implicit in the *a priori* position that the semi-proletarianised labourer in Africa is a 'transitional' class category. But there is no inherent reason why a low-wage, migrant labour economy, drawing labour from a subsistence sector which is marginal but not in collapse, cannot persist for a very long time. South Africa is perhaps the best case in point. Some labour protest, but hardly a revolution, could be expected. Why then, in Kenya, did the Mau Mau rebellion and massive social change result?[1]

In such a perspective Southern Rhodesia's migrant labour economy gave rise to the 'labour protest' of 1948, while Kenya's gave rise to

99

the Mau Mau 'revolution'.

In this chapter I want to stand Stichter's question on its head and to ask not why a Mau Mau did happen in Kenya but why a Mau Mau did *not* happen in Southern Rhodesia. In doing so I want us almost to forget for a time that no such outbreak in the end took place in Rhodesia: I want us to keep open in our minds the possibility that such a rural rebellion *might* have happened there in the late 1940s or early 1950s. By so doing I hope to reinstate the Rhodesian rural crisis of those years as a key topic of historiographical inquiry and to put into question the assumption that the future of African protest in Rhodesia lay with the urban working class rather than with a passive peasantry. Nor is this a sort of intellectual con trick, borrowing the bloody plumes of Mau Mau to deck out the Rhodesian peasantry in appropriately militant garb. As I shall hope to show, there really *was* a rural crisis in Rhodesia in the 1940s, and this crisis contained many of the elements which in Kenya produced Mau Mau. As I shall hope to show also, there were plans for and fears of peasant resistance in an area of Rhodesia which had many parallels in its agrarian experience with the Kikuyu country in which Mau Mau took place. In Chapter 2 I went a good way towards demonstrating why anything like a Mau Mau was very unlikely in Mashonaland or Manicaland. But Matabeleland's agrarian history was a different matter.

In order to explore the similarities – and the ultimate distinctions – between the Kenyan and the Rhodesian rural crises, let me draw briefly on recent accounts of the background to Mau Mau. To do so I want to cite three papers by John Lonsdale. Lonsdale tells us that the late 1940s in Kenya witnessed 'another crisis created by War' in which the colonial state strove to mediate 'contradictory developments at the Imperial and local levels'. 'But,' he continues, 'at the local level the settlers were riding high, in no mood to share power. The war had relieved them of debt; more importantly, it had enabled them to capture large sectors of state power.' Meanwhile, Africans were organizing themselves also:

and on the same basis as enjoyed by settlers: greatly expanded demand for agricultural produce during and after the War – but Africans were *divided* by this prosperity while settlers tended to be united by it. Three major African divisions [existed] (especially in Kikuyuland):
i) *aspirant bourgeoisie* of farmers-traders-teachers, the leaders of the Kenya African Union . . .
ii) '*middle peasants*', especially those on the settler 'White Highlands' who from 1944 forcibly resisted transformation from labour-tenants to wage-workers. These farm 'squatters' are themselves the best evidence for African class-formation, since many of them had been pushed off their

ancestral lands by 'accumulators' in the African Reserves. In the 1920s they had sought 'Land and freedom' as individual families on the White Highlands; now facing a Second Alienation they had to resist as collectivities: the origins of 'Mau Mau'.

iii) *urban poor*, tending to be divided between the 'guerrilla army of the underemployed' and the would-be 'respectable' workers, but both pushed together by wartime and post-war inflation and by the state's slowness to recognise as legitimate any African urban 'Estate'.

The conflicts between these three groups and competition for leadership between them are essential to understanding 'Mau Mau'.[2]

In another paper Lonsdale emphasizes that Mau Mau had to happen in Kikuyuland. Elsewhere in Kenya 'differentiation could barely be perceived as stratification'; 'all agricultural societies other than the Kikuyu had considerable reserves of uncultivated land . . . Most were ill-placed to exploit the communications infra-structure of export production.' But:

Kikuyuland was quite different. It was an agrarian society virtually unique in settler Africa, in that while some of its land was alienated to white ownership, the bulk of it which remained was fertile and centrally placed. The Kikuyu were able to exploit their close access both to the road and rail communications which were laid out to service the settlers and to the growing market for meat, vegetables, grain and fuel provided by the capital city on their doorstep, Nairobi. Like their fellows in other cultivating communities the Kikuyu colonised the local state apparatus and the mission schools. But unlike their fellows the powerful among them could exploit their more open market access only by the exclusionary accumulation of land within a frontier which was closely circumscribed by white settlement; they had to become rural capitalists. Those whose rights were extinguished had little option but to become the farm tenants of landlord Kenya on the 'White Highlands'; by the late 1940s they numbered almost one third of the Kikuyu population . . .

It was this double peculiarity of the Kikuyu, land concentration at home and a farm tenantry outside, which determined that they, and they only, would be the seat of a violent agrarian revolt which not only set Africans against whites, but Kikuyu against Kikuyu too. . .

[So] the clash came in Kikuyuland, coinciding as it did with the reflux of 'squatter' families who refused the new proletarian conditions of employment on the White Highlands, and the bitterness of underemployed landless Kikuyu in Nairobi. The cause of the poor in all three areas, the Highlands, Nairobi and the Kikuyu reserves, was championed by urban politicians whose recourse to violence split a nationalist movement hitherto dominated by the class of rural accumulators.[3]

And a final citation from a third paper:

For the squatters, restriction orders on their crops and cattle broke the moral order which, they had assumed, tied them to their settler patron with mutual obligations. The same moral order was also being transgressed by the spread of capitalist relations in the Kikuyu heartland, in the reserves. Whereas the demands of land colonization in the nineteenth century had encouraged the multiplication of people on the right-holder's land, all with varying claims on its use, capitalist accumulation required these claims to be repudiated. By the 1940s Kikuyu land law had ceased to exist, though the courts were thronged. Where there is no law, self-help is the only defence, and so, on the Highlands and in the Kikuyu reserves, men took up the panga and the gun.[4]

Now, in Rhodesia in the later 1940s many of these same elements can be seen. There, too, settlers were 'riding high' and settler agriculture was booming for the first time in its history. There, too, 'squatters' on white land were being forced off it unless they would accept 'labour agreements' in a process which certainly amounted to a 'Second Alienation'. There, too, the urban poor suffered from inflation and the state's slowness to recognize as legitimate any African urban estate. There, too, the peasant 'moral economy' was being violated as the great investment companies which had subsisted off peasant rents for so long suddenly demanded that their land be cleared of African producers, and as the peasant option within the Reserves was threatened by overpopulation and official coercion. All these elements applied to Rhodesia as a whole. But there were additional similarities between Matabeleland in particular and the situation in Kikuyuland as described by Lonsdale. Many Ndebele peasants and cattle-owners lived, until the 'Second Alienation', close to Bulawayo, the largest urban market in Rhodesia; like the Kikuyu, the Ndebele had a keen sense of their historic rights to land and a keen sense that these rights had been betrayed; this gave rise to rural political movements which could make connection with the urban politics of Bulawayo. Unlike the peasants of Mashonaland and Manicaland, the interests of Ndebele cultivators *were* championed by urban politicians. Finally, while the plough entrepreneurs had been undercut in Mashonaland and Manicaland, cattle-based inequalities of wealth survived in the Reserves of Matabeleland into the late 1940s.

The essential point at which to begin the story of the Rhodesian rural crisis is the post-war eviction of Africans off white land into the Reserves. Here Paul Mosley can provide me with a text. Once again comparing the two countries, he describes how dynamic white farming in both Kenya and Rhodesia needed for the first time room to expand. 'The squatter problem became more urgent', particularly the problem of 'squatters' on the huge investment estates in the white area. 'Very little attractive land within the European area remained unalienated, so that space could only be made for new settlers by getting existing owners to sell.' To clear this land, he says, possibly 100 000 Africans were evicted from white areas in Kenya; some 85 000 African families in Rhodesia. 'This process involved the movement of Africans to arid outlying districts, a reduction in their real income, and violent African resentment of Europeans, which in Kenya has been linked to the "Mau Mau" uprising of 1952–54.'[5] We may well ask why, if some 100 000 Africans were evicted in Kenya and some 425 000 were evicted in Rhodesia, the uprising should have taken place in the former rather than the latter.[6]

The Rhodesian Native Department was in fact seriously worried that the evictions of the later 1940s would cause serious discontent. During the war itself they had been able to defer any large-scale implementation of the Land Apportionment Act. In July 1940, for example, the Chief Native Commissioner circulated all districts informing them that 'While it is not desirable that there should be a general standstill order in the implementation of the Land Apportionment Act, large removals of natives which may cause hardship or discontent should not be initiated this year by the Department . . . in view of the situation.'[7]. Again, in December of the same year the Chief Native Commissioner ordered:

it will be necessary to further postpone the date up to which certain rent agreements may remain in force . . . Present conditions necessitate the temporary slowing down of the implementation of the Act in order to avoid anything in the nature of mass movements of Natives. Whether the Act should be enforced in any case is therefore dependent on whether suitable land is available in the Native areas to which the Natives affected can be moved without causing them hardship . . . In cases where the removal of the Natives cannot be effected without causing hardship and the tenants are under notice to quit because of the landholder's belief that it will not be legal for him to charge rent after July 1941, Native Commissioners are authorised to communicate [this] information to the landholder or his agent with a view to the notice being rescinded.[8]

After the war, however, the Department could no longer resist the clamour for 'mass movements of Natives'. The boom in European agriculture, and especially in ranching and tobacco production, led to the great investment estates being broken up into workable farms or ranches for sale or lease to whites. The investment companies, which had for so long wanted to keep rent-paying Africans on their land, now wanted to clear them off it as rapidly as possible. In January 1947, for example, the Native

Commissioner, Essexvale, Matabeleland reported that a request had been 'received from the Agent for the Rhodesia Corporation to break down huts and destroy gardens on Willsgrove. 'After kaffir farming this land for a generation the Corporation expected immediate total compliance with their order to quit.'[9]

Whatever the resentment of the Native Department, however, white public opinion now demanded enforcement of the Land Apportionment Act and the Government gave undertakings that implementation would be carried out rapidly. Thereafter the Chief Native Commissioner's warnings grew gloomier and gloomier. In 1948 he predicted that African unrest would become acute in view

not only [of] the difficulty of physical re-location, but all the economic and emotional disturbances arising from the uprooting of [a] population from the only areas they have ever known. The Natives that have to be moved have been on these large tracts of land for generations and so in equity equivalent land, on which they will have security of tenure, should be found for them by the Government.[10]

In 1949 he wrote:

Land is often alienated without any provision being made for Natives on it who have been in occupation for years, to the detriment of relations between Natives and European settlers. The vast majority of Rhodesian Natives are inherently loyal, peaceful, law-abiding and reasonably amenable to authority, and continue to be so when they have a sense of security, but elsewhere many tend to feel that Government is heedless of their legitimate grievances or that the administration is weak and unable or unwilling to secure their redress. Self-seeking agitators and organisations which offer no constructive criticism whatever, and whose main aims seem to be disruption and non-cooperation, have not been slow to take advantage of the situation, and, playing upon the susceptibilities of the irresponsible elements of the population already embittered by their real or imaginary grievances, have fanned the discontent which in some instances has shown itself in openly expressed contempt for the Government and its officials. Although such extreme attitudes are fortunately localised, their seriousness cannot be minimised, and to restore confidence in the administration amongst the masses, it is absolutely essential to obtain an early settlement of the land problem. . .Several Native Commissioners comment on the fact that . . . if [the Africans] see the grievances of others . . . going much longer undealt with, it would be difficult for many to resist the eventual enlistment of their sympathies on the side of their own people in active opposition to the Government.[11]

It was the most serious warning issued by the Department before the guerrilla war.

But not much attention was paid to it. In November 1950 the

Chief Native Commissioner wrote to the Native Commissioner, Lupani, in Matabeleland, instructing him to take in more cattle than the assessed carrying capacity of his district allowed in order to accommodate 'displaced Natives':

I am afraid the whole question is very difficult . . .As you know, the Minister promised in the House that all Natives on Crown Land be moved within 5 years, and he has told me to draw up a 5 year plan showing exactly how many Natives from each Province I will move each year and to where they will go. This as you may imagine is a very difficult, in fact well-nigh impossible, job, because the amount of land we have so far been given is not sufficient to take anything like the total number of natives to be moved unless they go in with no stock at all. . .As Shangani-Lupani is at the moment the only area in Matabeleland available for the transfer of displaced Natives, and as I have to move 815 families next year . . . you may have to be content with an assessment of 20 acres per beast . . . I am afraid that, faced as I am with dozens of families to move and limited land to which to move them, we must compromise.[12]

It was, in fact, an impossible job almost everywhere if the viability of African farming and stock management was to be preserved. In the Inyanga district successive Native Commissioners had long dreaded the day of the implementation of Land Apportionment. In July 1942 Native Commissioner Jowett of Inyanga had explained to the Natural Resources Board Native Enquiry that the Natural Resources Act and the Land Appointment Act 'work against each other'.

The actual settlement of new kraals in the Reserves is a very big thing. If the natives are to be given adequate land and if the land for each kraal is to be properly allocated it is a very big thing indeed. . . especially in this district where the arable land is very, very difficult to find. . . To carry out the terms of the Land Apportionment Act in this district I must double the population in the Reserves and that is absolutely impossible.[13]

'It is most unfortunate that the Natural Resources Act did not precede the Land Apportionment Act', wrote Jowett to the Provincial Native Commissioner; 'Even if native husbandry ultimately reaches a higher standard than that so far achieved by Europeans, and if individual holdings are strictly limited and supervised, close settlement, in this district, will not be possible'.[14] His successor noted in despair in January 1946 that 'the end of the war brought an immediate demand for the removal of tenants from farms in the European area and there is no available land to which these tenants, numbering hundreds, can be moved.'[15]

The Native Commissioner, Makoni, contemplating the task before him in 1942, told the Natural Resources Board that he had:

directed Chief Chipunza, who lives on a Lonrho farm quite close to
Rusape, to move into the Southern portion of the Chiduku Reserve . . . but
I am not quite certain about the wisdom of this measure of making greater
congestion in the Reserves . . .When one bears in mind that there are
another 8,000 natives to be settled in the Reserves if the Land
Apportionment Act is enforced and another 10,000 cattle to be
accommodated, one can just leave it as a big question mark in one's mind
as to how it is to be done . . .

I would like to mention a doubt I have as to the economic advisability of
reducing the Colony's stock holdings by congesting all native-owned stock
in the Reserves and perhaps reducing the Colony's stock holdings as much
as 50%. The stock holdings are a national asset; they provide hides and
cheap meat for industry and I have doubt as to the advisability of leaving
large areas which could be grazed by these native stock unoccupied and
making the native reduce his stock and move into a Reserve. . .

There are two chiefs with all their followers who live on European farms
in this district and it seemed that these chiefships . . . would have to be
distributed among other chiefs in order to make available to them land in
the native area, and one feels that where a chief and his followers are
situated in the European area they should be settled as an administrative
community, an administrative block, in a single area in the native area
rather than split up.[16]

Nevertheless, in Inyanga and Makoni after the Second World War
thousands of people *were* moved into the Reserves, endangering
subsistence in the first case and threatening the viability of the
peasant option in the second. The African herd *was* greatly reduced
by destocking. The people of one chiefdom were often scattered.
Chad Chipunza gives one example:

When the whites arrived the people of chief Chipunza lived in the west of
what is now Makoni district and extended as far as Macheke and
Headlands, now the heart of the commercial farming area, while chief
Makoni and his people had moved across the Lesapi River to the east. The
Chipunza side of the Lesapi was all beautiful farming land, and in the end
the whites took almost all of it, leaving a good deal of Makoni's land. In the
1940s the Chipunza's were finally scattered about all over the district and
many had to move outside it altogether. Some remained at Epiphany
Anglican mission; others went to Tanda in the north-east of the district;
others went out of the district into Wedza and Mtoko; yet others went as far
as Charter or Maramba. The land given to the chief was small. All this was
bitterly resented but when you have been divided and removed you are not
in a position to exploit the group spirit.[17]

But where the job really *did* seem impossible, and certainly
impossible to be achieved without the 'group spirit' bursting into
revolt, was in the core area of Matabeleland, extending in a great

circle around Bulawayo. It was here that a Rhodesian Mau Mau was going to break out if it was going to happen anywhere. In the first place, this inner core of Matabeleland was much more intensely affected by the evictions than anywhere else. After the 1893 war most of this land had been alienated to whites. When Cecil Rhodes negotiated with the Ndebele commanders in 1896, however, he promised them that they would be able to return to these lands. As Robin Palmer writes:

The Ndebele had just grounds for complaint. They had surrendered voluntarily to Rhodes in the impregnable Matopos on the understanding that they would be allowed to return to their homes. They believed, and were entitled to believe, that they would be guaranteed undisturbed possession. But as a result of the 1893 war their homes had become European property, the Company could not afford to buy the land back and was able only to lease two areas for five years, to make use of one of Rhodes' farms, and to guarantee two years of undisturbed tenure elsewhere. Thereafter the Ndebele were at the mercy of European landlords. The belief that a solemn promise was broken persists to this day.[18]

The implications of this took some time to work themselves out. European farming was slow to establish itself; the existence of the Bulawayo market and of the need for rations for labour on the mines stimulated Ndebele cereal production; *indunas* and others who owned large herds of cattle were able to find grazing land even if they had to pay rents and dipping fees. Hence a lot of land in Matabeleland was owned by land companies which preferred to raise rents from African 'squatters' than to sell farms to whites. Mosley cites an observer who described in 1908 the 'hundreds of thousands of acres marked off in farms, with one white man as caretaker, and the natives there . . . paying rent to land companies.' 'In Matabeleland,' this observer continues:

the average rent paid was £2 per head, so that £80 per year could be obtained from one farm, which amounted to 10% interest on £800. Very few of the settlers who came to this country could afford to pay more than £400 for a farm. Was it not a great temptation for a company, or an individual, who owned a lot of land, if he could draw £80 a year from each farm? Was he not likely to stick to the land rather than sell the farm for £400?[19]

In such a setting Ndebele peasant consciousness established itself.[20] But Ndebele 'squatters' were less secure than the peasant producers of Chiduku Reserve. They were subject to two pressures – land companies could raise rents and fees, and land could be taken over for commercial farming and ranching. In 1911 the Native Commissioner, Bulawayo, reported that:

there is a diminution in the amount of ground cultivated by natives in the vicinity of Bulawayo as compared with that cultivated in 1909 and 1910. The reason is that white men are settling around Bulawayo in increasing numbers and the native is being forced to seek land at a greater distance from the town. Large numbers have left this year, many to settle on the reserves, while others intend to leave after the next harvest.[21]

In 1912 he added that 'not only have the natives had to contend with adverse conditions as regards the seasons but also in many instances, European landowners have charged additional rentals in respect of grazing fees which the natives have had to pay owing to the restrictions on movements of cattle.'[22]. These pressures produced a peasant alienation from the regime in Matabeleland earlier than elsewhere. In 1914 the Native Commissioner, Bulawayo reported that:

The natives have evinced as full a measure of loyalty as we have the right to expect. This loyalty is of a passive nature and would not, perhaps, stand any considerable strain. The chief reason for the discernible lack of enthusiastic loyalty is afforded by the land question. It has always been unfortunate that the dominant native section of Southern Rhodesia – the Matabele – should have suffered more than the other tribes from European occupation in respect of their lands and homes. I mean as to their deep-seated preference for the pasturage and the loams which occur in the shale, gold-bearing geological formations, which are further the best sites for farms from the European point of view. The natives accepted Mr Rhodes' invitation to return to their old homes, mainly on land in occupation for urban, mining and farming purposes, but the passage of time has proved their development to be incompatible in many respects with the increase in the European population and the needs of the European settlers. The increase in their herds and flocks has called the farmer's attention to his own acute need for conserving the limited pasturage for his own cattle which are likewise increasing. The necessity for removing natives to distant reserves has thus become apparent.
This in itself is a sore grievance, as the natives are not nomadic and only remove from their homes under pressure. Their obligation to their landlords and their juxtaposition to industrial centres has tended towards the rapid disintegration of their tribal customs and tribal unity . . .Much of the coercive legislation passed and the manner of its administration have not tended towards the happiness of the natives.[23]

But the wholesale removal of the Ndebele to distant Reserves was long postponed. There *were* many evictions in the 1910s and 1920s, but much land continued to be held by investment companies and Ndebele cultivators and cattle herders continued to live on this land, even if with feelings of insecurity and resentment at increasing charges. Nor was it only factors of comparative economic return which maintained the rental system. There were too many Ndebele 'squatters' and too many cattle; the Reserves were too distant, arid and unsuitable. As early as 1920 the Native Commissioner, Gwanda, warned that he 'would be unable to locate in the reserve Africans who would be moved off European farms in future'.[24] The Native Department regarded with foreboding the prospect of a mass eviction of the Ndebele. Hence in the Land Apportionment Act of 1930 it was stipulated that no rent agreements were to remain in force in the European area after the end of March 1937, *except* for those already in existence in central Matabeleland which would continue to operate after that date. Palmer points out that throughout the 1930s 'a battle royal developed between the Native and Lands Departments. . .The Lands Department wanted the African "squatters" cleared off the land . . . whilst the Native Department, in Matabeleland in particular, often claimed that it had no land onto which it could move them.'[25] Thus in 1933 the Chief Native Commissioner protested that if he were forced to move Africans in Insiza district 'the enormous difficulties of the situation will be unduly precipitated.'[26]

As we have seen, implementation of Land Apportionment was in any case delayed during the Second World War. After it, however, no amount of pleading the special case of the Ndebele could avert the consummation of the long-feared catastrophe for Ndebele cultivators and herders. It was now profitable for the investment companies to clear the land of squatters: the government decided to move Africans off all Crown land. The consequences for central Matabeleland were immediately apparent. In 1946 the Native Commissioner, Matobo reported:

an acute land problem in this district . . .With more and more families being given notice to quit private and Crown farms, the land question becomes more alarming. The largest single block of ground to be depopulated will be the National Park. According to the report on this area 320 families with 2,430 stock equivalent, must quit by next year. Actually many more families will probably leave as none has evinced any interest in future labour agreements.[27]

'During the year,' wrote the Native Commissioner, Insiza, in 1946, 'I had to find room on Crown lands in the European area for natives who were moved from the Gwatemba Division [Native Purchase Area] and from certain alienated land. It will not be possible to find room for all these people within this district.'[28] By May 1950 the

Provincial Native Commissioner, Matabeleland, was obliged to expostulate to the Chief Native Commissioner. 'Successive Native Commissioners in the Insiza district,' he wrote, 'despite reports *ad nauseam* as to the inadequacy of land for natives in that district, have been compelled to allow displaced persons to settle here, there and everywhere. Hence the present chaotic state of affairs. To move the people referred to into the areas you name . . . would merely result in more trouble in the future.'[29] In Gwanda in 1946 it was reported that 'the uncertainty of the future particularly among natives residing on Alienated and Crown Lands in the European Area, many of whom are already under notice to quit, is creating a growing feeling of unrest and despondency. The necessity for destocking is not appreciated and is regarded by many as a distinct threat to their insurance against poverty.'[30]

The second reason why central Matabeleland was the area most likely to break out in protest against the evictions lay in its very specific traditions of politics. The Ndebele were like the Kikuyu at least in that they had developed a strong cultural nationalism, a myth of the past and of their betrayed rights. In my *African Voice in Southern Rhodesia*, which deals with African politics up to 1930, I showed how Ndebele agrarian protest was co-ordinated by the Matabele National Home movement and by the movement to restore the Ndebele kingship.[31] While Shona-speakers remained unaware of any shared Shona identity,[32] the sense of Ndebele identity grew stronger and more precise. It fed partly off white stereotypes of the Ndebele as mighty warriors – stereotypes which gave a definite advantage in the urban job hierarchy. It fed also off the feeling that Bulawayo was, or should be, an Ndebele town. The so-called 'faction-fights' which raged in the Bulawayo African areas in the 1920s were certainly mostly about access to jobs rather than expressions of inherent ethnic hostility, but they had the effect of sharpening ethnic distinctions and further defining Ndebele identity.[33] And in particular it fed off the historical record of white negotiations with the leaders of the Ndebele *state*. Grievances about land, which in Shona-speaking areas could only be articulated in a piecemeal way, could be expressed for central Matabeleland in terms of the rights to an Ndebele homeland recognized by Rhodes in the 1896 negotiations. 'After the rebellion when we were in the "Gusu" we were told to return, as we would be given land,' complained Chief Mdala of Insiza in 1931. 'This promise has not been carried out. The Government has sold the land to the Europeans.'[34]

What I did not appreciate at the time the *African Voice* was published was that this Ndebele protest tradition continued unabated into the 1930s. The Land Apportionment Act did not seem a final word on land rights so far as Ndebele spokesmen were concerned; the decline of the kingship movement did little to undercut 'national' claims to land. And the intensified grievances of the 1930s accentuated rather than dulled Ndebele resentments. I argued in Chapter 2 that Shona-speaking peasants knew what was happening to them in the 1930s but found no way to translate their understanding into political action. It was different in Matabeleland.

Ndebele peasants and herders certainly had every reason to protest. They did the worst out of the Land Apportionment Act, for example, since not only would the final implementation of the Act evict them from central Matabeleland but the areas set aside as Native Purchase Areas consisted almost entirely of arid and useless land. In 1928, for instance, Lobengula's cousin, Sikonkwane, was evicted with his herd of 1500 cattle from Craigola Ranch. The Native Commissioner, Gwelo, sought to settle him on a designated NPA. 'He was very upset and asked me if I considered the ground was fit for human occupation. It is certainly useless both from an agricultural and a pastoral point of view and I had to admit it.'[35] 'Very little of the land allocated for Native Purchase . . . is of any use for the purpose,' wrote the Superintendent of Natives, Bulawayo. 'The vast bulk of it is either waterless or in the Teak Forest Belt and its only value . . . is the timber it produces . . .The areas in Matabeleland, north of the Railway line, which have been recommended for Native Purchase, are almost useless; every native to whom they have been offered has declined to live on them.'[36] Throughout the 1930s it proved very difficult to find individual purchasers for Native Purchase farms in Matabeleland; Ndebele spokesmen constantly urged that if the land were to be used at all it should be used for additional collective grazing.

Maize Control, when implemented in Matabeleland in 1934, had a more far-reaching effect on the Ndebele agrarian economy than might have been expected from the customary emphasis on Ndebele pastoralism. 'It is quite a mistake to assume that all natives have lots of cattle,' wrote the Superintendent of Natives, Bulawayo, in 1934, 'some have none . . .There are quite a number of poor natives who rely on selling a few bags of mealies and others whose wives and daughters have small quantities.'[37] Indeed there were also quite a number of more entrepreneurial peasants in Matabeleland who prior to the 1930s had developed maize production. But if Maize Control affected Ndebele producers as well as Shona, the measures taken by the government to benefit European cattle-ranchers struck at the Ndebele particularly hard. As Murray Steele writes:

The 1930s constituted a decade of almost continuous crisis for African cattle-owners. Prices collapsed in the wake of the inter-war trade depression, a sequence of natural disasters beset African herdsmen and recovery was further hindered by a number of statutory measures designed to assist European producers. . . . The post-depression recovery of the African stock industry received a severe setback as a result of Government measures such as the Beef Bounty and Cattle Levy Act, the purpose of which was to subsidize the export of predominantly European-produced high-quality chilled and frozen beef; the export bounty was to be financed from a 10s per head slaughter levy, payable by butchers who slaughtered more than five cattle for local consumption . . .In practice, the levy was passed back to the African producer, depressing his level of return even further.[38]

The 'continuous crisis' of the 1930s provoked protest and that protest was voiced not only by Ndebele chiefs but also by urban associations. The Matabele Home Society, though based in Bulawayo, certainly did not restrict itself to the concerns of the would-be permanent urban dwellers but continued to take up the whole issue of Ndebele land rights. Where the Industrial and Commercial Workers Union (ICU) failed in Mashonaland to make any effective connection with rural grievance, in Matabeleland it served to co-ordinate rural opposition in the early 1930s. The Native Boards, with whose establishment the government hoped to defuse opposition, became instead the articulators of protest.

The first meeting of the Umzingwane Native Board in May 1931, for example, was attended by Masoja Ndhlovu of the ICU and by Mandaba of the Matabele Home Society. Masoja told its members that the Board would be 'useless, as the resolutions would never reach the Government.'[39] Mandaba demanded 'a proper constitution.'[40] But meanwhile Chief Ntola made use of the Board even as it was in order to present the basic Ndebele demand:

Mr Rhodes had promised them a Reserve in this District, and the promise had not been fulfilled: that the good land in the Reserves . . . in other districts were fully occupied, and that the only land now available for them was bad or waterless and in remote and unhealthy parts: that if windmills were provided they would go wrong and it was hard to pump water for their stock: that they wanted to remain in the district where they had lived all their lives, but that they were always being cleared off farms and had no place to which they could go.[41]

Reporting this to the Superintendent of Natives, Bulawayo, the Native Commissioner remarked that the 'natives appear to have convinced themselves that Mr Rhodes did make them a promise about a Reserve in this District . . .It is a fact that they are continually cleared off farms, and that it is very difficult for them to find new homes. They absolutely refuse to move to Reserves in Charter District.'[42]

Two years later the third meeting of the Umzingwane Board was 'lively, and in some instances speeches almost reached the invective':

Native Ngubo asked for a reply from the Government to their last resolution regarding the provision of extra land . . .He was informed that Government did not contemplate purchasing additional land, and that those who did not desire to avail themselves of the land now provided in the Settlement Area, could proceed to Reserves. Ndhlabulala stated that the Reserves were thickly populated and that further 'As we understand that Mzingwane [meaning the Settlement Area] is not a Reserve, we would ask for one. It must be realised that we are agriculturalists, and depend to a large extent upon our European market, and to go to Reserves would mean the loss of our livelihood.' Mtshotso remarked . . . that there would always be discontent until better provision was made. Mahalihadi remarked 'After the Matabele War, the Government promised to give us land, but we are still waiting.' Magwa then advanced and remarked that the Board was useless and to attend it served no useful purpose . . .Chief Ntola proposed 'That the Government be asked to declare his area a Reserve and to refrain from charging rent . . .' Loud acclamation followed this utterance . . . Chief Mvutu brought forward a matter affecting his people. He said 'I was told by Mr Taylor and Mr Jackson that the land in the vicinity of Heany Junction was for my people, that Mr Asserman was only herding his cattle there. Now I find that Mr Asserman is said to be the owner of the land.'[43]

The administration took a hard line in response to such articulate protest. 'I do not agree with the Superintendent of Natives, Bulawayo, that it is the normal practice of the Amandabele to couch their complaints or criticism in insolent language.' wrote the Chief Native Commissioner after the Umzingwane Board meeting. 'My own experience is that latitude . . . very soon develops into licence. It is better to check insolence at once.' Chief Ntola was to be told that since his people used their land 'in a wasteful manner' and 'are reluctant to accept advice on overstocking,' it was 'better that it be divided into small farms, for sale to those Natives who wish to live there.' And in general the Ndebele were to be told that they must make use of the land allocated for Native Purchase before they could be considered for any further communal land. 'The policy of the Government,' wrote the Chief Native Commissioner in June 1933:

is to re-organise and develop the Native Reserves to the fullest extent before considering the acquisition of more land. It is noticeable in

Matabeleland that the Natives are not availing themselves of the land set aside for them under the Land Apportionment Act, while in Mashonaland land is being taken up readily. Protracted delay in acquiring land may result in those who want it finding that it has all been taken up. The Matabele should be capable of doing what the Mashonas are doing in this matter, and until they have taken up all the land which has been provided for them, their cry of insufficiency of land will not be very convincing.[44]

The Ndebele themselves consistently refused to accept that Native Purchase land was relevant to their problems. In September 1932 the Native Commissioner, Matobo, warned the Shashani Board that:

saturation point in Reserves in this district was rapidly being approached and that when the full provisions of the Land Apportionment Act had materialised the position would be still more serious. The Chairman pointed out that if some of the bigger cattle owners could get together and sell sufficient cattle to buy land in purchase areas it would be a good thing to do as the land would be theirs 'in perpetuity' whereas vast herds of impoverished cattle with pasturage becoming yearly more inadequate in ratio to the increase of the cattle, would eventually leave them with little more than a recollection.[45]

But at its sixth meeting in March 1934 the Board proposed that the purchase area should be used exclusively for extra grazing. 'Ntelela,' it noted, 'pointed out that this area has always been used for grazing when water failed at various points in the Reserve. If a large population were placed in this area there would be nowhere to graze their stock during bad seasons.'[46]

Nor did the Native Boards only protest in the interest of cattle holders. When the Maize Control regulations were extended to Matabeleland in 1934, the Boards were quick to expostulate. On 14 June 1934, the Shashani Native Board minuted that the 'extension of the Maize Control Act to Matabeleland was explained. In practice this means that natives in this area cannot sell surplus maize. The board wanted to know why Native Demonstrators had been sent into Native Reserves to teach them modern methods of growing maize.'[47]

In Insiza district the Minister of Agriculture visited in June 1934 in order to explain the operation of the Act to local white farmers but did not make the time to explain it to Chief Ndala and his elders. The Native Commissioner was himself obliged to do so:

There was general and great dissatisfaction owing to the price of 4 shillings a bag for mealies. The prospect of participation in the pool early next year did not appeal to them at all. There were vociferous requests that, as they were formerly able to get from 7 shillings to 8 shillings a bag, and now could only get 4 shillings, that the Hut Tax should be reduced from £1 to 10 shillings. Natives in the Fort Rixon area of the Insiza District have been accustomed for years to obtain revenue for taxes by sale of mealies.[48]

And as the Superintendent of Natives, Bulawayo, reminded the Chief Native Commissioner in July 1934, Maize Control was bound to intensify the 'dissatisfaction which undoubtedly exists among natives' because it particularly affected the poorest:

There are a number of poor natives who rely on selling a few bags of mealies to raise their taxes . . .As many of these men are elderly and cannot readily obtain employment, there is bound to be a considerable falling off in Revenue. It is quite a mistake to assume that all natives have lots of cattle; some have none. They merely have cattle which have been 'sizaed' to them, and which they cannot dispose of.[49]

In this way the Native Boards expressed the discontents both of the rich cattle owners and of their poor clients to whom they lent out cattle. Nor did they forget the central issue of the Ndebele homeland. Thus a meeting of the Umzingwane Native Board on 29 January 1937 was characteristic for the later 1930s. It began with a proposal that: 'native maize should be exempt from the Maize Control, as the present arrangements cause undue suffering to native maize growers . . .Before the Maize Control came into force natives obtained 10 shillings and sixpence a bag for their maize and now they only recieve 6 shillings and sixpence to seven shillings a bag. Seconded by Ngubu. Carried unanimously.'
And it went on to demand:

Additional land for natives. This topic dominated the whole meeting. All natives spoke. . . 'We are always asking the Government but nothing is done.' The Matabeles in the Mzingwane district were the first to agree to pay tax. The first Native Commissioner in Matabeleland was appointed at Mzingwane. Ntola, the principal native chief lived here and now his successor lives here and Mzingwane should be made the Native Capital of Matabeleland with a permanent Native Commissioner and not an official who is always being transferred. Matabeles outside Matabeleland are unhappy and full of disappointment. We want the Government to provide land here for us as this is our home and the cradle of all Matabeles . . . land should be given to us here to perpetuate the memory of all great Matabele.[50]

It was this capacity to appeal to Ndebele *national* rights to land which prevented the development of class tensions within Ndebele agrarian politics in the 1930s. The third reason why Matabeleland might have been the setting for a Rhodesian Mau Mau was that distinctions of wealth and power within the rural areas were sharper and more entrenched there than in Mashonaland or Manicaland.

Some of these inequalities took the form among the Ndebele too of large-scale maize production. During the opposition to eviction of families from Rhodesdale estate in the Ndebele-speaking area of the Midlands, in 1950, for example, the Provincial Native Commissioner alleged that 'the fuss has been caused by one John Jack and several of his sons who own over 1,000 head of cattle, and has fenced 500 acres of arable land for himself.'[51] Five hundred acres would have surpassed the ambition of most of the maize-producing entrepreneurs of Mashonaland, and by 1950 none of the Reserves entrepreneurs there could have been farming on anything like that scale. Often though the Ndebele protested against having to live on privately owned land rather than being given adequate Reserves, at least this had meant that centralization had affected few producers. But the real contrast between John Jack's family and the plough entrepreneurs of Mashonaland was their thousand head of cattle. And cattle ownership was the basis of differentiation in Matabeleland.

Many men in Matabeleland owned very large herds of cattle in the 1930s. We have seen already the case of Sikonkwane with his 1500 head. Steele cites the cattle census carried out in the Shangani Reserve in 1933 to show the character of differentiation there. One man grazed nearly 2000 head of cattle in the Reserve. In general 'although the average holding was about 40 head, 175 owners had 14,569 cattle (a mean of 83 head) and the remaining 1,125 owned in total only 28,431 head (a mean of 25).'[52] There was thus a clear hierarchy of cattle ownership. Moreover, inequalities of cattle ownership found expression in Matabeleland within 'traditional' forms of patronage and clientage. As Steele writes, 'large stock-holders acquired prestige by leasing out cattle to less fortunate men, making them into virtual clients. Cattle thus became an important agency in social stratification . . . The "herding out" system was also a convenient way of securing adequate grazing for large herds and reducing the level of risk from localized natural disasters facing the big owner.'[53] And this led to a further contrast with inequalities of wealth in Matabeleland and Mashonaland. In Mashonaland the chiefs and headmen took very little part in cereal production for the market, relating to the new inequalities of wealth mainly by the fees they charged for the allocation of land in the Reserves to the plough entrepreneurs.[54] In Matabeleland important chiefs were amongst the largest owners of cattle. Nor was this a mere carry over from the 'traditional' economy. Steele emphasizes 'the dynamic response of African pastoralists to the incentives and disincentives of the new economic order, initiated before the start of the colonial era and gaining considerable momentum by the Second World War.'[55]

Ndebele chiefs had a keen interest in the operation of the colonial economy. They also felt that their economic position was threatened by insecurity of tenure on their rented grazing lands. For these reasons the administration had less success in Matabeleland than in Mashonaland in its policy of backing 'traditional' authorities against labour migrants in order to maintain rural order during the 1930s. In Filabusi, for instance, there was great difficulty in setting up a Native Board at all. An initial meeting of chiefs and headmen was held in May 1931 'before ICU propaganda had obtained the same hold which it now possesses', as the Native Commissioner complained in June 1933. Thereafter, later in 1931 and throughout 1932 the cultivators and herders of Filabusi looked to the ICU and especially to Masoja Ndhlovu to voice their grievances for them. 'Two committees and one sub-committee of the ICU [were] formed and strongly supported . . .Regular meetings of these committees were held at the kraals of Chief Maduna, Headman Gwadalala and Masisinga. There was also a committee of the Matabeleland Home Society which held its monthly meeting at Lotje's kraal.'[56] The Assistant Native Commissioner decided that he would try to set up a Native Board by co-opting local ICU members: 'to keep in touch with the progress of the ICU' by bringing their Filabusi leaders, Nduna, Mapolisa, Bizeni and Mfitshane on to a new Board, together with Lotje to represent the Matabele Home Society; six 'traditionalists' made up the number, so that the Board represented 'all lines of thought'. Bizeni, the secretary of the Nyatini committee of the ICU and a graduate of Fort Hare, agreed to act as secretary of the Native Board. But this interesting experiment did not work.

On the day of the new Native Board meeting Nduna told the Assistant Native Commissioner that he would only serve on such a Board if Masoja Ndhlovu were to be chairman. 'These Boards,' Nduna and Mapolisa told the other members, 'are like the *Ibunga* of the native territories, which have broken down the native people in the Transkei. These people now have no land and no cattle and are all living on plots, where a man must work for the white man, also his wife and children must work. All this was caused by the *Ibunga* and the same will happen here if Boards are accredited.'[57] At another attempt to set up a Board a few days later the Acting Superintendent of Natives, Bulawayo, found nobody ready to discuss it, but all 'extraordinarily keen on discussing the restrictions placed on Masoja, Secretary to the ICU. I explained to them that

Masoja had brought this about by his exhibition of bad manners in not obtaining permission to hold meetings.'[58] Faced with this opposition, the Assistant Native Commissioner changed his tactics completely. He recommended that 'In view of the democratic constitution of the ICU I submit that at present an effective counter would be the fostering of the Matabele Caste system in this area and that a more pronounced traditional control would secure better administration than "Vox Populi" methods.'[59]

But the point really was that the representatives of the 'Matabele Caste system' in Filabusi were themselves working closely with the ICU in the early 1930s. One of the ICU committees was based at Chief Maduna's kraal and enjoyed the chief's patronage. The Native Commissioner, Insiza, was firmly of the view that it was Maduna himself who was determined not to allow a Native Board to be set up and who preferred to work rather with the urban politicians.[60] Once Masoja and other ICU leaders had been effectively excluded from the rural areas and the organization itself fell into decline, the Native Boards were left to articulate Ndebele grievances by themselves. But the potentiality of combination with urban movements remained very real. And in the 1940s the development of Bulawayo was considerably more dynamic than that of Nairobi, as an infant secondary industry grew up in the town, accompanied by low wages, high prices, appalling living conditions, and all the other factors which precipitated the railway workers' strike of 1945 and the General Strike of 1948. Inevitably this labour unrest spilled out into the countryside so that peasants were able to draw on urban models of protest. Inevitably too, given the legacy of the ICU, the leaders of the Bulawayo urban associations went out into the rural areas around Bulawayo in the late 1940s to co-ordinate rural opposition.

So the context of protest and potential revolt in central Matabeleland has now been established – a 'squatting' peasantry, fearful that eviction will reduce it to immiseration; interaction between rural and urban unrest; a sense of betrayal both of historical obligations to the Ndebele nation and of the implicit promises made to African producers in the Demonstration programme; a sense of outrage at the sudden ending of the quasi-feudal relations between African tenants and the land companies; a lively cultural nationalism; sharp distinctions of wealth within Ndebele rural societies. It all sounds a little like the background to Mau Mau. How did it work out in the event?

At the opening of the crisis in Matabeleland the Native Department comforted itself with the illusion that, whatever their grievances, the Ndebele would react to the situation in a pre-political way. In August 1947 the Chief Native Commissioner described reponse to 'the worst drought . . . since the occupation of the Colony' in Matabeleland:

Another crime which is starting up again is witchcraft. This is due to the drought. Numbers who are seeking for the cause of the drought attribute it to the sins or omissions of others. This results in individuals being accused of having failed in their customary observances, thus calling down on the tribe the wrath of the ancestral spirits.[61]

In 1948 the District Commissioner, Matobo, recorded another reassuringly 'traditionalist' response. Zionist prophets had been attracting many converts in Matobo – just as the Depression years of the 1930s were the era of prophetism in Mashonaland, so the agrarian crisis of the 1940s saw its expansion in Matabeleland. The Native Department was pleased to note tension between the sect and Ndebele chiefs:

Chief Ntelela Malaba in his effort to discourage this sect ordered a raid on Zhouyaba Hill during the course of one of their ceremonies and the hill was surrounded at night. For fear of some of the children hurting themselves the advance was delayed until dawn. After listening to the singing and shouting the whole night the posse ascended. . . They 'arrested' a Zionist preacher.[62]

This was the world in which the Native Department felt at home. 'The population,' wrote the Native Commissioner, Matobo, in 1946, 'has shown little political consciousness . . . The older Natives like being left alone to their own devices. They are mainly occupied in making a living from the soil and in stock-raising, an increasingly difficult vocation. . . The Government is still looked upon as being there by virtue of the fact that the European law prevails through conquest.'[63]

But as it became more and more difficult to make 'a living from the soil', and the threatened evictions seemed likely to undercut the Ndebele rural economy, the elements which I have outlined above began to make their appearance, constituting a complex ideology of rural resistance. Once again there was the specific appeal to historical rights. In Matobo in 1948 there was an 'extremely acute necessity . . . for more land'; in Matopo Reserve there was 'an actual antagonism towards the Agricultural Demonstrators . . . The limitation of the size of the lands and the prohibition of the cultivation of sponges has a great deal to do with this'; there was hostility towards recruitment of labour for official projects and 'so soon as Messengers are sent to obtain labour, large numbers of youths flee the Reserves to obtain work in other places. . .' The Native Commissioner, who had found no 'political consciousness' in 1946 was now compelled to admit that:

Politically the natives of this district cannot be ignored. The movement of a portion of the population from the National Park . . . has created an uneasy stir in the native residents of this area. There have been frequent meetings, both general and of the 'inner circle'. With the approval of a large number, native Nqabe has become their accredited leader in spite of the fact that they look to Nzula as their Chief . . .The offer of the Government to allow 1896 residents and their direct descendants and all people turned off Rhodes Matopos Estate and their descendants to remain has made no difference to their attitude and the leaders are obviously hoping that *all* will remain and that there will be a State within a State. The Matabele Home Society has associated itself with this matter and there was a meeting sponsored by this Association on the 12th December. There is apparent a growing opposition to destocking partly because some natives who have *siza*-ed cattle are losing these whilst in the hands of the caretakers, and partly for the reason that they feel they are packed too closely in their areas and should have more land. Nqabe said they were overstocked and overpopulated because the Europeans have large farms and turn the natives off the land they have occupied for years. . . There is a spirit of nationalism amongst these people and the situation calls for careful handling if the link between nationalism and communism is not to be formed.[64]

In Filabusi in 1948 the Native Commissioner discerned 'a certain *social* unrest . . . due to the alienation of Crown land where Natives have been settled for generations, and in respect of which occupation they allege in some cases that they were given a Government guarantee of undisturbed tenure.'[65]

The 'nationalism' of Ndebele protestors found a ready expression in support of the Matabele Home Society. Just as in the early 1930s the people of Filabusi were resistant to the formation of a Native Board, so in June 1949 the people of Nkai/Shangani refused to nominate any candidates for a Council:

They could see no need of a Council . . . Native Commissioners wished to hide behind Councils and pretend that they were carrying out the wishes of the people . . .The highlight of the meeting was 'We have never seen the constitution of the Native Council but the Matabeleland Home Society has a constitution which is being taken to the High Court in Bulawayo and the Government will be forced to recognise the Matabeleland Home Society as the 'Voice of the People'. . . [At meetings the MHS discusses] more land for Africans, destocking, labour for repair of roads, Land Apportionment Act and the exclusion of European traders.[66]

But this 'nationalist' dimension was not the only component of peasant protest ideology in central Matabeleland. 'The link between nationalism and communism' so feared by the Native Commissioner, Matobo, was threatened by the influence in the Ndebele rural areas of urban models of organization. Thus in September 1949 it was reported from Nyamandhlovu district that 'during the quarter certain allegations were made by the Gwaai Workers' Benefit Society against the Assistant Native Commissioner's administration of the Reserve. . . As a result certain natives were moved to other areas by order of the Governor.'[67]

In Gwanda in 1948 it was reported that:

Much Communist (Bolshevist) propaganda comes into this country from the South. Natives of this district habitually serve at least one term of employment in the Union, and return with much ill feeling against the white man's Government. It is true too that large scale population removals brought about directly because of the Land Apportionment Act serve well the cause of these 'malcontents' . . .In the area openly showing disaffection, Wenlock Block, the people are largely swayed by Sofasihamba ('We die if we go') Society.[68]

The administration had some hopes of defusing this populist indignation. In Mashonaland and Manicaland it had acted against the Reserves entrepreneurs to ensure a sort of equalization of immiseration. Now in Matabeleland there was the prospect of using destocking in something of the same way. If destocking could be directed mostly against the larger cattle owners, it was thought, the measure might even become popular. Thus when the members of the Natural Resources Board Native Enquiry pressed the Chief Native Commissioner on the need for compulsory destocking in 1942, one of them suggested a strategy for Matabeleland. 'Natives,' he informed the Enquiry, 'come and discuss it with me and they are all against a percentage reduction but they are rather keen that the top man should be knocked. I have figures here for the Plumtree district: those owning from 1–20 head of cattle [are] 73½% so that if any destocking came about I suggest you would have 73% on your side.'[69]

In the destocking measures of the later 1940s precisely this strategy was put into effect. In June 1950, for example, the Assistant Native Commissioner, Que Que, summoned to his office the 320 men from Rhodesdale 'who have 20 head of cattle or more.' 'Some of you,' remarked the Assistant N.C., 'have 100 head.' He then harangued these more substantial cattle owners. 'We cannot,' he told them, 'allow you to continue destroying the grazing, and the land itself and the water supplies . . .By the end of next year you must all have reduced your stock to 10 head . . . per man. . .Sooner or later you must leave Rhodesdale . . . I do not think you will be permitted to take large herds.'[70]

This tactic had little chance of success. Unlike the Reserves entrepreneurs in Mashonaland and Manicaland, the larger cattle owners in Matabeleland could command clients and supporters. Moreover, while the implementation of centralization was resented by almost everyone in the Shona Reserves, and not only by the hard-hit entrepreneurs, nevertheless centralization did not strike at the poorer peasantry anything like as savagely as the eviction from central Matabeleland. Hence the administration could not separate poorer from wealthier peasants, nor persuade the former that their sufferings were the fault of the latter. It was all too clear that both suffered because of the government's insistence on implementation of its intolerable land policies. In 1942 the Assistant Native Commissioner, Essexvale, had explained that the Land Apportionment Act was *impossible* to implement; pointing out that 'We have nowhere to place them. We can't take them off . . .We are begging the owners not to shift them . . .It simply comes to this: that the Government have passed a law which they are not able to carry out.'[71] Now, however, the impossible was to be enforced – and the wealthier peasants and cattle owners were well-equipped to take the lead in protests against it.

As we have already seen, opposition in Matobo in 1948 was led by 'natives who have *siza*-ed cattle [and] are losing these whilst in the hands of the caretakers.' Rhodesdale protest was attributed to John Jack and his sons, with their huge herd and 500 acres. But the 320 owners of more than twenty cattle from Rhodesdale turned out to be fully capable of asking some very awkward questions on their own behalf:

On de-stocking generally. Do the European-owned cattle not cause as much damage? Why force only the natives to de-stock? Have our cattle got two mouths? Is Rhodesdale a new thing that we cannot claim it as home? Were not most of us here present actually born here? Is Rhodesdale not overstocked because farms have been sold to Europeans and we have been forced, all together, into one corner of it? . . .During the war we were told 'After the war you will all live in freedom'. We were told 'Help us to buy an aeroplane and after the war you will all be free.' We helped. Now see what happens to us. Is this freedom?[72]

Cattle owners on one of the new ranches carved out of Rhodesdale refused to go to the remote region of Gokwe; they demanded land 'on some other part of Rhodesdale' and if they were not given such land, they said, 'they would be troublesome next year.'[73]

The Assistant Native Commissioner summed up the state of popular consciousness in Que Que in June 1950. 'I get the impression,' he reported, 'that there is as yet no bitterness among the natives or very little. But they are disturbed and unhappy. As they said, "Our hearts are very sore". I do not think there is as yet any undue amount of serious discontent. But they are certainly ripening nicely for any agitator who may come along.'[74] And in fact the whole complex mix of Ndebele rural protest – of ethnic nationalism and 'traditional' leadership, of migrant-worker organization, of large cattle-owner indignation, of small peasant fears of total immiseration – *was* given co-ordination by 'agitator' and one 'agitator' in particular. From the last months of 1948 the lead was taken by Benjamin Burombo of the British African National Voice Association, vigorously seconded by a revived Masoja Ndhlovu. Burombo has yet to receive a full treatment by historians of Zimbabwe. At the moment his position in the literature is equivocal. On the one hand he appears in African nationalist reminiscences as a titanic popular leader. Lawrence Vambe, for example writes that:

Sooner or later African fury went into the area of bad wages and the rising cost of living. By the beginning of 1948 this feeling had become explosive. This time the Africans of Bulawayo took the lead. Matabeleland is a dry country and it has never been easy for the Africans there to make a decent living on the land. Therefore, paid employment has always meant more to the people living in Matabeleland . . .Naturally this harsh position of Africans in Matabeleland has bred in them a practical approach to labour problems. Fortunately for these people there were among them two fiercely nationalist personalities from Mashonaland who were determined to achieve practical unity through trade unionism. One was Jasper Zengeza Savanhu . . .The other was dynamic, ebullient twenty-stone Burombo, who came from the Fort Victoria district. Benjamin Burumbo established in 1947 the British African Workers' Voice Association. Clearly the Bulawayo workers were better organised in this respect than those in Salisbury . . .The Bulawayo Africans pinpointed their grievances to wages and confronted their employers with specific demands . . .The workers of Bulawayo grew tired of speeches. They opted for a strike.[75]

Burombo is similarly praised by Enoch Dumbutshena, who writes that:

Of all the African political leaders of the time the most effective was the late Mr Benjamin B. Burombo. For many years Burombo had worked in South Africa, where he had come under the influence of Kadali . . .It was the success of the 1948 strike which inspired one of its leaders, Benjamin B. Burombo, to intensify his fight against the Land Apportionment Act.

Burombo's British African Peoples Voice Association campaigned against the removal of Africans from their homelands and destocking.[76]

On the other hand, recent historians of the 1948 strike have presented a much less admiring picture of Burombo, whom they see as having lost control of the Bulawayo workers to more radical men and as having brought the strike to an end by falsely announcing that the employers had conceded a major wage increase.[77] However this may be, there is no doubt that the 1948 strike made urban politics more sharply relevant to rural Matabeleland than they had been since the days of ICU influence in the early 1930s. Nor is there any doubt that once the strike was over Burombo began to move out into the Matabeleland countryside.

In Matobo in 1948 the 'accredited leader' of resistance, Nqabe, 'enlisted the help of Burombo, whose prestige had advanced since his part in the strike and subsequent escape from conviction.'[78] Burombo had been a solicitor's clerk and one of his chief uses to Ndebele protestors was his ability to bring cases on their behalf. In 1948 the Provincial Native Commissioner reported that:

This year has been one of uncertainty following the strike in April. Self appointed leaders have been very vocal. The proposed eviction of Natives from the National Park in Matobo District has been a universal subject of discussion, and Burombo from Selukwe, who had so much to do with the April disturbances, has been interesting himself in the matter. One Masotsha, until recently quite inarticulate, has come into the open, and is beginning to work with Burombo . . .The Natives, or rather their leaders, are not slow to obtain legal advice in all doubtful matters.[79]

In June 1949 two quarterly reports documented Burombo's shift of interest from urban to rural issues. The Native Commissioner, Bulawayo reported that:

Complaints and queries in regard to the labour award have practically ceased and it would appear that natives have settled down under the award. Some reason for this may be found in the fact that Associations such as the Voice are now turning their activities to rural matters such as the Land question and destocking and do not appear to be interesting themselves in local labour.[80]

At the same time the Matobo report recorded that 'an unofficial meeting of Chiefs and Headmen was held in Bulawayo. The gathering was presided over by Burombo who appears to be gaining some importance in political matters affecting natives.'[81] Burombo, together with 'natives in Matabeleland in general' regarded 'the Park affair as something in the nature of a test'[82] and he co-ordinated evidence to be given to the Commission inquiring into the matter; on 26 June 1949 there was 'a meeting of natives in the National Park', which collected money 'to continue their resistance to removal from the Park if they are not satisfied with the findings and recommendations of the Commission.'[83]

But Burombo did not limit his activities to Matobo. In June 1949 the Native Commissioner, Nkai/Shangani reported that 'during the past six months meetings have been held in the Reserve addressed by men from Bulawayo. Burombo etc have been holding meetings in the Matobo and Gwanda districts' where Burombo was taking up the cases of those threatened with eviction.[84] Indeed Burombo did not limit his activities to Matabeleland. In Gutu District to the south east:

Some Chiefs asked permission to send representatives to Burombo's meeting in Bulawayo. Those who went without leave were rebuked. Council members were also invited and several went in their private capacity. I had told those who sought my advice before going that Burombo was not likely to produce a solution to any of the problems he had on the agenda and the meeting would amount to nothing more than 'hot air' with the idea of making Burombo appear a big man at their expense.[85]

In May 1950 Burombo arrived in the office of the Native Commissioner, Gwelo:

He said that 24 Association Members residing on Rhodesdale had visited him in Bulawayo to tell him of the present reduction of stock taking place on Rhodesdale by the Assistant Native Commissioner, Que Que. They had invited him to Rhodesdale to explain this 'new law', (as he put it), to them. He asked me whether the new destocking regulations were now being introduced. He went on to say that when a deputation from the British African National Voice Association interviewed the Minister for Native Affairs on 2/8/49 the Minister had said that the Native Department were working on the Destocking Regulations in order to make them as equitable as possible. I told Burombo that the Assistant Native Commissioner, Que Que was merely carrying out the regulations laid down in Government Notice 45/1946, Section 5 (h). He said he had been unaware of these regulations, thanked me for enlightening him and said he would make the position clear to the Rhodesdale Natives. He assured me of his wish to be co-operative and remove any suspicions that the Rhodesdale Natives might have.[86]

The result of Burombo's visit was a meeting at Somerset of more than 300 delegates from 'many parts of Que Que district', all allegedly members of the British African National Voice Association. They passed a resolution:

The British African National Voice Association Appeals to the Respectful-
ly Provincial Native Commissioner and Native Commissioner Gwelo
through the Assistant Native Commissioner Que Que district That for the
time being and until the grievances have been considered of amendment of
the land apportionment act Compulsory destocking or forced Sales of
Cattle and the Native Occupying Crown act . . . should be suspended.[87]

By July a tense situation had developed on Rhodesdale. The
Provincial Native Commissioner explained to the Chief Native
Commissioner the elements of the problem:

Rhodesdale was owned by the Lonhro company as a Ranch with section
managers in charge. Natives resided on this property under the Private
Locations Ordinance. After the War this land was bought by the
Government – surveys into farms and ranches took place as Natives living
on them moved or were moved off into the unsurveyed portions. The
surveys moved forward and the Natives with their stock became more
crowded on the remaining Crown lands. . .Congestion had reached the
stage that something had to be done to control a situation that was getting
out of hand . . .According to the Assistant Native Commissioner he made
representations which went unheeded particularly with regard to further
alienations. The policy of surveying and alienating land had reached the
stage where [further alienation] could not be done without taking a big slice
of the congested area. The result was that the land allocated to Brig.
Dunlop took in such a heavy population that a problem was created. . . He
was unfortunate enough to acquire a piece of land three quarters of which
was already occupied by Natives and their stock to the full extent of its
carrying capacity. Had a few families only been involved, I have no doubt
the 'shooing' formula could have been carried out. Under the circumstances, however, the Assistant Native Commissioner endeavoured to
come to some understanding.

This had been difficult to reach since Dunlop insisted that no land
should be cultivated by Africans: he was backed by other white
farmers 'of the locality' who felt 'strong resentment to the continued
residence of Natives on Rhodesdale.' The Civil Commissioner, Que
Que expressed his fear that 'Europeans would set themselves out to
make things uncomfortable for the Natives and most probably
offend the law'; the Provincial Commissioner warned him in turn
that 'there was just as much likelihood of reprisals if unconsidered
action was taken.' Meanwhile 'it is rumoured' that Africans on
Rhodesdale had engaged 'legal assistance in readiness for any
action by the Department.'[88]

Through July and August 1950 pressures built up both from
whites and blacks upon an uncomfortable Native Department. The
Minister of Mines, lobbied by his constituents, urged the Minister of
Native Affairs to act drastically to evict Africans from Dunlop's

farm and the rest of Rhodesdale. 'Burambo [sic],' he wrote, 'has been trying to stir up trouble. The longer they are left, therefore, the more likely it is that you will have trouble with the natives and the higher Burambo's stock will rise.'[89] On Rhodesdale itself yet other newly arrived white farmers ordered Africans off their land – 'it almost looks as if there is an anti-Rhodesdale Natives campaign going on,' bemoaned the Provincial Commissioner. The Assistant Native Commissioner warned Rhodesdale Africans that they would have to move to the remote bush area of Gokwe, though he knew that the carrying capacity of Gokwe could only cope with about half of the families he had to move. For their part Africans on Dunlop's farm declared that 'they would only move to Gokwe if their Headman and all his people moved with them this year, otherwise they would remain on Brigadier Dunlop's Ranch . . . but they would be troublesome next year.'[90]

Developments at Rhodesdale were reproduced all over the Ndebele rural areas. By the end of 1950 some sort of clash between blacks and whites, with the Native Department caught in the middle, seemed highly likely. There seems no doubt that Burombo's association was gaining many new members in readiness. In March 1951 Masoja Ndlovu, now living as a rent-paying tenant on Aberfoyle Ranch in Selukwe, called a meeting of the Voice Association there. He asked those who attended 'if they were content with destocking and limitation of arable policies in the Reserves'; they replied that they were not; forty men joined the Association, and Masoja and one Mhaso were elected as delegates to the forthcoming Bulawayo Congress.[91] 'Judging from the meetings I have had recently with Chiefs and others,' reported the Provincial Commissioner, 'the stock question is going to cause a lot of trouble.'[92]

The Voice Association conference in Bulawayo in March 1951 represented the climax of Burombo's attempts to pull protest together. Burombo claimed forty-four branches across the country – one of them, incidentally, in Makoni, though I can find nothing further about it. Delegates debated both an urban and a much longer rural agenda – 'Land Apportionment Act, Limitation of Acreage of African Lands, Destocking of African Cattle, Removal of Africans from their Reserves, Forced Labour, Native Marriage Act, Subversive Activities Act, Husbandry Bill, Plot Holding and Title Deeds for African farmers, Reduction of the number of Chiefs in the Reserves.' Its main purpose was announced as endorsement of a petition to the Governor, 'asking that the Minister for Native Affairs will instruct all Government officials and local authorities throughout the Colony of S. Rhodesia to *cease unnecessary interference with the African people* . . . in matters affecting the daily lives of the people.'[93] The conference was addressed by Masoja Ndhlovu and by Burombo himself, who stressed that 'the land we are given is too little for us. Redivide the land and give Africans a better share of it. The Government is like a leopard, which has many spots – white, black, yellow: if it licks the white spots and leaves the black ones, is that leopard clean? No!'[94]

But Burombo was not content with petitioning. In 1951 the whole issue was coming to a head. Government planned to resettle 4482 families. On the other side more and more African 'squatters' were digging their heels in and threatening to be 'troublesome next year.' In the Matopos National Park over a hundred and fifty family heads refused to move into Prospect Special Native Area:

they say they will not move and only recently a deputation of approximately 100 came to the Native Commissioner and told him that they refused to go . . . They also refused to leave his office, but when later he told them of the powers which will be given him under the new Act, the deputation left . . . Nquabe, the arch-agitator in the Park, has been to the Native Commissioner and asked him to arrange for 600 families with 10 head of cattle each to be moved at Government expense to Northern Rhodesia . . . merely another delaying action.[95]

The Chief Native Commissioner's report for 1951 tells us what happened. 'To begin with there was no trouble but after a few weeks passive resistance became apparent.' Burombo led this passive resistance, arguing that evictions should have been postponed in view of the poor harvest and near famine. Government only managed to move 1569 families: the rest remained where they were. The Native Department prosecuted those who refused to move. And it was at this point that Burombo scored his greatest success. From the earliest days of the operation of the Land Apportionment Act there had been uncertainty about the legal basis of eviction orders under the Act.[96] Now Burombo brought to court appeals against many of the eviction orders. And as Malcolm Rifkind tells us, 'because of the complexity of the procedure and technicalities in the law many of the defences were successful.'[97] It looked as though the Ndebele protest movement was going to succeed. And Burombo's influence had spread to Charter, Victoria and Chipinga districts as well as throughout Matabeleland. At the end of March 1952 the Provincial Commissioner, Matabeleland, summed up by pointing out that the 'political situation at the moment is not easily defined. It may be stated that there is a bridge between the Rural and Urban populations, but that the latter are for ever seeking to influence the former in one way or another. . . Our intelligence system is not of the best.'[98]

Godfrey Huggins, still Prime Minister, was prepared to an extent to take this African response into account. In August 1949 he told senior Native Department officials that:

We have got to recognise that the whole thing is changing. The Native is trying to take all his fences in one and he is going to be very difficult, I think, for quite a long period, and the difficulties will be largely political . . .We have got any amount of self appointed leaders in the Colony at the present time . . . They may be an unsatisfactory people and it may be that they are not going very far, but as human beings they are extremely like the Europeans, especially the Europeans that you know by studying the history of the social rise of the masses in Europe . . .The old days when the Native did exactly what he was told have passed. We are getting passive resistance in certain parts of the colony and to a certain extent we have got to handle them with a different technique.[99]

But Huggins was not prepared to accept Burombo's all-too effective passive resistance to the evictions. An amending Act was passed by the end of 1951 defining as a squatter 'any African who was occupying Crown land in the European Area or other areas without formal title'; evictions could now take place merely on proclamation by the Governor. This made Burombo's legal tactics of resistance no longer pertinent. It remained to be seen whether extra-legal tactics would now be adopted. If there was going to be any sort of Mau Mau in Matabeleland, 1952 was the year for it.

In the event there was anti-climax. Government announced that in 1952 it intended to move 3569 families at a cost of £130 000 for transport alone. The movements were effected even in those areas where violent protest had been expected. Seven hundred kraals were moved from Filabusi to Shangani, 200 miles away. 'The expected resistance did not materialise.'[100] After all the appeals to history, all the organization of protest, all the appeals to the law, the clearance of central Matabeleland took place. So far from being the transition to a newly radical peasant protest, the Ndebele protest movement of the late 1940s and early 1950s turned out to be rather the end of a long but ultimately unavailing Ndebele political tradition. After all my elaborate setting up of the comparison with the Kikuyu, this outcome may appear to be a sad letdown, though I think anybody interested in Rhodesian history and hitherto unfamiliar with the data will have been surprised by the extent and seriousness of this rural opposition. Still, even if it helps put the 1948 strike in perspective, it was certainly in the result no Mau Mau. Why not?

I think that *three* main differences between the Kikuyu and the Ndebele situations emerge. One relates, of course, to the overall stage of political development in the two territories at the end of the 1940s. In Kenya the notion of African paramountcy was in the air; in Rhodesia it certainly was not. Another relates to the contrast between the Kikuyu passion for education and the ferment of Christian independency in Kikuyuland and the wary lack of response to Christian missions in Matabeleland. The third, and perhaps the most important, relates to the processes of differentiation among the Kikuyu and the Ndebele. One could certainly not say about Matabeleland as Lonsdale says about the Kikuyu that 'the colonial absolutist state had failed to reconcile an emergent African capitalism with a settler capitalism.' Ndebele men of power and wealth were certainly *not* becoming a land-owning capitalist elite, potential allies of the colonial state against the landless. They were themselves very much the victims of state policy. Nor did the administration succeed in playing off class jealousies in the Ndebele countryside as it had hoped to do. Ndebele clients were content to follow the lead of Ndebele patrons in the opposition to measures which threatened all alike. This made for a more *united* protest but it also made for a less militant one. The urban politicians in the Ndebele case were men who had in fact tried to avoid mass confrontation with the authorities in the towns, not men already committed to violence like the Kikuyu trade union radicals. Ndebele peasants were prepared to put their faith in the leadership of chiefs and of men like Burombo: in the tactics of vocal protestation, passive resistance, legal recourse. When these failed there was no-one to lead them into violence nor were they yet ready to go that way themselves.

So there was no Mau Mau. On the other hand much too much has sometimes been made of this negative fact. Thus in 1967 Richard Greenfield published an essay entitled 'No Mau Mau in Rhodesia'. In this he was concerned to argue that even as late as 1967 African Nationalism in Rhodesia compared very unfavourably with its earlier manifestation in Kenya:

At the recent Cairo conference, President Julius Nyerere called on Rhodesia's African population to rise in revolt. But there seems little sign of this happening. Serious enquiry into the difference between Algerian or more pertinently Kikuyu and Kenyan nationalism and that of 'Zimbabwe' is revealing, for even if it is true as ZAPU and ZANU's exiled leaders claim that the world press ignores acts of sabotage in Rhodesia, they are at most sporadic and isolated. There is no Mau Mau in Rhodesia!

Greenfield went on to make a series of points which must read very oddly in the light of the material presented in this chapter. 'After the battle of Bembezi the Ndebele chiefs accepted defeat. . . Significantly, in Kenya, although the so-called "pacification" of the Kikuyu involved much bloodshed and havoc, the many African defeats were nonetheless local. At no time was there one ceremonial and symbolic moment of surrender . . . as there was in the Matopos Hills of Rhodesia.' This seems a perverse way to interpret the 1896 negotiations between Rhodes and the Ndebele which, as we have seen, constituted the main justifying 'charter' for Ndebele land claims. The Land Apportionment Act did not arouse 'significant African criticism'; 'not even compulsory movements of Africans from newly designated "European" areas was resisted, as it was in Kenya' – remarks which hardly require refutation at the end of this chapter. Greenfield concludes that the Rhodesian 'rural areas had seen less political activity even than comparable areas in South Africa . . .The much-talked of "sons of the soil" did not sufficiently understand their role . . . and how could they? They had never been adequately appealed to!'[101]

It has been the whole argument of this chapter that the fact of 'No Mau Mau in Rhodesia' did not imply a lack of rural political consciousness. Historians of the 1948 strike have recently concluded that it did not mark a crucial transition to proletarian power. It was rather a tactical and temporary coming together of the semi-skilled, aspirant 'permanent working class' and the great mass of migrant labour: a coming together which soon gave way to the pursuit of separate interests. Some of these historians have suggested that the rural protest of the late 1940s was more significant in the long run, boding forth the populist alliance of urban politicians and aggrieved peasants on which the later nationalist movements were to be based.[102] I have a good deal of sympathy with this point of view, as will become clear in Chapter 4. And even if the events in Matabeleland were in some ways the *end* of a long political tradition rather than the beginning of a new one, there was one further significant difference between them and Mau Mau. It is sometimes said that in Kenya the defeat of Mau Mau and the isolation of Kikuyu action from other peoples in the territory meant that the eventually successful Kenyan nationalist movement was largely a coalition of the educated elites of the various Kenyan regions. By contrast, one might say, the defeat of the Ndebele protest in the late 1940s left the way open to the development of a mass nationalism which could flourish outside the confines of what was always bound to be a minority political tradition. Protest against the evictions and against destocking, though most articulate in Matabeleland, had not been restricted to it; Burombo had received support in many other areas. And even in parts of the country where there was no protest recorded in the late 1940s the events of these years nevertheless laid, as we shall see, the foundations of a radical peasant nationalism which was to come fully into the open only with the guerrilla war.

NOTES

1 Sharon Stichter, *Migrant Labour in Kenya. Capitalism and African Response, 1895–1975* (London: 1982), p.83.

2 J.M. Lonsdale, 'Unhappy Valley: state and class formation in colonial Kenya', unpublished paper February 1982, pp. 10–11.

3 J.M. Lonsdale, 'A state of agrarian unrest: colonial Kenya', in *Agrarian Unrest in British and French Africa, British India and French Indo-China in the Nineteenth and Twentieth Centuries*, (Oxford Past and Present Society, 1982), pp. 5–6, 8.

4 J.M. Lonsdale, 'The growth and transformation of the colonial state in Kenya, 1929–1952', paper presented to Institute of Commonwealth Studies Seminar, 1980, p. 14.

5 Paul Mosley, 'The settler economies: studies in the economic history of Kenya and Southern Rhodesia, 1900-1963', (University of Cambridge: PhD thesis, April 1980), pp.30-33.

6 I have used a multiple of five to arrive at the total number of people affected by the eviction of 85,000 families. Some comparative idea of the scale of this Rhodesian operation can be obtained from the fact that in September 1980 the Zimbabwean government 'launched the intensive resettlement programme with the overall objective of resettling some 18,000 families . . . over a period of three years.' B.H. Kinsey, 'Forever gained: resettlement and land policy in the context of national development in Zimbabwe' in J.D.Y. Peel and T.O. Ranger (eds.) *Past and Present in Zimbabwe*, (Manchester: 1983), p.96.

   The comparison with Kenya in the late 1940s gains force when it is remembered that the 1946 African population figures for Kenya were 4,060,000, while those for Southern Rhodesia were only 1,533,000.

7 Chief Native Commissioner, Circular Minute No.60/39, Addendum A, 6 July 1940, file. S.1619, National Archives, Harare (NAH). The circular added: 'Strong persuasion should be brought to bear on landlords to induce them and their Native tenants to transform rent-paying agreements to labour agreements which need not be of a stereotyped form'.

8 Chief Native Commissioner, Circular Minute, No.60/39, Addendum B, 31 December 1940, file S.1619, NAH.

9 Monthly Report, Essexvale, January 1947, file S.1619, NAH.

10 Chief Native Commissioner's Report, 1948, as cited in Malcolm Rifkind 'The politics of land in Rhodesia' (University of Edinburgh: MSc thesis, 1968), p.77

11 Chief Native Commissioner's Report, 1949, cited in ibid., p.78. Rifkind comments that by 1949 'the individual rural villages were forging links with the towns and other rural areas and realising the possibility of resistance to the autocratic white Government.'

12 Chief Native Commissioner, Lupani, 7 November 1950, file S.160.LS 100/3A/50, NAH. This file contains correspondence about removals from Insiza and Matobo into Shangani. See also files LS 100/3B/50, NAH which also concerns resettlement in Shangani, and LS 100/3C/50, NAH which concerns the resettlement of 1500 African families in Matabeleland in mid 1951.

13 Evidence of L.V. Jowett, Native Commissioner, Inyanga to Natural Resources Board Native Enquiry, 16 July 1942, file S.988, NAH.

14 Native Commissioner, Inyanga to Provincial Native Commissioner, Umtali, 22 July 1942, file, S.988, NAH.

15 Monthly Report, Inyanga, January 1946, S.1619, NAH.

16 Evidence of W.H. Stead, Native Commissioner, Makoni to Natural Resources Board Native Enquiry, 15 and 16 July 1942, file S.988, NAH.

17 Interview with Chad Chipunza, Harare, 2 April 1981.

18 R.H. Palmer, *Aspects of Rhodesian Land Policy, 1890 – 1936* (Salisbury: 1968), p.17.

19 Mosley, 'The settler economies', p.24. Mosley is citing a speech by one Brown in the Legislative Assembly on 25 June 1908.

20 Sarah Brown, 'The Ndebele, 1897–1912: aspects of religious, economic and political life in the early colonial era' (Manchester University: BA Honours thesis, 1983), Chapter 2, 'Ndebele agriculture'.

21 Annual Report, Bulawayo, 31 March 1911, file NB 6/1/11, NAH.

22 Annual Report, Bulawayo, 1912, file NB 6/1/12, NAH.

23 Annual Report, Bulawayo, 1914, file N 9/1/17, NAH.

24 Cited in Palmer, *Aspects of Rhodesian Land Policy*, p.37.

25 ibid., p. 53.

26 ibid.

27 Annual Report, Matobo, 1946, file S.1563, NAH.

28 Annual Report, Insiza, 1946, file S.1563, NAH.

29 Provincial Native Commissioner, Matabeleland to Chief Native Commissioner, 13 May 1950, file LS/100/3Y/50, NAH.

30 Annual Report, Gwanda, 1946, file S.1563, NAH.

31 Terence Ranger, *The African Voice in Southern Rhodesia, 1898–1930* (London: 1970), especially Chapters 2 and 4.

32 Terence Ranger, 'Missionaries, migrants and the Manyika: the invention of ethnicity in Zimbabwe', paper presented to International Conference on the History of Ethnic Awareness in Southern Africa, Charlottesville, April 1983.

33 C.van Onselen and I. Phimister, 'The political economy of tribal animosity: a case study of the 1929 Bulawayo Location "faction fight" ', *Journal of Southern African Studies*, vol.6. no. 1 (1979), pp. 1–43.

34 Palmer, *Aspects of Rhodesian Land Policy* p.18, citing minutes of the

Native Board meeting at Fort Rixon, Insiza, 27 March 1931, file DO 35/389, NAH.

35 Native Commissioner, Gwelo to Superintendent of Natives, Bulawayo 15 August 1928, file S.138.21.Vol.2, NAH.

36 Superintendent of Natives, Bulawayo to Chief Native Commissioner, 18 June and 21 August 1928, file S.138.21.Vol.2, NAH.

37 Superintendent of Natives, Bulawayo to Chief Native Commissioner, 4 July 1934, file S.1542.M2, NAH.

38 M.C. Steele, 'The economic function of African-owned cattle in colonial Zimbabwe', *Zambezia*, vol.9, no.1, 1981, pp.44–5.

39 Native Commissioner, Mzingwane to Superintendent of Natives, Bulawayo 27 May 1931; Chief Native Commissioner to Secretary, Premier, 8 June 1931, file S.1542.N2, NAH. The CNC expressed the view that elections to the Native Boards should be open to anyone 'who is not a professional agitator such as Masoja, Mzingeli and other active members of the ICU, whose sole object would be to introduce dissension.'

40 Minutes of Umzingwane Native Board, 21 May 1931, file S.1542.N2, NAH.

41 ibid.

42 Native Commissioner, Mzingwane to Superintendent of Natives, Bulawayo 27 May 1931, file S.1542.N2, NAH.

43 Assistant Native Commissioner, Mzingwane to Superintendent of Natives, Bulawayo, 26 May 1933; Minutes of Umzingwane Native Board, 18 May 1933, file S.1542.N2, NAH.

44 Chief Native Commissioner to Secretary, Premier, 6 June 1933, S.1542.N2, NAH.

45 Minutes of Shashani Native Board, 16 September 1932, S.1542.N2, NAH.

46 Minutes of Shashani Native Board, 15 March 1934, S.1542.N2, NAH.

47 Minutes of Shashani Native Board, 14 June 1934, S.1542.N2, NAH.

48 Native Commissioner, Fort Rixon to Chief Native Commissioner, 29 June 1934, file S.1542.M2, NAH.

49 Superintendent of Natives, Bulawayo, to Chief Native Commissioner, 4 July 1934, file S.1542.M2, NAH.

50 Minutes of Umzingwane Native Board, 28 January 1937, file S.1542.N2, NAH.

51 Provincial Native Commissioner, Gwelo to Chief Native Commissioner, 1 July 1950, file LS 104/1/50, NAH.

52 Steele, 'The economic function of African owned cattle', p.41, citing Assistant Native Commissioner, Shangani to Native Commissioner, Bubi, 16 May 1933.

53 Steele 'The economic function of African owned cattle', p.30

54 Terence Ranger, 'Survival, revival and disaster: Shona traditional elites under colonialism', Paris June 1982.

55 Steele, 'The economic function of African-owned cattle', p.48

56 Assistant Native Commissioner, Filabusi to Native Commissioner, Fort Rixon, 13 March 1933, file S.1542.N2, NAH.

57   Assistant Native Commissioner, Filabusi to Native Commissioner, Fort Rixon, 15 June 1933, S.1542.N2, NAH.
58   Acting Superintendent of Natives, Bulawayo to Chief Native Commissioner, 23 March 1933, S.1542.N2, NAH.
59   Assistant Native Commissioner, Filabusi to Native Commissioner, Fort Rixon, 15 June 1933, S.1542.N2, NAH.
60   Native Commissioner, Fort Rixon, to Superintendent of Natives, Bulawayo, 20 June 1933, S.1542.N2, NAH.
61   Chief Native Commissioner's Report, August 1947, file S.1618, NAH.
62   Annual Report, Matobo, 1948, file S.1563, NAH.
63   Annual Report, Matobo, 1946, S.1563, NAH.
64   Annual Report, Matobo, 1948, S.1563, NAH.
65   Annual Report, Filabusi, 1948, S.1563, NAH.
66   Quarterly Report, Nkai/Shangani, June 1949, file S.1618, NAH.
67   Quarterly Report, Nyamandhlovu, September 1949, S.1618, NAH.
68   Annual Report, Gwanda, 1948, file S.1563, NAH.
69   Examination of Chief Native Commissioner by the Natural Resources Board Native Enquiry, 19 November 1942, file S.988, NAH.
70   Assistant Native Commissioner, Que Que to Native Commissioner, Gwelo, 7 June 1950, file LS 104/1/50, NAH.
71   Evidence of H.M. Fletcher to Natural Resources Board Native Enquiry, 30 September 1942, file S.988, NAH.
72   Assistant Native Commissioner, Que Que to Native Commissioner, Gwelo 7 June 1950, file LS 104/1/50, NAH.
73   Provincial Native Commissioner, Gwelo to Chief Native Commissioner, 7 August 1950, file LS 104/1/50, NAH.
74   Assistant Native Commissioner, Que Que to Native Commissioner, Gwelo 7 June 1950, file LS 104/1/50, NAH.
75   Lawrence Vambe, *From Rhodesia to Zimbabwe* (London: 1976), pp. 242-3.
76   Enoch Dumbutshena, *Zimbabwe Tragedy* (Nairobi: 1975) pp.26, 44.
77   This is the view taken in as yet unpublished studies of the 1948 strike by Ian Phimister, Stephen Thornton and John Lunn.
78   Annual Report, Matobo, 1948, file S.1563, NAH.
79   Annual Report, Bulawayo, 1948, S.1563, NAH.
80   Quarterly Report, Bulawayo, June 1949, file S.1618, NAH.
81   Quarterly Report, Matobo, June 1949, S.1618, NAH.
82   Quarterly Report, Provincial Native Commissioner, Matabeleland, September 1949, S.1618, NAH.
83   Quarterly Report, Matobo, June 1949, S.1618, NAH.
84   Quarterly Report, Nkai/Shangani, June 1949, S.1618, NAH.
85   Quarterly Report, Gutu, June 1949, S.1618, NAH.
86   Native Commissioner, Gwelo to Provincial Native Commissioner, Midlands, 26 May 1950, file LS 104/1/50, NAH.
87   Benjamin Burombo to Provincial Native Commissioner, Midlands, undated file LS 104/1/50, NAH.
88   Provincial Native Commissioner, Midlands to Chief Native Commissioner, 1 July 1950, file LS 104/1/50, NAH.

89 Minister of Mines to Minister of Native Affairs, 13 July 1950, file LS 106/1/50, NAH.
90 Provincial Native Commissioner, Midlands to Chief Native Commissioner, 7 August 1950, LS 104/1/50, NAH.
91 Native Commissioner, Selukwe to Provincial Native Commissioner, Midlands, 19 March 1951, file MC 103/2/51, NAH.
92 Provincial Native Commissioner, Midlands to Assistant Secretary, Administration, 28 March 1951, MC 103/2/51, NAH.
93 Invitation from Burombo to 'all members throughout the Colony', MC 103/2/51, NAH.
94 M.L. Rifkind, 'The politics of land in Rhodesia' (University of Edinburgh, M.Sc thesis, 1968), p.94.
95 Notes on a meeting on the Matopos National Park, 23 August 1950, file S.160. LS 103/3/50, NAH.
96 Chief Native Commissioner's Circular Minute, No.42, 16 August 1934, S.1619, NAH.
97 Rifkind, 'The politics of land in Rhodesia', p.92.
98 Quarterly Report, Provincial Commissioner, Matabeleland, March 1952, file S.1618.
99 Minutes of Native Affairs Advisory Board, 15 and 16 August 1949, file S.160 GC1–GC2.
100 Rifkind, 'The politics of land in Rhodesia', pp. 92–3.
101 Richard Greenfield, 'No Mau Mau in Rhodesia', *Legon Observer*, vol.11, nos 12 and 13 (June/July 1967).
102 John Lunn, 'The political economy of protest: the strikes and unrest of 1948 in Southern Rhodesia' (Manchester University: BA Honours thesis, 1982).

4

Mau Mau
and the guerrilla war
in Zimbabwe:
the lost lands

In Chapter 3 I described how the long tradition of Ndebele protest politics came to its climax in the early 1950s. Despite the evictions, a good deal of this complex Ndebele tradition remained vital and no doubt underlay the open mass nationalist movement in Matabeleland in the later 1950s. Equally, Ndebele aspirations for the recovery of their lost homeland no doubt played an important part in mobilizing peasant support for guerrillas during the 1970s. I say 'no doubt' in both cases because no study of the nationalist or guerrilla periods in Matabeleland has yet been made. Such a study is, I think, urgently necessary in order that the specific character of Ndebele peasant experience and grievances can be understood. In its absence, however, I am obliged in the rest of this book to draw mainly on the evidence from the Shona-speaking rural areas of Zimbabwe.

In any case it is to these areas that my argument now has to return. At the end of Chapter 2 Shona-speaking peasants were left in a state of increasing resentment and awareness but also in a state of political impotence. In the 1950s, however, a sense of Shona cultural identity belatedly emerged and this interacted with yet more intense peasant grievance to give the main impetus to African nationalism. At its highest stage of development this fusion of Shona cultural nationalism and peasant radicalism proved potent enough to allow the spread of ZANLA's guerrilla action across two-thirds of the country in the 1970s; it was also the powerfully mixed emotion which swept Robert Mugabe to power in the 1980 elections. Only after that have the two traditions had to confront each other – Shona cultural nationalism fused with peasant radicalism might effectively win the rural war in most of the country, but it cannot in itself offer solutions to the problems of Matabeleland, crucially intensified as they have been by the consequences of the clearances of the late 1940s.

But these are considerations for a later chapter. What I need to do now is to trace how what I have called peasant radicalism grew up among the Shona peasantries. And I think I can do this by means of yet another comparison with Mau Mau. This time I want to take up some of the questions raised by Robert Buijtenhuijs in his recent *Contributions to Mau Mau Historiography*. In the sections of his book which I want to cite he is not so much concerned with the origins of Mau Mau as with its character as a movement of violence. He proposes a comparative study:

It is extremely difficult, under the conditions prevailing in Africa south of the Sahara to launch a successful peasants' revolt. This was already so during the colonial era when the situation was relatively clear, because it was easy to identify the common enemy. The failure of the Mau Mau revolt in Kenya, of the 1947 Madagascar war and of the UPC insurrections in Cameroun strongly remind us of this difficulty. As far as one can judge, conditions are even less favourable in post-colonial Africa.

In the light of these considerations, a comparative study of the three peasant revolts that did occur in colonial Africa (Madagascar, Kenya, Cameroun) seems to be a path of research that could yield interesting results.[1]

In a footnote he adds that the 'revolutions in the ex-Portuguese colonies and in Zimbabwe, in my opinion, belong to a slightly different category, as they took place at a time when most of the other African countries were already independent, but the comparative study I am proposing could eventually be enlarged to include these cases.'[2]

Yet Buijtenhuijs himself does in fact make a preliminary comparison:

On the grass roots level [of Mau Mau] the land question seems to have been all-important, and this leads us to an interesting question. As has been noted by J.R. Sheffield only seven percent of Kenya's land was alienated to European settlers. Even when taking into account that these seven percent included over one-fifth of all available agricultural land with high potentialities for successful cultivation, this seems a relatively minor portion, considering that 49 percent and 87 percent respectively were taken by European settlers in Rhodesia and South Africa. Yet, as far as I know, the anti-colonial struggle in Kenya became much more focused on the 'stolen lands' aspect of colonial rule than has been the case in Zimbabwe or South Africa. It would be an interesting theme for comparative research to find out why this has been so . . . For the Kikuyu, even in pre-colonial times, the question of land tenure has always been paramount, as it was, in Kenyatta's words, 'the key to the people's life'. It is possible that most Zimbabwean and South African ethnic groups have a less direct and sacred bond with their land and that this is one of the reasons why the land question never took on the same proportions as it did in Kenya.[3]

It is this interesting theme for comparative research that I want to take up in this chapter. We have seen already that relative lack of concern over the 'stolen lands' was hardly characteristic of the Ndebele. But what about the Shona-speaking peasantry? On the face of it there does seem something in Buijtenhuijs' contrast so far as they are concerned. If there was no Mau Mau in Matabeleland, there was even less resistance or threat of resistance to the evictions of the late 1940s in Mashonaland and Manicaland. But it will be my argument in this chapter that in reality the evictions and their consequences did mark a key turning point in the development of peasant consciousness and that the peasant radicalism of the 1960s and 1970s was essentially derived from them.

This argument can best be made with reference to a particular case study and once again my case will be that of the Makoni District. And Makoni makes a very striking instance of my general prosposition. The district seemed to accept eviction and its consequences placidly in the late 1940s, but it was one of the first areas of intense peasant support for nationalism in the late 1950s and early 1960s; it was also an area of deep peasant commitment to the guerrilla war from the mid-1970s. I want in this chapter to explore the inner, agrarian, history of Makoni in these decades in order to show the consistency of peasant consciousness.

In the late 1930s Native Commissioners in the eastern districts of Zimbabwe had predicted that enforcement of the Land Apportionment Act would cause violent protest. In October 1937, for instance, the Native Commissioner, Umtali, noted that under the terms of the Act some 5500 Manyika were due to be turned off alienated land in 1941:

The Manyika Natives are pre-eminent among the Natives of Mashonaland for intelligence and initiative. They can be found in almost every large town of Southern Africa drawing comparatively large wages. As loyal subjects they can be most useful: as disaffected ones they may cause considerable trouble . . . It will require a special force even to expel them from their ancestral home.[4]

In the event, however, it did not require a special force, or the use of violence at all, to carry out the evictions in Umtali District, nor in Makoni, whose people had come to be classified as Manyika.[5] It seemed on the face of it that 'the Manyika' remained 'loyal subjects'.

Thus during the later 1940s the Annual Reports for Makoni consistently record both the continuing process of eviction and also the productivity, prosperity and contentment of the people. Their atmosphere could hardly have been more different from the reports I cited in the last chapter on the districts of Matabeleland. In 1944, for example, it was noted that 'the population in the Reserves had been increased by the movement of considerable numbers of Natives to them from Alienated land in the European area. Most of the people moved went to the Chiduku and Weya Reserves. The Makoni Reserve is heavily over-populated.' But it was also reported that well over 100 000 bags of grain had been marketed. The Makoni District Annual Report noted that traders and farmers reported 'a real improvement [in the grades of grain produced] over a period of years . . .At Rusape during the past season no maize was graded lower than B.1 . . .There is keen competition for Native grain and transport, today's great problem, is usually undertaken by the trader.' Equally the report recorded that 'destocking will be commenced in both Reserves [Makoni and Chiduku] during the coming year' and that labour 'conscription is not popular and the Native will avoid it if he can.' Nevertheless, it concluded that the 'year has been a good one from the Native viewpoint. Crops, prices and the demand for native produce rose . . .Work at fair wages was available for all who wished to work and it is probable that the people have never before been so prosperous.'[6]

It was the same picture in 1945, when the consistent recovery and expansion which had taken place in peasant production from the late 1930s reached its peak with the sale of no less than 150 700 bags of grain, including 124 500 bags of maize of 'good quality':

Large scale movements of tenants and squatters from Alienated Land in the European Area began to take place towards the end of the year. Many families are going to the Mangwendi Reserve in the Mrewa District and others to the Tanda Division, Native [Purchase] Area . . . Crops were heavier than average and because of the proximity of the Reserves to rail and improved communications within the Reserves themselves it was possible to market a considerable amount. . . The maize now produced is of good quality.[7]

The 1946 report showed how far the process of implementation of the Land Apportionment Act had already gone in Makoni District. The total African population was estimated at 56 227 and of these only just over 2000 remained as 'squatters' on the two huge investment estates, Inyati Block and Rathcline. The report noted that there would have to be some delay in moving the 2000 squatters since 'the Reserves are already over-populated' and 'it would be impossible to find room for them in the Natives Reserves in this district.' Negotiations were going on with the Commissioners of other districts to find room for them. Meanwhile, however, steps were being taken to deal with the problem of the 'over-populated' Reserves. The report noted, for example, that meetings had been held throughout the Chiduku Reserve with African cattle owners to explain the necessity of reducing stock numbers. There had been an 'excellent response'; without need for compulsory destocking the peasants of Chiduku had sold nearly 5000 head and slaughtered 6000 more for domestic consumption. Chiduku men had also worked without protest in 'a soil conservation gang', merely asking 'that their wages be reduced in return for their being allowed to perform the least possible tasks each day', so that they could put maximum labour into cultivation. And despite these pressures, the Native Commissioner was once again struck by the viability of the Makoni peasant option. 'So far as the indigenous native is concerned,' he noted, 'there does not seem to be the same need for acquiring money through employment as is the case in less favoured districts. He can find a ready market for his cattle and produce and in that way can acquire currency without having to perform personal service for a wage.'[8]

In 1947 the completion of the process of eviction was announced. Room had been found in Mrewa District for 170 families. As for the rest of the 'squatters' on Inyati and Rathcline:

Their removal from these two estates is now required by the owners and arrangements are at present under way to locate these people in the Tanda Native [Purchase] Area, Chikore Native Reserve, and in those areas of the Chiduku Native Reserve occupied by headmen Masoswa and Nedewedzo. This will complete the removal of natives from European areas in this district: only those on Mission Lands or under authorised labour agreement will remain.

The new order was coming rapidly into existence in Makoni. 'Large company-held land has been divided and sold, and the European population has considerably increased.' On the other hand, in the Reserves there was a 'vast effort to combat soil erosion . . .The cumulative effect of antierosion measures in the Reserves over the last few years can be clearly seen from the air and it is a source of wonder to European farmers who have flown over these Reserves.' 'Voluntary de-stocking' had cleared all the Reserves except the Makoni Reserve of excess cattle. Agricultural Demonstrators were enforcing agricultural rules, including the prohibition of cultivating rice and green maize in the *vleis*. 'They have also assisted in . . . the placing of natives from European areas in the Reserves.'

In addition to all this, the 1947 harvest suffered badly from drought, cutting the marketed grain surplus from 150 000 bags 'in a normal year', to only 23 373 of which only 9501 bags were maize. 'Some areas where good harvests can generally be expected reaped virtually nothing and many natives reverted to barter.' By this time the relative autonomy of the Makoni peasant economy had been sufficiently undermined for such a collapse of harvest to have an immediate effect on the supply of local labour to European agriculture. 'It was significant,' the 1947 Annual Report noted, 'that during the drought practically all the farmers had very much less trouble with their workers and the labour output per individual employee was greater.' In short, 1947 looks pretty much like a crisis for the Makoni peasant option. And yet the Native Commissioner, while finding farm labourers to suffer from 'that disease of mind . . . which appears to have infected the labouring classes throughout the world', was nevertheless able to assert that his peasantry was completely 'non-political. . . There is no doubt of their present contentment; it would be enlightening to some members of the United Nations Organisation to visit the Reserves and see the obviously well-fed, well-clothed and well-contented people.'[9]

As we shall see, the Native Commissioners were being in some ways blindly complacent. And yet at the time there clearly *was* a real contrast with Matabeleland. The evictions in Makoni had been carried out before the Native Department had steeled itself to attempt any in central Matabeleland. Indeed, by the early 1950s Makoni District was in many ways the model district in the eyes of administrators, agriculturalists and conservationists. Native Commissioners there had defined the problem of their Reserves as 'primarily soil conservation' from the early 1940s. In 1942, for example, Native Commissioner Stead stated that 'We are moving more and more natives from the farms into the reserves and this intensive cultivation in the reserves makes protection of the soil an essential method. There is a comprehensive scheme . . . to put about 23 000 acres under protection in the Chiduku Reserve . . . The scheme is to get the natives to build their own contour ridges.'[10] Stead's scheme was regarded as an important pioneering precedent by conservation experts. It was commended by the Technical Assistant for Soil Conservation, Douglas Aylen, in the *Rhodesia Agricultural Journal* in mid-1942:

There was little appreciable erosion when the native scratched out about an acre of garden among trees and scrub, and then abandoned the garden after a year or two leaving it to recover for many years before the land was again used . . . fertility is soon restored. Today he ploughs ten times the amount of land he used to hoe, clears it, and uses it for many years . . . Unfortunately conservation lags behind centralisation . . .This year it is intended to complete the protection of a large block of land in one fairly well populated Reserve (Chiduku) where during the last few years 7,000 acres have already been contour ridged, by undertaking the work on the remaining 23,000 acres of arable land within this block. The works will be set out for the natives and under the powers conferred by the Natural Resources Act, they will be ordered to construct them. Such an order would only be possible where the natives have already reacted favourably towards soil conservation, and in this case this attitude has been brought about by the work already done, and the interest taken by the Native Commissioner of this district. Next year no natives will be allowed to cultivate unprotected land within this area.[11]

The Soil Conservation Officer for Reserves, K.J. McKenzie, noting that Makoni was 'the only instance where people have been compelled to turn out and build their own ridges', thought that 'Stead's scheme is very interesting and if it can be made to work there is no cheaper way of doing it.'[12] In short, Stead was the darling of the experts, who increasingly favoured compulsion – for them Stead was 'a man who keeps them moving. . . .' Chief Native Commissioner Simmonds was less sure of Stead's methods. He pointed out that 'There would have been a little trouble [in Chiduku] if the Native Commissioner hadn't decided to take full responsibility. He had to inflict a few fines to get it done. Whether there was any legal sanction for that I am not prepared to say, but by the infliction of fines the work was done.'[13] In this respect Stead was a man of the authoritarian future.

Stead worked by 'the infliction of fines', but it also seems clear that the dogged peasant producers of Chiduku, who once had flourished on extensive shifting cultivation, were now determined to get the best they could out of permanent intensive cultivation. For this reason, Chiduku was the only Reserve in the country to adopt a communal development approach in the late 1940s. The Land Development Officer, Gorringe, set up a series of committees which were the envy and wonder of administrators in other districts:

Areas were divided up into chiefs or sub-chiefs areas and a Development committee was formed consisting of the chief or if he was unintelligent and non-progressive, a man was appointed whom the chief stated publicly he would recognise as his representative on the committee, three of the most progressive headmen, three progressive men, one progressive woman, the

demonstrator and two reserve overseers who had been trained in
maintenance work and crop rotations . . .As soon as an area is completely
protected and crop rotated, etc, the demonstrator informs me, I check the
area and block it off in black for 100% protected and properly farmed, in
green for protected only . . .A prize and certificate is given to the best
demonstrator and committee each year. The committee whose area is not
progressing satifactorily is brought into the office, shown the map, and how
their area shows up with others . . . The Natural Resources Act is read to
them, stressing the fact that if land was not looked after the Government
would naturally think that the people in that area had too much land to look
after.

After 1946 Gorringe's committees were allowed to run a maize
bonus scheme, allocating a bonus to 'progressive kraals in their
area', rather than to individual producers as was the case elsewhere
in the territory:

My whole system is based on the kraal system, the individual might be
worthy, but unless co-operation of the masses is obtained, my experience is
that development will fail. Particularly in the maize bonus scheme, if you
pay out selected individuals, their lands will be over-run by unknown cattle,
and they will be the butt of all slackers. . .In 1944 we could get no labour,
today we have no labour troubles, the committees turn out the gangs. Mr
Tracey, a well known authority on farming was amazed at the progress in
the Chiduku Reserve, and a well-known progressive farmer . . . stated that
he ought to be getting back to his farm, as these fellows were showing him
up.[14]

Chiduku retained this star status into the 1950s. In August 1951,
for instance, the Provincial Agriculturalist, Manicaland, com-
mented on 'the really excellent Show held in Chiduku' and on the
'literally hundreds of exhibits' shown by this 'progressive
community.'[15]
In 1952 it was reported that about half the arable areas in Rusape
South had been winter ploughed, compost making was proceeding
very satisfactorily and Soil Conservation had reported favourably on conservation in the area. Each week the Chiduku Farmers
Association met for lectures on good farming methods.[16] In
September 1953 the acting Provincial Agriculturalist hailed Chiduku's as 'certainly Manicaland's most impressive show', and noted
that a 'steady rate of progress in agricultural methods, particularly
in the dry land areas of Inyanga, Rusape and Umtali is taking
place. Soil Conservation is progressing well and costs have dropped in these areas owing to the cooperation of the Chiefs who have
influenced tribesmen and their followers to construct contour ridges
voluntarily and without remuneration.'[17]

Nor was all this merely a matter of officials putting a good face on things in their reports. Father Peter Turner, farm manager at Triashill in the 1950s, recalls that in the 'early 1950s Land Development Officer West took the line that it was impossible to make an impression on the whole area he had to cover so he decided to concentrate on Chiduku. He put a bridge over every stream in the Reserve. In the 1950s Chiduku was the show piece. But by the 1970s it was pretty desolate.'[18] Moreover, oral informants from the area themelves testify to the urgency with which they sought to acquire in those years the skills of intensive farming. Mbidzeni Luciah thus recalls that:

she was good at farming and when *Chidhumeni* [intensive farming] was introduced in western Chiduku . . . although her husband declined to join, she practised it without registering and did well in crop production. She made a lot of surplus. She was fortunate to have her children's labour and that of those who sought piece-work for salt, sugar and soap which her husband supplied in bags and cases. Surplus crop products were sold to Margolis and Inyazura for 15 shillings a bag of maize.[19]

Mandironda Beatrice recalls that:

Her husband Shonhiwa went to work in Salisbury and used to send money to her. They bought two head of cattle and a plough. In the 1950s *Chidhumeni* was introduced to Dewedzo. They joined it, hoping to go to African Purchase Areas if they qualified. They learnt crop rotation, soil conservation, maintenance of farm implements, rearing domestic animals and maintaining a good home. They qualified and got a Master Farmer's Certificate . . . They stayed in Dewedzo growing crops according to the way they had been taught. Her husband died in 1970 yet she remained at home working in the fields to produce crops for selling. Their main aim was to grow cash crops so that they could manage to educate their children. When she was widowed she continued to produce crops with this aim in mind.[20]

It looked, in fact, as if the one place where the government might succeed in implanting its vision of a contented intensive farming peasantry was Makoni District and Chiduku Reserve in particular. Readers will have been thinking that there is not much sign yet of the promised peasant radicalism. Yet all this reported contentment was much too good to be true for long. When the open mass nationalist movement began in the late 1950s it soon became clear that Makoni District was one of the most responsive to its message of all the districts in rural Rhodesia. The confrontations between peasant nationalists and the administration in the northern reserves of Makoni were the sharpest of any in the open nationalist period.

Why was this? And why did the aspirant Master Farmer, Mandironda Beatrice, come to feel that compulsory contour ridging was 'one of the main causes of the war of liberation'; come to support the ZANLA guerrillas unreservedly; and come to vote for Robert Mugabe in the hope that his government 'will soon attend to the land problem'?

There are broadly two answers, one most applicable to the northern areas of Makoni District, the other most applicable to Chiduku and Makoni Reserves. Both were in fact foreshadowed in amongst the self-congratulations of the district Annual Reports. As early as 1942, Native Commissioner W.H. Stead put his finger on what was ultimately to be the cause of radical nationalism in Chiduku. The self-help soil erosion scheme was going well, wrote Stead; 600 conscripts had been recruited to work for European food producers; there was no sign of disloyalty. And yet he felt:

constrained to write about certain factors which bear upon the future political situation . . . I have in mind particularly the position as it occurs in native reserves. From the agricultural side we have a dictum that 4 acres is as much as a man can cultivate thoroughly with 2 acres for each additional wife. Have we, on the other hand, an economic dictum that a man can maintain himself and his family on 4 to 6 acres? If so, at what minimum prices for his products, and at what standard of living? If these and many other allied problems are not thought out and planned for, then unfortunate political trends are certain to develop. One could wish that there existed an institution in the Colony to serve as an organ for social and economic planning so that consideration could be given at this stage to problems which are certain to arise and which should be prepared for before they constitute the basis for strong political antagonisms.[21]

The peasants of Chiduku ultimately turned to radical nationalism because despite all their efforts in intensive cultivation, peasant production increasingly failed to offer a viable economic return. It took them some years to reach this conclusion. The peasants of the northern areas of Makoni, however, attained to radicalism much earlier.

The peasants of the north knew more or less from the moment of their eviction and resettlement that the peasant option was ended for them. As early as 1948 both their predicament and their co-ordinated, disgruntled response to it emerge from the Annual Report:

The Inyati Block has been cut up into farms and many of them have been occupied by Europeans. The unauthorised squatters have moved to the Chiduku Reserve and to the Tanda Native [Purchase] Area. Before removal they were advised to enter into labour agreements with the new settlers but so far no applications for agreements have been made. The reluctance of the natives to remain on, or go to, European farms under labour agreements appears to me to have been organised. They will occupy land in the European area while such land is unoccupied but as soon as a European appears they move beyond his control. In a way, the Europeans are to blame for this state of affairs as so many of them ruthlessly demanded the immediate removal of all natives from their farms. Owing to the over-crowding of the Reserves and Native Areas many of these unfortunate natives had to be moved to unsuitable areas, and often, far from relatives and friends.[22]

The predicament of those who were moved into the Tanda Division is spelt out very clearly in Norman Thomas' excellent unpublished thesis on religion and politics in Manicaland:

Under the terms of the Land Apportionment Act Tanda was designated as a Native Area suitable for purchase by qualified African farmers. For fifteen years, however, it remained largely forgotten as those who wished to own farms secured more fertile land closer to markets. In 1945, however, the government decided to displace large numbers of Africans from their ancestral homes in European designated lands of the Makoni District and move them to Tanda . . .The land inspector's report on the potential of the Tanda division was not encouraging. The bulk of the land, he disclosed, 'was never intended by nature to be used for agricultural purposes' (Land Inspector to Director of Native Agriculture, 26 January 1945, file GN 202/45, District Commissioner's office, Rusape). He estimated that 15% was arable land, 75% grazing land, and 10% waste land. Since the land was 'of that type of country that quickly deteriorates if over-populated' the inspector recommended that not more than two hundred families be resettled on it.[23]

In fact 619 families were moved into the area between 1945 and 1947 'as there was nowhere else for them to go'[24]; many more followed in the next few years. At the time there were no facilities at all on the land – no schools, clinics, dip-tanks, access roads. But people kept coming in. By the early 1960s there was a population of 7350 in Tanda with 7000 cattle. The result was as the land inspector had predicted. In the period 1945 to 1947 'virgin lands provided yields of 20–40 bags of maize per acre in the first year, but once ploughed the rains washed away the finer and more fertile particles of clay, silt and humus. Within four years output dropped to 2–5 bags per acre.' Nor were there any available local markets. There soon came to be a high rate of labour migration: 'in every village,' writes Thomas, 'the number of married females far exceeds that of males.'[25]

All this gave rise to discontent enough, but the unfortunate new occupants of Tanda Division had yet other uncertainties to face.

Some agencies of government had been rattled by Burombo's movement of opposition and were anxious to avoid giving him obviously valid grounds for further criticism. They were extremely conscious that by moving peasants off European land into areas set aside for Native Purchase they were in breach of the bargain enshrined in the Land Apportionment Act.

In February 1950 the Natives Advisory Board deplored the fact that there were 2000 outstanding applications for Native Purchase Farms but that there were hardly any surveyed and prepared farms to allocate to applicants. A member of the Board, one Brent, emphasized the political consequences of this further undercutting of would-be entrepreneurs:

We are accepting these people and most of them will be dead before they get title. . .It is becoming most embarrassing. It is important politically as well as administratively . . .Why I attach such great political importance to it is that our friend Burombo goes round. He says that reserve work is only putting it in order for Europeans to take it away. He is murmuring about the Native Purchase Areas being only a bluff. If it meant taking the Land Inspectors and cutting it up into something, we could at least beat Mr Burombo . . . We would be at least one jump ahead of Burombo.[26]

But this desire to press ahead with the settlement of yeomen farmers so that evictions from 'European' land would be balanced by settlement of African rural entrepreneurs, clashed directly with the fact that Native Commissioners had only been able to carry out the evictions by making use of Native Purchase Area land. The two sections of the Land Apportionment Act clashed with each other, and in the struggle over which should prevail the Tanda area became a key battleground. The peasant families evicted into Tanda 'held temporary permits to use the land until it would be needed as a purchase area. Each man was expected to pay 15 shillings annual rent, carry out conservation measures, and limit cultivation to ten acres and stock to six head of cattle.'[27] Meanwhile the Native Department and the Native Land Board, which was responsible for the administration of the Native Purchase scheme, fought over the ultimate use of the land. In April 1950 the Native Land Board discussed a proposal to 'sub-divide Tanda Division, Makoni District, into farm holdings'. The minutes record that the 'Chief Land Officer explained the position to the Board and after a full discussion it was resolved to agree to the proposal in principle and that the Tanda Division be inspected . . . as to whether it is suitable to be cut up into farm holdings.'[28] The Native Commissioner urged that there was nowhere to move the present occupants, but in October 1951 'the Board resolved that we continue surveying from 50 to 60 holdings this year, which the Native Commissioner should arrange to alienate next year.'[29] As Thomas writes, the people who had been evicted into Tanda now watched 'surveyors peg their fields for division into purchase area farms. The crowding of additional families into Tanda . . . due to a redefinition of the border with the European area, only increased their apprehension.'[30]

This apprehension continued through the 1950s. The Native Department continued to press that there should be no further evictions. The Native Land Board continued to demand that the promise of land for purchase should be honoured. 'It would appear,' wrote the Chief Land Officer in 1952,

that all Divisions of the Native Purchase Area in Manicaland are filled to capacity by Crown Land Tenants. No matter which division is cut up for sale, there is nowhere to place natives who may have to be moved. The Provincial Native Commissioner is thus reduced to the expedient of recommending that a Division (Tanda) be cut up for sale to those occupying it at present under communal tenure. The size of the farms recommended is such that . . . only subsistence farming can be practised.

So far as Manicaland is concerned the Land Apportionment Act cannot be implemented in one of its most fundamental particulars . . . When this becomes known to the native population, I need hardly describe the political situation that is likely to arise. Unless we are to break faith with the native people in this most important point, our only alternatives are (1) to make available further land for purchase by natives, or (2) return to the status quo prior to 1930, when natives could purchase land anywhere.

The suggestions for Tanda were, he thought:

a travesty of the intentions of the Land Apportionment Act. There is no evidence that the Crown Land Tenants have the least desire to purchase the land they occupy communally, but they are to be practically forced to do so, to the exclusion of those natives who do genuinely wish to acquire their own farms . . . The suggestions put forward are dictated purely by expediency, which has been allowed to obscure the moral obligations implicit in the Land Apportionment Act.[31]

The Native Department had a different view of the African political universe. They thought that it would be very inexpedient to force already evicted peasants to move yet again and feared 'the political situation that is likely to arise' from doing so. Some of them felt that it would also constitute a breach of the 'moral obligations' owed to the evicted by the administration. Feelings became so high that a meeting of senior Native Department officials in September 1954 called for the abolition of the Native Land Board.[32]

Meanwhile, however, the Land Board presssed on with its attempt to make a reality out of the Native Purchase scheme. In April 1952 it demanded 'the speedy elimination of squatters from land in the Native Purchase Areas required for alienation.'[33] It insisted that fifty farms be surveyed and demarcated on Tanda and allocated to purchasers and that the previously evicted peasants now on the land be evicted yet again. In September 1952 the Land Development Officer for Rusape North visited Tanda with the Provincial Native Commissioner and the Native Commissioner, Makoni, 'to investigate the possibility of moving in people to Chikore [Reserve] ex Tanda'.[34] By September 1953 Purchase Farms in western Tanda were beginning to be taken up by their new owners.[35] This was in fact the end of Native Purchase allocations in the area, but the evicted peasants were left in uncertainty for a further ten years, during which time they continued to pay annual rents for 'temporary' residence. Then at last, 'in 1962 the Government devised a compromise. Hiving off the North West corner of Tanda, they allocated fifty-one purchase area farms to qualified master farmers from other parts of Rhodesia. Crowding those displaced from these farms into the remaining area, they reclassified it as tribal trust land.'[36]

It was hardly surprising that the peasants of Tanda became some of the most embittered opponents of the administration. In December 1965, after several years of nationalist activity in the area, the Internal Affairs Delineation report for Tanda remarked that:

The two headmen [Maparura and Makumbe] have little or no control; the area is the political 'hot-bed' of the district and the politically inclined have dominated the thinking of the people for many years . . . The European areas of Mayo and Rathcline are continually inconvenienced by cattle which trespass from Tanda . . . The community spirit has been of a low order over many years. Tribesmen have been intimidated into thuggery, acts of violence and opposition to law and order . . . Agricultural staff are not popular . . . The agitators have warned people against helping themselves, saying 'The Government does not give you clinics, roads or water – do not co-operate!' Until such time as these people can be left in peace by their own agitators, development by the people will not make a start. . .

The majority of [Maparura] people lived in the Inyati Block until 1949 . . .

The people are backward and politically inclined. . .

[Makumbe's people] moved from European farms into Tanda purchase area originally, then moved out into the T.T.L; this possibly explains why they are such a disgruntled people. . . There are no council or self-help projects. . . Political agitation and intimidation preclude constructive thought.[37]

But the special problems of Tanda merely added to the more general grievances of all the peasants of northern Makoni. Very many of those evicted had been pushed not into Tanda but into the small and arid northern Weya Reserve, to the west of Tanda. What happened in Weya is graphically described in a long minute, written in 1976 after the Reserve had become a haven for guerrillas, by the District Commissioner, Makoni, who was seeking to give an account of events 'as I believe the tribesman sees them':

At the end of the second world war [came] the breaking up of the large tracts of European owned estates of Mayo, Rathcline and Inyati to make way for farms for returning ex-servicemen. These large ranches had been owned by overseas land and mining companies who had permitted the land to lie dormant, and who had further permitted the tribesman who was in occupation, to continue to scratch the soil and hunt the game without interference . . . Suddenly this was all changed, and these scattered family groups were forced into two tribal trust lands, leaving behind their ancestral graves and refuges. These people arrived in the Weya and Tanda T.T.Ls, and after some jockeying around, settled down after a fashion . . . They now came under the dominion of Chendambuya whom . . . they regarded as having failed them because he acquiesced to what they considered was the theft of their land by the Europeans.

Here then was the situation in the early 1950s, a group of people comparatively better educated than other tribesmen, seething with hatred at the wrong they believed had been committed against them by the European Administration and with no proper tribal structure . . . What better place was there for the seed of African Nationalism to germinate, grow, and as the 1960s were to display, flower?

This 'seething hatred' was the reality that underlay the bland reports of administrators in the late 1940s and early 1950s so far as northern Makoni was concerned.

Other disruptions were to follow. The evictions and the demands for intensive farming, which had already so much changed 'traditional' peasant agriculture, were now followed by sweeping changes in tenure and land allocation procedures under the Land Husbandry Act of 1951. As the District Commissioner, Makoni continued in 1976:

The Administration was then able, in the eyes of the tribesman, to further aggravate the situation by again, in the tribesman's view, threatening his tenure over the land by the introduction of the African Land Husbandry Act. This Act required the tribesman to move from the land that he had recently acquired, and ensured that those who did not hold land prior to the introduction of the Land Husbandry Act, returned to the T.T.L. to lay stake to a piece of land. The situation thus developed where tribesmen had their holdings reduced . . .

1960 saw a decline in the value of tobacco, and the once prosperous tobacco farms on the borders of the T.T.L. fell into disuse, and were in some instances abandoned, although some were turned into cattle ranches. The tribesman in Weya turned his eyes to the land from which he had been so recently evicted, and decided that it would not be long before he returned to those lands, as the European was apparently abandoning farms. This belief still prevails. Support for the belief came from outside quarters, and was brought into the area by the African nationalists. Their message was that the hated European was leaving Africa, and soon the country would once again be ruled by blacks. The tribesman believed this, and once again, as he sees it, the European has wronged him by not leaving the country. But before this further belief of being wronged took root, the tribesman in Weya and Tanda set about trying to evict the European, and embarked upon a typical Mashona campaign of disorder and disobedience.[38]

From the early 1950s, then, there was no doubt that the peasants of Weya and Tanda wanted to express their 'seething hatred'. The question was how they could do it. As we have seen already, they began with an 'organized' refusal to enter into labour agreements with the new European owners of their homelands – 'as soon as a European appears they move beyond his control.' Beyond this passive resistance they could hit back at the white farmers by driving cattle on to their land – 'the European areas of Mayo and Rathcline are continually inconvenienced by cattle which trespass from Tanda.' But there was little they could directly do to 'evict the European' until the guerrilla war transformed the prospects for action. Before the war what enabled the peasants of Weya and Tanda to do more than merely withdraw their labour from European farms was the administration's ever-increasing intervention in peasant production.

Weya Reserve had been centralized in 1938, thereby bringing about 'closer settlement'.[39] Nothing had been done in Tanda. But now, as far too many people and cattle were pushed into these fragile lands, there really *was* an ecological threat. Yields collapsed; erosion was extensive; grazing was exhausted. The peasants and the administration explained these disasters in diametrically opposed ways. The peasants knew that they were the result of eviction and resettlement. The administration increasingly came to explain their poverty and the degeneration of the land in terms of the backward farming methods of Weya and Tanda cultivators. The peasants were determined not to have to invest all too scarce land and labour in conservation measures. The administration was determined to achieve directive control over the northern Makoni Reserves and to enforce a multitude of agricultural rules.

In 1951 Weya was re-centralized to deal with 'shortage of grazing
. . . one of the unfortunate consequences of over-population'; it
was hoped that 'individual allocation would . . . result in some
surplus which could go over to grazing.'[40] At the same time the
Chief Native Commissioner summoned all the chiefs of Manicaland
to Umtali to discuss land, telling them that some people would have
to move to remote areas such as the Zambezi valley. As a result 'so
many rumours [were] going around' Weya that the Native Commissioner considered it 'very serious'; the somewhat eccentric Chief
Chendambuya under whose traditional jurisdiction Weya lay
'called a meeting of all his heads to pass on what he had been told
. . . Chief Chendambuya informed the people that he had been told
by the Native Commissioner that as there were many natives in
Rhodesia the Natives would be shifted to Nyasaland; this included
the natives in Weya Reserve.'[41] Thereafter each new administrative
intervention gave rise to renewed suspicions that the ultimate aim of
the Europeans was to drive those 'who wished to be agriculturalists'
out of the Reserve altogether. In March 1953 a survey was carried
out in Chikore Reserve 'where close supervision is necessary, with a
view to centralisation and demarcation of Water Supplies.'[42] As for
Tanda, the Native Commissioner admitted in September 1951 that
peasants there could hardly be compelled to carry out conservation
work – 'it would not be fair to call on the inhabitants to turn out for
this work if they may have to be expelled in the near future.'[43] But
this forebearance soon gave way to what seemed the urgent
ecological necessities.

In February 1952 it was reported that throughout northern
Makoni 'meetings of Headmen have been held to collect labour for
roads and soil conservation.'[44] Thereafter the monthly reports of
the Land Development Officer for northern Makoni document a
massive intervention – drain strips, gulley dams, contour ridges,
rotational grazing, all these and more were enforced. More and
more demands were made – there was to be no intercropping; no
cultivation of wet gardens near streams. The peasants of Weya and
Tanda bitterly resented having to waste labour in soil conservation
work, which did nothing to increase productivity, or to give up an
insurance against famine in the wet gardens. By the end of 1952
there were clear signs of opposition. 'Owing to non-co-operation by
two villages,' recorded the Land Development Officer in October
1952, '48,152 yards of Grass Strips have had to be repaired'; '31,963
yards of Grass Buffer Strips had to be repegged [in November
1952] after having been destroyed by landholders'.[45] Meanwhile
hardly any labour was forthcoming from Tanda for conservation
work.

It was at this time, too, that the African Demonstrators, once the valued collaborators of entrepreneurs, came to be seen as hated agents of unjust and arbitrary authority. An African Community Adviser, J.C. Kandiero, looked back in 1976 at the situation as it had existed in Weya and Tanda in the late 1950s:

[In all conservation measures] the people were not consulted, neither was there time to advise these people at grass roots level why this was being done. . . Due to the powers which were at that time instituted . . . people were arrested for failing to comply with the laws of the Land Husbandry Act. Demonstrators were used or behaved like police . . .This did not go without its aftermath. Some people who failed to acquire land or felt the land they were getting was not what they expected moved to Zambia. Those who felt things were unfair or could be improved had to seek for help from legal advisers or found themselves in the hands and advice of the African National Congress which was at that time looking for membership. And thus Weya became a stronghold of the A.N.C. with the motive of fighting against the then Demonstrator who was at that time the field administrator.[46]

Amon Shonge, a long-time nationalist activist in Weya, says:

The people in Weya have been fighting since 1957. Many thousands have been jailed over the years. . .There were some good farmers but they did not have markets. I remember in the 1950s people had to sell their crops to the nearby European farmers who would sell them again at a profit . . .Because they could not sell their crops people did not have money to buy scotch carts. Only a few could qualify as master-farmers. People were anxious to pick up new things but the way they were introduced did not give the people any choice. It was without any good introduction. And also threatening people, fining them, punishing them. This made people very angry. Definitely if there had been a proper agricultural education scheme people would have wanted new things. But when it was forced they would not have it. Since the enemy were using these things the people thought that the only thing to do first was to destroy and then build later.[47]

This was the background to the establishment of the African National Congress in Makoni District from late 1957 onwards. The leading Congress activist in the district was John Mutasa, then farm manager at the co-operative farm which had been developed at St Faith's mission in central Makoni by Guy Clutton-Brock. One of the reasons why Makoni became a leading Congress district was that the influence of the ideas from St Faith's radiated out from it to the primary school teachers of the neighbouring Reserves. But Weya made its own direct contact with Congress as soon as the news filtered through that its inaugural meeting had been held, peasant leaders in Weya sending an emissary to Salisbury to tell George

Nyandoro that they wanted a Congress branch. In September 1982 I interviewed John Mutasa about the early days of nationalism in Makoni. He contrasted the two halves of the district. In Chiduku and Makoni Reserves, where peasants were still clinging to the ideal of successful intensive farming, 'people were very hesitant, so afraid, so doubtful, saying: "These Europeans are very clever, you are surely joking." People would not believe that the organization could assist them. [But] it was widely known that people in Weya, Tanda and Chikore were more hostile to the administration. I knew this because I used to go to buy cattle for St Faith's up there.'[48] So after the Rusape branch, the second branch of Congress in Makoni was formed in Weya, and unlike the schoolteachers and traders who held office in the Rusape branch, the Weya Chairman was 'an old man, now dead, Chigudu, who was just a peasant.'

Despite the greater militancy of the north, however, peasants in Chiduku and Makoni Reserves were themselves beginning to move towards open discontent. Land shortage, as more and more people were pushed into the Reserves, changed the role of the Demonstrators there as well. Demonstrators came to be the effective allocators of land and some extracted bribes for giving a little more land or for not reporting conservation offences. In 1949 Chidakwa, headman of Musengiyina's kraal testified that:

In 1944 my kraal was moved to its present locality in Chiduku Reserve. From 1944 to 1947 I approached Chief Chipunza, on behalf of my kraal, for land for ploughing. I also approached Native Agricultural Demonstrator Tendani . . .In June 1948 I saw a native called Chayipa who gave me a letter from Tendani. As a result of this letter I gave Chayipa the sum of £1.10 . . .I understood that I should be given some land for ploughing if I paid this money . . .Later the Native Commissioner allocated me some land.[49]

Similarly, acting headman Mugodo of Nedewedzo testified that:

Demonstrator Dozen came to me and told me my people had been ploughing in the grazing area and told me to gather all my people together. I did this the next day. A native called Benhanah suggested to me that all the people should pay ten shillings so that they should not be taken to the Native Commissioner's office . . .Dozen Jenje told me that the money would be accepted. I collected ten shillings from each person which amounted to £21 in all. I handed this money to the accused . . .My people continued to plough in the grazing area.[50]

Moreover, 'honest' Demonstrators were acting as policemen to enforce what seemed arbitrary and capricious rulings.

Thus in 1958 there arose an occasion for John Mutasa, Maurice Nyagumbo and the other Congress leaders, to articulate peasant discontent. John Mutasa recalls that:

The Demonstrators were ordering people to uproot all sweet potatoes and telling them that no mixed crops should be found in any land. People were punished if they disobeyed. The peasants became very annoyed and that time we went in very strongly, telling people 'Don't obey, don't obey, don't listen to that Demonstrator'. The instructions had come from Rusape and applied to the whole district. I went with John Ruredzo Makoni and Maurice Nyagumbo to see the local member of parliament, Straw, to ask him why it was happening. He disclaimed any knowledge of it and agreed to meet with us at the District Commissioner's office the following Monday . . .The Native Commissioner also disclaimed all knowledge of the instructions and blamed the Land Development Officer; he also said the rules would be changed. He did not realise that we were officers of Congress; he thought we were members of Chief Makoni's family, come to complain on his behalf. Then we said we would like a meeting with all Chiefs and headmen so that he could explain to them that the rules had been changed and that he had never issued the order. A date was fixed.
So all the Chiefs and headmen gathered, each with their followers and all the kraal-heads, outside the District Commissioner's office. But we talked to them first, telling them about all the evil things the Demonstrators were doing. We told the Chiefs and headmen, 'The D.C. is not your chief. Your chief is Chief Makoni. The D.C. is just your Secretary.' After an hour the D.C. came out and addressed the people saying that the Demonstrators had made a mistake and that he had issued no order. Then I asked Chief Zambe Makoni for permission to speak. The D.C. said 'Ah, no John, you have spoken already at our meeting.' But Zambe gave me permission. So I told the public what the D.C. is, that he is not the Chief. In future, whenever you find any order given that is difficult, don't just go mad and rush to obey it. First of all come to us and find out.
The Native Commissioner was very angry but the people were now very angry too. They started asking difficult questions to the D.C. The D.C. replied 'Ask your Chief.' But Chief Zambe Makoni got up and said that he had not approved the order. 'You have never seen the day when I came to your yard to see how you were planting.' So I said it was no use crying over the past but in future they were to come and ask us. That was the very beginning of having the people in Makoni. They said 'Ah! They can talk to the D.C. like that.' From then on they started to invite us to address meetings. During Congress Makoni had more people supporting the nationalist movement than any other district. The main issue was the way the Demonstrators used to behave; the way the Cattle dip supervisors used to treat the people.[51]

The ban on Congress in 1959 and the detention of the local committee members checked enthusiasm for the movement in southern Makoni. It had little effect in the north. Thomas describes the progress of peasant radicalism there. In Tanda there had only been 150 fully paid-up members of Congress: membership of the successor movement, the National Democratic Party (NDP), rose to 1700 or 62.3 per cent of the adult population. Local leaders were drawn from peasant farmers and:

from among those ambitious young men who could not achieve status and leadership roles in tribal politics or the church. Most of the activists were labour migrants who had retained close rural ties – builders, carpenters, bus-drivers. etc . . .The small educated elite of teachers and businessmen, however, did not provide nationalist leadership in Tanda to the extent which they did in other parts of Rhodesia . . . [since they were] distrusted as outsiders.[52]

In 1961 NDP leaders collected over 1000 rent cards in Tanda and dumped them on the Native Commissioner's desk as a protest 'against taxation of the land. . . .' The embarrassed headman, Maparura, who was 'co-operating well with improved agriculture', hastened to assure the Land Development Officer that 'the action of certain people in this area in refusing to pay Crown Land Tax was entirely without his approval.'[53] A subsequent refusal to dip cattle and pay dipping fees led to the arrest of ten village heads and 300 heads of households. In 1962, now as members of the Zimbabwe African People's Union, nationalist youth in Tanda attacked the local churches for advising moderation. They 'chose to blame the moderates even more than the government'; in October 1962 four churches and three schools were burnt down. 'By 1963,' writes Thomas, 'Tanda was widely known as one of Rhodesia's rural trouble spots.' There were further arrests but 'such repression only led to a further blow-up.' In February 1964 there was 'another mass refusal to dip cattle. This time dip tanks were filled with stones or destroyed. Before the year-long protest was quelled by the arrival of troops in helicopters, 400 cattle-owners were jailed and 3,000 cattle died from tick-borne diseases.'[54]

John Mutasa says that 'it was only at Tanda that such clashes with the Government took place.' One of the Tanda leaders was a Headman, Magwaza; another, Chikomo, had a carpenter's shop in Weya. They were 'very much in command . . .They said to the people, "It is these government men who make us suffer more." '[55] But Weya itself was only a little behind Tanda in its nationalist ardour, and by 1964 many areas of Chiduku were also beginning to move into strong protest. Mhondiwa Remus Rungodo described in 1981 how he became a nationalist activist in western Chiduku. Having worked for many years as a waiter and chef in South African hotels, Remus returned to help run a bakery in Nedewedzo. He soon became involved in politics:

In the 1950s the introduction of soil conservation brought a lot of miseries to many people. They were asked to make contour ridges which took an awful lot of time and fined for not making them to a given standard. People were shifted from their original villages to be concentrated into lines and land allocated into grazing and arable. Often a few acres were allocated to a family. This system led to the reduction of numbers of cattle to be owned by people. Permits were granted to a few. He was unfortunate for he had no dip-card and it was difficult for him to secure one. He had no single head of cattle. . . .He had no plough, nor anything needed in spanning oxen. He brought a second-hand plough from a neighbour . . .He later bought two heads of cattle . . .From these scratchings he has built his home.

In 1960 he heard of a political meeting . . . and he attended. He was influenced by the speeches given but took no active part or response. When another was called for in 1961 by ZAPU they were told by the nationalists addressing the meeting that the 'Boers' were to go together with their oppressive laws. He was fully impressed and at the end of the meeting went to ask one of the nationalists how he could become a member of ZAPU. He was given a receipt book and told to enrol members . . .He enrolled 76 members between April 1961 and September 1962. When ZAPU was banned the affiliated members held meetings in the mountains by day or night. He organised these meetings . . . Then Chief Nedewedzo was murdered. All suspects and prominent nationalists in Dewedzo were rounded up and gathered at Nyahawa dip-tank where they were interrogated and tortured . . .Remus was released in 1964.

Reports by informers often went to Rusape that Remus was continuing to organise political meetings. He was arrested and sent to Gonakudzingwa detention camp in 1966. Between 1964 and 1966 Remus kept in touch with detained nationalists and was often encouraged to go ahead organising and informing ZAPU members in his area about the political developments.[56]

Meanwhile Chief Zambe Makoni, so long regarded by the administration as totally loyal, was taking his own protest action. In February 1963, the District Commissioner wrote that:

Chief Makoni has been allocating land to all and sundry in various Headman's areas, without reference to me . . . [Zambe said] he had done this because he was tired of being faced with demands for land by his people and he considered that many had been allocated unfertile lands and should be permitted to move . . .He blatantly indicated that he was Chief Makoni and as such should have power and authority to allocate land.[57]

In April 1963 the District Commissioner reported interaction between Chief Zambe's defiance and the campaign of the ZAPU 'Land Freedom Farmers', who were moving into grazing land and empty 'European' land as squatters:

Chief Makoni was given explicit instructions by me during February . . .

that he was not empowered to allocate land in Tribal Trust Areas and the practice was to cease immediately. . . Chief Makoni has blatantly ignored the order and continues to allocate land in the grazing area. In doing so he has undermined the authority of this Department, Chief Tandi and Gandanzara. . .

A three day patrol was made by me in the Makoni Tribal Trust Area. Some of the 'LAND FREEDOM FARMERS', in my opinion, genuinely believe that Makoni now has jurisdiction in all land matters. On several occasions, however, people refused to impart information even as to names of Kraals and individuals. They were insolent, contemptuous and uncooperative. On one occasion when talking to people of Chikomwe kraal, several in the background were giving them instructions to . . . refrain from assisting me in my inquiries. Politics are no doubt the main cause of this behaviour, but I am sure a close second is due to Makoni's gradual influence over the people convincing them that he holds all reins of authority in this district.[58]

In August the Secretary for Internal Affairs, together with the Provincial and District Commissioners summoned Zambe for formal rebuke. The late Roland Hatendi, who was present at this interview as interpreter, recalled it in 1981:

The Secretary of Internal Affairs spoke to Zambe in Shona. Zambe would not answer him and asked Hatendi what he said. Hatendi said 'He is speaking to you in your own tongue.' 'Ah, I will not heed him. He speaks like a little child.' So the Secretary had to speak in English. Zambe was allocating lands to young people, just married and with no lands to plough. He said 'I had to take the responsibility of allocating land because you have failed to find my children work in the towns.'[59]

Zambe went on ignoring and counterbalancing Land Husbandry allocations right through the 1960s.

It seems clear, then, that in the open nationalist period most elements in Makoni District were moving into radical opposition to the government over the question of land – the embittered peasants of Weya and Tanda; the returning labour migrants in Chiduku and elsewhere, who found themselves without land or cattle entitlement; Chief Zambe Makoni, outraged both by the curtailment of his traditional rights over land and by the predicament of his people. But what happened after the government sought to bring an end to such opposition with its final ban on the nationalist parties in 1964? Thomas suggests that even in Tanda this ban *did* lead to the sort of inward-turning, non-political disillusionment which has been asserted for other parts of Rhodesia.[60] Peasants had come to support the nationalist movements, it is argued, because of their millenarian promises: when these were proved false, peasants lapsed into apathy and atomism. Thus, Thomas writes, the 'united support for Joshua Nkomo had prevented a spread to Tanda of that internecine warfare between political factions that plagued the country during 1964–5. [But] cowed by fear of police informers and reprisals, they could boast of only one change: the arousal of unrequited discontent.'[61]

My own research in Makoni District suggests that it did not need nationalist politicians to arouse discontent; nor did the banning of the nationalist parties result in a cowed and passive peasantry. Peasants in Makoni had resisted local administrative interference before the establishment of the nationalist parties, and they continued to resist after the nationalist parties were proscribed. On the other hand, the linkage with a national movement, once effected in the late 1950s and early 1960s, had permanent consequences. Peasants did not fall back on purely local traditions of thought and action. The parties may have been banned; many local leaders may have been detained and restricted; but in a very real sense nationalism continued to function at the local level. In Makoni District this meant that the Zimbabwe African People's Union continued to function. The contestation between ZAPU and the challenge of ZANU in 1963 and 1964 was differently resolved from district to district. In Makoni the pioneer nationalists of St Faith's backed ZANU: so did 'nationalist businessmen' in Makoni Reserve, like Maurice Nyagumbo and Columbus Makoni; so did many of the inhabitants of Vengere Township in Rusape; so did a number of secondary school and university students whose families lived in the district. But everyone else continued to back ZAPU, which had come by 1963 to be so closely identified with peasant radicalism. Thus John Mutasa, himself a supporter of ZANU, recalls that 'at the time of the split, especially at Tanda, Weya, Chiduku, ah, they were still very loyal to ZAPU, and from Rugoyi to Gandanzara in Makoni Reserve.'[62]

In Weya and Tanda, where as Thomas remarks energies were not dissipated into fighting between the parties, everyone backed ZAPU and continued to do so long after the formal ban in 1964. Amon Shonge recalls that 'I was ZAPU. In 1963 I remained ZAPU until the boys introduced ZANU into our area in the war, from 1976 onwards. The people were quite deep in ZAPU in Weya. After 1964 everybody supported ZAPU underground . . . They remained ZAPU right up to 1976.'[63]

In the western parts of Chiduku, so Peter Chakanyuka recalls:

By 1963 Dewedzo was fully ZAPU, even the children. When ZAPU was banned there were meetings in the mountains; there was much sabotage;

and the headman was killed because he had given the whites information about ZAPU activities. Many people were arrested and we were beaten ourselves when the headman was killed. People in Dewedzo were anti-government, I can assure you, because they had been mostly moved into that area off the farms . . . Right up to 1970, to the war situation, in fact, the whole area was ZAPU, except for a few secondary students like me. Everybody hated the split, I can assure you.[64]

As for the ZAPU detainees in Nedewedzo, 'when released they met and continued with their activities'.[65]

This underground peasant nationalism was able to organize collective strategies of resistance to the enforcement of agricultural rules. It was also able to make contact with ex-ZAPU national leaders, who continued to operate under the cover of one or other umbrella organization. This comes out most clearly in the case of Weya.

After the banning of the parties in 1964, the administration went into Weya with the intention of restoring its full authority. In December 1969 the District Commissioner reported that:

Weya T.T.L. is one of our endemic problem areas. During the 'Troubles' life was quite difficult there for all Ministries. Since then there has been considerable improvement but all is not yet well. Payments of Personal Tax and later Prescribed Areas Tax were very low, and payments of dip fees were considerably in arrears. Practically all land allocated under Land Husbandry and fully protected with good contours was abandoned and new lands opened up, some on very steep slopes and all unprotected. Part of the rehabilitation campaign has consisted of re-establishing discipline. More tax is being collected; arrears of dip fees have been considerably reduced; the Land Inspectorate has been active and have stopped 95% of stream bank cultivation; patient persuasion has resulted in half the arable area being pegged and contoured.[66]

The District Commissioner believed that the majority of the population was prepared to co-operate but that there remained 'a core of dissidents'. But all other evidence suggests that these 'dissidents' commanded the backing of the great majority of Weya peasants.

A later District Commissioner evaluated the 'rehabilitation campaign' more realistically. 'For the next ten years from 1965,' wrote Bickersteth in December 1975:

the Administration . . . reacted violently to any apparent opposition by the tribesmen, by mounting large-scale exercises to 'beat some sense into the tribesmen', which, although in the short term has proved successful, in the long term has been of doubtful benefit, and tends to make the tribesman more dissatisfied than he was before . . . We have tribesmen in Weya who see the Administration in all its forms as an enemy who attempts to thwart their aspirations. They are distrustful of anything Government does.[67]

At the end of 1976 the African Community Advisor, J.C. Kandiero, looked back on what had happened after the Rhodesia Front government had abandoned the Land Husbandry Act and restored powers over land to the chiefs. This had been intended to buy off peasant opposition and to placate chiefs like Zambe. But:

When land power was given to Chiefs this was done with very short notice and very few people at village level knew exactly why this was being done. The then leaders (political) told people a battle had been won. The demonstrators no more had powers. What followed – Despondency, unco-operation, illegal land allocations, ignoring the Chiefs. No conservation and destruction. [When] Government adopts Community Development as policy the concept was not at home with many Government Departments and some did not accept or realise its long term effect. Inasmuch that by 1976 this had not reached the people of Weya Reserve who still think they have to be fathered OR OPPOSE AND RESIST. . . More powers for the Chief came to end up nowhere but in the brain of the politician who believed and told people he was responsible for the changes.[68]

Thus neither administrative authoritarianism nor concessions over Land Husbandry managed to break the radicalism of Weya. Moreover, the leaders of 'dissidence' were not landless young men or itinerant traders but members of the chiefly family, headmen and male peasant elders. When Chief Chendambuya died in July 1970, it was reported that 'the younger brother is very anti-government and known to be under the influence of ex-restrictees'; no acting Chief nor any successor acceptable to the administration could be found because the Chendambuya family were believed to be strong supporters of ZAPU.[69] In December 1969 five Weya headmen presented their grievances to the *Rhodesia Herald* which publicized them under the headline 'Headman Tell of Unemployed African Youth'. Headman Pitirosi Chibanda:

apparently acted as leader. The investigating District Assistant reports that . . . he was told that their complaints were that:
(a) They were being chased off the land by Government and Missions just at the start of the rainy season:
(b) There was a general shortage of money for tax and school fees;
(c) They are being forced by Government to dig contours;
(d) Many children are leaving school because of lack of money . . .
(f) School leavers unable to find work, having no money to pay taxes and therefore unable to be granted lands.[70]

Reflecting on all this, the District Commissioner concluded that 'Weya can be defined as a problem area, it has been such for a long time and . . . will continue to remain so until some sort of tribal authority is established.'[71]

But Weya opposition was yet more deeply rooted. In March 1976 J.C. Kandiero was posted there 'to study the general life of people living in Weya Reserve, causing acute resistance and ignoring of Government employees.' Although he reported that the kraal heads 'tended to hold up information or reject my doing this survey', he reached some general conclusions. He found that the key leaders of Weya opinion and opponents of the administration were male elders over 40 years old:

These are the people who mainly retain the traditional life of the kraal . . . and [are] commonly very resistant to change. These elders are usually left alone at home to look after a chain of daughter in laws, and the organising of all family affairs. These, forming 0.3% of the registered male population, usually have a very regulating effect on change . . . Because of their continuity at home you will find these on Kraalhead *dares*, School Boards, Church leaders etc. . . You will find the over 40s have a big influence for they are usually the ones with land, house and cattle. At the present moment sons getting married get land and cattle from their fathers. This is a reason why sons look at their fathers with respect as compared to the kraalhead if there is no extra land for the kraalhead to allocate. Fathers have retained their Land Husbandry allocations for their sons . . . You will find it is still the same [man] who has been in the area for a longer time who has much land. This land is usually reserved for the sons. When the people moved to plough in the grazing, they retained the right of ownership for their Land Husbandry allocations. It is in these allocations that the peasants are now allocating their married sons . . . Headmen are usually pushed around by some of their kraalheads and at times fall victims of ignorance and yield to useless ideas. This poses a main threat of resistance. I have seen most of the final decisions at their *dare* Chendambuya come from none but the most talkative kraalheads. The kraalheads are usually a one man's band and usually impose their feeling to the people.[72]

However active the young men may have been in the days of the ZAPU Youth League and were again to become during the guerrilla war, the core of peasant radical nationalism in Weya were the resident elders, determined to retain their hold on plots in the grazing land and determined to resist official interference with their farming. By the early 1970s the situation in Weya was again one of critical confrontation. Moreover, the elders retained their capacity to call on outside assistance. One man to whom they appealed was a labour migrant from Weya, Amon Shonge, a supporter of ZAPU and a member of the communal agricultural enterprise at Cold

Comfort Farm near Salisbury. Emissaries from Weya travelled to Cold Comfort to report authoritarian enforcement of agricultural rules. Shonge recalls that the:

Native Commissioner had sent messengers to burn gardens at Chimutuwa kraal, Weya. I went there specially to collect information about it and to help the people. The kraalheads were called to Cold Comfort Farm to consult lawyers. This was in 1970. In 1969 I had written a circular in Shona on the problems of Weya and sent it to influential leaders there. I wrote about forced labour in Weya, mentioning contour ridges and the harassment of the people. I said that it was the intention of the Smith Government to take those without land and put them in a location in Headlands or Macheke to provide cheap labour . . . When Cold Comfort was closed down in January 1971 the police searched everywhere and found these circulars. So I was arrested . . . because I had told the people that we should refuse these things.[73]

And refuse them they did. When the Land Inspector with African administrative assistants and some of Chief Makoni's councillors went to Chimutuwa's kraal in October 1970 to destroy gardens made along the stream-banks, acting Chief Chendambuya refused to guide them there:

He said 'I am not going to work with you.' I asked him why and he said he was afraid of the people. I asked whether he is no longer going to carry out his work as Leader of a tribe and he said 'Yes, I feel I am not concerned now' . . . It was obvious to us that Chief Chendambuya is not cooperating with either ourselves or the Government and further he is siding with his people in everything that goes on in his area.

People at Chimutuwa's kraal resisted the destruction of their gardens and a Chief's Messenger was assaulted with a hoe:

This non-cooperation existing among the Weya people was proved by us when we went to Charambawamwe kraal . . . One man started beating a drum, the action which was uncalled for. The other picked up a stick and beat it on the ground. The other asked me . . . does a judge ever execute a pregnant woman? The women at Chimutuwa said the Land Inspector is a Chombe and Smith. The other said such an act can only be done by Aliens and not people in your position of Chiefs. One Mangwiro said, Do you *Machinda* [Councillors] think that what you are doing pleases the country?[74]

But the best insight into Weya peasant radicalism at this time (and into its links with nationalist leadership) is provided by Arthur Chadzingwa's letters to Guy Clutton-Brock. Chadzingwa, a ZAPU leader, had initiated a body called the African Peoples Association

– 'an attempt to get the people united and active at ground level.'
On its behalf, and later in the name of the African National Council,
Chadzingwa 'travelled through the rural areas [and] so gained a
good knowledge of the peasant particularly.' On 6 July 1971 he
wrote to Clutton-Brock:

The people at Weya have for the past month been subjected to a reign of
terror. Several men have been detained at Rusape for questioning. This
includes some of those who have been to Gonakudzingwa [restrictees]. The
police are saying Weya people are holding illegal meetings in the mountains, that they collect money for the legal defence of people like Amon
who fall into trouble, and that it is due to considerable agitation that many
of the men and women refuse to pay fines, preferring to go to prison. What
has annoyed the authorities is that while some of the people claim to be too
poor to pay fines, they deposit considerable amounts with the prison
authorities for safekeeping when they go in . . . Earlier this year I had to
ask the lawyer pursuing the matter of the burned down gardens to slow
down as we were not able to pay. Last week I asked him to keep the case
alive. . .

I must say straight away that legal aid will always be necessary in this
struggle. As much as possible we shall be cautious and impress upon the
people that it is not the lawyers who will solve our problems for us but a
preparedness on our part to make a stand openly. However we do come
against cases which need legal backing to strengthen the hand of the people
or in certain cases to keep useful people in circulation.[75]

Chadzingwa's assessment was even more correct than he realized. In December 1971 an event took place which was to lead to a
law case that greatly embarrassed the regime and gave the peasant
radicals of Weya their greatest victory before the guerrilla war.
Chadzingwa wrote that:

There were arrests in Weya on the 16th of November involving about
eleven people. On the 23rd of November 9 of them were convicted under
the Conservation Act and fined 30 dollars to 70 dollars. This was for not
having completed making their contour ridges . . . The Land Inspector,
Botha, is just being vindictive. The people chose to go to jail . . . However
they were given until the 7th of December to get the money. On that day the
people said they would rather go to jail. The magistrate imposed the fine
. . . by seizing cattle. Abel Tadokera who got the highest sentence . . . is
appealing.[76]

It turned out that Tadokera's case raised very important issues. The
administration in Makoni had continued to issue and enforce
conservation orders after the death of Chief Chendambuya but
under the law enacted by the Rhodesia Front government no conservation order was valid unless made by a Native Land Authority

under a Chief. The administration had chosen not to appoint a new Chendambuya because of the ZAPU sympathies of the chiefly lineages, and as a result, complained the District Commissioner, 'this office is in the position of having virtually no tribal structure through which normal day to day administration can be routed . . . The Lands Inspectorate and conservation staff in this Ministry are finding it virtually impossible to achieve any progress . . . having no tribal land authority as such to work through.'[77] As a result, also, the conservation orders and the fines imposed for breach of them were all invalid in law.

In February 1972 the presiding judge adjourned the case because, as Chadzingwa wrote:

he wants the full bench of judges and the Chief Justice. He wants the Attorney General to lead the prosecution. . . The reason why a simple peasant's appeal has been blown to such proportions is as follows. Our main grounds of appeal is that the order which led to the prosecutions . . . requires that the chief must be consulted before it is issued. Now there is no chief in Weya . . . If we were to succeed this would cost the regime a lot because it has already acted on 1,600 people. Thus they intend to invoke the doctrine of necessity which was used to justify the Smith regime as de facto and then as de jure . . . The matter is well in hand.[78]

It was. Tadokera won his appeal. On 8 June 1972 his conviction and sentence were set aside; so also were those of many other Weya men, including kraalhead Chimutuwa.[79] The District Commissioner gloomily admitted a major defeat:

There is no-one suitable in Weya TTL who can be appointed to act as Chief at the moment and command the support of the people. However, the work of the administration must go on. Tadokera and his fellow nationalist politicians have scored a victory and much of the good work achieved in conserving the arable land in this area during 1971 will be lost unless it can be seen that someone possesses the authority to enforce compliance with the law. I add at this stage to reinforce my point – that money to pay for Tadokera's appeal came from outside Rhodesia. Tadokera together with half a dozen or so former restrictees have since the fifties gone out of their way to hinder and obstruct the efforts of Government agencies operating in Weya and no doubt fired by this recent individual success and that of the nationalist factor as a whole in the rejection of the settlement proposals, will now be even more impossible to deal with.[80]

In fact in early 1973 all agricultural staff and African administrative assistants were withdrawn from Weya 'in view of the lack of interest and co-operation shown in the area.'[81] The Weya kraalheads, reported a police patrol, 'are now happy that the Field

Assistants were moved away from Weya to Chikore and Tanda TTL because they did not want them there. It seems to encourage the politically minded to be able to tell other people that they have chased them away from that area with their own power.'[82]

Thereafter the administration constantly planned 'to get the Agricultural Demonstrators back into Weya.'[83] They could find no rapid solution of the dilemma of the missing Native Land Authority. 'I have kept the inhabitants of Weya in isolation,' wrote the District Commissioner in February 1974, 'to such an extent that they now suspect some dastardly Government plan and are reported to have prepared themselves to counter that plan by being as co-operative as possible with the Authorities.'[84]. In reality, as he knew only too well, the peasants of Weya rejoiced in their immunity from interference. 'I have refrained from exercising any powers, allegedly vested in me as the tribal land authority,' he went on, 'for without doubt the traditional leaders and heads of kraals would refuse to support me.' No solution had been found by January 1975 when District Commissioner Bickersteth urged the abolition of the Chendambuya chiefship and the incorporation of the area into Chief Makoni's sphere of authority. This should be done 'as soon as possible to avoid any further likelihood of the many African Nationalists who live in the area being able to undermine the tribal authority. This area is near to the "Operational Area" and a tribal structure must be in operation without any due delay if we are to have any tribal government to combat terrorism.'[85] That same month, 'Warning to Report Terrorists' notices were posted throughout Weya.

Weya was put under Chief Makoni in May 1975 and in June the District Commissioner met with the Regional Land Inspector and the officer commanding the police to discuss how to enforce conservation in Weya. They were very cautious – they knew that once they knocked 'this bee-hive, the people will be galvanised into taking retaliatory action.' So 'it was considered undesirable at this present stage to transfer Demonstrators into Weya, as their role will be misinterpreted by tribesmen . . . We just cannot afford to make another mistake.'[86] Nothing had in fact been done by the end of 1975. In March 1976 Kandiero was sent to Weya to report on how peasant opposition might be overcome. He recommended that no agricultural officer should be seen to be linked with prosecutions:

Possible Resistance . . . At the moment there is quite a lot of ploughing in prohibited areas . . . The people might use this as a weapon when they are prosecuted that it is due to the E/A. Group approach to begin with would meet with direct resistance . . . [We need a man] popular with the people

. . . very current and conversant and able to mix up with different societies . . . The Land Inspectors should make use of the kraalheads and Headmen as much as they can. This would relinquish the E/A from any involvement of prosecution on conservation matters.[87]

But no such paragon had been found by December 1976 by which time guerrillas had established themselves in Weya. Aided by local peasant nationalists they attacked and damaged an administrative base.

Goaded beyond endurance, the District Commissioner abandoned the kid-glove approach to Weya. 'Whether it is terrorists or the locals who are responsible for the damage to the base,' he reported, 'it is my opinion that we must re-establish control over this T.T.L. forthwith. To fail to do so will mean that the locals will now receive confirmation that they can get away with virtually anything.' He suggested that all peasants in Weya be moved into protected villages; that fines be levied to compensate for the damage done; and a curfew imposed.[88] The protected villages were not set up. It was in any case too late: 'Right from the beginning,' says Amon Shonge, 'people knew that if the comrades got into Weya they could never be got out.'[89]

I have concentrated on Weya because of the remarkably full documentation available for the struggle of its peasant radicals. But much the same story could be reconstructed for Tanda, which was noted as a 'difficult area' for the administration throughout the 1960s; where nationalist meetings continued to be held 'very much under cover' right up to 1976; and where Headman Makumbe joined with the nationalist politicians to frustrate conservation enforcement. In July 1972 the District Commissioner reported that:

Makumbe's conservation met at the Rest Camp by themselves and talked about the possible implementation of a grazing scheme in the whole area, then went off to Makumbe with their plans. Makumbe called a meeting of all kraalheads on the 12th. Naison Chatsama, John Chigodoro and Onias Muwuru amongst others spoke up against the scheme, saying that the Committee should concern themselves with contours and nothing more. Makumbe was not strong enough to support his committee. Makumbe then told those present of the increase in dip fees. Before explaining the reasons for this he asked the people for their views. Garikayi Magwaza was the main speaker, saying people would pay no more than 30 cents and that they would all go and see the District Commissioner about this at the Sub Office . . . All Kraalheads have been told to produce 50 cents so that a lawyer can be engaged to fight the increase in dip fees . . . The political progress of this area is being thwarted by the efforts of nationalist politicians. Chatsama, Chigodoro, Magwaza and crowd, are proving to be the stumbling block to all efforts towards progress . . . Headman Makumbe would appear to be afraid of these people and thus to be on their side.[90]

It was reported that 'African National Council meetings are taking place throughout Makumbe's area but very much under cover'; when the time to collect the new dip fees came 'there was no-one present. By 1030 hours one kraalhead only had arrived. He refused to pay saying that he was not prepared to be the first to pay, that the Headman and other known politically oriented kraals must also pay before he did . . . Neither Headman Makumbe, his Messenger or anyone from his kraal attended or paid dip fees; in addition some 22 other kraalheads, including all the nationalist types, failed to attend.'[91]

The evidence for Makoni and Chiduku TTLs is more scattered but what there is suggests strongly that the story there too was one of continued underground organization. Moreover, the popular pressure upon chiefs and headmen ensured that many of them showed sympathy with peasant nationalism. During the 1970s the Rhodesia Front administration embarked upon the policy of building up 'traditional' authority and erecting a 'tribal government' structure which they could present as the legitimate alternative to nationalism. Chief Zambe Makoni died in August 1970 and the administration sought a more accommodating successor, whom they could make use of as the keystone of this traditionalist edifice. In May 1975 they sent Chief Muzanenamo Makoni to attend military demonstrations held in Weya and Tanda with the intention of overawing the radicals of those areas. The Chief rubbed home the message:

What has been demonstrated here is very great power. We have been left trembling with fear and are indeed very much afraid. We have heard that our children are fighting in the bush. We would question how they can fight people who fight on the ground as well as from the air . . . I wonder what our fate would be if, say, these bombs were directed on our houses. We would definitely be left hopeless and indeed dead. Let us now work and live in co-operation and peace.[92]

But Muzanenamo Makoni was not prepared to stand aside from his people's grievances over land. In mid 1975 many people were evicted from Rusape into a new township, Sansaguru. The District Commissioner asked Chief Makoni how he intended to govern the new settlement. Makoni replied that:

he did not remove the people from the area; Government had done so, and should he now take part in the administration of that area, the people would accuse him of having forced them out and would kill him. This, of course, alludes to the murder in 1960 of Headman Nedewedzo, who was killed by African nationalists in the height of the political uncertainty. We have the same position pertaining now. The Chief has obviously decided that the best horse to support is that of the African nationalists. It is therefore apparent that the Government must give a firm lead, so that the African people and their leaders can see that we intend to govern.[93]

It is time to return to the contrast developed by Buijtenhuijs. Plainly at the peasant level it is quite untrue to say that the struggle in Zimbabwe was not focused on the 'stolen lands'. I wrote earlier in this book that the loss of lands to the whites in the 1890s was not bitterly resented in the memory of Makoni elders because the peasant option had still remained open. The loss of land in the 1940s *was* bitterly resented, most of all in those areas of infertility and remoteness where the peasant choice was impossible from the first moment of eviction and resettlement, but also in areas like Chiduku whose prosperity gradually fell away from the 1950s on as population pressure and destocking took their effect. In Makoni District during the guerrilla war, which raged there from 1976 to 1980, the claim to the lost lands was both the ideological and the practical focus of resistance. One of the most popular Chimurenga songs in Makoni during the war runs in translation as follows:

They came to Zimbabwe from Germany, America, Britain, fleeing from hunger in their own lands, seeing it was a black land, full of milk and honey. *Our* land, we the black people. . . At first they came to hunt, then went home, these oppressors. People like Selous spied upon our life here in Zimbabwe so as to pave the way for their kith and kin who were to follow. It was not long before we saw them moving into our land of Zimbabwe. These oppressors were arrogant people, people with long trousers, who thought only of themselves and cared nothing for the Zimbabwean people, who were the rightful owners of the land . . . So we showed the people of Zimbabwe that when the oppressor is seen acting in such a manner it is time for him to go home; where his troubles are many and the women are lazy . . .

One day the District Commissioner gathered all the people in the village and amongst them was a ZANU comrade. The D.C. said 'We need to talk about these terrorists. A terrorist is a bad person' . . . The comrade stood up, the child of the soil, and began to question: 'What does this terrorist say he wants?' 'He wants the land'. . . 'O.K., oppressor, listen to what I have to say. I have some questions to ask'. The comrade goes and stands beside the *msasa* tree and asks 'Are not the tree and I similar in appearance?' The oppressor answers 'Yes.' Then the comrade stretches himself out in the grass, under the *mutondo* and *mupfuti* trees, and again they are similar. 'O.K., oppressor. I ask you to do exactly what I have done.' The oppressor goes and stands against the tree and the contrast is obvious. Therefore the answer is 'No – you do *not* belong to this land as we do.'[94]

As for the tactics of the war in Makoni, these consisted in putting the white farmlands under unendurable pressure, and in particular the white farm and ranch lands which had been established in the 1940s. As David Caute has written:

In June 1896, at the outset of the Shona rising, a triangle of territory . . . had become a place of terror: from Macheke to Mayo (at the apex of the triangle), then down to Headlands and, further south, Rusape, the whites had been compelled to evacuate their farms. Until the early months of 1976 the guerrilla war scarcely penetrated the triangle, but in August of that year the police post at Mayo was hit by a rocket . . . The belt of European farming land round Mayo lay trapped between tribal trust lands . . . Mangwende to the west, Weya to the south, Tanda to the east. Sandbags were now piled against bedroom walls.[95]

From out of Weya and Tanda came the guerrillas in attacks on farm compounds and farm houses; from out of Weya and Tanda came the sons and daughters of the peasant elders in attacks on standing crops and cattle. Back they poured in raids on their old lands – Mayo, Rathcline, Inyati Block, just as peasants from out of Chiduku raided the European farms from which they too had been evicted. It was of course the coming of the guerrillas that made this counterattack on the whites possible, but it was their deep concern for their lost lands that made these people, who had been 'ZAPU in their hearts' up to the 1970s, support the ZANLA guerrillas and so provide the additional manpower which broke all white farming in the district, save for the longest established and most productive.

NOTES

1 Robert Buijtenhuijs, *Essays on Mau Mau. Contributions to Mau Mau Historiography* (Leiden: African Studies Centre, Research Report No. 17, 1982), p. 207.
2 ibid., p. 217.
3 ibid., p. 143.
4 Memorandum by W.S. Bazely, Native Commissioner, Umtali, 1 October 1937, file S.1542.L4, 1933/1935, National Archives, Harare (NAH).
5 Terence Ranger, 'Missionaries, migrants and the Manyika: the invention of ethnicity in Zimbabwe', Paper presented to International Conference on the History of Ethnic Awareness in Southern Africa, Charlottesville, April 1983.
6 Annual Report, Makoni, 1944, file S.1563, NAH.
7 Annual Report, Makoni, 1945, file S.1563, NAH.
8 Annual Report, Makoni, 1946, S.1563, NAH.
9 Annual Report, Makoni, 1947, S.1563, NAH.

10 Evidence of Native Commissioner Stead to the Natural Resources Board Native Enquiry, 13 July 1942, file S.988, NAH.
11 Douglas Aylen, 'Conserving soil in the native reserves', *Rhodesia Agricultural Journal*, vol. 39 (May/June 1942), pp. 152-60.
12 Evidence of K.J. McKenzie to Natural Resources Board Native Enquiry, 19 November 1942, S.988, NAH.
13 Evidence of Chief Native Commissioner, 19 November 1942, S.988, NAH.
14 Land Development Officer Gorringe, Rusape to Native Commissioner, Rusape, 19 July 1949, S.160.GC1–GC2, NAH.
15 Provincial Agricultural Officer, Manicaland, Monthly Report, August 1951, file S.160.AGR.4/6/51, NAH.
16 Monthly Report, L.D.O., South Rusape, July 1952, file S.160.AGR.4/6/51, NAH.
17 Acting Provincial Agriculturalist, Manicaland to Director of Native Agriculture, 26 September 1953, S.160.AGR.4/6/51, NAH.
18 Interview with Father Peter Turner, Umtali, 14 March 1981.
19 Interview between Peter Chakanyuka and Mbidzeni Luciah, Nedewedzo, 18 January 1981.
20 Interview between Peter Chakanyuka and Mandironda Beatrice, Nedewedzo, 1 February 1981.
21 Annual Report, Makoni, 1942, file S.1563, NAH.
22 Annual Report, Makoni, 1948, S.1563, NAH.
23 N.E. Thomas, 'Christianity, politics and the Manyika' (Boston University: PhD thesis, 1968) pp. 83–4.
24 ibid., citing Native Commissioner, Rusape to Provincial Native Commissioner, Umtali, 3 April 1950, file GN 202/45, District Commissioner's office, Rusape.
25 ibid., pp. 87–8.
26 Minutes of Natives Advisory Board enclosed in Chief Land Officer to Chief Agriculturalist, 11 February 1950, file S.160.DMW.2/12/51, NAH.
27 Thomas, 'Christianity, politics and the Manyika', drawing on Native Commissioner, Makoni to African applicant for land in Tanda, 15 November 1947, file GN 202/45, District Commissioner's office, Rusape.
28 Minutes of the Native Land Board, 28 April 1950, file S.160.DMW.2/12/51, NAH.
29 Minutes of the Native Land Board, 29 and 30 April 1951, file S.160.DMW.2/12/51, NAH.
30 Thomas, 'Christianity, politics and the Manyika', p. 85
31 'Memorandum for Native Land Board. Points arising out of Tanda Correspondence', Chief Land Officer; see also 'Memorandum for Native Land board. Matters arising out of Tanda Division Correspodence', Acting Director of Native Agriculture, 1952, file S.160.DMW.2/12/51, NAH.
32 Minutes of Native Affairs Advisory Board, 21 and 22 September 1954, file S.160. DMN.2/33/53, NAH.

33 Minutes of the Native Land Board, 21 April 1952, file S.160.DMW.2/ 12/51, NAH.
34 Monthly Report, Land Development Officer, Rusape North, September 1952, file S.160.AGR.4/6/51, NAH.
35 Monthly Report, Land Development Officer, Rusape North, September 1953, file S.160.AGR.4/6/51, NAH.
36 Thomas 'Christianity, politics and the Manyika', p. 86.
37 Tanda TTL General Report, The Maparura Headmanship and Community, The Makumbe Headmanship and Community, Delineation of Communities, Makoni District, November/December 1965, pp. 78–81. I am grateful to Professor Marshall Murphree for making available to me his copies of the Delineation Reports.
38 District Commissioner, Makoni, to Officer Commanding, British South African Police, Rusape, 31 December 1975, file 'Weya/ Chendambuya', District Commissioner's office, Rusape (DCOR). When I was carrying out field research in Makoni in 1980/81 there were still many files in the District Office; I was able to work on those relating to chiefs, headmen and spirit mediums. There are now no files for the period prior to 1980 in the District Office; they are reported to have been sent to the Ministry of Local Government, though I do not know if all the material I saw in Rusape has reached there.
39 Annual Report, Makoni, 1938; Annual Report, Makoni, 1940, file S.1563, NAH.
40 Provincial Agriculturalist, Umtali, to Director of Native Agriculture, 13 April 1951; Director of Native Agriculture to Provincial Agriculturalist, 9 June 1951, file LS 101/3/50, NAH. According to the Director there were at this date 1253 families in Weya.
41 Officer Commanding, British South African Police, Umtali to Provincial Native Commissioner, Umtali, 23 August 1951; Native Commissioner to Provincial Native Commissioner, 29 August 1951, file 'Weya/ Chendambuya', DCOR.
42 Monthly Report, Land Development Officer, Rusape North, March 1953, file S.160.AGR.4/6/51, NAH.
43 Thomas, 'Christianity, politics and the Manyika', p. 88, citing Native Commissioner, Rusape to Provincial Native Commissioner, Umtali, 10 September 1951, file GN 202/45, DCOR.
44 Monthly Report, Land Development Officer, Rusape North, February 1952, file S.160.AGR.4/6/51, NAH.
45 Monthly Reports, L.D.O., Rusape North, October and November 1952, file S.160.AGR.4/6/51, NAH.
46 J.C. Kandiero, General Report on Weya, October 1976, file 'Weya/ Chendambuya', DCOR.
47 Interview with Amon Shonge, Weya, 25 March 1981.
48 Interview with John Mutasa, Makoni, 11 September 1982.
49 Evidence of Chidakwa, Rex versus Dozen, 29 July 1949, file S.1695. 1949, NAH.
50 Evidence of Mugodo, Rex versus Dozen, 25 July 1949, file S.1695.1949, NAH.

51   Interview with John Mutasa, Makoni, 11 September 1982.
52   Thomas 'Christianity, politics and the Manyika', pp. 111–12.
53   Land Development Officer, Rusape North, to Native Commissioner, Rusape, 13 April 1961, file 'Headman Maparura', DCOR.
54   Thomas, 'Christianity, politics and the Manyika, p. 114.
55   Interview with John Mutasa, Makoni, 11 September 1982.
56   Interview between Peter Chakanyuka and Mhondiwa Remus Rungodo, Nedewedzo, 30 January 1981.
57   District Commissioner, Rusape, to Provincial Commissioner, Manicaland, 28 February 1963, file 'Makoni', DCOR.
58   District Commissioner, Rusape, to Provincial Commissioner, Manicaland, 29 April 1963, file 'Makoni', DCOR.
59   Interview with Roland Hatendi, Tandi, 21 February 1981. The late Roland Hatendi was the leading local historian of the Makoni chiefship. He had written a manuscript history of the chieftancy which was unfortunately destroyed by fire. The District Commissioner's files on chiefs, however, are full of Hatendi's historical and ethnographic reports. I had several interviews with him in which he patiently answered questions on matters which he did not regard as properly historical. I regret very much that he will not be able to read this book.
60   Peter Fry, *Spirits of Protest. Spirit-mediums and the Articulation of Consensus among the Zezuru of Southern Rhodesia (Zimbabwe)* (Cambridge: 1976). Fry writes: 'Prior to the banning of the African Nationalist parties in 1964 . . . the Africans of Chiota were confident that majority rule would soon be established in Rhodesia . . . However, after the events of 1964 and 1965 hope turned almost to despair.' (p. 120).
61   Thomas, 'Christianity, politics and the Manyika', p. 115.
62   Interview with John Mutasa, Makoni, 11 September 1982. Columbus Makoni, now a ZANU MP told me on 30 January 1981, how he had been driven out of Makoni Reserve and had to take refuge in Umtali because of his support for ZANU in 1964. 'Maurice Nyagumbo was very much hated for his ZANU politics then. Today everyone in Makoni is ZANU. They talk about the glory of ZANU, ZANU. Now at home Maurice Nyagumbo's glory is wonderful. The people began to see the light in the 1970s and especially when the guerrillas came.'
63   Interview with Amon Shonge, Weya, 25 March 1981.
64   Interview with Peter Chakanyuka, Harare, 29 March 1981.
65   Interview between Peter Chakanyuka and Mhondiwa Remus Rungodo, 30 January 1981.
66   District Commissioner to Provincial Commisioner, 9 December 1969, file 'Weya/Chendambuya', DCOR.
67   District Commissioner, Rusape to Officer Commanding, British South Africa Police, Rusape, 31 December 1975, file 'Weya/Chendambuya', DCOR.
68   J.C. Kandiero, General Report on Weya, October 1976, file 'Weya/Chendambuya', DCOR.
69   District Commissioner, Rusape to Secretary, Internal Affairs, 2

February 1971, file 'Weya/Chendambuya', DCOR. See also District Commissioner, Rusape, to Provincial Native Commissioner, 29 January 1971: 'No acting appointment has been recommended to date as the man suggested is not acceptable due to his anti-government attitude. The position as far as this individual is concerned continues to deteriorate. Latest intelligence reports indicate his increased involvement with former restrictees.'

70   District Commissioner, Rusape to Provincial Commissioner, 9 December 1969, file 'Weya/Chendambuya', DCOR.
71   District Commissioner, Rusape to Provincial Commissioner, 29 January 1971, file 'Weya/Chendambuya', DCOR.
72   J.C. Kandiero, 'Analysis. Kraal Information for Development Purposes', Weya, 28 August to 21 October 1976, file 'Weya/Chendambuya', DCOR.
73   Interview with Amon Shonge, Weya, 25 March 1981.
74   'Soil Conservation Report – Weya T.T.L'. Statement of Leonard Murumbi, Takundwa Edward and Muchira, October 1970, file 'Weya/Chendambuya', DCOR.
75   Arthur Chadzingwa to Guy Clutton-Brock, 6 July 1971, Clutton-Brock correspondence, 1970–80. Several files of correspondence between Guy Clutton-Brock and nationalist leaders are in the possession of the author and will eventually be deposited in the National Archives, Harare. I am very grateful to Guy for allowing me to use this material.
76   Arthur Chadzingwa to Guy Clutton-Brock, 16 December 1971, Clutton-Brock correspondence, 1970–80.
77   District Commissioner, Rusape to Provincial Commissioner, 29 January 1971, file 'Weya/Chendambuya', DCOR.
78   Arthur Chadzingwa to Guy Clutton-Brock, 20 February 1972, Clutton-Brock correspondence, 1970–80.
79   Acting Director of Public Prosecutions to Scanlen and Holderness, 7 August 1972; Scanlen and Holderness to District Commissioner, Rusape, 10 August 1972, file 'Weya/Chendambuya'. See also Arthur Chadzingwa to Guy Clutton-Brock, 17 June 1972, Clutton-Brock correspondence, 1970–80.
80   District Commissioner, Rusape to Provincial Commissioner, n.d., 1972, file 'Weya/Chendambuya', DCOR.
81   Minute, 'Justification for removal of A/Ds from Weya', 2 February 1973, file 'Weya/Chendambuya', DCOR.
82   Provincial Special Branch officer to P.C., 4 January 1973.
83   District Commissioner, Rusape to Provincial Commissioner, 13 March 1973, file 'Weya/Chendambuya', DCOR.
84   District Commissioner, Rusape to Provincial Commissioner, 4 February 1974, file 'Weya/Chendambuya', DCOR.
85   District Commissioner, Rusape to Provincial Commissioner, 24 January 1975, file 'Weya/Chendambuya', DCOR.
86   District Commissioner, Rusape to Provincial Commissioner, 24 June 1975, file 'Weya/Chendambuya', DCOR.

87 J.C. Kandiero, 'Analysis', file 'Weya/Chendambuya', DCOR.
88 District Commissioner, Rusape to Assistant District Commissioner, 21 December 1976, file 'Weya/Chendambuya', DCOR.
89 Interview with Amon Shonge, Weya, 25 March 1981.
90 District Commissioner Rusape to Provincial Commissioner, 26 July 1972, file 'Headman Makumbe', DCOR.
91 ibid., citing Report no. 6/V1/72.
92 Speech by Chief Makoni, Tanda, 1 May 1975, enclosed in B.P.Kaschula, Combined Services Anti-Terrorist Psychological Operations, to District Commissioner, Rusape, 29 May 1975. Chief Makoni's speeches in Tanda and Weya were printed in Shona and in English translation and circulated widely in the district, DCOR.
93 District Commissioner, Rusape to Provincial Commissioner, 18 July 1975, file 'Makoni', DCOR.
94 'Maruza vapambi pfumi', collected at Mukute, Weya.
95 David Caute, *Under the Skin. The Death of White Rhodesia* (London: 1983), pp. 43–4.

5

Mau Mau, FRELIMO and the Zimbabwean guerrilla war: ideology

In Chapter 4 I completed my historical narrative of the peasant experience on the Shona-speaking plateau of Zimbabwe. By the time the guerrilla war began, I have argued, peasants had a long tradition of understanding what had been done to them. They knew that their land had been taken in order to establish white commercial farming and ranching; they knew that the Rhodesian state had discriminated in favour of white agriculture and had intervened in their own production in intolerable ways. Locally they fought during the guerrilla war for the recovery of their lost lands; nationally they desired a transformed state – a state that would back black farming against white, rather than the other way round. This transformed state would no longer interfere in peasant production but would content itself with ensuring high prices, good marketing facilities, supplies of cheap fertilizer and so on. *This* was the nature of peasant class consciousness by the 1970s and it was fully adequate to sustaining the horrors of a guerrilla war, even if it may not prove adequate to sustain and increase agricultural productivity in an independent Zimbabwe.

During the war the guerrillas encouraged this type of consciousness. They intensified the sense of resentment over the lost lands; generalized it by showing how land alienation had affected everyone in the whole country; and promised that when a ZANU/PF government had come to power the lost lands would be returned. But they did not seek to transform peasant consciousness so far as land or agricultural production was concerned. I found no evidence to suggest that in Makoni District the guerrillas preached the virtues of collective or even of co-operative farming: Amon Shonge, who was working with a handful of others in a communal farming project in Weya all through the 1970s, had to explain what they were up to to guerrilla bands initially suspicious of the idea though in the end the guerrillas became warmly supportive. In August 1982 I interviewed one of the young men who left Makoni District to cross over into Mozambique for training as a guerrilla. Caston Makoni lived on Makoni Farm, the area immediately around Chief Muzanenamo Makoni's residence. In 1976 he went into Mozambique where he received political education at Chimoio. In 1978 he became a member of the commissariat section of a guerrilla group operating in Mount Darwin, with the responsibility of reporting back to Mozambique on the relations of the guerrillas and the 'masses' and of giving 'continuous political education' to the peasant population. Caston, or 'Comrade Revenge', was working at the Shandisai Pfungwa Co-operative farm in Marondera when I interviewed him and is personally committed to co-operative production. But during the war:

We did not talk to the peasants about Socialism. Ah, no, we couldn't do that. The peasantry are very conservative and even today they know nothing about Socialism. We had to teach them first about the evil deeds and oppression of the regime and how we had tried to talk to the whites but failed, so that we had to take up arms.[1]

Another guerrilla who went into Mozambique from Makoni, Lameck Madzwendira, told me in February 1981 that his political education in Mozambique had been the most important part of his training. 'They taught us politics first. They showed us things we didn't have in our minds.' But when he came back into Charter district at the end of 1978 the lesson taught to the peasants at the night time *pungwes* was 'the history of how the whites took the land.'[2]

These impressions from my research in Makoni are confirmed by evidence published elsewhere. In her splendid *None But Ourselves*, Julie Frederikse cites both a ZANLA and a ZIPRA Political Commissar. The ZANLA Commissar Comrade Zeppelin, told her:

We would get into an area, study the problems in that particular area, and then teach those people about their problems, how we can solve them by fighting the enemy. You see, in the northeast, where I was operating, many people were far away from the good farming areas, so we told them that their land was very poor, since it is usually very hot and the soil is non-productive. So we would tell them, 'It's you, the people of Zimbabwe, of this area, who should have been in the areas where there are those farmers who are getting a lot from the rich land. They've thrown you out of the rich land so that you don't get anything', and of course, then the people would like very much to have that land which they did not have. In fact, overall, the land question was our major political weapon. The people responded to it. As for socialism versus capitalism, since the olden days of our ancestors our people used to work communally and live communally, which was almost the same as socialism.[3]

Things were much the same with the ZIPRA guerrillas in the west. Colin Matutu told Frederikse that:

People did not understand all that political jargon. What we had to do, in fact, was to tell them of the hard realities of life. People should get the message, that was the important thing. The simplest way was to learn their grievances. This was what was important, to get the people's ideas about their own grievances and what they thought about solutions to these grievances. How to approach them was what mattered. You don't talk about the capitalist state or the socialist state to them. What mattered to them was how to do away with their grievances at the present time . . . That political jargon is left to documents and other things. When you are dealing with the masses you have to talk about relevant issues on the ground.[4]

The guerrillas were not themselves highly trained theoreticians. As one sympathetic missionary wrote to another, in whose area guerrillas were about to penetrate:

If you hope for good conversations . . . I am afraid you will be disappointed. The intellectuals and the thinkers are in Mozambique, directing the war. The fighting men are simply fighting for their country, fighting to rid the place of colonialism, oppression, capitalism, racialism, etc. without distinguishing between what any of these particular things mean. Some of the commanders are very intelligent, but they are soldiers rather than politicians.[5]

Unlike northern Mozambique, no areas of Zimbabwe were fully and continuously under the control of the liberation movements during the war so that there was no opportunity to reorganize production or marketing, or to set up a regular school system. The same missionary went on to describe one of the two main tasks of the guerrillas:

to educate the people; 'to politicise the masses'; to conscientize the people. This involves telling them what the struggle is all about, to make them aware of the evils of the present system, and to prepare them to create a new system of justice where there is no exploitation. So the guerrillas spend a lot of their time addressing meetings with long speeches. Their speeches are very repetitive, with lots of singing and lots of slogan-chanting. They do not go into the problems very deeply, but, rather like a religious revival service, it rouses the people.[6]

The other main task of the guerrillas was 'to disrupt the civil administration and, ultimately, to cause it to collapse'; to undermine white rural economic activity. In this they depended very heavily on the peasantry. The peasants did not merely provide food and shelter and information; they also *acted* in the war. In 1978 Robert Mugabe told the Mozambican magazine *Tempo* that 'As we advance out of the rural zones [i.e. the TTLs] the people will have a very important part to play. The war turns into a people's war with the people struggling . . . and attacking the enemy. Our army will attack the most difficult targets and the people the easier ones.'[7] This was not revolutionary rhetoric but the plain truth. In Makoni, for example, the people of Weya, of whom I wrote so much in Chapter 4, struck mortal blows at the ranching economy around them by the rustling and killing of cattle. Amon Shonge describes how:

the people used to go on to European farms and drive away cattle. They never bothered to leave them alive. They killed them and ate the meat or left the carcasses to rot. If the army found any of the bones or any evidence of the cattle then you were in real trouble. They shot your cattle, burnt huts. All the people in Matongo village were forced to strip naked – men, women and children – and marched for a mile while their huts were burnt.[8]

As early as March 1977 the Provincial Commissioner imposed a collective fine of $35 000 on 'the inhabitants of the Weya Tribal Trust Land' asserting that:

between the 1st July 1976 and 16th February 1977 cattle numbering 3292 and estimated to value 326,950 dollars have been stolen from farms in the area known as the Dutch Settlement in the Inyanga District and from farms in the Mayo, Headlands and Macheke areas of the Makoni District;
that these cattle were driven into Weya, Tanda and Chikore and Zimbiti Tribal Trust Lands . . . and that of the 3292 head of cattle stolen 928 head valued at approximately 92,000 dollars have been driven into Weya Tribal Trust Land . . .
that the terrorists have held and are holding meetings in the Tribal Trust Lands mentioned above with tribesmen instructing them to steal European owned cattle;
that the tribesmen of these Tribal Trust Lands have willingly carried out the instructions in question and have assisted the terrorists and continue to do so in their declared aim of disrupting the agricultural economy of the areas mentioned above.[9]

The fine was levied by means of seizure of African stock – '37 Headmen were forced by a D.C's decree to collect from their people cattle to be handed over to Gvt. Each H/M had to collect 30 or more cattle'.[10]

Nor did the authorities restrict themselves to imposing fines. The *Rhodesia Herald* on 7 April 1977 reported that there were 'terrorists' in Chikore, Tanda and Weya. From Weya they had struck into the Mayo farming area and an anti-guerrilla operation had been mounted.[11] In May Amon Shonge wrote to tell Guy Clutton-Brock the character of this operation:

On the 5th April the Army rounded up all the people village by village in our area, collected all the biggest, best and fattest oxen they can find. Roughly the oxen could number between 300–400 beasts. Some families could have as much as 7 beasts taken, as long as they are the best in that village. All such unfortunate families have no oxen to plough with now. Not even a cent was offered for their beasts. This was said to be the punishment for feeding and sympathising with 'Terrorists'. The next day they dropped leaflets from a plane warning people that if they will continue they could face even more severe punishment in future . . . On Friday, April the 22nd soldiers took a young boy of about 15 years old from his parent's home, after beating his father badly. The boy was shot and killed with several bullets all over his body. This was only 100–200 yards away from his parents' home. The reason? 'Suspect' . . . There are many tricks which they are playing, pretending to be 'terrorists'. Some of the tricks include knocking on the doors at night and then ask for food. 'We are your sons in the jungle': if you are found to be a sympathiser then you are gone in the next few days to come.[12]

'People of Weya,' ran one of the leaflets dropped from the air:

You are warned that terrorists cause suffering. You were warned that if you help terrorists you will suffer again . . . What have the terrorists ever done for you? If they eat your *sadza* you will soon be without maize. Who will give you food when you starve? . . . Terrorists do not succeed. Even now many of them were killed in Weya. Turn against them now and remove them before time is finished.[13]

In this way the pattern of the war in Weya and Tanda was fixed. The contest proved to be an unequal one. The peasants were exposed to the fearsome military power which had so impressed Chief Muzanenamo Makoni – but they showed that it *was* possible after all to endure it. Peasant support for the guerrillas did not flag. For their part the white farmers and ranchers around Weya and Tanda found the pressure of guerrillas and peasants unendurable. By 1978 army intelligence maps of the Mayo area showed the extent of the white withdrawal:

Virginia, Martin. J. unoccupied – not farmed; Vrede, Martin and Son, unoccupied – not farmed; Rosendal, unoccupied – not farmed; Quando, Botha. L.M. unoccupied – not farmed; Koodoo Kop, unoccupied – not farmed . . .[14]

So ran the litany. The land which early Native Commissioners had wanted to use to enlarge the north Makoni Reserves; which had long lain idle in the hands of the investment companies; from which the peasants of Tanda had been driven in the 1940s; which had experienced a brief boom in the 1950s – the land was being reclaimed. Yet though the whites were withdrawing it was not time yet for the peasants of Weya and Tanda to re-establish themselves on the land. They had enough to do to survive in their arid enclaves. A report by the Catholic Commission for Justice and Peace in August 1977 catches the atmosphere of the secret and ugly war which raged in north Makoni. 'On 6 July,' it noted, 'members of the Security Forces were burning six villages in Tanda T.T.L. when they were attacked by guerrillas and nine were killed. The incident itself never appeared anywhere, and the names of only two of the soldiers were reported the following week as "killed in action" '[15]

Equally Amon Shonge's letters catch the atmosphere of this quintessentially peasant war, in which death went alongside the basic preoccupation with markets and yields. 'Unfortunately,' he wrote to Clutton-Brock in December 1977, 'we cannot cope up with the external markets, namely due to the war going on here. I hope you still remember Kraalhead Chimutuwa, who used to visit us at Cold Comfort Farm with his garden problems. He was murdered by Selous Scouts with several outstanding figures. It is difficult to know where it will happen next.'[16] In March 1978 he wrote that 'More and more deaths are taking place day after day in our area. We are expecting quite good yields in the fields. That means we can suffer, but we will be able to have some food to eat.'[17]

Everywhere in Zimbabwe there was this degree of participation by the peasantry. Garfield Todd was right when he wrote in 1980 that the '30,000 guerillas sharing in the life of the people' were 'well aware of the proportions of suffering of the people.'[18] The collective action and collective suffering of peasants and guerrillas produced a composite ideology in Makoni District and elsewhere in the country. The peasants of Makoni, where all the guerrillas were members of ZANLA, ceased being ZAPU in their hearts and swung behind the idea of Robert Mugabe's ZANU/PF as the ideal governors of the new state. For their part, the guerrillas came to admire the determination of the peasantry and to support them in their quintessentially peasant political programme – for the recovery of the lost lands and the cessation of state interference in production.

To this extent, then, in its deep commitment to the land, peasant war in Zimbabwe *was* similar to Mau Mau. But how similar was it in other ways? Robert Buijtenhuijs writes of Mau Mau as 'a movement of cultural renewal'; its rituals were 'not a return to the past, but a return to the sources of Kikuyu culture; they represented cultural innovation, the beginning of something new.' He describes the contribution made to Mau Mau ideology by Kikuyu religion; the leadership of the 'seers' in the forest. All this he sees as serving to deepen commitment and meaning. But he also emphasizes the limitations of these cultural and supernaturalist elements:

The culture its leaders and followers wanted to revive was a Kikuyu culture and in its ceremonies the movement used symbols that were essentially Kikuyu. This appeal to Kikuyu values, though undeniably a most powerful tool to unite the Kikuyu people, was nevertheless a double-edged weapon that finally harmed Mau Mau as an anti-colonial revolt . . . The more the organisers drew near to their aim of cementing the unity of their own ethnic group . . . the more difficult it became for a non-Kikuyu to recognise himself in the mirror Mau Mau held up to him . . Mau Mau as a movement of cultural renewal was incompatible with Mau Mau as an anti-colonial revolt.[19]

These criticisms of the supernaturalist element in the Mau Mau ideology are stated much more vigorously by other commentators. In a recent survey of peasant unrest in black Africa, Catherine Coquery-Vidrovitch describes Mau Mau as a 'xenophobic movement of a messianic type', and stresses the almost 'inevitable recourse to the supernatural' which characterized revolts limited to the peasantry. Her comment on Matswanism in the Congo brings out her view of the necessary consequences of supernaturalist rural ideologies: 'The movement,' she argues, 'based originally on the idea of Congolese nationalism, had regressed in the form of a religious sect with an ethnic and rural appeal, which recovered after the gap of several decades the millenarian accents of the beginning of the century. These had drained it of its dynamic political content.'[20]

Basil Davidson's assessment of Mau Mau is more favourable. It was 'a rebellion such as nobody in East Africa had seen before, whether in its force and drive, its manner of organisation and leadership, or its aims. In all these respects it made a bridge between the past and the future.' But in the forests, he argues, supernaturalism came to predominate:

In the early phases the Kikuyu *mundo mogo*, oracle spokesmen or diviners, had helped to enforce discipline and morale; now they began to undermine what they had helped to build, relapsing into magical explanations of reality, claiming to command operations by reference to their prophecies, spreading belief in the efficacy of charms . . . In this situation the 'joints' between traditional and modernising ideas and forms evidently continued to collapse. . . Superstition flourished. Discipline went by the board. . . fighters and commanders fell increasingly into actions of despair.[21]

The key variable which distinguishes between older style rural upheavals and a proper 'people's war', Davidson goes on to explain, is whether 'a leadership emerge[s] that can really lead "out of the past into the future"? Can the movement in question rise . . . above the bedrock of its rural culture, above utopian or messianic hopes, above magic and corresponding superstition?' What is necessary is 'a modernizing elite' that can stay 'close to the movement of rebellion'. Mau Mau 'never possessed any modernizing leadership save what they could produce out of their own ranks'. In the guerrilla movements of Lusophone Africa, on the other hand, a modernizing *elite* did emerge, stayed close to the peasants, and through the processes of a people's war, helped to carry them from superstition to rationality:

Village volunteers never had much difficulty in learning to handle, fire and even repair rifles and light automatics: the difficulty came in accepting secular explanations of reality in place of religious explanations. It was one thing to learn how to ambush an enemy, quite another that witches could not hurt you. This was the learning . . . which imposed the need for protracted war.[22]

Yoweri Museveni, now himself a guerrilla leader in Uganda, has vividly described this process as he saw it in northern Mozambique during the war against the Portuguese:

The peasants of Northern Mozambique have undergone the cleansing effect of revolution . . . The peasant in Cabo Delgado has participated in killing the white man – the former 'demi-god' . . . In the course of the revolution, the peasant is also liberated from parochialism . . . The peasant gains much ideologically from the intellectual . . . He becomes more scientific and discards most of the superstitions . . . and the whole magical superstructure that characterizes a frustrated colonial society . . . The transformation of the peasant into a rational anti-imperialist fighter becomes a must.[23]

Now, where does the guerrilla war in Zimbabwe stand in this continuum from superstition to rationality? What was the outcome in Zimbabwe of the interaction between peasant belief and guerrilla conscientization? Did the strongly peasant character of the war necessarily imply that its ideology was bound to be marked by the rural 'inevitable recourse to the supernatural'? And if so, did this prevent it being in a full sense a 'people's war'?

There is no doubt, to begin with, that peasants in Zimbabwe had responded to their experiences in the twentieth century by means of a number of different religious idioms. Some of these I have indicated in previous chapters. Thus I suggested that self-peasantization in the first twenty years of the century was accompanied by the development of a number of religious strata, each expressive of a different layer of peasant consciousness. In Makoni District, at least, one could discern the peasant entrepreneurs, inspired by the American Methodist mixture of ardour and discipline; the small marketing peasant Anglican; the folk Catholicism of the subsistence peasantry; the congruity between production for the market on a 'traditional' basis and the injunctions of the Mwari cult or of the spirit mediums. I have suggested also that in the 1930s in Shona-speaking peasant areas the crisis in consciousness produced by the Depression expressed itself largely in religious protest, prophetism and Revival. On the one hand there was a repudiation of the political economy of missionary Christianity, which expressed itself both in Apostolic prophetic movements and in renewed recourse to the spirit mediums; on the other hand, there was the recovery of morale and initiative by aspirant peasant progressives, by means of the revival movements within the mission churches. The ideologies thus enunciated and acted out were not political or 'rational' in Davidson's sense, but they were very relevant to peasant experience. They thus have to be taken very seriously by the historian of the peasantry.

In a recent paper I remarked that in much of the existing literature 'peasant religion is seen as "false consciousness", more or less damaging.' I went on to argue that:

we have to start from the assumption that peasants had and have a privileged access to many – to most – of the realities of their own existence. They do not respond to or talk about these realities *only* in terms of religion, but African peasant religious discourse is nevertheless a privileged language in which reality is categorised and transformed and to which the scholar has to struggle to gain access. . .

All forms of religion in Makoni adapted themselves to the realities of peasant society. The religious pluralism of the twentieth century fitted a differentiated peasantry. . . Of course, the fit between differentiated peasant experience and religion was not exact: even peasants were concerned with spiritual and material realities other than those of agricultural production . . . Nevertheless, in ways obviously much more complex than I have been able to show here agrarian innovation and religious innovation in the rural areas of Zimbabwe were inextricably intertwined. Any movement seeking to reach the peasantry, to mobilise them, would have to seek to understand what it was that peasant religion had to say about reality and about aspiration.[24]

But what I have not so far done in this book is to set out the religious consequences of the rural crisis of the late 1940s and of the emergence of radical peasant nationalism. Much of the available literature suggests that a major consequence was the increased significance of so-called 'traditional' religion. Thus the crisis of the open nationalist movements in 1963–4, with fierce competition between ZAPU and ZANU and the ultimate banning of both, was accompanied by open attacks on the rural mission churches in the name of the Spirits. Salathiel Madziyire, Anglican pastor in Marandellas, described how:

Many teenage boys have recently accepted spirit belief and been buoyed up by the pride of being possessed by the spirits. Many have claimed to act as foretellers of the future for the communities in which they live. They demand to be respected, feared, worshipped . . . These boys were practising Christians during their time at school. They obtained a reasonable education so far as Grade Seven but not enough to get them anywhere in the world. So they have returned to claim the power to tell the future, make rain, etc . . . This is a time of trouble for the Church. Many have hidden themselves during these terrible days of crisis in Rhodesia. Surely the politicians must have contributed something towards this and towards the desire to return to ancestor worship. Why have some Christians helped to burn down church buildings for which they helped to pay? . . . The teenager . . . used to take great pride in the 1950s in being seen walking with his friends to church on Sunday. But the teenagers now put themselves forward as spirit-possessed leaders of African communities, offering sacrifices to the ancestors, renewing the old religion.[25]

N.E. Thomas tells us that in Tanda the nationalist elders proclaimed 'traditional magico-religious taboos' and that these were enforced in Headman Makumbe's court. One man was 'charged £2 for publicly scoffing at the ancestral spirits when prayers to them did not end drought.' In 1962 the ZAPU Youth League began to say that 'Africans should return to the worship of Chaminuka' and burnt churches and classrooms.[26]

Now, it is obviously possible to interpret this sort of evidence much as Buijtenhuijs and Davidson interpret the religious elements in the Mau Mau ideology. The adherence of nationalist elders and of teenagers to 'the ancestral spirits' was part of a 'movement of cultural renewal'; the revival of traditionalism 'helped to enforce discipline and morale' within the nationalist movement. And it is possible to emphasize the negative side of such 'cultural renewal'. Indeed the fullest account of peasant religion in this period *does* see the rise of the influence of the spirit mediums precisely in terms of the collapse of nationalist 'rationality' and the inward-turning despair of a disillusioned peasantry. In this perspective Shona religion too undermined what it had helped to build; relapsed into magical explanations of reality; collapsed the joints between traditional and modernizing ideas.

The anthropologist Peter Fry, who carried out field work in the Chiota Tribal Trust Land in the first half of the 1960s, argues just such a case. He begins by documenting the rising influence of 'traditional' religion and its links with nationalism:

During my fieldwork . . . ZANU and the PCC [the cover organisation for ZAPU] were banned. Mr Smith declared unilateral independence from Britain . . . African leaders were rounded up and put either in detention or in restriction in camps miles out in the bush . . . From the start of my fieldwork I had intended not to be preoccupied with studying religion and ritual, mainly because of my interest in making a contribution to an understanding of what were considered to be more basic matters, but also because I had been led to believe that 'traditional' beliefs and practices were drying out and were of little significance to the contemporary situation. However, bit by bit I became aware of the fact that this was by no means the case . . . the number of persons who were succumbing to spirit mediumship was increasing, churches were being burned and stoned . . . It became quite clear that 'traditional' beliefs and practices were related to the rise of African nationalism.

And at the end of his fascinating book, Fry sums up the significance of the vigorous religious activity which he has documented:

The uneasy calm of post-UDI Rhodesia rested basically on . . . superior force . . . and should not be interpreted to mean that the African population had abandoned its nationalistic ideals. If anything nationalist sentiment became stronger, in reaction to the increasingly repressive nature of white domination . . . Spirit-mediums . . . are effective as a focus for nationalist sentiment because they bring the past to the present . . . above all because they are the people whose very authority is given by public opinion and who are unequivocally opposed structurally to Christianity.

So far, so positive. But Fry goes on to show what happened to revived 'traditional' religion after the defeat of nationalism in 1964, and here he highlights negative effects:

Prior to the banning of the African Nationalist parties in 1964 . . . the

Africans of Chiota were confident that majority rule would soon be established in Rhodesia. The spontaneous emergence of new spirit-mediums in Chiota was a popular manifestation of this confidence. However, after the events of 1964 and 1965 hope turned almost to despair . . . Africans began their hunt for 'sell-outs', those who had taken sides with the whites. The confrontation between black and white had been diverted into a search for the enemy within . . . The search for 'informers' and 'sell-outs' was accompanied in the religious sphere by a new preoccupation with witches and sorcerers . . . The most popular spirit-mediums in Chiota were those who were believed capable of detecting witchcraft . . . The conflict between white and black had been transmuted into a conflict between the ancestors and witchcraft . . . in Chiota the spirit-mediums who had once heralded the triumphant return of the ancestors and the realisation of nationalist ambitions were now the arbiters of despondency and despair.[27]

If Fry's conclusions hold good for Zimbabwe as a whole and for the whole period between 1964 and the arrival of the guerrillas, then it certainly would seem as if a religion 'with an ethnic and rural appeal' was draining peasant consciousness of 'its dynamic political content'. It would seem equally obvious that guerrillas could only lead the peasantry out of 'despondency and despair' by teaching them to be 'more scientific', so as to discard 'most of the superstitions'; and by transforming 'the peasant into a rational anti-imperialist fighter'. Even if guerrillas were prepared to intensify and enlarge peasant political consciousness, as I have argued, surely they could not make use of peasant religious ideas. If there was to be a people's war in Zimbabwe then the liberation movements would surely have to 'rise above the bedrock of rural culture'.

In fact in Zimbabwe things have not worked out at all like this. There *was* an effective guerrilla war but it was a war in which spirit mediums became more significant than ever. Peasant religion formed an indispensable part of the composite ideology of the war. Why and how did this happen? I shall argue that there were four main reasons. In the first place, 'despondency and despair' were by no means a long-term peasant reaction to the events of 1964 and 1965; even before guerrillas entered them, most rural areas in Zimbabwe had recovered their determination to oppose. Secondly, although there was undoubtedly a good deal of external and artificial interest in 'traditional' religion and the spirit mediums in the late 1950s and early 1960s, they were also, and for quite different reasons, important to the stage that peasant consciousness itself had reached by that time. Nationalist intellectuals and anthropologists and historians in search of the Shona past 'discovered' the spirit mediums – and some talented and entrepreneurial mediums responded by inventing a version of history which boosted the prestige of their own possessing spirits.[28] But peasant interest in the mediums had very little to do with intellectual nationalism. And this leads me to the third point I wish to make. Spirit mediums were significant to peasant radical consciousness precisely because that consciousness was so focused on land and on government interference with production: above any other possible religious form the mediums symbolized peasant right to the land and their right to work it as they chose. Hence mediums had already become important as articulators of radical consciousness even before guerrillas entered the rural areas. But finally, and fourthly, once the guerrillas *had* entered the mediums proved ideally fitted to play another and crucial role. It was they who offered the most effective means of bringing together peasant elders, who had hitherto been the local leaders of radical opposition, with the young strangers who entered each rural district, armed with guns and ready to administer revolutionary law. Hence not only peasants but also most guerrillas themselves came to draw heavily on the religious elements within the composite ideology of the war.

It will be recalled from Chapter 4 that although Thomas believed that from the mid-1960s the people of Tanda were locked in embittered futility, in fact the peasants of north Makoni were able to continue their contestation with the white regime right up to the point at which guerrillas entered the area. Nor were areas like Weya and Tanda, with their recent experience of land alienation, the only places where peasant radicalism awaited the coming of war. In 1970 ZANLA leaders first began to adopt the strategy of mobilizing the peasantry rather than relying on military-style incursions. A handful of ZANLA organizers entered the north-east of the country from FRELIMO-controlled areas in Mozambique. They came into areas very different from Makoni District; areas in which the peasant option had never been a possibility, where there had always been a high rate of labour migration, where there was little alienation of land to whites, and where the organizational networks of the open nationalist parties had barely extended. It may be that such areas had not experienced the traumatic shock of high hope shattered which Fry describes for Chiota, and Thomas for Tanda. At any rate, when the first ZANLA organizers went in they were surprised to find a rural population immediately responsive to the idea of armed struggle. 'The revolutionary situation was excellent'[29]; 'The people had been ready for armed struggle for quite a long period and nobody in the leadership had ever discovered what the people were capable of doing.'[30] One of the first four ZANLA men to enter the north-east has described how he found 'very, very poor people' there, and how he was able to set up many cells consisting of 'peasants only . . . not even teachers . . . a few, a very few, headmen.'. . . These recruits knew little of nationalist ideology. They were 'very very dull people; they never went to school, they don't have schools there, they just plough, they don't have cattle, they don't have anything, just people. They don't want to see any European there. They fight.' 'This area was a new area to us, a completely new area', but out of this apparently unpromising material there rapidly developed the first committed peasant participation in Zimbabwe's peoples war.[31] As we shall see, one of the things that the very different areas of north Makoni and the north-eastern border *did* have in common was that in both places the guerrillas found that spirit mediums exercised very considerable influence amongst the peasantry.

The idea that spirit mediums were important was certainly not taken to the peasants by cultural nationalist intellectuals. David Lan has carried out nearly two years research in the Zimbabwean north-east and has written by far the most profound study of the significance of the role of the mediums during the war. He emphasizes that the guerrillas:

did not enter Dande with the intention of recruiting the mediums. It was only after they ascertained that the mediums held the respect of the peasantry that the guerillas made attempts to win them to their side. . . The suggestion is frequently made that the only reason the guerillas approached the mediums at this stage of the war was that their leaders had read of the exploits of earlier *mhondoro* mediums in Ranger's history of the [1896] rebellion . . . This view severely underestimates the significance of the mediums in the life of the peasantry.[32]

What, then, was the significance of the mediums in the life of the peasantry? In the Dande area, largely unaffected as it has been by the commercialization of African agriculture or by any acute land shortage for subsistence production, it might perhaps be said that the mediums had 'preserved' a 'traditional' role as the ideologists of an unchanged rural economy – though Lan himself stresses the 'radical' character of Dande mediums in the twentieth century and their contribution to adaptation and change. In Makoni, however, the African rural political economy has obviously changed a very great deal. If spirit mediums were influential there in the 1970s it was not because they had 'survived'; it was because they had become increasingly relevant to the peasant dilemma and the state of peasant consciousness. In particular they were relevant to peasant resentment over land alienation and the enforcement of agricultural rules.

As I have argued in earlier chapters, mediums had *not* objected to peasants producing and selling a surplus. But they *did* object, just as much as did many peasants themselves, to the demands and prohibitions of the new intensive agriculture. Michael Gelfand, writing of the spirit mediums of the eastern border in the 1970s, quotes the medium of the Nyawada spirit, Diki Rukadza, an ex-labour-migrant:

According to Diki Rukadza, his spirit disapproves of certain developments introduced in modern days. For instance, it does not care for contour ridging because it causes too much work and has introduced features that were not in the landscape in former days. His spirit declares that there is no pleasure in walking the fields or bush as the contours make movement difficult. This innovation makes the spirit angry and as a result people are short of food. The tribal spirit, he says, dislikes the rising rates levied by rural councils in the TTLs . . . The tribal spirit gave people soil on which to grow their crops and enough water to enable them to flourish. But nowadays they were being told to plough here and not there, only in particular places, unlike the instructions of the tribal spirit, which were merely to plant and water would be provided.

There could hardly have been a more exact expression of the consciousness of radical peasant nationalists. And Diki Rukadza went on also to express small peasant hostility towards the rural entrepreneur. 'Very rarely do Africans die of starvation. They have enough. They can get help from others . . . relatives and friends . . . If one brother needs help, another must come forward and help . . . The sons of today expect something in return for what was given, but this is a European custom. Amongst the Shona there is no usury.'[33]

What happened in the Triashill area, on the eastern border of Makoni District, is pertinent here. As we have seen, Triashill farm was a core area of folk Catholicism for a largely subsistence peasantry. Two things happened there in the 1960s. One was that many Triashill peasants effectively entered the market for the first time: the other, only apparently paradoxically, was that the authority of the *mhondoro* spirits and their mediums over agricultural production was re-asserted. On Triashill farm from 1956, two Demonstrators, trained at Domboshowa, listed every family and all its members, making 'a mosaic of the whole farm'; land was reallocated on the basis of six acres per family, or four acres on the good red soils; those who had previously held more land than this surrendered it; contour ridges were introduced; people began to use fertilizer. In short, the Triashill cultivators belatedly experienced under mission control the transition to more or less egalitarian intensive agriculture which the adminstration had carried out in the neighbouring Reserves over the previous two decades. For the Triashill peasants it was all a much less traumatic experience than it had been elsewhere. Learning from the mistakes of the administration, the Triashill missionaries were careful to evict no-one. Instead of giving notice to half of the 395 families on the land, as government officials recommended, the mission actually brought another 195 families on to the farm by means of giving up much of the mission demesne. Instead of using Demonstrators as coercive policemen, everything was done through elaborate consultation. 'Everything that smacked of compulsion was out.' Moreover, the use of fertilizers quadrupled maize output per acre, and the good new road through to Inyanga, and the growth of the mission boarding schools provided good markets for the surplus. Very many men returned from the towns in order to invest their labour in agricultural production. 'It *was*,' says Father Peter Turner, Farm Manager in this period 'a great success. The District Commissioner wanted to use it for demonstration. But *he* just gave orders. Consultation was the root of our success.'

These rapid developments had a complex effect on peasant consciousness. On the one hand, the men who had returned from the towns were more concerned with fertility and productivity than ever before, and receptive to ritual means for assuring it. On the other hand, whatever the success of this belated production for the market, the new scheme of settlement at Triashill did involve a whole new set of rules and regulations which were often reluctantly accepted. 'If we heard the noise of a beer-drink we would keep away from that kraal so that no-one would say anything about the new scheme that they would regret afterwards.' Finally, the peasants of Triashill were in close interaction with those of the Manyika and the Makoni Tribal Trust Lands, where grievances against intensive agriculture were much more strongly felt. One of the results of all this was an expansion of the influence of spirit mediums, shown most clearly in the almost universal observation of the *chisi* rest days. According to Father Turner:

The Chisi rest day on Fridays was observed at Triashill. In fact it was coming in when I took over. It came from Manyika first, then reached St Barbara's and finally Triashill. Friday was kept as a day of rest at home, where no cultivation was done, in honour of the spirits. Sunday was kept as a day of rest away from home, in honour of the church. Chief Zambe Makoni was very strict in Chisi observance . . . The people said the observance was for Chaminuka.[34]

Early in 1981 Sister Emilia Chiteka carried out a series of

interviews at Triashill, from which there emerged clearly a picture of the growing significance of the mediums in peasant consciousness there. The testimony of a Triashill 'progressive', Denis Tahusarira Name, brings out very clearly both agricultural change and the more of less negotiated acceptance of the mediums' authority:

I was born on the twelfth of December 1918 . . . In 1933 at the age of fifteen I was able to help my mother in the fields . . . my special task was that of herding . . . When I had become a teacher in 1945 I continued to live as a partial subsistence farmer at home. The crops that we grew were maize, groundnuts, monkey-nuts, which could be sold to neighbouring villages should there be a low yield in the crop, *mapfunde* and *rapoko*. The use of cattle manure was still forbidden by the elders. Up to the fifties the system of subsistence farming which we used was not different save for the iron ploughs which we had begun to use in the early thirties. The change that I witnessed was that brought about in the early sixties when the agricultural demonstrators encouraged the use of cattle manure and . . . we began to make contours in our fields . . . The rise in the cost of living in the seventies meant that I had to step up in the methods of farming. This meant a step up in the use of fertilisers . . . As a result I have been one of those people in my village to sell surplus maize . . . However, this type of economy which had begun to flourish was disrupted by the war. . .

I know two spirit mediums by name. These are Murambachinya and Chikunguru. Their importance in the village was to tell the people when to sow the crops. Anyone who sowed earlier than the others was to suffer the consequence . . . They are the people who told the whole village when to brew beer in order to petition the ancestors to intercede for them so that they may get good rains and abundant crops. The spirit mediums are the people who pronounced the rest days. In this part of the country, it was Fridays and Mondays. These were . . . to honour the ancestors by not working in the fields. However, the people at Triashill made a petition to the mediums that because they also had to observe Sundays this would mean only four days in which they could work in the fields, so the Monday *chisi* day was dropped out.[35]

If the influence of the mediums increased in an area like Triashill where the 1960s brought a relative prosperity and actually opened up the peasant option, it can readily be imagined that in Weya and Tanda, where the peasant option had been foreclosed, the spirit mediums played a vigorous part in resistance to the enforcement of agricultural rules. And there, too the distinctions between the cultural nationalist enthusiasms for 'traditional' religion and the long-term interactions of peasants and mediums can be particularly clearly seen. In his analysis of the complex religious situation of Tanda, Thomas stresses that in the early 1960s there were basic tensions between the traditional religious leaders and the new nationalist political elite. The high tide of nationalist political activity in Tanda included numerous week-ends in which ZAPU youth drummed, danced and drank 'in honour of the *vadzimu*'. Their elders complained, however, that the traditional rituals were being carried out superficially . . . Fearing that the nationalist leaders were usurping their own roles as ritual leaders, the spirit mediums tended to be hostile to nationalist politics.[36]

Nothing could have been more different, as we shall see, than the relations which Tanda mediums established with the guerrillas ten years later. Between the hostility of mediums to young nationalists in 1961 and 1962 and their endorsement of the young guerrillas in 1975 there lay a decade in which the mediums in Weya and Tanda had no rivals as 'ritual leaders' and in which they came increasingly to symbolize peasant grievances against administrative interference.

The case of the Chendambuya chiefship and mediumship illustrates this admirably. The original Chendambuya had been one of the early holders of the Makoni chiefship itself. Subsequently the Chendambuya spirit had become one of the most important *mhondoro* in Makoni and its medium a man of great influence. According to the investigations of the administration's research officer in 1972:

During the last century the area over which Chief Makoni held sway was large and included the area between the present Makoni, Weya and Tanda Tribal Trust Lands . . . The senior medium of Makoni is Muswere and at that time this swikiro lived at Sangano, a place near to the chief's kraal. The swikiro's son lived . . . to the west of Weya . . . Chendambuya was, at that time, the second medium in the hierarchy and was represented by a medium who lived . . . near the chief's kraal. . . In this way the Chief was enabled to consult both maswikiro on any particular question and this he did. It will be appreciated that these maswikiro exercised influence over the Chief.
    Some time towards the end of the last century Chendambuya's swikiro decided to move to the Weya area because population pressure had built up around Makoni's kraal and he wanted a great area of land to cultivate . . . He moved into the area of Sadunu Mwendazuya . . . exercising authority over this area on behalf of Chief Makoni . . . At the beginning to the century Chendambuya was the favoured mudzimu of Makoni because of his ability to produce rain.

When the administration determined to do away with the Chendambuya chiefship in the early 1970s because of its involvement with ZAPU, it took the line that it had been a mistake to have such a chiefship from the very beginning. An early colonial Native

Commissioner had made the medium of the Chendambuya spirit a chief and put him in authority over Weya and Tandu, but 'a swikiro should not become a chief.' According to this version of the past, the appointment was an injustice to the Mwendazuya family and the cause of tension in Weya. In the atmosphere of artificially revived tradition within which the administration worked in the 1970s, they even offered a 'spiritual' explanation for the problems of Weya:

It would seem that Mwendazuya's mudzimu (ancestral spirit) was not very happy about the position and while this had no immediate consequences, the later results have proved serious . . . Local spirit authority [had been] in the hands of Mwendazuya's medium, who had always resided on the hill Ruchero . . . A serious error was made and the repercussions, stemming basically from spiritual sources, have been growing steadily worse. . . The people have demonstrated their disapproval . . . led without doubt by the spirits. . . The troubled condition of Weya was basically due to the disapproval of the mudzimu of Mwendazuya.

So the administration's recommendation was that the Chendambuya chiefship be abolished and that a Mwendazuya headman under Chief Makoni be reinstated. 'This would make the mudzimu of Mwendazuya happy and remove the basic cause of the trouble.'[37] Once this had been done, a Mwendazuya headman would be able to enforce agricultural rules.

In view of the deep-seated economic and political grievances of Weya this analysis must strike us as an example of how the district administration deceived itself with bogus traditionalism in the 1970s. But while no such changes could have made a transforming difference to peasant radicalism in Weya and Tanda, the administration's case possessed a degree of plausibility and needed to be combated on its own terms. This was achieved by the emergence of a Chendambuya medium who was able to insist that discontent in Weya was due to administrative interference. Tobias Chatambudza Chendambuya, a ZAPU supporter, and nephew of the deceased chief, emerged as the *svikiro* of the Chendambuya spirit, 'masquerading about dressed in black and muttering strange things to the consternation of the people', as the District Commissioner complained.[38] Tobias soon made himself a champion both of those who supported the Chendambuya family and those who resisted the enforcement of agricultural rules.

In April 1972 the District Commissioner's administrative assistant, Roland Hatendi, went to Weya on a 'Get to Know the People and their Problems' patrol. On this occasion Hatendi pursued another of the administration's strategies for building up local support against 'trouble-makers', appealing not to traditionalists but to successful entrepreneurs. In the absence of a Chief, he thought, 'it would be a good idea to meet people who had endeavoured to acquire something worthy of esteem and find out how they elevated themselves to that standard.' The headmasters, eating-house keepers and 'business-men' to whom he spoke assured him that 'the trouble-makers in Weya are not getting the usual support from the tribesmen [who] seem to have realised their mistake of listening to a person who is incapable of acquiring a substantial property . . . If only people could keep their hands busy there [would] be less troubles in the country as a whole.' One of them took Hatendi to 'see his crops and conservation work.' Another assured him that he did 'not believe that Tobias is a *svikiro* of Chendambuya but that he is a power hungry person.' But Tobias himself came to see Hatendi and turned out to be much more in touch with the 'tribesmen'. While the businessmen were worrying about keeping 'Hire Purchase Agreements up to date', Tobias came to complain of the 'handling of affairs in Weya T.T.L particularly the setting of fire on Chimutuwa's gardens.'[39] Indeed, Tobias himself was one of those prosecuted along with Chimutuwa for conservation offences; along with the others he declared that he would go to jail rather than pay fines, and consequently had his cattle seized. For some reason when the sentences on Chimutuwa and the rest were set aside in June 1972 in the aftermath of the Tadokera case, Tobias' conviction and fine was still allowed to stand.[40]

Marked out in this way by the administration, who refused to admit that he should be recognized as a medium, Tobias nevertheless played a role in frustrating the administration's plans for north Makoni. In May 1974 the plan for establishing a Mwendazuya headmanship and so reconstituting a legal Tribal Land Authority in Weya and Tanda suffered a severe setback. Of the kraalheads in the area, thirty-one out of forty insisted on remaining under a Chendambuya chief; only nine were prepared to accept a Mwendazuya headman. Reporting this to the District Commissioner, elder Chikukutu also insisted 'that Tobias Chatambudza is a Swikiro and that he speaks for the spirit of Chendambuya. I believe it to be the spirit of the man who was a Chief Makoni . . . He speaks of things that happened long ago before any of us can remember.'[41] Faced with this resistance, the administration was unable to carry through its 'tribal reorganisation' in Weya and Tanda so that conservation orders remained without legal force. Given all this it was not surprising that the District office collected and filed away all the information it could about mediums in Weya.[42] Nor was it surprising that 'when the comrades came to Weya Tobias, who claimed to be the medium of Chendambuya, worked with them and his son became a guerrilla. Tobias was shot and wounded by the Security Forces.' It is rather more surprising, but the clearest indication of how comprehensively the administration had lost this 'spiritual' war, that 'the main medium the comrades used was the chief svikiro of Mwendazuya, Mukuwamombe, the greatest spirit of them all. The svikiro had been living in Tanda but the comrades brought him into Weya. They wanted him here because he was supposed to be the one able to make this land safe for the comrades.'[43]

In the mid 1960s Thomas found that:

The majority of the Apostolics, Seventh Day Adventists and rural Methodists denied that an ancestor can present their requests to God. They reject prayers to ancestors . . . and consultation with spirit mediums . . . In Tanda members of these churches even refuse to contribute grain for the annual festivals of thanksgiving for the new harvest in April/May or for prayers for rain in September/October.[44]

In the 1970s things changed. Headman Makumbe, ally of the radical peasant nationalists of Tanda and later 'running with and actively assisting terrorists' during the war, campaigned against the 'hold the Apostolic Church is gaining over his people' and enforced the Friday *chisi* day.[45] When J.C. Kandiero carried out his investigations in Weya in 1976 he found that the resident elders who observed the spirit possession ceremonies 'are the same people who go to Church, School and nearly all activities. It is only the Apostolic people who sort of isolate themselves.' By the mid-1970s, in fact, Weya and Tanda Adventists, Methodists, Anglicans and Catholics had all come to recognize the mediums as controllers of the agrarian cycle. 'These mediums,' wrote Kandiero, 'are responsible for rain, good harvests, diseases and pests. Many things are observed by the people so as not to disappoint the mediums.'[46]

But of course the mediums were not only significant to peasants in the late 1960s and 1970s because they stood for a way of working the soil which contrasted starkly with authoritarian intensive cultivation. They were important also as symbols of the fundamental right of the peasantry to the land. This idea of the *mhondoro* spirits as the true owners of the land had already been made use of before the 1960s and 1970s in a whole variety of ways, sometimes to console an evicted community with the thought that nevertheless they alone really 'owned' the land; sometimes to seek to establish a claim to land in what had been defined as the 'European' area; sometimes to frighten away anyone who might come to take the land over. Three instances from Makoni or nearby illustrate this range of possibilities.

I described in Chapter 1 how white farmers under the leadership of Barnes Pope campaigned in the second decade of the twentieth century to reduce the extent of the Chiduku Reserve. In 1981 I found that Barnes Pope and other early white farmers of lands bordering on Chiduku are still remembered, and in a very illuminating way. The medium of the Akuchekwa spirit in the Tandi chiefdom, Chiduku, told of how:

All our holy mountains – Matowe and Nhowehuru and Shangwe, all except Fungwa – are on European farm lands. When we were driven off the farm lands long ago we came down here. Then it never rained. In those days Mr Pope was living on Alpha farm where Matowe is. He had a stone built house. He was driven away by the spirits. His washing, hanging out on the line, was carried away by baboons. The meat in his butchery kept on being thrown down on the floor in the dirt. When he went inside his house he found strange beings there such as he had never seen before. His bed used to be seen outside the house at night because he could not sleep inside. Then some wonderful force destroyed the house altogether. Pope left. Still it never rained. The tobacco on the white farms was drying up . . . They asked 'Who was living here before we came?' It was answered 'Chief Tandi and his svikiro (medium)'. So the farmers came to ask our svikiro and showed him all the dried up tobacco. He asked them who had cut down all the Mushakata trees on the land. They answered 'Pope'. He asked to be shown one tree only. He was shown one. He asked them for rapoko which he spread out on the rock. Before he reached his home again it was raining.[47]

Another variant of the idea was used by Chief Chipunza's people after the Land Appointment Act. In May 1936 the European owner of Lesapi Cave farm wrote to the Director of the Native Land Board:

When I bought this farm in 1928 there were a number of natives living on the place as tenants, all members of the tribe of Chief Chipunza – and as a matter of fact he was also living on the edge of this farm . . . As these natives were a hindrance to the development of my farm, I gave them all notice and they left. I have learnt since that this farm was actually Chief Chipunza's domain originally, and that the place is the ancestral burial ground for this particular tribe, and that they attach considerable sentiment to this place. Chipunza has been given notice to leave the farm he is now resident on . . . and some of the headmen have approached me, asking to come back here. I also hear that Chipunza himself is coming to ask the same question. I have told them that I cannot have them as squatters again, but that it might be possible for them to buy the eastern portion of this farm. They are tremendously keen on this . . . I am keen to sell the eastern portion of this farm, about 2,300 acres, and am willing to have it proclaimed a Native Purchase Area.[48]

But although Chief Makoni and his people were actually allowed to make a collective purchase of the land on which the Makoni Chiefs were buried and the senior spirit mediums were resident, this proposal for Chipunza was declared against the intentions of the Land Apportionment Act.

The spirits as owners of the land could be appealed to rather more aggressively in order to frustrate those intentions. In May 1934 it was reported that the people of Chief Zimunya in Umtali District were seeking to buy collectively 10 000 acres around Mount Rowa so as to prevent Native Purchase settlement on the land. The Native Commissioner wrote that 'Natives of Chitiyo's kraal appeared and reported that the tribal spirits [of dead chiefs] have ordered through the spirit media Mafuko and Chitowo that the sacred land south of Mount Rowa must not be cut up into holdings. . . The spirits threaten to visit their wrath on anyone who purchases land in this area as an individual.'[49]

With the rise of radical peasant nationalism and particularly with the coming of the guerrilla war it became possible to adopt a yet more aggressive strategy to recover the lost lands, and possible to back spiritual anger with armed force. Lan writes:

The most significant and pervasive inequality experienced by all Zimbabweans was, of course, that between blacks and whites. . . The most important aspect of this national inequality was the control of access to land . . . The consequent shortage of land for peasant cultivation was the single most significant incentive of the struggle. Now, throughout Zimbabwe, it is the particular responsibility of the *mhondoro* spirits to protect the land. It was precisely because the guerilas were able to convince the mediums that they were fighting to reclaim the land for its rightful owners, the peasantry, that they were given access to the symbolism and the ritual practice that lie at the heart of the authority of the *mhondoro* . . . The guerillas promised to liberate Zimbabwe . . . to free the land . . . and return it to the peasants who had barely enough to keep their families alive. The single most important function of the spirit mediums is to protect the land. From the grave, from the depths of the forest, from the body of a lion or of their mediums, the *mhondoro* control in perpetuity the land they conquered during their lives. The guerillas offered land as fertility and land as restored tradition . . . The support of the *mhondoro* mediums could not be withheld. The guerillas and the mediums shared a desire to regain the land, to renew its lost fertility and their lost wealth. From this common aim the sharing of ritual and weapons, of symbolism and strategy, the union of the mystical power of the ancestors with the military strength of the guerillas were to flow.[50]

In Makoni, as no doubt elsewhere, the natural desire of the peasantry to recover their lost and more fertile soils came together with the call of the spirit mediums that they should return to 'our holy mountains': In 1981 Chief Tandi's councillors recalled:

the days when we could freely sell our grain for good prices. It was not only centralisation that stopped it but especially the eviction of people from the farms in the 1940s so that people had to use the same land time and time again . . . We all very much want to go back to Matowe mountain and to the well of water on top of it where we go to drink when we want rain. We hope the Government will give it to us. But whether we are here or there the important thing is to keep the traditions.[51]

Chief Muzanenamo Makoni is a follower of the Mai Chaza church and expresses a proper Christian doubt: 'The Bible says there is one God but people still talk of the spirits. I myself am afraid of the Commandment "Thou shalt have no other Gods before me." When the svikiro calls I send my councillors and do not make the sacrifice myself.' Nevertheless Chief Makoni certainly sanctioned the protection given to the guerrillas by his senior mediums during the war, and his demands for the return of land are couched in the idiom of the spirits:

Chief Ndafunya Makoni was told that the land he lived on was European land. But he said he would not move because it was holy land. He raised enough money from the people to buy it. We know today that it is ours and we call it Makoni Farm. The Europeans called it the Tribal Trust Land – but we do not know what that means. Who were we supposed to trust? Yes, although it was ours, they enforced centralisation and destocking on the land. Nobody was free. . . On the land is the hill where the Makoni chiefs are buried and people make intercessions there. There is also a small pool on a flat hill where the rain ceremonies are carried out. The Makoni princesses are buried at Chitsotso. This was originally on the land we bought but in the 1950s the boundary was changed so that Chitsotso is now on Prospect Farm. We were very angry. As chief, I am still crying for that fence to be removed. But it is not only the land where the chief lives. All the land from Gwindingwi through St Faith's to Rusape should be ours because it belonged to the ancestors and the spirits. . . My people are not troublesome – I live very well with them – but they have been wronged. Now the war is over I have prohibited my people from taking the land by force but they cannot wait for ever.[52]

Thus the spirit mediums were significant to the peasantry because they stood against administrative coercion and because they symbolized the peasant right to recover the land. The adherence of the mediums to these positions was all the more important because in the late 1960s and early 1970s the administration did everything it could to co-opt mediums on the side of officially defined tradition and against nationalist guerrillas. In a recent article I have described the attempts by the Rhodesia Front regime to establish a fully 'traditional' tribal political structure in the rural areas as an alternative to nationalism. This involved ensuring that chiefs were selected only in the most elaborate 'customary' manner and the administration spent a lot of time trying to find spirit mediums who would select and install chiefs. The administration offered recognition and subsidy to mediums who were prepared to speak out against 'trouble-makers' and to report to the District Office when strangers entered the Tribal Trust Lands. District Commissioners even attempted to pre-empt the idiom of the spirits in their admonitions to the people. 'In your tribe,' the District Commissioner told the people of Chief Chiduku in December 1975, 'you have decided no longer to follow custom and it is quite apparent that your spirits are not satisfied with things . . . You have failed to put the spirits in appeasement . . . If no rain comes I will not be surprised. You have got yourselves into a dreadful state.'[53]

Some mediums did collaborate with the regime, the most prominent amongst them being Muchetera, who claimed to be medium of Chaminuka and who lived in west Chiduku, and Kupara, who claimed to be the medium of Mutota and lived in Dande. But these were men who had spent years building up huge supra-tribal networks. Mediums closer to the ground were careful to evade the administration's embrace. Some refused to have anything to do with Europeans or European-associated objects. By ritual avoidance they displayed their total distinctness from the bogus traditionalism of the Rhodesia Front. In Makoni the radical peasants withdrew their support from the mediums who collaborated with the regime. Peter Chakanyuka points out that:

When Muchetera first claimed to be possessed by Chaminuka very many believed him and came to his kraal. But when it came to the idea of nationalism he used to associate with the District Commissioner, had pictures of Europeans in his *banya* (spirit hut), stopped eating *sadza* (meal porridge) and depended on tea. He always wore his hair uncut and plaited, his black robe, to show he was a regional spirit medium, but he used to come to our family eating-house every day to eat buns and tea. He had ceased to be African. He rode a bike and never walked. He acted on the principle that if a person was well known to whites he would gain their support. . . In 1961 or 1962 when Dewedzo was fully ZAPU, even the children, my uncle threw him out of our eating-house. He caught him by the throat and shouted: 'You think that this country can be led by the whites'. He threw him out. Muchetera had to cycle all the way to Dowa Purchase Area to get his bread and tea.[54]

Numbers attending ceremonies at Muchetera's kraal fell sharply.

People in Nedewedzo began to turn to mediums of smaller spirits, linked with the particular history and land areas of their own district. These provided the peasantry with the capacity to repudiate the chiefs without repudiating their own past. As we have seen, in Makoni District the family of Chief Chendambuya was linked with radical nationalism and Chiefs Tandi and Makoni endorsed the right of the people to repossess the land which the spirits 'owned'. Nevertheless, the institution of chiefship as a whole was discredited even in Makoni by the administration's use of it and many chiefs and headmen were killed during the war.

As for the Dande, Lan's field work there has enabled him to make the point very strongly:

[In the north-east] the centre of political authority has progressively shifted from the chiefs to the mediums to the guerillas and, finally, to the newly established ZANU (PF) political committees . . . The interference of the white administration in the appointment of chiefs and in the operation of their traditional duties had the effect of delegitimising their 'ancestral' authority . . . willingly or otherwise, the chiefs became intimately associated with the white government. The mediums rejected it and demonstrated their rejection by their 'ritual' avoidance . . . Mediums may not ride in buses or cars. The smell of petrol is so dangerous that the medium of Mutota is said to have died of it. They may not enter shops or eat food produced by mechanical means . . . It is inconceivable that mediums would accept employment from a white person . . . Many mediums refuse to see white at all . . . an acting out of avoidance of whites based on experience of them in the past . . .

By accepting their lowly position in the government hierarchy, the chiefs had acquired the authority to receive a monthly salary, to collect taxes, to wear a flamboyant uniform, and to little else. Their followers were left with no authority but to do what the government required of them. The shift of 'traditional' political authority from the chiefs to the independent, nationalist *mhondoro* mediums provided the thousands of deeply discontented villagers in Dande with the authority to do what the ancestors required of them. They received the authority to resist.[55]

Thus when the guerrillas began to infiltrate into the rural areas they found that spirits played an important part in peasant ideology. What, then, were the guerrillas to do about this? What were they to tell the peasants about the mediums? Were they to seek to wean the peasants away from such irrationality to a 'scientific' understanding of the revolution?

This was very much an open question in the 1960s. For many years ZANU in exile depended on the financial support of Zimbabweans who had gone to Zambia in search of more opportunities for advancement than existed in Zimbabwe itself. Up to 1967 most of these were Zimbabwean 'business people' in the towns; after the Zambianization policy of 1967 which undercut the position of many of these urban entrepreneurs, 'we started expanding our operations in Zambia. Then the Zimbabwean farmers formed rural branches, collecting food' for the recruits under training in ZANU camps.[56] Most of these recruits during the 1960s were young men from Zimbabwean families in Zambia. None of them had any direct experience of the spirit mediums or the part they played in peasant consciousness inside Zimbabwe. Many Zimbabwean farmers inside Zambia, indeed, were members of independent churches and ascribed their striking economic success to their freedom from antiquated tradition. Young men from this background who had then gone on to political education somewhere in the Socialist bloc were hardly likely to be very sympathetic to the idea that the mediums might have a crucial role to play in guerrilla war. For its part, ZAPU, with a greater preponderance of Ndebele recruits and an alliance with the South African National Congress (ANC), was if anything less likely to develop such a notion. In any case in the 1960s few guerrilla incursions across the Zambezi made any effective connection with the peasantry and the debate about how best to relate to them ideologically remained a theoretical one.

One unexpected source gives us an idea of the inherent ambiguity of the guerrilla movements' relations with the spirit mediums in this period. In October 1969 the American radical magazine *Ramparts* carried a fascinating account of the debates, aroused by their experience in the field, which were taking place among guerrillas of the ZAPU/South African ANC alliance. A ZAPU/ANC band had scattered after a series of engagements with the Rhodesian forces. In a certain Shona village they found one of their comrades, hitherto given up for lost or dead:

He told us that the villagers who had hidden him and given him food were anxious to join our section. We felt that making such contacts was premature – probably wrongly. Then, almost casually, he related something which came to have a most important connection with what was to happen to us. The people with whom he had been staying had advised him to carry out the custom which every stranger for his own good must do . . . visit the local Maswikero (spirit medium). Only *he* would be able to say whether our stay would be safe . . . Some of the members of our group continued to talk about it. Eventually they raised the matter with the commander. The commander called us all together. He explained that we had received advice from the local people which some of the men strongly felt should be followed because we should respect local custom. Many of us spoke against it: 'We can't follow all the traditions in our special situation. If this is the tradition then the police must go there too . . .' . . . After two days of discussion, some of the fighters became impatient. 'You despise our customs,' one of them said. 'You undermine our traditions. Is it because you are communists? This is Africa and to achieve our aim we have to follow our own traditions.'

In the end one of the guerrillas *was* sent to consult the medium; the medium replied that he would 'arrange a mist to cover you on the route to any place you want to go'; as a result of the consultation the presence of guerrillas became known to the administration; 'the village was invaded by Security Forces; the guerilla's contact-man with the village was shot and killed.' The ANC narrator of this story ended it ambiguously:

It struck me later that after the disastrous fortune teller incident nothing at all was said of it in our detachment. No recriminations and no apologies. We were all close again. All understood now. It had to be learned, not from books, but from life. As for the mists, this was not the season for them. But we had learned that what will really keep us secure and covered in our route are our millions of oppressed countrymen who will throw up thousands of people like . . . all the people in *our* village.[57]

In the 1970s the ZANLA guerrillas coming in from Mozambique based their new strategy precisely upon mingling with the 'oppressed countrymen'. The opening of the Mozambique front meant that thousands of young men went over to join the guerrillas directly from the peasant areas of Zimbabwe. These young men, most of whom received a much less intense ideological training than their predecessors, found it natural to operate within the idioms of radical peasant consciousness. From the earliest penetration of the guerrillas into the north-east, spirit mediums began to play a crucial role. As Lan writes, 'the key to understanding' that role 'is found at the first moment of contact between peasants and guerillas. When the guerillas arrived in Dande and sought out sympathetic leaders of the local communities, they were taken to the villages of the spirit mediums'.[58] 'When we arrived in the area,' Mayor Urimbo told Lan, 'we had to start by talking to the masses. We spoke to the old people who said we must consult the medium. We were taken to Nehanda . . . We told her "We are the children of Zimbabwe, we want to liberate Zimbabwe". She was very much interested.'[59]
David Martin and Phyllis Johnson, also drawing on Urimbo's evidence, tell us that 'Urimbo, ZANLA's first provincial commander, and Chimurenga, the operational commander of ZANLA forces [in the north east], swiftly recognized the importance of the spirit mediums . . . they talked with the spirit of the first Nehanda, explaining that they were her children and that they needed her

guidance to launch the war of liberation. The guerrillas talked [with the spirit] about strategy, places to cache arms, places to hide and routes to take.' Thereafter they returned with the old woman to Mozambique.[60]

Josiah Tungamirai, later to become ZANLA's Chief Political Commissar, at first uneasy about the use of the mediums, later told Martin that, 'Mbuya Nehanda was ZANLA's most important and influential recruit . . . "Once the children, the boys and girls in that area, knew that Nehanda had joined the war, they came in large numbers." '[61] ZANLA war zones were named after Nehanda and Chaminuka. ZANLA songs, which played such an important part in the night-time politicization sessions, appealed to the memory of the great spirits. One of the most popular, broadcast on the night of Zimbabwean independence by the ZANU/PF Ideological Choir, ran:

> Grandmother Nehanda
> You prophesied,
> Nehanda's bones resurrected,
> ZANU's spear caught their fire
> Which was transformed into ZANU's gun,
> The gun which liberated our land.[62]

Nor was it only the great spirits and their mediums which proved of importance in the north-east. A ZANLA political commissar recalls:

We would learn the local customs and we would follow them. . . Even those of us who were not believing these things had to follow the traditions. We always met the elders first, so they could tell us what procedures to follow in their particular areas. You'd find there were sacred places they could tell you about . . . Most of the spirit mediums did support the struggle. They didn't tell people to support the struggle; they would just tell us what to do so that we would succeed in the armed struggle. You could see sometimes with those few spirit mediums who did not support the struggle, the spirits would vanish from such people. They would just end up a normal human being, and not get possessed again.[63]

How, then, are we to evaluate all this? Are we witnessing a treason of the modernizing intellectuals, a wilful failure to carry out their task of enlightening the peasantry? Are we witnessing a failure to achieve a true 'people's war? Were these transactions between guerrillas and mediums bound to limit the effectiveness of the war itself and bound to undercut the capacity of the Zimbabwean revolution to transform the lives of the people?

I would certainly argue that more was going on than merely a survival of 'superstition'; more than a merely cynical exploitation of peasant credulity. It is clear from what I have already said in this book that the spirit mediums had played a much more central 'structural' role in the history of the Zimbabwean peasantry than the 'seers' had played in the history of the Kikuyu peasantry. It is not helpful to lump mediums and seers together as part of a general and regrettable rural tendency towards 'magical religion' at times of armed confrontation with colonial regimes. Moreover, mediums did not only symbolically represent peasant grievances over lost lands and administrative coercion. They also helped radical peasants and incoming guerrillas to come together as one community of resistance. The systematic symbolic logic of this process in the north-east must await demonstration when Lan's doctoral dissertation is published as a book.[64] Meanwhile I can make some less profound points from my own data on Makoni.

Once the guerrillas had discovered how important spirit mediums were to the successful prosecution of the war in the north-east, they made contact with mediums as soon as, or even before, they entered any new war zone. Elleck Mashingaidze was carrying out historical research in the Mazoe area in 1972 and – after much hesitation and suspicion of him as a stranger – had been granted an interview with one of the influential mediums. On the day of his interview he had to wait while the medium received unexpected visitors. When these men emerged from their talk with the medium, having been assured of Mashingaidze's reliability, they told him that they had come from the north-east, where all was in readiness for the onset of an effective guerrilla war. They had come to tell the medium of what was planned, and they were going on to inform mediums in other areas.[65] I do not know whether any medium in Makoni District was in contact with the guerrillas as early as 1972, but there is no doubt that some of them were in touch before the actual outbreak of war in Makoni in 1976. In Makoni, as elsewhere, once the guerrillas had arrived the mediums helped to articulate liberation ideology with peasant aspirations.

This was a task that very much needed to be done. I have argued for a substantial continuity of peasant consciousness into the period of the war. But it has to be recognized that there were some substantial discontinuities also which made it difficult for there to be immediate or total collaboration between the peasant elders and the young guerrillas. To begin with the guerrillas *were* young and they were closer to the teenagers of Makoni District than they were to the resident elders. Men in their fifties, who had hitherto dominated Makoni peasant radicalism and who were used to controlling a flock of dependent women – wives, daughters, daughters-in-law – now found that the initiative had passed to young men with guns. These young men called upon the unmarried women of Makoni to act as their cooks, informants and messengers and in these latter two roles teenage girls were able to exercise a good deal of power, for the first time in Makoni's history. Moreover, the peasant resident elders of Tanda and Weya and western Chiduku had confronted the whites in the name of ZAPU, and by 1977 at any rate the incoming guerrillas demanded exclusive allegiance to ZANU/Mugabe. Those pioneer nationalists who could not stomach having to change parties at the behest of young strangers found it wise to leave the district and take refuge in Salisbury.

The great majority of Makoni peasants, as the war developed and they confronted the whites together with the guerrillas, came naturally enough to transfer their allegiance to ZANU/Mugabe. But even they needed some way of coming to terms with and exerting influence upon the unknown young men with guns. They could not do it in the time-honoured way of establishing kin linkages. It was ZANLA policy that men should not serve as guerrillas in their own districts. In this way guerrillas would not feel constrained by kin obligations if they had to mete out punishments; in this way the resident elders could not place the guerrillas in positions of subordination because of their youth. Moreover, the guerrillas were known only by their Chimurenga nicknames so that no affinities of clan could be established. In 1981 as I conducted interviews on the war, I soon came to recognize two repetitive themes. The young men who had left Makoni District to join the guerrillas in Mozambique would describe how they had been unable to make contact with their own kin as they passed back through the district; and peasants in Makoni would describe the first extraordinary experience of meeting the guerrillas with their unheard of names.

Lameck Madzwendira, whose Chimurenga name is Mutsawareyi ('working on the reactionaries') testifies that when he had finished his training in Mozambique, he:

was sent back in as part of a group of 100, guided by comrades who had been in the bush before. We came in through the Hondi Valley; then to St Barbara's mission, where we left ten comrades. Then we came across Kemp's Farm on the edge of the Makoni Reserve. This was the wet season of 1978. Then we came to Zonga mountain in Makoni Reserve and spent the whole day there. I was very close now to my relatives because the St Francis African Church, to which some of them belonged, had a farm at Zonga. During the day we spent there I could see the Sisters of St Francis working on the farm and *mukoma* Mavis herding the animals. I could see them but I could not call out to them. They thought that I was dead. So we went off into Chiduku on our way to Charter, where I served for the rest of the war.[66]

Isaac Tsungo, farmer and store-owner testifies that:

In February 1977 I received the first message from the guerrillas brought by two young boys who told me that the comrades wanted to see me. I went with them some three miles from the road in Makoni Tribal Trust Land. I was taken to them among the rocks. I shall never forget that day. Their leader was called 'Soveria'; then there was 'Action' and 'Pedzai Mabunu', 'finish the Boers'. Those were the days when they were called 'mangandan-gas'. They said to me, 'They call us mangandangas. Look, do we have tails?' I said 'I don't see any'. 'So we are human beings, you see, and we need your help'. I said I would do what I could. And after that meeting I became a *mujiba*, a helper and messenger for the comrades.[67]

Finally, the guerrillas with their strange names – Comrade Mao, Comrade Dracula, Comrade Evil Eyes, Comrade Uriah Heep, and the rest – could not be brought within the 'traditional' tribal political system and be made subordinate to chiefs and headmen. Even if some chiefs and headmen worked closely with the guerrillas, the system as such was discredited by the use the whites had made of it. In many parts of Makoni District peasants saw the guerrillas making attacks on 'tribal authorities'. All in all, some means was urgently required to give the guerrillas legitimacy in terms of Makoni's own past and to give the peasants some way of controlling the young men with guns.

The spirit mediums provided just such a means. In the pre-colonial past it had been the mediums who welcomed incoming fighting men to Makoni District. Peter Chakanyuka's summary of his interview with old Manyukire Gorembeu tells how in the early 1890s:

Manyukire's family migrated from Mangwende's area. . . They went into *rimuka* (thick forests) hunting elephants in Makoni's area. They carried out their hunting trips with the help of Muswere who was Makoni's chief spirit medium. This spirit medium played a big role by introducing these hunters to Makoni, the king of the area, who was living at Sangano. A ceremony was organised for their reception at the *muzinda*, the capital. . . The ceremonies were repeated annually . . . On each ceremony Muswere was given a wife or herd of cattle by Makoni.[68]

Now in the 1970s the mediums could play the same role, not now welcoming incoming fighting men to the service of the chief but to membership of the wider community of resistance. Headman Mpambawhale of Toriro in Chiduku testifies that in 1977:

Comrade Mao, Comrade Dracula, Comrade Rib-Crusher came to me with *swikiro* Sakureba. They all went into the mountain and Sakureba appeased the ancestors there. I went with them early in the morning to a special place where headmen sacrifice for rain. Sakureba told me what to say to the ancestors and I did it. My ancestors have been living here for centuries. My area was used as a route through Makoni district by the guerrillas and they needed the favour of the ancestors. Then Sakureba and the comrades went back to report to Chief Makoni that it had been done. Sakureba gave me a white cloth and a black cloth. A *swikiro* from Mozambique had come first and given white and black cloth to Chief Makoni. It was this *swikiro* from Mozambique who had gone to seek out Sakureba and then Sakureba had escorted the guerrillas through the district. We knew Sakureba. People would go to him for rain.[69]

Rituals such as this gave the guerrillas access to 'the secrets of our strongholds' as well as ensuring them the favour of the ancestral owners of the land. The strongholds, secure caves and other places of retreat in the granite hills, had been much used in the first *Chimurenga* of 1896. Their secrets were preserved by elders and headmen in Makoni through the long colonial peace. In 1930 that irate Jesuit, Father Jerome O'Hea, complaining of resistance to Triashill mission stimulated by the young migrants returning from the towns, declared that:

Nothing but a rod of iron is any use for these people . . . It is hard . . . to humble a people whose age-long vice has been cowardice, when that very vice is looked upon as a great virtue: to point to great rock caverns and subterranean dwellings where they crept like rabbits in quaking fear, rather than fight like men, and to know that they smugly congratulate themselves on having sneaked away.[70]

O'Hea's words were echoed by the whites in the late 1970s who constantly called upon the guerrillas to 'fight like men' in pitched combat with the Rhodesian army. But the guerrilla strategy, of course, was precisely to sally out of their secure bases and guerrillas made great use of all the strongholds of Makoni, many of which remained unknown to the whites. In particular, they were able to use the 'holy mountains' which no ordinary Makoni peasant was allowed to approach. As Archdeacon Alban Makoni recalls:

At this stage of the war (1976) the comrades were very hostile to Christianity. 'We don't want to hear about Jesus. Jesus can do nothing'. In the crisis of the war they put emphasis on the spirits. In Chiduku Reserve the chief base for the comrades was Ruwombe mountain, the second most important base for them in the whole of Manicaland. Ruwombe was a holy mountain, on which offerings were made for rain. It became a major reception centre for comrades coming in from Mozambique and passing on through the district, at the rate of 50 a day. Ruwombe was attacked by the Army but no guerrillas were killed – they said because of the protection of the spirits. In a similar way Muwona hill in Makoni, was the hill where the chiefs were buried. When I was a boy I used to be told never to point at Muwona, but indicate it if necessary with my fist clenched. Muwona became a firm stronghold for the guerrillas after certain ceremonies had been carried out to make this possible.[71]

It was indeed the guerrilla use of the burial hill of the Makoni chiefs which showed most dramatically the status which the mediums were able to confer upon them. In the 1970s the burial rites of the Makoni chiefs were still surrounded in mystery and awe. The councillors of Chief Makoni very properly would not talk to me about them in 1981 – 'we must keep *some* secrets from the Europeans.' In 1974, however, the District Commissioner compiled a report based on information given by his African assistants:

The only 'MHONDORO' or 'Lion' that I know is the one that appears the night following the installation of a Chief. On that night the people are told to stay close at home and see that their children do not wander about . . . This MHONDORO, or lion, last appeared when they carried ZAMBE's dried body from the BVEKERWA area of Chiduku to bury it at MATOTWE HILL for burial. Those people did something wrong so the lions chased them until they dropped the body and ran . . . They had previously appeared when the Chief died. That night they came and rubbed themselves against the huts and the people were afraid to go out. These MHONDORO of the VAUNGWE are born of the liquid that comes from the body of the chief as it is drying. Those responsible for that work collect that liquid in a very big pot. They carry that to MATOTWE where, after the body has been placed in a cave, the liquid is poured into a prepared 'grave' situated to one side. That is closed and the top carefully swept. The people who look after the graves then inspect the surface every day, watching for a hole to appear there. Once the hole appears, they announce that the Chief's 'Mhondoro' has come out. The bodies themselves are seated in their places in the cave and it is the duty of the new Chief to provide them with new cloths. The caretakers take these cloths and, addressing each body by name, they tell it who the cloths come from and that he is the new chief.[72]

And yet the guerrillas were given access to this most sacred of places.

In February 1981 I interviewed George Bhongohozo, intelligence officer for the guerrilla groups in Makoni in 1978 and 1979:

In 1978 I found that the guerrilla platoons had fall-back hideouts. In
Makoni detachment area there were . . . Mugumabwemairi hill near St
Barbara's. Here the hill was honey-combed with caves and at one point a
small crevice in the rock led into a large chamber where many could hide in
safety. Our ancestors took refuge there in 1896. The guerrillas on Mugumabwemairi used to keep in touch with Father Kenny at St Barbara's, a
very good man . . .
Then there was Matotwe mountain, the burial place of chief Makoni.
Special ceremonies were carried out there by two mediums, an old man and
an old woman, who had inherited their role. They allocated caves in the
mountain to the comrades where they could not disturb the spirits . . .
In Chiduku detachment area there was Romwe mountain, another place
where people hid in 1896. Here again the spirit mediums showed the
comrades where they could hide . . .
Of course we used to work with the mediums. The two near Matotwe
used to foresee and then warn us of enemy attacks. A very young medium at
Nyachibva hill, which was another of our bases, also used to help in the
same way. Many of the guerrillas were also themselves mediums. They had
spirits helpful to war . . . Indeed, the masses used to believe that we moved
supernaturally and not on our own feet. The enemy attacked where we had
been and we were not there any more. They did not know that we had been
warned by the mediums at Matotwe.[73]

With this kind of endorsement there was no danger that the
guerrillas would be repudiated by the peasant elders. Maurice
Nyagumbo has recorded what happened to the very first 'trained
boys with weapons' to penetrate the Makoni District. This was 'a
group of about ten trained boys with weapons' sent in by ZAPU in
November 1964:

[They] went to Rusape and reached Njanike village. They then took their
weapons into one of the mountains and hid them, leaving themselves with
revolvers. As three of the boys belonged to this village, they decided to stay
there and lived in one house for the purpose of co-ordinating their
activities. During the mornings, the boys would go up into the mountain
and practise with their big guns. But in the afternoon, the boys would
rampage the beer parties which were mainly attended by the elderly men
and women. They demanded money from these elderly people and those
who could not produce it were threatened with the small guns.
After several weeks of this state of affairs, some of the elderly people
decided to report the matter to the police. All the boys were arrested and
those precious weapons confiscated.[74]

Twelve years later the peasant elders backed the guerrillas in the
people's war. Still, even now that the guerrillas were ZANLA men

and women specifically trained to respect the peasantry, there
remined a need for that peasantry to be able to articulate norms of
conduct to which they wanted the guerrillas to conform. There is no
doubt that even in the late 1970s ZANLA guerrilla groups lost
peasant support when they were perceived to be acting arbitrarily
and without respect for the moral economy of the war. Once again it
was the spirit mediums who most effectively laid down this moral
economy.

In February 1981 I interviewed the medium of the Akuchekwa
spirit of Tandi in Chiduku and his acolyte. They told me of the
central role of the spirit in Tandi and of the relations of its medium
with the guerrillas:

The Tandi spirit is that of Akuchekwa. The living Akuchekwa was the son
of Mutorio son of Tandi . . . You ask why it should have been Akuchekwa
rather than Tandi or Mutorio who became our great spirit. This is because
when he was alive it was he who went . . . to the home of the Old Rozwi and
he was given a cup and a corn stalk and the power to make rain. The *swikiro*
who has his spirit had the power to call together all other *swikiros* in Tandi
and can tell which is genuine. A *swikiro* of Akuchekwa can send a great
wind to blow locusts away from the lands. And in 1958 there was a plague of
hyenas attacking the cattle. They appealed to the then *swikiro* who was the
present incumbent's father and he said in the spirit 'Within two weeks there
will be no hyenas' and indeed they all vanished . . . The present *swikiro*
became possessed only in 1979. His father died in 1968. He was for many
years an Apostle and a farm guard at Wakefield but he gave both up when
he became a *swikiro*. . .
    In 1979 the guerrillas used to come to consult the spirit . . . Akuchekwa
told the boys he would protect them but that they must not do the things
which the spirits disliked. The spirits refused to accept the shedding of
innocent blood. If 'sell-outs' went to the boys and said 'This one is a witch',
'this one is an informer', they were not just to kill them. The boys obeyed
the spirits. Things were quite perfect then. And the spirits protected the
boys. But unfortunately Muzorewa's Auxiliaries did not obey the spirits.[75]

Amon Shonge, who witnessed the interaction of mediums and
guerrillas in Weya, sums up this particular function:

This use of mediums was the same everywhere. The comrades had to
contact the spirit medium first to introduce themselves. Then they would be
told what to do. They were told which were the holy places and given some
sort of bye-laws to guide them. They were told that them must not kill
innocent people. Nearly everyone then started to feel that the mediums
were very important people. The mediums felt that they had been forgotten
but now they were remembered.[76]

It seems clear, then, that the composite peasant/guerrilla ideology of Makoni included not only a common focus on the 'lost lands' but also a common belief in the protection of the spirits. It also seems clear that the practical effects of such a composite ideology were not damaging to the success of the guerrilla war. Buijtenhuijs concluded that in Kenya the use of Kikuyu religion within Mau Mau, though 'a powerful tool to unite the Kikuyu people', proved 'incompatible with Mau Mau as an anti-colonial revolt.' That this was not so within ZANLA's guerrilla campaign was due to three factors. The first was that the relationship of the spirit mediums to Shona-speaking rural society in Zimbabwe was much more central and more closely connected with the basics of the peasant economy than was the case with the 'seers' in Kikuyuland. Another was that the culture area in which this 'movement of cultural renewal' was taking place was so much larger than Kikuyuland. The composite peasant/guerrilla ideology proved exportable across at least two-thirds of rural Zimbabwe. The third was that there was a strong element of pragmatism in the religion of the spirit mediums. Lan writes that 'few, if any, of the guerrillas relied exclusively for their safety on the magic means of protection which the *mhondoro* mediums supplied, nor would the mediums have expected them to. Sound planning, courage and discipline were the recognised requirements of a successful operation.'[77]

The idiom of rural Zimbabwe during the war was taken up by ZANU/PF candidates in the 1980 elections. Davis Mugabe thus addressed a peasant audience in an election rally in Munyikwa TTL in Gutu District:

[The ZANLA guerrillas] were fighting so that you and me may be free . . . They were fighting for you. They were fighting for me. Then today you say you want to run a store, and you join forces with Smith – the ancestral spirits of Zimbabwe will say 'No!'. The ancestral spirits of Zimbabwe absolutely refuse . . .

Now the war was . . . right in the heart of Zimbabwe. The whites continued to wail. They cried and wailed. Till they decided to call upon one of their political mentors [Dr Kissinger]. But they can't mess with the spirits of Zimbabwe, or the country suffer real bloodshed. Do you realise that the children [guerrillas] you used to cook for were being looked after by ancestral spirits? Ask those who have been there. . . It's true we once went to mission schools. We prayed every day, but the best lessons were in the bush – that this country is under the rule of the ancestral spirits. Sometimes Muzorewa's war planes came in big numbers . . .[but] the children survived. Who then would dare to tell me there is no such thing as an ancestral spirit? He will be kidding. This country belongs to spirits. . . If you should be bribed to vote for Muzorewa, the spirits will seek revenge on you. Our ancestors are too good to betray.

As for Muzorewa, said Davis Mugabe to great amusement, all *he* had learnt was 'how to venerate and propitiate the spirits of the white man . . . He was so good he even got possessed . . . with the spirit of a white man.'[78]

My conclusion, then, is the same in this respect as in the question of the 'lost lands'. Mau Mau was in many ways similar to the guerrilla war in Zimbabwe's peasant areas. If Mau Mau failed it was not so much because of its supernaturalism *as such* but because its cultural nationalism was too narrow; because it had no external suppliers of guns or training facilities; because the Kikuyu 'Home Guard' held the Reserves against it; because the Kikuyu had been so profoundly influenced by mission and independent Christianity that they had little but the most marginal religious 'traditions' to draw on. On the other hand, my conclusion is *not* that the guerrilla war in rural Zimbabwe was so like Mau Mau that it belongs to some relatively primitive category of peasant struggle rather than to the category of a 'people's war'. It seems to me that the guerrilla war in Zimbabwe was quintessentially a people's war, in which the people were able to contribute much of their own experience and ideology.

The emphasis on the lost lands, after all, and even the emphasis on the spirit mediums, did not stand in the way of building up a complex network of elected ZANU/PF committees in the rural areas. Nor did it stand in the way of peasant solidarity with Mozambique and other international guerrilla struggles. Rollisa Machaba, a peasant woman in Chibi TTL recalls that:

The comrades told us to look after our houses and look after our gardens and to send our children to school. And they told us the people will decide how our country will be after liberation. In the meantime we were deciding how things should be in this area. We divided this whole place up into districts. We decided to call our area 'Maputo', that is for Machel, who was helping us so much with our struggle. Also we had a district called 'Namibia' and another called 'China'. They are good names because those are the countries which helped us in the war to conquer our enemies.[79]

In Chiduku the band of territory across the TTL which guerrillas used as a transit route was similarly divided up into zones known as 'Ogaden', 'Viet-nam', and other names proclaiming international solidarity. No one in the district found any incongruity in the fact that each of these zones also had its spirit medium who interceded with the spirits for the safety of the guerrillas. Nor did anyone in Zimbabwe feel any incongruity when on the evening of independence Thomas Mapfumo sang on the radio:

All ancestral spirits adore the liberators
Congratulations, Mr Machel.[80]

Two things, however, remain to be said. One is that the whole tradition of peasant Christianity did not disappear during the war; nor did all peasants who remained practising Christians become supporters of Bishop Muzorewa, though some of them did. In many areas Christians picked up the general peasant/guerrilla ideology and sang the *Chimurenga* songs addressed to the spirits. In Dande, Lan found, 'joining the resistance required a rejection of Christianity which was firmly associated with the white state. For some members of established churches, their past affiliation to both belief systems allowed them to, as it were, put Christianity into neutral and concentrate exclusively on the other for a time.'[81] It was not quite like that in Makoni, where the different mission Christian ideologies had correlated to different layers of peasant experience and where core areas of 'folk Christianity' had developed. The core areas of folk Methodism naturally enough followed Bishop Muzorewa, the head of their church. The core areas of Anglicanism and Catholicism collaborated intensely with the guerrillas. Both the Anglican centre of St Faith's and the Catholic centres of Triashill and St Barbara's were guerrilla strongholds. In these places guerrillas made some attempt to appeal to belief in spirit mediums *against* folk Christianity. But in the long run they found themselves obliged to respect the rather different customs of these particular groups of peasants. It will perhaps have been noticed that while George Bhongoghozo found the guerrillas at Matotwe and Romwe mountains collaborating with the mediums, he found those at Mugumabwemairi keeping 'in touch with Father Kenny at St Barbara's, a very good man'. In such areas of folk Christianity, I have argued in a recent article, it was Christian holy men who played the essential role of mediator between guerrillas and peasants. Irish Catholic priests at Triashill, St Barbara's and St Killian's in the Makoni TTL, African Anglican priests and evangelists at St Faith's and Toriro in Chiduku, procured supplies for the guerrillas, obtained legal aid for arrested and tortured *mujibas*, lent their sacred authority to the guerrillas' cause, and imposed the bye-laws and ground rules for guerrilla interaction with a Christian peasantry.[82]

The second qualification is a significant modification of my general position in this chapter, namely that the peasant religious element in the ideology of the war had largely positive consequences. Wide though the Shona cultural nationalist zone was, it did not, of course, embrace the whole country. Sooner or later the ZANLA guerrillas were going to come across peasant populations to whom their composite ideology was not going to be attractive. This happened when ZANLA guerrillas entered into southern Matabeleland. Lionel Cliffe, Joshua Mpofu and Barry Munslow have described what happened. 'The ZANLA guerrillas established their politico-military structures in the entire Filabusi District, most of rural Essexvale . . . a "good portion" of rural Gwanda', areas which readers will recognize as a good part of the region which expressed such fierce resentment against the evictions of the late 1940s, a resentment then partly cast in the idiom of the Matabele Home Society. 'The typical ZANLA base area committees, *mujibas* and *chibwidos* were established to involve the masses in the struggle.' Yet though they were supported by the peasant population during the war, the guerrillas had alienated these Ndebele voters and ZANU/PF gained no seats in the elections. One local man testified that he would have 'voted for ZANU-PF if [they] had treated me and my family properly. But they did not treat us in a good way. They tried to compel us to speak Shona. They were ruthless on those who asked why. All the slogans and songs were in Shona and they were not to be translated into Sindebele. Everything tended to "change" us to Shona.' The ZANLA guerrillas were not sufficently flexible to be able to adapt the composite ideology which had served them so well throughout two-thirds of the country. In 1980 Ndebele peasants flocked instead to Nkomo's election rally – held, significantly enough, at the senior shrine of the High God cult at Njelele in the Matopos.[83]

And that is a good place to end this chapter, not only with the limitations of the composite peasant/guerrilla ideology which had developed in the Shona-speaking rural areas during the war, but also with a confession of the limitations of my own knowledge. The Njelele rally reminds us that there must also be a history of the interaction of religion and the war in Matabeleland. It is merely one of the indications of our current ignorance of rural Matabeleland's recent history that I have no idea what it has been.

NOTES

1 Interview with Caston Makoni, Marondera, 28 August 1982.
2 Interview with Lameck Madzwendira, Makoni, 15 February 1981.
3 Julie Frederikse, *None But Ourselves. Masses vs. Media in the Making of Zimbabwe* (Johannesburg: 1982), p. 61.
4 ibid., p. 60.
5 'Letter from one missionary to another, 1979', ibid., pp. 300–2.
6 ibid., p. 301.

7 Robert Mugabe, 'The Patriotic Front is a creation of Zimbabwe', in *Zimbabwe, The Final Advance* (Oakland: LSM, 1978), p. 28.

8 Interview with Amon Shonge, Weya, 25 March 1981.

9 'Collective Fine in Terms of Section 3 of the Emergency Powers (Collective Fines) Regulations, 1973', 28 March 1977, file 'Collective Punishment', Catholic Commission for Justice and Peace Archives (CCJP Archives) Harare.

10 'Communal Punishment Report', 25 April 1977, *ibid.*

11 'Forces Can Hold Down Any Terror Threat', *Rhodesia Herald*, 7 April 1977.

12 Amon Shonge to Guy Clutton-Brock, 29 May 1977, Clutton-Brock correspondence, 1970–80.

13 Translated leaflet dropped over Weya, April 1977.

14 Rhodesian Intelligence Corps Mapping and Research Unit, 12/78, Map Munda 1732C3.

15 Catholic Commission for Justice and Peace, Fact Paper Series, August 1977, file 'Civilian Deaths', CCJP Archives, Harare.

16 Amon Shonge to Guy Clutton-Brock, 1 December 1977, Clutton-Brock correspondence, 1970–80.

17 Amon Shonge to Guy Clutton-Brock, 3 March 1978, Clutton-Brock correspondence, 1970–80. Accounts of the war, experience of members of the Mukute Farm Society, the co-operative founded by Shonge in Weya, are given in full in A.K.H. Weinrich, *Struggle For the Land. A History of Co-operatives in Zimbabwe*, (Harare: forthcoming). In Chapter 4 Dr Weinrich cites the testimony of Cedric:

The army became very bothersome to us, invading our area with motor cycles and horses. 16 Km from here they had their base. During the night they would sleep in the mountains. Early in the morning they would come down to us to search for comrades. One day in 1978 they attacked us here on our farm and four of us were tortured and taken to their base near Macheke. Torture there was even worse, and then we were taken to Mayo, another and biggest police camp . . . The Security Forces thought we Makute Bros were a dangerous group . . . They simply could not understand who we were.

18 'The Speech that says it all – in silence', *Rand Daily Mail*, 25 July 1980. Todd's speech, intended to be delivered to the University of the Witwatersrand, was banned by the South African government. It continued:

We, the ma-Zimbabwe, will not forget the sacrifices made, nor will we prove unworthy of the heroes we are to remember on August 11th and 12th of each year. We will accept our heroes, not as demi-gods or even only those who died in battle, or were executed by the state . . . but the ordinary people of the villages who suffered most cruelly and who were killed in thousands by the security forces.

19 R. Buijtenhuijs, *Essays on Mau Mau. Contributions to Mau Mau*

Historiography, (Leiden: African Studies Centre Research Report No. 17, 1982), pp. 135–6.

20 Catherine Coquery-Vidrovitch, 'Peasant unrest in Black Africa', in *Agrarian Unrest in British and French Africa, British India and French Indo-China*, (Oxford: Past and Present Society, 1982) pp. 14, 23, 33.

21 Basil Davidson, *The People's Cause. A History of Guerrillas in Africa*, (London: 1981), pp. 92, 97.

22 ibid., pp. 113, 117, 124.

23 Y.T. Museveni, 'Fanon's theory of violence: its verification in liberated Mozambique', in N. Shamuyarira (ed.), *Essays on the Liberation of Southern Africa* (Dar es Salaam: 1972), pp. 14–15, 20, 21.

24 Terence Ranger, 'Religion in the Zimbabwean guerrilla war', History Workshop, Religion and Society, London, July 1983.

25 S.K. Madziyire, 'Heathen practices in the urban and rural parts of Marandellas area and their effects upon Christianity', in Terence Ranger and John Weller (eds), *Themes in the Christian History of Central Africa* (London: 1975), pp. 80–1.

26 N.E. Thomas, 'Christianity, politics and the Manyika', (Boston University: PhD thesis, 1968), pp. 98, 114.

27 Peter Fry, *Spirits of Protest. Spirit-mediums and the articulation of consensus among the Zezuru of Southern Rhodesia (Zimbabwe)*, Cambridge, 1976, pp. 1, 3, 109–10, 120–2.

28 Two mediums in particular built up very extensive networks of influence by means of acting as informants to historians and anthropologists. One of these was Muchetera Njuru, who claimed to be the medium of Chaminuka and who lived in west Chiduku. For him see Terence Ranger, 'The death of Chaminuka: spirit mediums, nationalism and the guerilla war in Zimbabwe', *African Affairs*, vol. 81, no. 324 (July 1982), pp. 349–69. The other was George Kupara, who claimed to be the medium of Mutota, for whom see David Lan, 'Making history. Spirit mediums and the guerrilla war in the Dande area of Zimbabwe' (London School of Economics: PhD thesis: 1983), Chapter VII, 'The politics of tradition I: the making of Mutota'.

29 Interview between John Conradie and Josiah Tongogara, Maputo, 20 August 1979.

30 Interview between John Conradie and Kumbirai Kangai, 21 August 1979.

31 Interview between John Conradie and Samuel Mamutsi *aka* Mrimbo, 23 August 1979.

32 Lan, 'Making history', p. 273.

33 Michael Gelfand, *The Spiritual Beliefs of the Shona* (Gwelo: 1977), p. 134.

34 Interview with Father Peter Turner, Umtali, 14 March 1981.

35 Interview between Sister Emilia Chiteka and Denis Tahusarira Name, Mawango Village, 11 January 1981. Thomas noted that 'Roman Catholics at Triashill Mission in 1966 asked for official church approval for their family *vadzimu* worship and their intercessions for rain to the tribal spirits', Thomas, 'Christianity, politics and the Manyika', p. 166.

36 ibid., pp. 174–5.
37 'Chendambuya' August 1972, file 'Weya/Chendambuya', District Commissioner's office, Rusape (DCOR).
38 District Commissioner to Provincial Commissioner, 13 March 1973, file 'Weya/Chendambuya', DCOR.
39 Roland Hatendi, General Patrol, Weya, 17 April 1972, file 'Chikore', DCOR.
40 Acting Director of Public Prosecution to Scanlen and Holderness, 7 August 1972, file 'Weya/Chendambuya', DCOR.
41 Notes of a discussion between District Commissioner and delegation of elders, 28 May 1974, file 'Weya/Chendambuya', DCOR.
42 File 'Spirit Mediums, Weya', DCOR.
43 Interview with Amon Shonge, Weya, 25 March 1981.
44 Thomas 'Christianity, politics and the Manyika', p. 160.
45 F.A. White to District Commissioner, 29 January 1971; District Commissioner to Provincial Commissioner, 24 August 1977, file 'Headman Makumbe', DCOR.
46 J.C. Kandiero, 'Analysis', 1976, file 'Weya/Chendambuya', DCOR.
47 Interview with the medium of the Akuchekwa spirit, Tandi, Chiduku, 27 February 1981.
48 E.C. Harrington to Director of Native Land Board, 18 May 1936, file S.924.G1.5, National Archives, Harare (NAH).
49 Native Commissioner, Umtali to Chief Native Commissioner, 18 May 1934, file S.1542.L4. 1933 to 1935, NAH.
50 Lan, 'Making history', pp. 16–17, 272.
51 Interview with the councillors of Chief Tandi, Tandi, Chiduku, 27 February 1981.
52 Interview with chief Muzanenamo Makoni and councillors, Makoni, 8 Feburary 1981.
53 'Minutes of a meeting held at Chiwetu', 17 December 1975, file 'Chief Chiduku. Chiduku', DCOR, cited in Terence Ranger, 'Tradition and travesty: chiefs and the administration in Makoni District, Zimbabwe, 1960–1980', *Africa*, vol. 53, no. 3, (1982), p. 35.
54 Interview with Peter Chakanyuka, Harare, 29 March 1981. Fry, *Spirits of Protest*, pp. 43–4, records an analogous story:

In October 1963, *Drum* magazine published an article about a medium whom they called the 'Wild Man', who lived near Chiota at a place called Chitungwiza and who claimed to be the medium of *Chaminuka* . . . Soon after this publication the *Drum* offices were visited by one Muchatera who himself claimed to be the true *Chaminuka* medium . . . *Drum* therefore arranged for the two mediums to meet at Chitungwiza. The meeting was reported as having been dramatic. The 'Wild Man' took the offensive and, dressed only in a leopard skin, denounced Muchatera for wearing a suit, tie and shoes. and for having travelled by car . . . The meeting ended soon after this when the 'Wild Man' and his followers demanded the withdrawal of

Muchatera who was obliged to leave to the derision of the 'Wild Man' and his followers.

See also M.W. Murphree, *Christianity and the Shona* (London: 1969). Murphree remarks (p. 48) that Muchetera 'in spite of the fact that he has little connection with any tribal leadership . . . has been implacably opposed to nationalist politics, an attitude which has led to the burning of his huts in retaliation.' (p. 154). Murphree also describes how Muchetera arranged an interview with the Prime Minister, Sir Edgar Whitehead, calling for 'a convocation of all the national political leaders, who would then be instructed by him "on how he wished the affairs of the country to be run".'

55   David Lan, 'Spirit mediums and the authority to resist in the struggle for Zimbabwe', seminar paper, Institute of Commonwealth Studies, London, 14 January 1983, pp. 2, 4, 6, 8.
56   Interview between John Conradie and Kumbirai Kangai, Maputo, 21 August 1979.
57   Anon., 'Southern Africa: a smuggled account from a guerilla fighter', *Ramparts*, vol. 8, no. 4. (October 1969), pp. 8–18.
58   Lan, 'Making history', p. 14.
59   Mayor Urimbo as cited in ibid., p. 28.
60   David Martin and Phyllis Johnson, *The Struggle for Zimbabwe. The Chimurenga War*, (London: 1981), p. 75.
61   ibid., p. 78.
62   Frederikse, *None But Ourselves*, p. 326.
63   Ibid., p. 131.
64   Lan, 'Making History', p. 7. Lan's argument in condensed form is as follows:

During the colonial period, the chiefs were incorporated into the white-dominated state as low level administrators. Powerless to prevent the large-scale loss of land and forced resettlement, as well as taxation and forced labour, they were believed by the people of Dande to have betrayed their followers and to have been rejected by the ancestors. With the rise of the nationalist movements, reaching a climax with the entry of the guerrillas into Dande, the insurgents were incorporated into the ritual and symbolic frameworks which had previously been occupied by the chiefs. This incorporation was effected through the agency of the spirit medium thus allowing the perpetuation of the traditional symbolism of political authority.

As the ideology of the guerrillas promoted the ownership of the land and control of the political process of all categories of people irrespective of ancestry, the symbolism of the royal lineage was expanded to refer to all the people of Dande, and that of the spirit province to refer to the emergent state of Zimbabwe which was believed to have been taken under the protection of the ancestors.

65   Personal communication from Elleck Mashingaidze.

66 Interview with Lameck Madzwendira, St Francis Church, Makoni, 16 February 1981.
67 Interview with Isaac Tsungo, Makoni, 14 February 1981.
68 Interview between Peter Chakanyuka and Manyukire Gorembeu, Nedewedzo, Chiduku, 4 January 1981. Two interviews in the National Archives of Zimbabwe Oral History project are to the point here. An interview between Dawson Munjeri and Aaron Mutambirwa Makoni on 10 and 17 of May 1979, AOH/54, discussed how in earlier days the medium of Muswere had allocated the various chiefly houses of Makoni their respective lands:

We settled in Chidovha. My 'father', Mutambirwa of the Zendera 'house' was appointed chief by the *svikiro*, Muswere. You see these matters are complicated and not to be published. His nephew was given a region of his own. Nyamombe was given the region near the Sungwidzi river. Mupambawashe was given the region on the Rugowe river. All these were apportioned land by the Muswere *svikiro*.

Aaron Mutambirwa also threw light on the role of the mediums in linking the memories of the past *Chimurenga* to the present. He spoke of the execution of Chingaira Makoni by the whites in 1896, saying that 'no-one knows' where he is buried. 'This is not allowed to be said and the *svikiro* does not want us to say the story. We are young but what I tell you is that what was written is not true at all. No-one saw him . . . If the situation in our country was all right, I would have told you to go to our home and to speak to the *svikiro* which would tell you everything . . . The word from the *svikiro* is the true one.'
    An interview between Dawson Munjeri and Sylvester Mushauripo on 14 February 1980, National Archives Oral History Project, AOH/65, provides a variant. His 'great-grandfather Madziyeninga went into Makoni's territory and became a leading warrior of Makoni, in the very old days. He fought in the wars of Makoni until he died. He died as a "pillow of Chingaira". He was succeeded by a son, Revesai . . . They were warriors, hunters and also traditional healers, possessed with their ancestral spirits. Madziyeninga himself was a very good warrior. He came to Makoni guided by his spirits . . . Revesai was a spirit medium and he was a healer . . . Chingaira was executed at the same time as my ancestor, Madziyeninga. They were shot in front of a cave when they emerged from it after dynamite had been thrown into it. Madziyeninga was Chingaira's right hand man, more so because . . . he was a spirit medium.'

69 Interview with Headman Mpambawhale, Toriro, Chiduku, 24 March 1981. According to other informants, the Sakureba medium was 'very well known in the war' and was killed by the Security Forces in a bombing raid on his village. In April 1974, before the war began in Makoni, information given by African assistants of the District Commissioner held that 'SAKUREBA is the first Swikiro of the Vaungwe

. . . When Nyamatore speaks with SAKUREBA's voice he will prophesy the weather and say if the rains will be good or bad. He is also known to be able to say whether disaster, in the form of war, pestilence or human illness, will come about.' The District Commissioner tried but failed to discover who the current Sakureba medium was. 'The Vaungwe: Chief Makoni and Chipunza (Wamhina)', notes by G. Broderick from information given by Roland Hatendi and D/A Sgt. Gumunya, 16 April 1974, file 'Makoni. Chief Makoni', DCOR.

70 Father O'Hea to Monsignor Brown, 11 September 1930, Box 195, Jesuit Archives, Mount Pleasant, Harare.

71 Interview with Archdeacon Alban Makoni, Rusape, 2 February 1981.

72 'The Vaungwe: Chiefs Makoni and Chipunza (Wamhina)', 16 April 1974, file 'Makoni. Chief Makoni', DCOR. The anthropologist, Leo Frobenius, managed to penetrate the burial cave. Father Conrad Answenger recalls that 'one thing he wanted to see was the cave where the Makoni Chiefs were buried. He lived, not as a Christian, in the kraal of the Chief for a week until he got permission to enter the cave. Our Catholic people were very shocked and asked where Frobenius had been brought up to behave in so dreadful a way. I said he could not have been brought up as a Christian. But Frobenius was very pleased and told me he had seen eight or nine bodies wrapped in cowhide'. Interview with Father Conrad Answenger, Macheke, 17 March 1981.

73 Interview with George Bhongoghozo, Rusape, 16 February 1981.

74 Maurice Nyagumbo, *With The People. An Autobiography from the Zimbabwe Struggle* (London: 1980), pp. 189–90.

75 Interview with the Akuchekwa medium and his acolyte, Tandi, Chiduku, 27 February 1981. 'Before the war a lot of people were Christians,' said the *svikiro*, 'but now they are believing in the spirits. Everywhere people are brewing beer for the spirits. There are many smaller *svikiro* in Tandi and Akuchekwa has to tell us which are genuine.' I am very grateful to S.D. Madziwandzira who took me to meet Chief Tandi and his medium and acted as interpreter.

76 Interview with Amon Shonge, Weya, 25 March 1981.

77 Lan, 'Making history', p. 290.

78 Translation of a campaigning speech in Munyikwa TTL, Gutu, by Davis Mugabe. Recording by Kees Maxey, translation by Eustacius Valisai. I am grateful to Kees Maxey for making a copy of this translation available.

79 Frederikse, *None But Ourselves,* p. 309.

80 ibid., p. 328.

81 Lan, 'Making history', p. 72.

82 Terence Ranger, 'Holy men and rural communities in Zimbabwe, 1970–1980', in W.J. Sheils (ed.), *The Church and War*, (Oxford, Studies in Church History, vol. 20: 1983), pp. 443–61.

83 Lionel Cliffe, Joshua Mpofu and Barry Munslow, 'Nationalist politics in Zimbabwe: the 1980 elections and beyond', *Review of African Political Economy*, no. 18 (May/August 1980), pp. 62, 64.

6

Mau Mau,
FRELIMO
and the guerrilla war:
rural class struggle

In Chapter 5 I concluded that there *was* a people's war in rural
Zimbabwe and that the differences between ZANU/PF and FRE-
LIMO were partly differences of historical context. In Mozambique
there were few attacks on white settlers since FRELIMO's main
enemy was the metropolitan Portuguese regime. In Zimbabwe, on
the other hand, the main target had to be the settler economy and
peasants could be used directly in the assault upon it. (Ten times
more whites were killed in the Zimbabwean war than in the Kenyan
emergency). In Mozambique it would not have been possible to
work along with the belief in spirit mediums in the Shona-speaking
areas of that country because these represented a relatively small
proportion of the total African population; in Zimbabwe it was
possible to work with the mediums across two-thirds of the country.
In Mozambique there was a large liberated zone in the north of the
country in which FRELIMO was able to set up an administration
which directed production and provided services. In Zimbabwe
there were few if any liberated zones of this kind so that peasant
agricultural production was seldom if ever directed into new channels under guerrilla command.[1] All these differences, together with
the evolution of a radical peasant consciousness of the ways in which
the settler state had operated to exploit them, meant that in
Zimbabwe the peasants made a greater proportional input into the
ideology and programme of the war.

In this chapter I want to examine a final aspect of the Zimbabwean guerrilla war. In the cases of Kenya and Mozambique,
interpreters have stressed that the struggle between black and white
in the countryside became also a struggle between one black class

and another: an internal civil war. Thus G. Lamb opposes the forest fighters to Kikuyu 'loyalists':

The active loyalists were government servants such as chiefs, and those Kikuyu who by commercial activity or the acquisition of non-*mbari* land had acquired an interest in the system which the forest fighters threatened. Sorrenson's assertion that the active loyalists were from the 'landed and wealthy classes' is supported, for example, by an analysis of the Githunguri Home Guard (Kiambu) by the District Officer in charge of it. Eighty-four per cent of the Unit's leadership was classified as 'rich or very rich', and of the rank and file numbering 609 men, just over 50% fell into the same category, with a further 23% listed as 'above average in wealth' . . . At the other end of the scale, the core of the forest fighters, or at least of that majority which came from the rural areas, consisted of those who had little or no land – dispossessed *ahoi*, repatriated migrant labourers, and former holders of *githaka* plots which had been taken over by more fortunate or more astute lineage members. Allied to them, it appears, were the bulk of the small peasants, who had been subject to increasing pressure in the years preceding the Emergency, from the breakdown of the communal system and population increase.[2]

The administration's handling of the emergency had very different effects upon these two groupings. 'Individual forest fighters were punished with the loss of their land'; 'Home Guards and other trustworthy individuals were allowed to grow coffee and other cash crops.' Land Consolidation benefited 'the rich, the powerful and the loyal'. So the Emergency consolidated 'the position of the pre-Emergency powerholders in Kikuyu society. . . The Emergency ensured that the nationalist leadership . . . was physically removed from the scene, the peasantry suppressed by military repression of an exceptionally violent and thorough kind, and the way opened for rural elites to consolidate their economic and social primacy.'[3]

The northern Mozambique case is different from this straightforward account of class battle lines drawn up even before the struggle began and intensified by it, if only because there had been much less stratification in northern Mozambique than in the Kikuyu Reserve. Nevertheless, there was some. This has been most effectively explored in Allen Isaacman's paper on the emergence of cotton co-operatives in northern Mozambique. In 1955 the system of forced cotton production was modified by a new law allowing for the organization of 'autonomous' co-operatives. And in 1957 'a dozen northerners led by Lazaro Kavandame formed the nucleus of the Mozambican Voluntary Cotton Society.' Kavandame had been one of those Maconde migrants into Tanganyika about whom

Edward Alpers has recently written. It will perhaps be remembered that Alpers believes that 'Maconde immigrants in Tanganyika remained overwhelmingly a class of peasants with clearly defined peasant interests right into the early 1960s.' For him, 'the political implications of this analysis are that peasants could certainly be mobilized against any colonial regime that sought to restrict their economic opportunities, but that they were not, therefore, likely to become a radical or revolutionary force without considerable political education.' Moreover, 'by the late 1950s, a few of these individuals among the Maconde were carrying out the logic of their peasant aspirations by attempting to transform themselves into small capitalist farmers and traders. The best known example of such an individual is Lazaro Kavandame . . . Kavandame returned to Cabo Delgado in 1956, invested capital accumulated during his career as a labour recruiter for the Tanganyika sisal plantations in a small shop and agricultural commodity production.'[4]

Isaacman writes:

From the sanctuary of the mission station Kavandame advocated the formation of an African cooperative. Initially, many of the parishioners and surrounding peasants were either skeptical or afraid, but Kavandame rallied a small number of adherents. As a group, the founding members possessed a higher degree of literacy and education as well as broader wordly experience than the overwhelming majority of the rural population. They also had a somewhat privileged economic position . . . Their ranks included four missionary teachers . . . a mason . . . a catechist . . . and a cook . . . From the outset the founding members of the cotton cooperative shared two explicit objectives – ending the most abusive and degrading aspects of the cotton regime and improving their relative economic conditions.

The co-operative leaders organized secret night-time meetings in the bush in order to plan the establishment of an anti-colonial nationalist party. Meanwhile, however:

The Mozambiquan African Voluntary Cotton Society provided a convenient vehicle for the self-advancement and self-aggrandizement of a small number of ambitious individuals who themselves exploited less fortunate members of the rural population. As President of the cooperatives, Kavandame used his position of authority as well as his entrepreneurial skills to introduce capitalist relations of production into the cooperative system. Unlike most of the members, Kavandame did not work the land himself but hired a number of laborers from the pool of unemployed or impoverished who were either afraid of being arrested on vagrancy charges or were on the verge of starvation . . . The availability of cheap labour motivated Kavandame . . . to acquire additional land beyond the four hectare tract allocated to each member . . .During the organization's short lifespan, each year he sold between 150–300 fifty-kilo sacks of cotton, generating profits of more than 1,000 dollars per annum. With a portion of the capital which he accumulated, Kavandame enlarged his shop . . . and opened up a second store.[5]

Alpers sees in the entrepreneurial activities of men like Kavandame, as also in the beginnings of sale of land in northern Mozambique, clear indications of 'the emergence of a local petty bourgeoisie'. This class adopted a form of 'populist ideology'. Its aim was to 'build a political movement that would serve the interests of the Maconde petty bourgeoisie', and since its own acquisitions were 'carrying out the logic of peasant aspirations', 'it was not difficult to appeal to Maconde peasants . . . that this kind of politics was in their best interests.' As Alpers writes, 'the Maconde remained overwhelmingly peasants and many of them . . . no doubt shared . . . the deeply rooted vision of a mobile peasantry.' To transform them into 'a revolutionary force' required a 'transformation of political consciousness.' This took place during and as result of the armed struggle in northern Mozambique, so that:

when Kavandame and his cohorts tried to resurrect a Maconde separatist movement in 1968, history had made this kind of petty bourgeois politics transparently antithetical to the interests of Maconde peasants, who would have not part of it. The Mueda massacre of 1960 and the political success of FRELIMO since the armed liberation struggle began in 1964 had made Kavandame irrelevant.[6]

Peasant repudiation of Kavandame also had a great deal to do with their own perception of a clash of interests. Isaacman points out that 'Kavandame became Director of FRELIMO's Department of Commerce in Cabo Delgado. By 1967 he had come under repeated attack from peasants who complained that he speculated in products in short supply, employed laborers in his private fields and generally abused his position.'

Isaacman sums up by pointing out that:

Forced cotton production in northern Mozambique increased existing rural differentiations creating the conditions for the formation of a nascent class of capitalist farmers . . . For some of the leaders of the cooperative, most notably Kavandame, the Mozambique African Voluntary Cotton Society offered a vehicle for prosperity and power and an opportunity to mobilize deap-seated anti-Portuguese sentiment . . . His central role in the early independence campaign demonstrates that FRELIMO, like other nationalist organizations in Africa, was initially open to all social classes, while his removal marks the beginning of a campaign to prevent an internal bourgeoisie from dominating the movement.[7]

What, then, was the case within Zimbabwe's rural guerrilla war? Was there a situation such as Lamb postulates for the Kikuyu, in which rich peasants, already in possession, stood 'loyal' to the government and opposed to the landless and to poor peasants, ultimately to be rewarded with yet greater wealth and power through the mechanisms of land redistribution and concentration? Or was there a situation such as Alpers and Isaacman postulate for northern Mozambique, in which resident rural entrepreneurs, involved directly in agricultural production, took an early lead in nationalism, mobilized the peasantry behind a populist programme beneficial to entrepreneurial interests, exercised power and influence during the early stages of the guerrilla war, but were ultimately exposed and overthrown? By now, readers will not be surprised to learn that in my view historical differences in the patterns of rural inequality and in the character of the guerrilla war meant that neither the Kikuyu model nor the model of northern Mozambique were repeated in Zimbabwe. In Zimbabwe there were no rich peasant Home Guards in the Tribal Trust Lands, nor have there been redistributions of lands there which have benefited an entrepreneurial minority. On the other hand, rural entrepreneurs in Zimbabwe did not take the lead in nationalism as well as in cash-crop production; nor has any section of the rural nationalist alliance come to be systematically repudiated and denounced as 'exploiters of the people'.

Indeed, the difficulty of analyzing the various Zimbabwean nationalist and liberation movements in class terms has become notorious, leading some commentators to conclude that conflicts arising out of rural differentiation played no significant role in Zimbabwean liberation history. Thus L.H. Gann and T.H. Henriksen emphasize that the liberation movements mirrored the full range of differentiation in Zimbabwean African society:

The partisan movement's sociological structure reflected that of African society at large. Supreme political direction fell largely . . . to the new class of professional men. The permanent cadres and field officers mostly had a high school education . . . [combining] literary skills with solid combat training . . . The bulk of the full time fighting men . . . had worked both in the villages and in the towns [and] were familiar with a simple form of English; they were labour migrants in arms . . . The ordinary volunteers stood at the bottom of the guerilla pyramid . . . the African villager, good at survival.[8]

Given their scholarly advocacy of the interests of Southern Africa's white regimes, Gann and Henriksen might be suspected of seeking to discredit the liberation movements' claims to radicalism by laying stress on this hierarchy of command. But commentators within the liberation movements themselves have largely eschewed analysis based on rural class contradictions. A ZAPU Party Document of November 1976, for example, runs:

Comrades, we should all appreciate the fact that ANC ZAPU is a *movement*. Like all movements it contains all political tendencies brought together at this stage of the struggle by the common desire to defeat colonialism . . . No one stratum can succeed in the colonies without the cooperation of the other strata. It is in this context that ANC ZAPU sees the unity of all social strata *that can be united* as crucial in the struggle for independence . . . We know from our experience . . . that there are always contradictions, including antagonistic ones, in such a movement. . .We should handle all contradictions correctly. There are those among the people, and those between the enemy and the people. The former should be solved by education and persuasion, while the latter are settled by the destruction of the enemy. Only where an individual, group, or whole class has made common cause with the enemy must he or it be treated as an enemy.[9]

In February 1979 at a conference in The Hague attended by both ZANU/PF and ZAPU, J.W. Murisi delivered a paper on 'The history of class consciousness in Zimbabwe'. Murisi depicted a continuous national resistance to the whites dating back to the 1890s:

The present Chimurenga or people's war in Zimbabwe has reflected the uninterrupted class/national struggle which has been waged against the European ruling class. The nationwide uprising in the Chimurenga of the 1890s demonstrated the high degree of solidarity and political consciousness among the people of Zimbabwe. After the bloody repression of Rhodesian colonialism was instituted, the Zimbabwean nation continued to struggle, especially against efforts to exploit the labour power of the peasantry by forcing Zimbabweans out of agriculture and into semi-starvation. Persistent efforts to severely restrict the African peasantry and to maintain a large, rural-based semi-proletariat helped to forge solidarity and a common awareness of the common enemy – imperialism. Attempts by scholars . . . to illustrate the lack of political consciousness and class struggle on the part of Zimbabweans by pointing to ineffectual protest groups neglect the constant struggle by the vast majority of the African people against exploitation and oppression. In a way, the Chimurenga was continued underground and at the local level after 1897 . . .
The strategy of the Rhodesian ruling class consisted of confining the African peasantry to the poorest land and creating a limited population of

tenant farmers. The prevention of African land holdings and the maintenance of communal patterns of land ownership in most areas precluded the
emergence of an African rural bourgeoisie; these measures also impeded
capitalist development in African agriculture which would have led to
substantial proletarianisation. . . The 1950s . . . brought the expropriation
of even more land from the African peasantry . . .The expulsion of 85,000
African peasants from their land . . . brought the African peasantry into
closer union with the African proletariat and with the nationalist movement
in Zimbabwe.

   Admittedly, Murisi continues, in the 1950s there had been 'some
efforts to shift from a policy of separate development to one of
racial partnership.' Realizing the 'increasing frustration of the
African petty bourgeoisie and proletariat, combined with the growing discontent of the pauperised peasantry', the whites tried 'to
create an African middle class to ease intensifying contradictions.'
They 'attempted to forge an alliance of sorts with African bus-
owners, master farmers, contractors and senior employees.' But
these attempts were sabotaged by the white 'rural bourgeoisie and
the white working class'. The struggle of the people as a whole
continued, and 'in liberating Zimbabwe, the people of Zimbabwe
have become revolutionised. Attempts to arrange a neo-colonial,
"Internal Settlement" have come a decade too late. In effect, the
Smith regime has dug its own grave.'[10]
   Zimbabwe's rural areas did not look very different from this in
the perspective of a group of scholars at the Centre of African
Studies in Maputo. In 1977 they described the emergence of a
Zimbabwean petty-bourgeoisie, 'the highest class position which
Africans can attain within a colonial or settler dominated state.'
They found the Zimbabwean petty-bourgeoisie to be 'highly heterogenous, including self-employed artisans, traders, professionals,
clerks, small farmers or kulaks, shopkeepers, bus and taxi owners,
teachers, non-commissioned ranks in the army and police, intellectuals, and even chiefs.' It was possible to discern four main groups:
'the self-employed, the kulaks, a comprador group and the embryo
of a bureaucratic petit-bourgeoisie.' The significance of this class as
a whole lay 'not in its numerical significance at present but its
potential for expansion and class domination in an independent
Zimbabwe. . . .' But so far as a rural petty-bourgeoisie was concerned, they found:

The Unilateral Declaration of Independence by the racist regime and the
subsequent imposition of international sanctions changed the nature of
agricultural production quite drastically . . . All government investments
and subsidies went to sustain the settler community, while the African

peasants were left to pay the bill . . . The switch was away from tobacco to maize, cotton, sugar and beef. Thus the previous division of labour was radically changed, with settler production now becoming the competitor . . . of the African peasantry. The result upon the African peasantry was disastrous . . . The obvious result of this has been that the development of an African kulak class was severely restricted in this period . . . To allow for its own diversification, the settler community had to destroy the African kulak class which had become competitive with it . . .

The massive NO which the Pearce Commission received in early 1972 was in part due to the process of impoverishment which the years 1966–70 had brought to the African rural population. Subsequently the nationalist movements turned to guerilla warfare . . . The racist regime realised that within the 1966–70 period it had effectively destroyed what might have constituted conservative allies of the regime among the African population, namely the African kulak class. . . However, the racist regime could not seriously advance a policy for the development of a strong African kulak class because this would directly conflict with the interests of the settler community . . .It is thus unlikely that the regime succeeded in establishing a conservative base within any faction of the rural population. On the contrary the brutal oppression of peasant communities which supported the guerilla struggle alienated the countryside from the state.[11]

I shall not in this chapter dissent from this consensus, nor argue that particular African political movements correlated with particular classes, nor describe an intra-African class war in the Zimbabwean countryside. But I shall argue that if rural class distinctions were not determinant in these ways, nevertheless one *can* discern them operating at particular conjunctures as one among the many forces operating to shape the course of the guerrilla war. To do this I need to go back to the point at which I left the question of rural differentiation and to summarize what I have said in previous chapters.

Briefly, I have argued that during the 1930s the Rhodesian government set its face against the kind of ploughman entrepreneurs who were emerging on a significant scale within the Reserves; that the redistributive procedures of 'centralization' and ultimately of Land Husbandry were used to undercut such men; and that destocking of cattle was similarly used to reduce differentiation among cattle owners. The official model for an acceptable rural entrepreneurial cluster was an African yeomanry based in the areas set aside for African purchase under the Land Apportionment Act. But I argued that during the 1930s a Native Purchase yeomanry grew too slowly to be a significant factor, and that the eviction of peasants in the 1940s was only carried out by means of allowing large numbers of communal tenure peasants to settle on land originally set aside for purchase. Up to the early 1950s the government showed 'indifference to the new landowning class it had created', and African peasants showed an intense and often effective hostility towards the establishment of black farmer landowners in areas which they regarded as rightfully their own.

The case of Makoni District once again shows how very painfully and slowly the transition was made from one kind of rural entrepreneur to the other. Let us take as a beginning a record of a meeting between the Native Commissioner, Makoni and the chiefs and headmen of the district in April 1937:

Natives asked for higher prices for maize: told that such was frivolous, as, this year, they had received 7/6d per bag through the Maize Control Board as against 3/6d to 4/6d in the past. Natives asked for government to provide transport for grain to railways: informed that if such were arranged the maize-growers would have to pay for the transport: further, there were Indians and natives with transport in all reserves, and this request was not reasonable. Further pointed out: native Sirewu passed 301 bags of maize through this office; Nakayanga 140 bags; Manditowepi 143 bags; many natives 100 bags; and that transport arrangements must lie in the hands of growers. The meeting was addressed on overstocking the reserves with cattle: soil erosion: intensive cultivation of the soil with a view to allowing natives on farms to return to their reserves. In reply many natives who lived on farms asked that government buy the farms from Europeans. Reply was that the reserves as at present set aside, are more than capable of carrying the natives, but wasteful tilth of the land must be stopped to allow this to be proved.[12]

Some of those who had been 'wastefully' tilling the land through extensive plough cultivation *did* manage to make a rapid transfer to the new order. Thus Sirewu, registration X 3184, Rusape, was approved by the Native Land Board for a Native Purchase farm at Dowa, to the north-west of Chiduku, on 12 October 1938.[13] But for many others it was a more agonizing business. Here, for example, is the story of one of the men 'who lived on the farms'. Peter Chawandamira recalls that his father:

was a 'squatter' on a farm owned by a European from the 1920s. He had to do three months in the year labour for Mr Kilpin as a rent. Later on he paid a money rent instead. Kilpin had a vast estate which ran from Macheke to Eagle's Nest along the railway and the main road between Salisbury and Umtali. Kilpin did not grow maize or any other crops. He specialized in cattle-ranching. The 'squatters' on his land herded his cattle during their three month's work, though my father worked in Kilpin's kitchen. For the rest of the year they were allowed to grow what they liked wherever they liked and on as much land as they liked. Kilpin had many stores dotted about his estates at which his tenants had to sell their grain. Maize had to be sold at these stores, you were not allowed to sell anywhere else. Besides we did not even have a scotch cart. Even to get to his store was five miles carrying grain on our heads, The maize was bought at a very low price. But my father preferred being on this land. He liked it very much. There wasn't much interference from Kilpin, to be honest. If you were in the Reserves the Demonstrators ordered you about. If you were on other white farms, like Fischer's, you were bullied all the time. But Kilpin just told men not to cultivate by the water and that was all – no contour ridges, nothing.

My mother and father worked on one field together, but my mother had her own quarter of an acre in the *vlei* where she grew *senza* roots which sold by the railway line at Eagle's Nest. In this way she got money for dresses. My father was a very, very good gardener. He had a plot on which he grew cabbages, carrots, onions, rhubarb. Those are the things that educated me. We never tasted any of them because they were all sold at Macheke to the European households there. It was a good life. Honestly my father had a big land. Every man round there could plough as much as he liked, whatever he could manage. Those who had many children could plough more. My father had 20 cattle and a plough; others had 50 or 60 cattle. My father was a Catholic. He did not keep the *chisi* days, nor brew beer for spirits. But he brewed beer for work parties at harvest time. One year he had 50 bags of *rapoko* and it took two days to thresh for a big work party. The beer that was brewed was very much.[14]

This idyllic existence came to an end in the mid-1940s:

Kilpin didn't want to move anyone from the land. But in 1945 they were all moved off. It was against the wishes of Mr Kilpin. But it was now the wishes of the government of the day, whether he liked it or not. They were offered a place either in Chiduku or in Mrewa, outside the Makoni District altogether. My father tried Chiduku but couldn't see where there was to settle there. So at last he was sent to Mrewa. Muzorewa's father went there at the same time. Oh, it was hard going then for him. The kraalhead he went under disliked the Wa-ungwe. So there was this forced labour, where you had to go and build the roads and dip-tanks. Each time no matter what the season or what work he had on his lands the kraalhead would send him. He only had one acre for maize; a quarter of an acre a garden. As he couldn't tolerate the conditions he had to think about pur hasing a Native Purchase farm in Zivyambe. In Mrewa there we met Demonstrators. Fortunately he was so clever at doing crop rotation that he became a Master Farmer and was then entitled to a plot in Zivyambe. Zivyambe was a very dry land and he could not have a garden there. There was an arrogant Native Commissioner there. He was often very annoyed. But he was not so much annoyed as he had been when he was forced to leave Kilpin's farm.[15]

Bishop Muzorewa's father, whom we have seen happily farming fifty fertile acres in Chiduku in the 1930s, suffered similar traumas in the 1940s. Bishop Muzorewa writes:

Cattle were sold, farmlands surrendered to others . . .These were trying years for my parents. They had accepted land in Chief Mangwende's reserve which was almost desert-like in comparison with our former home. . . His solution was to go to South Africa to work . . . My father began to work in Cape Town as a waiter . . . Amid the political changes of 1948 in which Afrikaners gained power in South Africa, my father determined to return home. Having heard no reply to his application to purchase a farm in Rhodesia, he decided to go back to his home area in Makoni District. Still the odyssey continued. After one year's residence at Sharara, the white government decided that Makoni District was overcrowded and forced my parents to return to the poor soils of Mangwende Reserve.

As Bishop Muzorewa remarks, 'such disappointments would have broken the spirit of most persons.' But persisting in his efforts, his father began to raise carrots as a cash crop on a half-acre plot. At last, in 1957, he too was able to buy a farm in Zviyambe Purchase Area.[16]

By the 1960s, then, both old Chawandamira and old Muzorewa were Native Purchase Farmers, but they were hardly secure or contented members of a collaborative petty-bourgeoisie. Chawandamira kept out of politics as a good Seventh Day Adventist. Old Muzorewa, however, became a staunch ZAPU man. A stranger in the district in which Zviyambe was situated, he was ZAPU along with rather than at the head of the peasants of the Tribal Trust Lands. If he was not a rich and loyal Kikuyu landowner, no more was he a Kavandame. Rather he was a member of ZAPU as a 'movement'. His son describes how, when ZAPU was banned, and white police were confiscating party cards, old Muzorewa told them: 'You have taken away my party card and the cards from so many people, but does that take away the party cards lodged in our hearts? How are you to impound those?'[17]

Within Makoni District itself there was little opportunity even for such difficult attainment of Native Purchase status. The Land Apportionment Act had set aside a number of areas in the district for purchase. We have seen already that the Tanda area was fiercely contested and that most of it eventually became communal land. The Zonga area, adjacent to Makoni Tribal Trust Land, was also not fully opened up to purchasers: in fact, the farm sold there to one Tangai in 1931 remained the only one alienated in the whole area. Later purchasers of Tangai's title remember the intense hostility shown by the surrounding peasant 'squatters' whenever they travelled to the farm.[18] Only one of the areas set aside became a fully functioning Native Purchase Area. This was Dowa, to the north-west of Chiduku. Chiduku peasants bitterly resented the loss of Dowa, which had once been part of Chiduku Reserve, which had been removed initially as part of Barnes Pope's scheme to undercut peasant production, and which was now set aside for African yeomen purchasers. But there was little they could do about it, and Dowa gradually filled up, at first largely with men from outside Makoni District.[19]

These first Dowa farmers remember how very difficult life was for them in the early years. Dowa was far from the line of rail and markets. Solomon Chavunduka, who had worked as an Agricultural Demonstrator for ten years and then applied for and occupied the first farm to be sold in Dowa, recalled that 'In those early years life was very difficult. At the time I took the farm I could only get 30 cents a bag for maize. Transport was so difficult, no roads, no bridges over the Macheke river, no traders. I had to carry all my own maize to Rusape.'[20] Although Chavunduka possessed a plough, a scotch cart and wagons, and employed two men at five shillings a month, his agricultural achievement in this period was not in any way remarkable.

By far the most evocative account of Dowa in its early days is given in Stan Made's autobiography. Made's father was 'by origin and tribe a foreigner, a Sena.' He had settled at Rusape in 1913, beginning as shop cleaner in an Indian store, and thereafter becoming a tailor. He established a village two miles out of Rusape where he 'organized dancing sessions . . . women and beer and gambling'. 'It is said,' Made writes, 'that when the passenger train came from Umtali my father would arrange to have his fellow tribesmen from the Eastern Border transported in dozens on bicycles to his village to imbibe the waters of immortality and have their fill of pleasure before proceeding further to Salisbury where they would be recruited for the mines.' The enterprising Sena used his profits to establish himself in Makoni society. He took three local girls to wife – one from chief Makoni's village, another from Tandi in eastern Chiduku and the third from Nedewedzo in western Chiduku. Stan Made was born in 1935 to this third wife in Befa village in Nedwedzo. Then:

In 1938 a new 'native' farming area was defined and demarcated from the source of Nedewedzo Range towards the west where there were plains and wood with sandy soil up to the European farming area . . . The new native purchase area was called 'Dowa', meaning a place of dew in the morning. My maternal uncle, Timothy Dupxa, who was the elder brother to my mother and the first son in their family, was one of the first to buy a farm in Dowa. His was No. 4 farm and as it was, it just stretched from the beginning of Nedewedzo Mountain for up to three miles southwards and about two miles wide . . . My mother's family literally just moved from the eastern side of Nedewedzo to the western side of it.

Timothy Dupxa had also been a tailor in Rusape. Now he surrounded himself with his extended polygamous household and ran it in a businesslike way;

There was my uncle Timothy with a crowd of my mothers. He had five sisters and three half-sisters. The great grand Dupxa was a polygamist and two of his wives lived with him on Farm No. 4 . . . In the early mornings all my mothers would be ordered to the fields . . . Timothy himself generally sat by a small shady tree running tailoring, but in an open enough space to see everybody who was working. Then there was the swarm of us kids. I think we numbered up to about twenty-seven at that time . . . We were assigned whatever should be done in the kitchens, the milking of cows, chasing baboons . . . Our fathers worked far away in towns or farms. Clever Uncle Timothy had managed to impress the husbands that their wives were far better cared for if they remained on his 'big' state.

Made's own father, however, decided to become a Purchase Area farmer himself. In 1948 he qualified as a master farmer – 'a great achievement for an all-time town pleasure lover.' In 1949 he settled at Farm No. 133 in Dowa, gathering his own polygamous household around him. Made describes the farming season of 1950/51:

The whole summer we worked hard in the fields . . .My father who had never used a plough or cultivator before, would also rise up early with us boys so that he could do his share in ploughing and cultivating so as to encourage us, but by 7.00 a.m. he would . . . retire to take a bath and then afterwards engaged himself with tailoring . . . Very often he would pack a bag of farm products like cucumbers, cassava and vegetables and ride to neighbours' European farms to sell. He knew many Sena 'home boys' on the European farms and it was very easy to dispose of his goods of the day.[21]

It is plain that neither Dupxa nor Made were large-scale, modernizing cash-crop farmers. And yet in other ways an elite was germinating in Dowa and Zviyambe. What all the men I have been describing had in common was a commitment to the education of their children. Peter Chawandamira's father's vegetables were 'the things that educated me'. Bishop Muzorewa writes of his parents that 'determined to educate their children . . . they concentrated all their efforts on raising carrots as a cash crop. The hours of fertilizing, planting and watering by hand, reaped surprising results year after year. In fact, my brothers, sisters and I all had school fees paid during those years through father's sale of carrots.'[22] For Solomon Chavunduka education for his children was 'the big thing in my heart.' Stan Made tells us that 'Uncle Timothy concurred with my mother that I must go to school for the benefit of them all. In the whole family among the old ones it was only Uncle Timothy who could write a letter . . .It was the beginning of a long road to my education through my mother's toils. My mother virtually worked for Uncle Timothy for my school fees and clothing.'[23]

Schooling in Dowa was not easy. The first school in Dowa did not open until 1943. Roland Hatendi, who was its headmaster until he joined the Native Department in 1945, recalled in 1981 that 'when the school started many farms were still vacant. There were only 42 farmers in Dowa then, though there were many children because so many were polygamists. The farms were scattered about and children had to travel long distances.'[24] Made tells us that:

Dowa School was still bush in 1945 . . . I and my three cousins left home in the morning at about 6.00 a.m. every day and trotted the four odd miles to be in time . . . The age range for primary school at Dowa was very wide, I think pupils were between six years of age and thirty years . . . As Dowa School was in the centre of the whole community we came from different directions, and so we divided ourselves according to the direction from which we came . . . into boxing groups.'[25]

Conditions at some of the longer-established schools in the Reserves were certainly better than this.

And yet the investment made by Native Purchase farmers in education paid rich dividends. One of Solomon Chavunduka's sons, Gordon, is today Professor of Sociology at the University of Zimbabwe; another son, Dexter, is now Permanent Secretary in the Ministry of Agriculture. Their cousin, Sarah, daughter of another pioneer Dowa farmer, was the first African female student at the University College of Rhodesia and Nyasaland and is now Assistant Permanent Secretary at the Ministry for Community Development and Women's Affairs. Stan Made is now Librarian at the University of Zimbabwe, after having worked as a teacher for some years. Abel Muzorewa's later career is well enough known. Peter Chawandamira became a teacher at St Faith's where he 'first came to know what [he] was politically.' Becoming a teacher was impressive enough. Stan Made tells us that his father was delighted with this achievement – 'Who else had a son who had trained as a teacher at my age?' But Made himself was determined to prepare 'for a better future through education', and not to remain content with teaching.[26] It was the disproportion between the sums that had to be invested in education and the ultimate rewards in terms of professional salaries which made the Native Purchase Areas into an effective mechanism of differentiation. But in investing in the education of their children, the farmers of Dowa and Zviyambe were preparing a national elite rather than a local one. These educated sons and daughters were not going to return to cash-crop production in Makoni District.

In the late 1940s and 1950s, however, the Native Purchase farmers began to look as if they would themselves blossom into a significant class of rural entrepreneurs. In the boom period for white farming, competition from African yeomen ceased to be feared. In order to refute the charges of Burombo and others that the Land Apportionment Act had been betrayed, some gestures of support had to be made towards the Native Purchase farmers. Oliver Pollak writes:

Slowly the government put into motion carefully measured concessions to the African Farmers' Union. [It] substantially differentiated between the reserves and the purchase areas and separate agencies and services were gradually developed . . . In late December 1951 the Land Board accepted the principle of issuing original title deeds . . . The discriminatory marketing legislation of the 1930s was modified and sales opportunities for African and European agriculturalists and ranchers equalized . . . In 1957 the advisory services in the European areas were extended to the purchase areas and small loan schemes were made available . . . Special conservation subsidies were granted . . . separate purchase area funds were being allocated for roads.[27]

Numbers of NPA farmers grew, eventually to reach some eight-and-a-half thousand by the 1970s. 'A distinct class of African farmers had developed,' writes Barry Munslow, 'which employed 56,000 African labourers' by 1960.[28] In Makoni District Dowa began to fill up with farmers.

Many of these farmers had connections with either the 'traditional' or the 'modern' sources of influence in Makoni District. Members of the Makoni chiefly families, African administrative assistants, leading figures in the Makoni Christian churches, all acquired farms in Dowa. While retaining their connections with the wider Makoni community, these men began to organize their own political bodies. In early 1948 the Dowa Farmers Association passed a resolution calling for a Council; the Native Commissioner advised them to wait until 'approved applicants for farm holdings in the Division, who are at present undergoing a course of agricultural training, will have returned and taken up residence', but before long a Division Council was established and holding regular meetings.[29] Moreover, as communications improved so grain from Dowa began to flow into Rusape. In September 1948 it was reported that Dowa farmers had surrendered 2195 bags of 'A' grade maize to the Maize Control Board. In June 1949 the Chief Native

Commissioner and members of the Native Land Board inspected Dowa where they visited several farms and were impressed with general progress. In September it was reported that African farmers from the Dowa Native Purchase Area had delivered over 2000 bags of maize to the Maize Control Board and had sold considerable quantities of groundnuts and small grain.[30] Dowa looked as though it might become a nucleus of economic and political power in the district.

The general political consequences of this period of growth and relative prosperity were significant. As Pollak tells us:

The AFU [African Farmers Union] earned a new measure of 'respect' from the government as a result of the rise of nationalist politics in the reserves in 1956. Both government and the AFU leadership opposed the nationalists. Jacha, who had been an early member of the Bantu Congress and had been instrumental in reviving the African National Congress in the mid-1930s, had left the ANC when the movement outspokenly militant . . . Jacha claimed to represent the more stable, constitutionally oriented middle-class, and felt the AFU would grow from 'strength to strength . . . [on the] policy of fruitful cooperation with Government'.

Even after Jacha was replaced as leader of the Union by William Henry Kona, who in mid-1961 aligned himself with the National Democratic Party, his programme was still very much conceived in the interests of a distinct yeomanry. Kona 'called for accelerated land disbursement . . . [he] wanted government to live up to its pledge of 7½ to 8 million acres [for African purchase] and at one point called for 10 million acres . . . The AFU felt that the communal agriculturalists – 'squatters' – who occupied purchase lands should be removed as was done to blacks occupying European lands.'[31] In this way the spokesmen of the purchase farmers palely reflected first the Kenyan and then the northern Mozambican models – with Jacha offering a 'middle-class' alliance to the government, and Kona seeking to participate in a populist nationalist movement whose success would benefit rural entrepreneurs. Both attitudes were even more palely reflected in Dowa.

By this time the purchase farmers had other potential 'petty bourgeois' allies in the rural areas, who might have assisted in building a significant class presence in rural politics. These were the so-called 'rural businessmen'. In Makoni there had been signs in the 1930s of an aspiration to business enterprise. 'Enlightened natives are most keen on entering business on their account,' noted the Native Commissioner in 1938, though he added that they 'are seldom very successful.' In that year there were thirty-one African builders, seven carpenters, ten brickmakers, five well sinkers and a number of urban craftsmen in Makoni, but no store-keepers, butchers or eating-house owners.[32] After the Second World War, however, these rapidly developed. In the neighbouring Wedza area the Assistant Native Commissioner noted in 1946 that there was 'a scramble for business activity in the Reserve.' There were six general dealers with nine others about to start; three butchers with ten about to begin; three eating-house proprietors with six applications for licences, together with millers, tailors and a bus-owner.[33] In Makoni itself in 1947, while the African grain trade was still dominated by European and Indian traders who sent 'fleets of lorries into the Reserves to bring out the surplus grain', nevertheless Africans in Makoni were 'showing a strong inclination for business' and were 'establishing stores, butcheries, tailor's shops, native eating-houses, mineral water businesses, carpenters' shops, and greengroceries, in all native reserves and areas.' They were also 'taking advantage of the better roads' and had 'established public transport services.'[34] In 1948 it was remarked that the 'number of native owned businesses have shown a notable increase . . . A number of general dealers have their own transport and are assisting to bring native produce to the European market.'[35]

Some of these business enterprises were closely connected with the Native Purchase areas and the Native Land Board minutes record many applications to open up stores, butcheries and eating houses in Dowa and Tanda. How closely the various types of entrepreneurs – yeoman farmers, businessmen, government employees – could be linked comes out very clearly in a letter from a Dowa farmer to the Director of Native Agriculture in March 1948. 'My son Richard Boniface Mukonyora is your Agricultural Demonstrator at Bannockburn South Inyanga District,' wrote Boniface Mukonyora from Dowa Cash Butchery:

I kindly request the Director to do me a favour by transferring him near my farm No. 18 Dowa Division . . . where I am farming, trading as a general dealer in the reserve near my farm . . . [Please transfer him to Dowa or Nedewedzo] where he will spend week-ends improving my farm, poultry, sheep management, etc. This was my sole aim in getting him trained as an Agricultural Demonstrator.[36]

But the great majority of 'businessmen' were different from the purchase farmers in one vital respect – they operated in the reserves and directly among the peasantry. For this reason they were more likely to provide a populist political leadership to a peasant nationalist movement.

The anthropologist A.K.H. Weinrich worked in the rural areas in the 1960s on the relative influence of chiefs, teachers and business-men. She found that businessmen were in many ways the most influential:

Businessmen derive one of the major sources of their power from their control over the network of communication in rural areas. Their stores are always situated on important roads, either near bus stops or at cross roads, but never in villages . . . They are always situated at strategical points to give easy access to a large number of people. The central position of their stores contributes to the influence of local store owners . . .
Businessmen, who advance goods on credit, make their debtors depen-dent on them . . . Popular traders are the social kingpins of their communi-ties because their stores are the social centres where men gather to discuss local events and politics. Here housewives, peasants, teachers and travellers meet and rapidly pass on . . . information . . . Their stores, therefore, provide traders with many opportunities to convert their econo-mic power into social influence . . . Most businessmen are keenly in-terested in politics . . . businessmen enjoyed not only strong economic but also political influence.[37]

In what direction, then, were rural businessmen likely to use this influence? Did their stores become nuclei of 'loyal' collaboration with the authorities, no-go zones for nationalism? Or did they seek to put themselves at the head of rural populism? To answer this question one needs to appreciate that the expression 'business-man' covers a great variety of people, from very prosperous owners of many stores, lorries and buses to owners of one small and ill-stocked shop. In Makoni District, for instance, some store-owners were ex-Reserve entrepreneurs who turned to commerce when they lost opportunities to produce maize; others were returning labour migrants who were unable even to get a footing as a small peasant in the reserves.

A striking example of a pioneering Reserves entrepreneur who became a pioneering businessman is Michael Jack Nyamusamba. Nyamusamba was one of the first converts of the Trappist mission-aries at Triashill and became one of their most successful teachers. From 1915 onwards he was in charge of a school in the Makoni Reserve and cultivated 'the surrounding hundred acres'. In 1922, when mission 'progressives' were still highly esteemed by the administration, his school was visited by Inspector Condy who reported it to be 'the best of the six schools I saw. The teacher is enterprising and has much influence in the district . . . The teacher has two carts and a plough. He has 46 head of native cattle . . . Last year he reaped 60 bags of mealies and 16 bags of wheat. A progressive man like Michael must set an excellent example to those around him.[38] Nyamusamba got rid of his hundred acres long before the campaign against the Reserves entrepreneurs began in the 1930s. In 1925 he made a deed of gift of 'my kraal for a mission station with a European staff. The surrounding hundred acres, which I cultivated for the last ten years, are for their own use.'[39] Thereafter, with a good claim to be regarded as the founder of St Killian's mission, he returned to teach and live at Triashill.

At Triashill he made his home in Muchenu village on the mission farm where he continued his agrarian entrepreneurial activities. His son recalls that 'we were one of the few families who owned ploughs and we also used to plough for other families . . . paid in money or grain.' Nyamusamba finally gave up most of his land during the reorganization of the mission farm in the late 1950s, accepting the standard six-acre holding as 'an example to the others'.[40] Long before this, however, he moved his emphasis from grain production to business enterprises. His son Isidore recalls that when he in turn began to teach at Triashill in 1937, 'they used to give me very little money, £1.10s a month and their reason was that my father was very rich and that I did not need any money. True, my father owned a butchery, a store in Inyanga and a store at St Killian's but I did not like the poor salary which they gave me.' Isidore went off to Salisbury where he found work as a lorry driver – 'it did not take me long to get a licence since my father owned a car and he had taught me how to drive before I went to town.'

An African businessman with a car was a rare figure indeed in the Rhodesian rural areas before the Second World War. But after the war Nyamusamba grew yet more prosperous. 'During the fifties,' says Isidore, 'my father's business expanded and he opened two more stores, one in the Manyika Reserve and the other in the Inyanga District.' His lorries as they travelled between his stores carried building materials for the establishment of new mission schools and hospitals.[41]

At the other extreme were the returned labour migrants who had lost land and grazing rights under the Land Husbandry Act. Thus when Mhondiwa Remus Rungodo came back to Nedewedzo in 1950 'he was unfortunate for he had no dip card . . . He had no single head of cattle.' He clubbed together with Takapera Moda Chakanyuka to set up an eating-house:

Remus was more than pleased to become a businessman and actively ran it as a hotel, baking buns and bread, the work he had partly done in South African hotels. They were making very little profit but managed to pay the lease and rents most of the time from their sales. At times they had to pay from their pockets. The most difficult times he saw were the 1950s and 1960s and the recent war.[42]

Rungodo was plainly a 'businessman' of a very different sort from Nyamusamba. So too was Maurice Nyagumbo. He had spent years of wandering and working in South Africa. His immediate problem when he came home to Makoni in February 1955:

> was how to earn a living. I did not think it was possible for me to work for a white man in this country. I also realised that I had not enough money to establish myself in a business. The little money I had brought had already found its way out of my pocket . . . Just before the end of February, I took an interest in a man who was about to sell his premises at a business centre about three miles from my home [in the Makoni Reserve]. After a few days of negotiations he agreed to sell the property to me for two hundred pounds. It was a half-built store which needed completion. Early in March, I went to Salisbury to buy groceries for the little shop.

In April 1955 Nyagumbo married. He recalls that 'When I arrived home in February 1955, land allocation and cattle destocking had already taken place in Makoni area. Since it was not possible for Victoria and me to get land allocated to us, we decided to remain at our little shop and depend on the proceeds from it.'[43]

The political positions of Nyamusamba on the one hand, and of Rungodo and Nyagumbo on the other, were bound to be very different. Nyamusamba was a hero figure in Triashill folk Christianity and to the Catholic missionaries. His Golden Wedding was celebrated in 1960 in Triashill church with 'a very big attendance'. In January 1962 his funeral was accompanied by a solemn Requiem Mass celebrated by four priests, nuns from several stations, and the whole Triashill community.[44] His politics were identical with those of the mission – an attempt to hold the Triashill farm community for 'moderation' and against 'communism' by means of an active lay Catholic Association. It was to men like Nyamusamba that the Triashill fathers gave thanks for the relative tranquillity of their peasant flock in the open nationalist period. 'Special Police patrol arrive today', runs the diary entry in the Triashill log for 13 September 1961. 'Suspected trouble from the N.D.P. in reserves but thank God everything is quiet on the Farm. Dip tanks burned at Inyanga and Headlands, but people here are quite willing to dip and no trouble.'[45] It was all a long way from the atmosphere in which Nyamusamba's son Isidore had to operate during the folk Catholic commitment to the guerrillas in the 1970s.

But Rungodo and Nyagumbo were already living in a political world which was not so far away from the peasant/guerrilla alliance. We have already seen how Rungodo became a ZAPU activist in Nedewedzo and how he was arrested there after the banning of the party; we have already seen how Nyagumbo worked to establish

Congress as a party of peasant grievance. Thereafter both men continued their commitment to a radical nationalism; Rungodo in a sequence of detentions and underground activity in western Chiduku, Nyagumbo as the internal co-ordinator of ZANU guerrilla action and as the longest-serving political prisoner in Zimbabwe. Between these radical small 'businessmen' and the establishment figure of Nyamusamba stretched a whole variety of intermediate figures, divided in mind between the sort of collaboration with the authorities which would allow them to continue to operate and the resentment which they felt against all the restrictions which segregation and paternalism imposed upon their business activities.

During the open nationalist period many of these men opted for support and indeed for attempted local leadership of nationalism. Weinrich found that:

In the 1960s, most businessmen were critical of local chiefs on economic as well as political grounds. Before they could open their stores, they had to offer gifts to the chiefs . . . Also, most of the businessmen interviewed were nationalistically inclined and resented the leadership positions given by the European-controlled government to chiefs. . . store owners often fomented local opposition to traditional leaders . . . Most businessmen are keenly interested in politics . . .Several . . . were paid up members of a nationalist party. One had personally organized the incipient nationalist movement in his chiefdom . . . The possession of cars and lorries turned businessmen into effective supporters of the nationalist parties. When rallies were announced in the early 1960s, the businessmen were ready with their transport to bring villagers to the meeting places. The speakers on such occasions were often teachers, but the organizers businessmen . . . By the mid-1960s, when all nationalist activities had been banned, businessmen in two adjoining chiefdoms formed a local businessmen's association which overtly aimed at protecting their trading interests. Its hidden function, however, was to keep alive nationalist aspirations . . . When African businessmen compare their own opportunities with those of Europeans they often feel discriminated against. Many can see only one way out of their difficulties: an African government . . . economic need spurs many African store owners to support nationalist movements.[46]

And in central Makoni businessmen were active in the African National Congress. In February 1959, Patricia Chater wrote from St Faith's that:

On Wednesday night or rather early Thursday morning the C.I.D. came out and took John [Mutasa], Peter Chawandamira and Ernest . . . Their houses were searched and left in an awful mess and all John's Congress treasurer papers taken . . .Since when the Police and Territorials have visited us a few times . . . People here are bewildered as it was so sudden, but taking it very calmly . . . already the chaps are looked upon as heroes.

Whitehead has said that the majority of leaders are men without any standing and without regular employment . . . but this is patently untrue as far as this district goes . . . there are teachers, missionaries and business-men detained.[47]

In March, she wrote that 'One knows of some 10 of the detainees – 4 headmasters (one of an upper primary school), 3 teachers, two businessmen in Rusape and Inyazura area, Patrick Matimba who has just started his own printing business, and John. . . One wonders whether our area is an exception, or whether there are many teachers and business people detained.'[48]

Chater's listing of headmasters and teachers detained in 1959, her further comment that 'from hearsay we have heard of seven or so teachers from Roman Catholic and Methodist Missions in the area', and Weinrich's picture of nationalist meetings organized by businessmen but addressed by teachers, naturally brings us to the third potential constituent of a rural petty-bourgeoisie, the young educated sons and daughters of the Native Purchase farmers and of the more aspirant Reserves peasants. I wrote above that the most highly educated of them were a potential national elite rather than constituting a local leadership group. But this was not true of the teachers. In 1948 the Chief Native Commissioner noted the existence of ' "leaders" Associations which have sprung up in the Reserves, instigated and staffed largely by demonstrators and teachers – a combination which can have a most powerful influence providing they can avoid the danger of setting themselves apart as an aristocratic intelligentsia.'[49] Weinrich found that 'teachers represent the largest and most powerful group of the modern elite in rural Rhodesia . . . [They] form a powerful body influencing public opinion. . .Because of their kinship connections with the people and their easy association with them in their daily lives, teachers are a powerful force in the rural villages.'[50] In Makoni District not only teachers but also students sought to play a leadership role. There were no secondary schools within the district, but numbers of Makoni students achieved places in boarding secondary schools elsewhere. In 1955 a number of them formed the Makoni Students Association:

We should seek for light and guidance from those who know and when we have got it we should do what we are required to do, despite the dangers which may be involved . . . [Our aim is] to secure unity of all the students in the Makoni district. To study educational, social and material problems affecting Africans especially in the Makoni district, and to promote African welfare . . . to establish a link between chiefs, elders, teachers, demonstrators, and students . . . to encourage students to aspire for higher education and self improvement.[51]

Teachers and secondary school students had essentially the same choices as purchase farmers and businessmen – they might bid for a privileged role by means of an alliance with the administration; they might bid for leadership of a populist nationalism, whose success would open limitless opportunities; they might throw in their lot with radical peasant nationalism. In Makoni District there were plenty of bids for a position of influence within the official system from men whose qualification was superior education. Thus there were many attempts to achieve chiefships or headmanships for educated men. In October 1951, for example, William Chigutsa Rugoyi wrote to the Native Commissioner, Makoni, pointing out that:

From the time I became a man and able to watch the progress in Makoni Reserve, I have been doubly disappointed with the way the Chiefs have been working. Being the son of that Reserve it burns my heart to see such a terrible slow progress going because of the Chief's laziness. For instance just where the Chief has been living people sale beer, drinking hard, doing no work. Very little attention is paid to soil conservation . . . If I were the Chief at all the first thing I would do with that ground called Makoni Farm, is to have thorough allocation of lands, thus have every bit of that soil well served.[52]

In 1951, J. Makoni wrote to the Assistant Native Commissioner, Rusape:

I feel much pressed . . . when I look, hear and know how Mrewa district under a young chief is progressing . . . Now looking to our district as it has had only the rule of old and uncivilised chiefs, commissioners of different ranks still find it very hard and difficult to develop our people . . . A new broom sweeps clean . . . Schools need the chief's help, hospitals, demonstrators will be helped greatly if this man of modern acting is chosen . . . Josiah was only eight years old when he began to reign.[53]

And such appeals continued after the nationalist period. After Zambe Makoni's death, Maynard Makoni, previously an active member of the Makoni Students Association and now a teacher, wrote to the District Commissioner in 1971:

It has been a bother to me and perhaps to many others about to whom the Makoni Chieftanship should be . . . In my own point of view, our next Makoni Chief should be a man apt to understand the importance of unity with the Government. So by so to rule his people, the Chief wouldn't mistake his chiefship for opposition to the Government . . . [He] should be an ex civil-servant . . . with responsible ex-working mates to support his being fit in a Chief's position.[54]

As late as 1975 the Methodist kraalheads of Gandanzara appealed for an educated headman who could preserve their 'progressive' tradition:

The late headman was a Christian, his influence did spread to the village that we were all brought up under church . . . His village became a centre of civilisation and attraction which made it easier for the District Commissioners and missionaries to contact other districts, making his village as an example of what the D.Cs wanted to produce . . . e.g. people of Makoni as a whole had refused the idea of contour ridges but because this man Gandanzara went to Domboshowa for training he introduced the idea . . . Today a confusion was brought about by certain people who are claiming to be a successor . . . Most of them ended up in prison . . . [Some] set fire to the dipping tanks . . . [We ask for Naboth] that the standards of the area may not go down.[55]

Even the Makoni Students Association, which Didymus Mutasa has described as an important forerunner of nationalism in Makoni, was initially prepared to adopt the stance of a 'progressive' ally of the administration. As Didymus Mutasa himself remarked in the first MSA news-sheet, 'It is our duty to struggle hard to build a bridge between those in the Reserves and those ruling us. We should be the middle man and serve the community well and faithfully.'[56] The MSA report of December 1955 carefully explained the effect of the Land Husbandry Act; pointing out that the 'bad farmer will, after due warning, have his farm taken from him. The Government will control marketing of produce. The effect of the plan will be that many who now hold land will either have to farm well or give up their land and go into town to work . . . Although it may cause hardship now, members thought the plan would be a good thing for the future.'[57] In September 1957 the MSA held a conference at Chingono in Makoni Reserve. John Mutasa 'gave good advice by saying we should have a District Council so as to show improvement for our country which is still in a dark position. When a Council is there then we shall have good roads and many highly educated people of our own.'[58] In the third MSA News-sheet issued in November 1957 under the heading 'Shall we not partake also?' Maynard Makoni stated the case for 'progressive' participation in the governance of Makoni district:

For many years we have gradually developed in efficiency as farmers, builders, businessmen, teachers, demonstrators and influential parents. Is this all we can achieve? I feel strongly that we have a greater part to play than we are playing at this moment . . . The Government has played its part in developing the district and it is now looking to us to see if we realise the progress done by responding to it. We can surely respond by helping to make some necessary improvements such as building community grinding mills and bridges . . . It is very desirable that we have a number of tractors working in the District for the good of everybody. Where are they and who is to blame for the lack of all these things? The answer is simple and clear. You and I are to blame because we have always shunned responsibility . . . It is impossible for one man to rule the whole of Makoni District, and I cannot see any reason why we should be reluctant to help our honourable Chief in the smooth running of the District. I strongly look forward to the day when there will be a District Council helping the Chief to run the District and improve it.[59]

Support for Land Husbandry and for Councils could hardly have been more in contrast with the policies of the nationalist movement when it got under way. And yet the dividing line between these 'progressive' manifestos and support for nationalism was very thin. With no apparent sign of incongruity the November 1957 News-sheet reported both that 'the President and Vice President, representing the Association, attended the inaugural meeting of the Southern Rhodesian African National Congress', and that 'a delegation called on Chief Makoni shortly after the Conference and discussed with him the question of the formation of a District Council.' Equally, on the agenda for the MSA executive committee meeting in January 1958 were both 'Report on District Councils' and 'Affiliation with S.R.A.N.C.'[60] The claim to have a right to run Makoni District was logically connected with the claim to have a right to run the country. The minutes of that other forum for the opinions of the educated of Makoni, the St Faith's Discussion Group, reveal their groping towards a political position, their sense of their own readiness to take responsiblity, their resentment at European refusal to admit them to influence, and their eventual endorsement of Congress. In March 1956, for example, there was a discussion on the franchise:

There were those that strongly advocated for universal suffrage for all . . . We do believe that there is sense and wisdom in the unqualified ordinary people. The other stream of thought was for rule by the able without racial consideration. If power is given to ignorant people who do not appreciate what a civilised African . . . values there is a danger that our civilisation may share the fate of the classic civilisation which was destroyed by Barbarians.[61]

But the Discussion Group was deeply cynical about European readiness to accept educated Africans into the defence of 'civilisation':

Mr J. Mutasa said that African priests always had a white one over them . . . Mr Mutseyekwa said he was dissatisfied by the missionaries because they brought and preached the Christian doctrines and made the African drop his old customs for the new ones but now was afraid of letting the Africans go on the same line with them. . .Most of the audience thought there must have been a certain Society which has wisely formed this Christian Society so that Africans are deceived . . . Europeans are afraid of [abandoning segregation] unless there was fear of ugly things like what the Mau Mau terrorists are practising. War is the best remedy to achieve harmony . . . Mr J. Mutasa suggested that the only best method was to go about in the reserves holding meetings with the elders explaining in details what we are aiming at, and this resolution was passed unanimously.[62]

It comes as no surprise to read the ecstatic minutes for the meeting of 18 June 1958 addressed by one of the Congress leaders, Paul Mushonga, 'whose talk was so thrilling'. Mushonga spoke on how Congress was fighting against 'these barriers' between black and white opportunity: 'Our children must have schools if we are to be any people on earth.'[63] By this time leading members of both the Makoni Students Association and the Discussion Group had assumed office in the Rusape branch of Congress. At a meeting in August 1958 John Mutasa, now Treasurer of the Congress branch, sought to shame more cautious members of Makoni's educated. 'The irresponsibility of the Government has made the people form this Congress,' he declared. 'Most people do not want to join Congress because they think it is still at lowest stage. But those mainly in the Reserves who have gained a few things through the help of Congress are very eager to join.'[64]

In an interview in 1982 John Mutasa insisted on the importance of teachers and other educated Africans in the emergence of Congress in Makoni:

During Congress Makoni had more people supporting the nationalist movement than any other district . . . St Faith's was really the nucleus at this time. The meetings and discussions there made people to rethink. The week-end courses attracted so many teachers from all over the district. They became office holders in small branches in the villages. They were able to talk to the children and through them to the parents.[65]

Weinrich writes that 'In many areas teachers formed the backbone of the nationalist movement almost from its beginning . . . Teachers form the most outspoken critics of the European government and the strongest supporters of African nationalism in many areas . . . Teachers reached the height of their influence in the early 1960s.'[66]

There can be no doubt, then, that purchase area farmers, businessmen and the African educated were important in the politics of Makoni District and of very many other districts in Southern Rhodesia. One certainly has to add their activities and aspirations to the peasant radicalism of Tanda and Weya and Nedewedzo and to the cussedness of Chief Zambe Makoni in order to get the full flavour of the open mass nationalist period in Makoni. There is no doubt either that aspirations towards both the Kenyan 'rich' landholder bargain with the regime and a Kavandame-style leadership of populist nationalism were articulated by these groups. But it is important to understand that *neither* aspiration had a chance of being realized. To begin with, these groups, even in combination, just did not seem plausible to the administration as 'loyalist' allies. This was partly because the white regime would not give African farmers or businessmen the economic opportunities which would have been necessary to win them over. But it was also because the administration did not believe that they had enough local influence to deliver the goods. The Native Department, and its successor the Internal Affairs Department, were primarily concerned to control the zones of communal peasant agriculture. They did not think that this could be done by making use of purchase farmers or storekeepers or educated young men.

Native and District Commissioners in Makoni were never very much enamoured of the Purchase Areas, which they regarded as taking up land that could better have been used for communal peasant settlement and as being anomalously outside the control of 'tribal authority'. In 1942, for example, Stead stated that he felt that:

individual tenure has only a limited period of survival . . .The native, having paid £60 or £80 as a purchase price, gives you the idea that he has a right to the property whereas under a leasehold arrangement . . . if he did not actually occupy it he would have to go. At present we have no system for determining the extent to which these arable lands are occupied. A block of land may be cultivated by 40 natives whereas it may be capable of carrying 200 if each holding were limited to 6 acreas.[67]

'The centralization scheme is better than the native tenants scheme,' said the Provincial Commissioner, 'simply because land is very limited . . . and this native purchase scheme is not the most economical way of sharing out land to natives.'[68] We have seen already how officials of the district and provincial administration fought to prevent Tanda from being developed as a Purchase Area. They continued to regard Purchase Areas as so obviously antithetical to the interests of peasants in the Tribal Trust Lands that there was no prospect of purchase farmers being made use of as a stabilizing influence on the peasantry. Nor was there any chance of the remote and scattered Purchase Areas becoming bastions of government power during nationalist or guerrilla upheaval. Administrators felt that it was much more likely that they might become bases for troublemakers. During the guerrilla war no military protection was offered to purchase farmers. And in 1977 an attempt was made to liquidate a Purchase Area altogether, though admittedly a recently established one. After the collapse of the St Faith's co-operative farm, a Purchase Area was set up at Epiphany on which ex-members of the co-operative might purchase farms. In April 1977 the Assistant Secretary of the Purchase Land Authority recommended the elimination of the whole scheme. During December 1976, he said, a dip tank had been destroyed there and a bullet wrapped in a threatening note left for the District Commissioner. In February 1977 the army had encountered guerrillas on the land. The Land Inspectors demarcating the farms had been advised that it was unsafe to enter the area. The District Comissioner was convinced that guerrillas were being given shelter there by the Epiphany purchase farmers 'and preparing a build up to attack the Inyati Copper Mine as well as European farms.' It was suggested that Epiphany Purchase Area be declared a 'No Go Area' and that all thirty-eight families be evicted from it; the land would then be 'consolidated with adjacent European farms. . . .'[69] Admittedly, the District Commissioner belatedly decided that it 'might be inappropriate to take any action against the inhabitants of Epiphany . . . If we move them are we not likely to alienate what little loyalty they might still have to Government and make enemies where we desperately need friends.'[70] So far as the Purchase Areas in general were concerned it was a little late to think about that.

It was a similar story with the rural businessmen. In the 1970s both Roland Hatendi and J.C. Kandiero advised that the administration should seek to work through businessmen in Weya and Tanda. But as we have seen businessmen in fact possessed little influence either as 'loyalists' or as leaders of nationalism in those zones of radical peasant politics. In central Makoni it was a different matter. Businessmen were undoubtedly influential there and by no means all of them had thrown in their lot with nationalism. But once again the administration believed that the interests of African storekeepers and those of peasant producers were manifestly antithetical. African businessmen were thought of as less efficient and more exploitative than white or Indian traders. In September 1951 the Chief Native Commissioner wrote that crop failure had 'shown up the inability of African traders to meet the needs of local people, who still have to look to European traders to stock food supplies in times of scarcity. In several districts it is stated that Africans with food to sell are exploiting the situation by demanding excessive prices from their less fortunate brethren.'[71] Far from fostering African businessmen, the administration kept its heavy hand upon them. 'I think that the Native Department should be abolished,' wrote Basil Nyabadza, church leader, purchase farmer and store-owner at Makoni Farm:

It has become a dictatorship and the Native Commissioners have enormous powers over the lives of Africans who are completely at his mercy. To be in the N.C.s bad books can mean having to face many difficulties over licences, business transactions, etc . . . As a farmer I am very much opposed to the Land Apportionment Act . . . Europeans are extremely ignorant of conditions in the African area, and they think they know the African when they see their cookboy . . . I feel strongly that the leaders of the National Democratic Party . . . best represent the views of African people.[72]

As for the young educated, the administration reacted to their bids for a 'progressive' alliance with a mixture of scorn and fury. In 1944 the Provincial Commissioner, Manicaland, expressed admiration for Chief Mangwende – 'a particularly enlightened Chief; one treats him as if he were a European' – but also asserted that he was 'the greatest believer in indirect rule.'[73] It was the second view that triumphed over the first. As Mangwende emerged as a leading critic of the Land Husbandry Act and was eventually deposed, indirect rule came more and more to mean a blind commitment to 'traditional' chiefs, which in turn meant a sequence of very aged men. The District Commissioner, Makoni, responded to Maynard Makoni's plea for an efficient and educated chief in 1971 by scribbling in the margin of the letter the words 'utter tripe!'[74] This was the response to all attempts to have educated men appointed as chiefs. Occasionally the administration was appalled at the consequences. When the ambitious Chad Chipunza was repulsed as a candidate for the Chipunza chiefship his aged uncle Chiwongote was appointed instead. 'Tradition' was thus upheld but at a cost. In 1970 the Provincial Commissioner wrote that:

Ever since I saw Chief Chipunza for the first time at the recent election, I have been haunted at this awful example of what the tribal system can throw up as a ruler. He simply won't do. Please tell the tribal elders that we require a deputy Chief, able bodied and in possession of such sense as the African normally has, at the earliest possible moment. The man should be acceptable to you, to the tribal elders and should not, if at all possible, be Chad.[75]

This 'awful example' had no effect. The invented 'traditionalism' of the 1970s prohibited any attempt to find 'progressive' chiefs.

Meanwhile the mild discussions of the Makoni Students Association and the St Faith's conferences struck the Native Commissioner as 'odious and harmful'. In May 1957 the Native Commissioner wrote that he was:

confident that Clutton-Brock is the schemer and guiding force behind all these happenings. He is no doubt an idealist with his own schemes to forward but in effect, I consider these to be downright evil. He holds himself out to be one who supports and champions the underdog. In the efforts of the Mission to do this it turns out a type of Native youth . . . lazy, lacking in any sense of responsibility . . . and to cap it, impudent, complaining and even patronising. . . Respectable natives . . . dislike the manner in which their children are taught to behave, their indolence and disrespect for their elders and betters. Chief Makoni is most scornful; says the products of St Faith's are upstarts and ill-mannered. . .

September 1956 Clutton-Brock entered Makoni Reserve and gate-crashed a large meeting called by Chief Makoni to discuss certain tribal affairs . . . A small group of youths known as the Makoni Students Association, instigated by Clutton-Brock, had also called a meeting at the same place and before the large gathering . . . Clutton-Brock spoke condemning the recent increase of tax . . .

St Faith's has its own discussion group . . . After a meeting had been attended by a local M.P., so shocked was he at the subversive talk that he refused to attend again.

The authoritarianism of the administration's whole agrarian programme seemed particularly threatened:

Members of our own Native Agricultural Department . . . have attended and given lectures at Clutton-Brock's organised courses. This has caused considerable embarrassment to general administration in the district owing to the misunderstanding of the subject matter . . . on the part of the Native Mission youths and others. Native Agricultural Demonstrators were later confronted by such youths . . . and were told that their [the Demonstrators] methods are incorrect and forsooth against policy. The Demonstrators were informed that they are not Policemen and had no right to report Natives who destroy soil conservation works, plough in grazing areas, etc . . . When asked where they had received such information, contradictory to all the L.D.O's had taught and implemented, these people answered that the Director of Native Agriculture had told them so at one of these courses.[76]

Given all this, it is not surprising that few members of the Makoni 'petty-bourgeoisie' persisted with an attempt to forge a 'loyalist' alliance with the administration. The key question, therefore, is whether any of them managed to bring off the Kavandame strategy. I think the answer is that they did not. The administration's attitude was plainly highly racist and arbitrary but their feeling that the purchase farmers, businessmen and secondary-school students could not command the support of the Makoni peasantry seems to me to have been an accurate one. Of course, the administration was totally wrong to suppose that chiefs and headmen did or could command such support. My own emphasis would be, as it has been already, upon the impulses which sprang from the peasantry themselves. At the national centre the policies and intentions of the nationalist parties may have been designed to further petty-bourgeois interests. In the rural areas nationalism had to be seen as taking up the case of the peasantry. John Mutasa's warning to the St Faith's discussion group that 'those mainly in the Reserves' were making the running in Congress was much to the point. As members of the Makoni Students Association became nationalist office holders and members they had to abandon any idea that Land Husbandry might be a progressive measure; any emphasis upon building community bridges or rapidly developing higher education gave way to telling the Demonstrators that they were not policemen. Moreover, even at the basic level of patronage the purchase farmers, storeowners and teachers could not compete with the radical nationalist resident elders of Weya and Tanda who had *land* to give their sons – provided that Land Husbandry collapsed and Demonstrators could be forced to stop acting as policemen, that is. In short, even in what is often referred to as the petty-bourgeois stage of open mass nationalism I do not find that peasant protest in the localities was co-opted or harmfully diverted. And the dominance of a radical peasant ideology was, of course, even clearer during the guerrilla war.

But while I do not see either a Kenyan or a Kavandame model as relevant to the Zimbabwean rural areas, I do not think that the existence of purchase farmers, businessmen and teachers among the peasantry had *no* impact upon the war. In fact, I think that some sort of class analysis is necessary in order to understand at least three developments of the 1970s. The first of these is the whole complex question of rural support for Bishop Muzorewa and the African National Council. The second is the key structural position, indeed the key structural predicament, of teachers and businessmen during the war. The third is the evidence for a deliberate attack on 'petty-bourgeois' elements in the countryside by some guerrillas in

1978 and 1979. I shall discuss these three in turn. But in order to arrive at some more or less secure conclusions I need first to take the analysis of rural differentiation one stage further and to examine what were the significant inequalities within the Tribal Trust Lands and among the peasantry which lived there.

A recent Agritex research report remarks that most predictions about the effect of agricultural extension work in the communal areas depend upon 'assumptions about the existence of different layers or strata among people using crude socio-economic criteria (of poverty and wealth). Yet there is little data to date on which to test these assumptions.'[77] I certainly possess little reliable data on which to base an account of differentiation in the Makoni Tribal Trust Lands. Administrative statistics were confessedly often guess-work and this was especially the case with estimates of production per acre. But there exist three rather subjective and inadequate but still useful sources from which one can obtain at least an impress-ionistic picture.

One of these is Norman Thomas' description of Tanda in the mid-1960s. I have hitherto written about Tanda peasants as if they shared a common predicament, though emphasizing the gener-ational distinction between resident elders and their sons. Yet even in Tanda there were significant distinctions of output, education and attitude not only between peasants on the one hand and teachers and store-keepers on the other but also among peasants themselves. Thomas' account of them is focused on what correla-tions can be made between religious affiliation and economic or political conduct – a question of much significance when we come to consider the sources of support for Muzorewa. Thomas writes that:

Within a radius of five miles from sub-chief Makumbe's kraal four de-nominations have built churches and schools. In addition three indepen-dent churches have a following there . . . The Makumbe ward has in recent years been one of the most politically active rural communities in Manica-land. Within it wide variations in attitude toward the nationalists occurred in the past according to religious affiliation and can be observed today.[78]

Thomas' picture is more complicated than the neat fit between type of peasant status and type of religious affiliation which I drew for the early decades of the century. For one thing religious affiliations were initially brought into Tanda from outside it rather than developing as a response to its own particular problems. 'No established congregations,' he writes, 'existed in the central area of Tanda prior to the 1945–48 resettlement . . . Immigrants brought each of the four major denominations of Manicaland into Tanda . . . They entered Tanda as village groups under their headmen, and the church lay leaders among them were zealous to continue meetings for prayer.'[79] In this way a pattern of single-religion kraals built up, some Anglican, some Catholic, some Methodist and so on. This pattern was then overlaid by an intense competition among the churches to build schools and win converts in Tanda. The end result of this was that just over 30 per cent of adult peasants in Tanda were Catholics; just under 25 per cent were Anglicans; around 15 per cent were Adventists; only 7 per cent were American Methodists and just over 10 per cent were Apostolics.

For another thing the characteristics of the various forms of Christianity had changed since the 1920s and 1930s. Thus in the earlier period American Methodist educational provision had been superior to Catholic; in Tanda in the 1960s Catholics had 'an unbeatable lead' in educational provision while Methodists were 'far behind'. 'Significant differences exist in Tanda in levels of education according to religious affiliation'; in the 1960s Catholics were the best educated and Apostolics, of course, the least. Yet here was another change. The Apostolics had originally emerged as a challenge to both peasant and proletarian status. By the 1960s, however, some Apostolics were amongst the most successful peasant producers. Despite little education, Thomas writes, 'in economic status some among the Apostolics are at the apex of the farming community. Apostolic leaders own the only three tractors in Tanda. They display that compulsion towards hard work and thrift that was characteristic of Puritans and Wesleyans in Europe', or, he might have added, of American Methodists in an earlier period in Manicaland. Plainly it is difficult to correlate prosperity and belief; Catholic education gave advantages in the migrant labour market but Apostolic zeal produced agrarian surpluses. Thomas tells a story which neatly illustrates the religious strategies required of anyone who wished to combine both. A man he calls Mr D, a resident elder, had been for many years an Apostle and claimed to be the leading prophet in Tanda. 'Blessed with fertile, well-watered fields and gardens, adjoining European farmland, he developed them with startling success. Today he is the most prosperous farmer in Tanda, with a well furnished home, motor-cycle, tractor, eighty head of cattle, and an annual income in excess of £300.' Mr D wished to educate his children so he put them into mission schools and himself 'accepted church discipline'. But he planned to assume his prophetic role so soon as his children had finished school.[80]

Despite these complications, significant differences of political attitude existed between peasants of varying religious affiliations towards nationalism. Thomas explains these in terms of differential commitment to religious belief and practice. Apostolics in Tanda were very regular in attendance at their religious observations. Caught up in a religion of 'social control through incapsulation' they had 'no need to follow those who seek to reform society – the nationalists' Methodists were also very much focused on their church as the key social institution. Like Apostolics they largely abstained from nationalist politics in the early 1960s. Catholics and Anglicans, on the other hand, did not regard their churches as providing anything like a total answer to their social and economic problems. 'In Tanda Roman Catholics have been the most active in political groups and the least approving of Europeans.' Apostolics and Methodists were bitterly opposed to the emphasis upon the ancestral spirits which was becoming so much an aspect of rural nationalist ideology; a majority of Tanda Catholics and Anglicans, however, 'testified to an unbroken practice of traditional family rituals in their home.' In Tanda in the 1960s, therefore, there were significant religious and political differences which did not correlate exactly with but nevertheless related to different economic positions and activities.[81]

The second available attempt at a social survey is J.C. Kandiero's kraal analysis of Weya in 1976. Kandiero found religious affiliation still important, though there were by now fewer single-denomination kraals and the control over schools by 'religious conscious school committees' had broken down so that 'parents now send their children to school of their wish regardless of religion.' In Weya 'the Roman Catholics and the Methodists share the command over the number of followers.' Ten years after Thomas' survey of Tanda, Kandiero found fewer people standing aloof from either nationalist opposition to the administration or to ancestral observations. In fact he depicted a society dominated by the nationalist resident elders and committed to the radical nationalist ideology. 'There are no interest groups in Weya. When they try to form they are usually threatened and discouraged.' But Kandiero did find one area of differentiation:

Cattle fattening looks to be a major interest of people in Weya. You will find cattle being fed for sales and this is mainly done by those in the teaching field, and farmers who are more established to obtain the cattle and feeds. . .

The society in Weya looks apathetic though a few individuals; i.e. mostly teachers and businessmen are making use of this opportunity. That is they buy cattle from the inactive people, fatten them and sale them to improve themselves and their families.

Farmers in Weya still farm at subsistence level but the businessman is running his business for profit. Though the businessman encourages the farmer to grow more crops he discourages organisations [for fear] of losing customers who sale grain through him. The prominent farmer looks to be embarking on cattle fattening and improving of his housing. This is mainly done in family groups. . .

The biggest number of cattle owners amongst the over 40s . . .A small number of women also have cattle. These they get on behalf of the marriage of their daughters or a widow whose husband died and left very small children, who are not old enough to run the house. It is in this field that a few people are buying cattle from others in the kraals, and have taken up fattening for sale. . . They seem to take advantage of those who do not know the best idea of disposing their cattle.[82]

Even in radical Weya in 1976, then, there were peasants who were more prosperous and who allied themselves with teachers and businessmen 'to take advantage of those who do not know the best idea.' So far as Kandiero was concerned, this enterprise was much to be commended – the ex-teacher who had pioneered cattle fattening 'has spread quite good influence.' His own recommendation was that the administration should seek to re-enter Weya by sending a man to work with the larger peasant farmers and 'prepared to mix up much with teachers and businessmen.'

A third source enables us to contrast these northern Tribal Trust Lands with other areas of Makoni. In the mid-1970s the administration collected a series of 'Kraal Information Sheets for Developmental Purposes', in which they made a breakdown of the residence, education and employment of every member of the families resident in the kraal, though not including data on the families' agricultural output. It is illuminating to take what we might anticipate to be an extreme contrast between a radical nationalist kraal in Tanda and a well-known centre of entrepreneurial Methodism in Makoni Tribal Trust Land, between Headman Maparura's kraal in Tanda and Headman Gandanzara's kraal in Makoni. We have seen already that Gandanzara kraal regarded itself in the mid-1970s as 'a centre of civilisation and attraction'. What this meant emerges from the kraal analysis. In Gandanzara thirty-three of the forty-three cultivators were using chemical fertilizers in 1975; all used manure and compost. There was a Savings Club, a Co-operative, a Woman's Club, a long-established Methodist school, 'our denomination'. Even in Gandanzara by this time many male family heads were away in paid work so that thirteen women were cultivating on behalf of their absent husbands. But none of these men nor their sons were employed on European farms, that most hated form of work. Some still kept up the Makoni tradition of hotel work, like family-head Makoto who was a barman in La Bohème, Salisbury, or family head Nyasha of the Flamboyant Motel in Fort Victoria.

But there were two teachers belonging to the kraal, one headmaster and two in teacher training; there were five men working as drivers; and many in urban employment. Particularly striking was the educational advantage of Gandanzara children. In some families all of six or seven children were in school, either in Gandanzara primary school or boarding at Old Umtali.[83]

It was very different at Maparura kraal in Tanda, whose headman was recorded as 'suspect towards the administration. One brother active in politics. Whole family have been involved in political activity at some time or another.' There were five 'carded' nationalists in the kraal. Nothing is said here of the use of fertilizers or of any voluntary associations; many of the men were working on European farms. Five family heads worked on the 'Inyati Block Farms' and other men worked on farms in Mayo, Macheke and Rusape. One daughter is recorded as being a 'prostitute on Macheke farms'. Only one child was in secondary education.[84] It is clear, then, that there were substantial differences in peasant prosperity from one part of Makoni to another. It is also clear that there were sharp differences *within* Gandanzara kraal. While some families had all their children in school or their elder children in good jobs, the kraal widows were less well off. Of widow Josephine's nine children, for instance, none was in school and only one had a job.

An Agritex study of Wedza communal area, which borders Chiduku, produced in January 1983 remarked that 'the socio-economic differences between the "better-off" farmers and the sample as a whole are not really very great in universal terms.'[85] The same could be said of the distinctions which existed in the 1970s in Tanda, Weya and Makoni. Nevertheless they *did* have some political effect during the emergence and development of Muzorewa's African National Council and during the guerrilla war.

In previous chapters I have written about peasants in Makoni who changed their loyalties from ZAPU to ZANU/Mugabe during the guerrilla war. I have said nothing about the intervention of the African National Council. Yet as we have seen Muzorewa's family lived in Makoni during his boyhood and he himself had his first parish there. Makoni was thought of, indeed, as one of the core areas of support for Muzorewa's African National Council. In Makoni as elsewhere the question is an enormously complicated one. The ANC began with *wider* support than any previous nationalist movement and over the years fell away until it came to represent only a minority of interests. At its beginning many peasants supported it as a cover for continuing ZAPU or ZANU activity, and when it had fallen away it could nevertheless still achieve in 1979 electoral support from many people who were not committed followers in any sense. The question of the class basis of such a shifting and amorphous movement is clearly very difficult.

When it first emerged in order to fight the British government's settlement proposals in 1972, the ANC was clearly not merely an expression of the class interest of the petty-bourgeoisie or of the 'better-off' peasants in the Tribal Trust Lands. The ANC itself claimed to be above all 'truly a grass-roots organisation in its very scope, membership and spirit'. 'The Zimbabwe political scene was transformed,' wrote Michael Mawema in August 1972. 'The people emerged as a united people. It became clearer and clearer that the masses had achieved such total unity as had never been witnessed in the whole history of Zimbabwe.'[86]

In March 1972 Guy Clutton-Brock produced a background assessment of Muzorewa himself for the use of *The Observer*:

I think that Muzorewa emerged from Old Umtali Mission and America as in no way radical . . .His home was a simple middle-class one with all the right European stuff laid out for tea . . . He was not involved in past parties . . . Those who formed ANC and are now its leaders, are not a special tribe of African nationalists. They are a mixed bag, people of moderate influence in various spheres . . . Some were detained, but not for doing anything much. But they sensed the feeling of their people and got together to express it. Muzorewa was drawn into leadership and has responded to the mood and been drawn out by it. His current performance is a revelation of the African tradition, difficult for us Europeans to understand, the people feeling strongly and inspiring the Chief and the Chief then responding and knowing what to say. As he was carried from the airport, so he is spiritually born up by his people, more and more as he becomes more widely known . . . Muzorewa himself was like a little ecclesiastical nut. Smith has cracked the nut and it now breaks forth with new life. Much the same has happened to the people of Rhodesia. Smith and Home are nut-crackers. Now Muzorewa is a Man and no longer a Bishop, as he says, one of five million, producing five million men.[87]

After such eloquence, accurately capturing the hope-intoxicated atmosphere of 1972, I am reluctant to focus on the 'simple middle-class' characterization of Muzorewa. But I think it is important. As we have seen, in the Makoni context Muzorewa's father pre-eminently represented the rural entrepreneurial tradition. Attracted to the American Methodist 'progressive' doctrine; becoming a successful Reserves entrepreneur; mutating from that to become a Native Purchase farmer; all the time deeply committed to the education of his children, old Muzorewa represented all the ambiguity of a man whose achievements had only been accomplished in the teeth of constant interference by the white administration and constant discrimination in favour of white agricultural producers. It becomes necessary, then, to ask to what extent Abel Muzorewa's ANC essentially represented the grievances and aspirations of the frustrated achievers.

In the middle of 1972 the Research Projects Sub-Committee of the Catholic Justice and Peace Commission carried out an inquiry into the ANC. Its findings, which were amplified in a longer account by Weinrich two years later, are pertinent to my question. The Sub-Committee found that the 'men in the streets . . . indeed supported the ANC'. It found that in 1972 there was 'greater support for the ANC among the poor than among the better off Africans.' In short, it found that the ANC was a genuine mass movement. The question, however, is whether it attracted elements over and above the previous mass movements. The Sub-Committee's inquiry suggests that it did. Among its leaders were 'radical nationalists who have remained intensely loyal to their first nationalist leaders', but there were also men who 'had never been a member of ZAPU or ZANU' because they had deplored nationalist violence and faction fighting. These new, respectable, elements in the ANC appealed to those businessmen, purchase farmers and educated men who had not committed themselves to earlier nationalism:

Businessmen are an essential element of the emerging African middle class . . . their ability and willingness to support a political movement is highly desirable . . .In 1972 . . . whereas the wealthier businessmen were cautious, the smaller businessmen spoke more enthusiastically about the new movement. When their attention was drawn to the more reticent support by bigger businessmen, the small store-owners accused the more successful entrepreneurs of being traitors, since they cared more for their money than their country. The reason is that the small store owners often go bankrupt and have little to lose, but much to gain, whereas the affluent businessmen stand great risks in any political transition period. By 1974, however, even the wealthier businessmen took the ANC seriously, and many of them met privately with Bishop Muzorewa to learn more about his policy and plans. Most of the businessmen interviewed in 1972 held a very high opinion of the president [Muzorewa] and vice-president [Banana], but they rejected the behaviour of many ex-detainees on the ANC executive.[88]

As for the purchase farmers, many members of their AFU executive hastened to join the ANC. Their evidence to the Pearce Commission gave cogent expression to rural entrepreneurial frustrations:

For the past seven years, this Government embarked on a policy which gave the African little or no opportunity to acquire property which would make him qualify [for the vote]. In the African Purchase Area, the

Unreserved land which was introduced by the U.F.P. Government in order to enhance the chances for Africans to acquire meaningful land stakes was abolished by this Government. Land allocations to African farmers were reduced to the barest minimum and the cancellation of leases was accelerated. . . Unreserved land . . . was withdrawn from the African farmers and only made available for European occupation. . . No irrigation schemes were introduced in the African Purchase Areas as was done in the European Area . . .Loàns for development purposes and for production purposes in the African Purchase Area have never existed as an economic proposition. . . The Africans have lost a whole generation in time and human development in the field of education . . .Should opportunity avail itself, the attempt will be made to isolate African agriculture from European agriculture in order to apply discrimination more effectively . . . We reject these Proposals in order to avert a bloody revolution which may be the result of oppression and frustration. No sane person can expect any people to brook frustration indefinitely.[89]

The AFU found the prospects of violence 'the most horrible future'. But they were reassured by the leadership of Muzorewa. As the Justice and Peace Sub-Committee found, 'the present clerical leadership seems firmly in command of the A.N.C., and are held in respect . . . They are believed to be strongly opposed to violence.'[90]

To investigate the position of the ANC in the rural areas, the Sub-Committee chose Mrewa District, Here, too, it found a combination of 'grass-roots' support from peasants and resident elders and an involvement of local entrepreneurs:

The local branch of the ANC in that area was founded in April 1972 by some ex-detainees whom the tribesmen trusted . . . The people in Mrewa rejoiced when the Commission returned its NO verdict . . . They thought that all their grievances would soon be redressed, such as land shortage, reduction of cattle herds, poverty . . .

At times the ANC office was crowded by men in their fifties and sixties who, before they came to the office, walked through the township and asked everyone who could read what the current political news in the press was. . . After such interpretations of current events they talked about the golden past and compared it with their own miserable lives. Finally one man concluded: 'God knows it all, he is no fool. The time will come when we shall get back our own country.'

The secretary and the organising secretary [of the Mrewa branch] were prosperous local farmers who grew beans and vegetables for sale. One executive member owned a butchery.[91]

The situation was much the same in Makoni. Those who had led and supported the previous nationalist movements turned to the ANC as a way of resuming open activity. Those in the Tribal Trust Lands who had stood aloof from the old movements now came enthusiastically into the ANC. Thus in the early 1970s there was a very broad coalition of radical peasants and 'progressive' entrepreneurs.

In many areas of Makoni, as we have seen, radical peasant nationalism had continued unabated after the ban on the parties. In these areas peasants felt the continuity between their membership of the open mass nationalist movements, their resistance to enforced agricultural rules and their backing for the guerrilla war. They came to terms with the apparent discontinuities of successive parties claiming to represent the will of the people. The emergence of the African National Council in 1972, indeed, was the easiest of these developments to come to terms with because it seemed so manifestly an opportunity to organize more openly the activities already on foot. Arthur Chadzingwa, known to the peasants of Weya and Tanda as a firm ZAPU man, had been their link with legal representation in Salisbury. Now that he was Deputy National Organizing Secretary on the Central Committee of the ANC he went on with his grass-roots mobilization in exactly the same way as before.[92] Amon Shonge describes the transitions in Weya:

When the ANC came people used it only as a cover. They remained ZAPU right up to 1976. Then when the boys came in everyone turned out to support ZANU. Now they think of ZAPU as a past story . . . Those few who wanted to go on supporting ANC have left the area . . . The comrades came in September 1976 . . . by way of Avila Mission, Nyamaropa, Chikore and Tanda . . . At first the groups which came gave slogans about ZANU – one of them wore a Sithole hat-band – but they said 'We don't have a leader. We are only fighters and don't have a leader yet.' In 1977 they began to say 'Now we have a leader. It's Mugabe.' At first the people were suspicious of them and they were suspicious of the people because they knew Weya was a ZAPU area. They used to say 'We don't trust anybody. I don't trust my shadow. This is war.' But the people came to support ZANU. Even before this people had given money to be sent to the comrades through the umbrella organisation of the ANC. A lot of young people had gone over to Mozambique.[93]

In western Chiduku, says Peter Chakanyuka, people 'thought that the African National Council was a way of reviving ZAPU.'[94] The nationalist activist in Nedewedzo, Mhondiwa Remus Rungodo, describes the transitions there:

In the long run they began to hear of guerrillas organised externally. It was difficult to tell whether they were pro-ZAPU or pro-ZANU. In the early 1970s he was happy to find people united behind ANC led by Bishop Muzorewa. The unhappy days of faction fighting he had witnessed in Salisbury African townships were over . . . Somewhat convinced that

ZAPU and ZANU days were over he went to Umtali to seek help so that he might start or continue organising the people under this umbrella of ANC which was accepted as the only party by then. He later took donations to the headquarters in Umtali. . . Meanwhile the guerrillas were beginning to infiltrate Dewedzo . . . They were called to a meeting at night . . . At this first meeting they were told about the differences in political aims and strategy between ZAPU, ZANU and UANC. This indoctrination was thoroughly emphasised at meetings and as a result most if not all the inhabitants became pro-ZANU. Remus was allowed to continue organising the people in Mutoko area and adjacent villages.[95]

Yet even in these areas of radical peasant activism, the African National Council mobilized other people who had remained aloof hitherto. As John Mutasa says, 'Muzorewa brought in people who had nothing to do with politics before, who were even anti-politics.'[96] In particular, he brought in the Methodists. Where Thomas shows the Methodists of Tanda seeking to keep aloof from nationalist activity in the early 1960s, Methodists everywhere in Makoni became stalwarts of the ANC in the early 1970s. The American Methodist church newspaper, *Umbowo*, became a main propaganda organ of the ANC: the formidable women of the *Rukwadzano* association became familiar figures in pro-Muzorewa political demonstrations. This was partly a result of a politicization of American Methodism which Muzorewa's predecessor as bishop, Ralph Dodge, had initiated. It was partly, of course, because Muzorewa had the church structures immediately at his disposal. But it was also partly because the quintessential American Methodist mix of 'progressive' aspiration and piety found a natural home within the ANC. So Gandanzara, that centre of civilization, prosperity and acquiescence in official agrarian rules, became as much a centre of nationalist activity as was Headman Mapurara's impoverished and embittered kraal. 'Gandanzara supported Muzorewa, of course,' says Columbus Makoni, 'because it had been for so long an American Methodist stronghold. And it went on supporting Muzorewa after other people had begun to realize that he was betraying the revolution. Gandanzara provided some of the recruits for the Auxiliaries who supported Muzorewa and fought the guerrillas in 1979.'[97] George Bhongoghozo, a guerrilla intelligence officer recalls that:

Early on Muzorewa had seemed to the people like a good man. The ANC had been widely supported and many volunteers had gone across to the guerrillas in Mozambique. But by 1978 it was clear that Muzorewa was betraying. From 1977 on we told the comrades already in the district so everyone of them was persuaded. But many of the people remained less clear. Gradually we persuaded them and they saw that Muzorewa was killing the boys in Mozambique. But Gandanzara remained loyal to him. There were two Auxiliary camps at Gandanzara. We guerrillas captured many of the leading American Methodists and interrogated them; we found that many were reliable. Those we killed were not killed because they were Methodists.[98]

Amos Waretsa, a deputy headmaster at Gandanzara in 1977, remembers that:

Before the war Gandanzara was prosperous. The comrades first arrived in September 18th 1977. About twenty-four of them came from Jenya at night. They collected all the villagers to come to the church, including the kraalhead and the Methodist minister. They met outside the church. The comrades introduced themselves by their Chimurenga names, Comrade Chicken, Comrade T.N.T., etc. Gandanzara had many UANC supporters but the comrades said 'Pasi ne Muzorewa'. I myself had supported Muzorewa in 1972 but had resigned in 1976. I am a Methodist and went to school in Gandanzara and Old Umtali. But many people in Gandanzara remained supporters of the ANC. Auxiliaries were based there to defend them and defend the church. The comrades came to attack the Auxiliaries. That was the day when all those buildings were destroyed; most of the Auxiliaries died that day. So at first the comrades regarded Gandanzara as an enemy but gradually they found many people coming to support them.[99]

These attacks on the impressive buildings around the church at Gandanzara was as close as Makoni came to class war. A final quotation – this time from a different perspective – makes the point. Langton Charidza, who remained UANC Provincial Organizer in 1981, testifies that:

In March 1978 I was elected to the Provincial level of the ANC. I moved to Rusape though I knew little about the area. It was a very difficult time. . . In 1976 Makoni had really been our area but then it became a home of the freedom fighters which we failed to penetrate. Even in 1977 we had a stronghold there, definitely. In 1978 our support began to fade. We could not move about freely. Our supporters warned us not to come. . .But the Auxiliaries protected our people. The Auxiliaries wanted the roads to re-open, cattle to go to the dip tanks, children to go to school. In areas where the parents would work with the Auxiliaries all that happened. In Gandanzara the people were freed by the Auxiliaries. In Tandi too they were successful. It was not so much that the people of Gandanzara belonged to the American Methodists. It was because they were very intelligent and progressive. They could see everything being destroyed . . . Ah, those people of Gandanzara, if they were left to themselves they would progress so much. They are dedicated people, very clever.[100]

I have said that this was as close as Makoni came to rural civil war but even here, of course, the correlations were not neat or exact. By no means all Gandanzara Methodists stayed with Muzorewa's party to the end. As for peasants in general, it was very difficult indeed for them to get access to the information required to make a well-founded decision. For a long time it was hard for them to know what was going on inside Mozambique; which party was in control of the guerrillas there and who that party accepted as its leader. Peter Chakanyuka's record of his interview with Mavengeni Annah in Nedewedzo in February 1981 gives a good notion of the confusion of the majority:

She was a ZAPU member. At some political meetings she remembers being told about party strife but could not make head or tail of the stories about party leadership. When Muzorewa appeared on the political scene she and most other people believed he was part of the liberation movement until the time the guerrillas infiltrated. At political gatherings the Comrades showed us his weaknesses and why they were not behind him. It was then that she learnt about Comrade Mugabe. Annah had been convinced that Muzorewa was a good nationalist leader, especially during the Pearce Commission exercise. Muzorewa fought hard to have prominent detainees and nationalist leaders released. He managed to organise people to reject the Pearce proposals and at one time united the factional parties ZAPU and ZANU under ANC. However she came to dislike Muzorewa's leadership especially when he formed a government in 1979. It was the time Security Forces carried out atrocities in Dewedzo. She has in memory two elderly people who were shot . . . at St Bede's school. Villages like Samukange's were set on fire and the Security Forces looted the villages, molesting girls whom they collected from the villages to their camp in Chiwetu. She came to support ZANU when the guerrillas politicised in the meetings they organised during the nights. Here they clearly distinguished the aims of the liberation movement from those of the internal political parties.[101]

Moreover, the potential differences of interest within the ANC front during the early and mid-1970s were not exploited by the Rhodesia Front regime. Even if there could be no clusters of wealthy Home Guards in the Tribal Trust Lands there could well be prosperous informers; the administration might have tried to make Native Purchase Areas into no-go zones by ringing them with police or African soldiers. None of this happened. Instead the government still further hammered the various strata of the rural areas into a single opposition. Take, for example, the setting up of the so-called Protected Villages. In his article on the rural African middle class, William Duggan remarked that the Protected Village system *could* have been used as a prelude to a sweeping redistribution of land in the communal areas:

The Kenyan experience becomes even more relevant at this point. As in Rhodesia, guerrilla war in the countryside was preceded by the settlers' staunch refusal to enfranchise a rural African middle class. The speed with which this enfranchisement was accomplished during the Mau Mau crisis was remarkable . . . The scale of intervention required for a Swynnerton Plan in Rhodesia would be massive . . . As in Kenya, for a rural elite to be given adequate land, the position of the poorer families would [have to] be so eroded as to make it possible to implement the plan rapidly only by military force. In Kenya this was done in the context of a civil war. In Rhodesia . . . there may be enough armable Africans willing to fight for the elimination of the vestiges of white political privilege as well as for the entrenchment of their own economic privilege to turn the current nationalist war into a bloody civil war.

From 1973, reserve residents in Rhodesia were herded into 'protected villages', a major feature also of the Kenyan government's anti-Mau Mau Swynnerton Plan in the Kikuyu reserves From this position the Kenyan government sorted out the Mau Mau 'sympathizers' and redistributed the outlying empty farmland to the advantage of a loyal minority who received ample plots. Reserve residents were recruited to protect this new order against the guerillas. . . the endurance of the protected villages leaves the reserves vulnerable to a Kenyan solution . . . A Swynnerton Plan in the countryside is therefore at least a possible option in Zimbabwe Rhodesia.[102]

But as Duggan himself remarks, the Rhodesia Front regime were highly unlikely to adopt such a policy wholeheartedly. 'The Zimbabwe Rhodesian authorities still refuse to redistribute reserve land in order to create a loyal middle class, for that class would compete directly with surviving settler farmers.' In the event, nothing could have been further from the *effect* of the Protected Village strategy, which yet further alienated rural 'progressives' rather than winning their support. Take, for example, the case of Chiweshe Tribal Trust Land, 70 km north of Salisbury, the inhabitants of which were moved into Protected Villages in 1974.

Chiweshe was an area of surviving peasant prosperity. The Catholic Commission for Justice and Peace representative, who toured Chiweshe after the removal of its people to the Protected Villages, was struck by the fact that the:

deserted villages [were] extremely well built in comparison to villages in Tribal Trust Lands in the more remote areas. We also noticed a number of deserted bungalow-type homes which must have been built at considerable expense. They were of a higher standard than the average Salisbury township house and would compare favourably with some of the better houses in Kambuzuma . . . Mr Johnstone said that it was unlikely that compensation would be paid to the owners of these homes . . . The area through which we travelled has produced some of the finest tobacco in Rhodesia. From the many tobacco sheds we saw on our way I would infer that cash-cropping must have been an essential part of the economic activities in that area.

The observer noted that the local District Commissioner was committed to the permanence of the regrouping and that he regarded the Protected Village system as inaugurating a better life, 'of a higher standard than the traditional way of life. . .' But this was not at all to be based on giving 'progressives' a free hand. Instead:

Land Husbandry would now be carried out as 'collective farming'. Referring to *nhimbe*, the traditional communal work party, [the District Commissioner] said that 'collective farming' had been a traditional feature of Shona culture . . . I was dismayed to hear the District Commissioner . . . and to note that he was preparing to solve the crucial land problem on the basis of this incorrect assumption.

The whole operation, concluded this observer, had nothing to offer a man 'who has built himself a good house and was working his land profitably and individually.'[103] Even the *Rhodesia Herald* protested that the Chiweshe regrouping amounted to 'a collective fine that bears hardest on those who made the greatest effort to better themselves.'[104]

Another representative of the Catholic Commission interviewed people inside the Protected Villages and found bitter resentment from Chiweshe 'progressives':

Mr C is about 35 years old. He is a Roman Catholic . . . He is highly esteemed in the community and is known as a very successful master farmer who used to grow tobacco and cotton. By African standards he is a very well-to-do person. Mr C is strongly opposed to the government action which put the people into protected villages . . . Mrs C believes that help would only dull the people's suffering and make them forget their plight. She wants the people to remain united and to oppose government's policy . . . She pleaded missionaries not to give any help so that the people's resentment against government was kept alive.

Mrs G . . . used to grow cotton and did very well economically . . . Mrs G feels very strongly about the government action and demands that the government not the missionaries assume responsibility for the people . . . Mr K is a local businessman and carpenter . . . Mr K challenges government to prove that anyone in the protected villages supports its policy. He is strongly opposed to the government . . . Mrs K is the wife of Mr K. Her husband and she owned a house worth 8,000 dollars which has had to be abandoned during the move. She greatly resents government action.[105]

The Mashonaland Central Provincial Commissioner and the Police Superintendent stressed that 'the principal short-term objective' behind moving over forty-six thousand people was to gain 'complete control over the people': 'all other ways of trying to obtain the cooperation of the Chiweshe people having failed, the concept of the Protected Village had become the only method to try and divorce the people from the guerrillas.'[106] *Yet the effect of the* move was to bind the different strata of the Chiweshe peasantry yet more firmly together.[107]

If the Rhodesia Front did nothing to detach businessmen and master farmers from the rural nationalist front, no more did the most militant spokesmen of a 'people's war' proclaim hostility towards 'petty-bourgeois' elements who might have been thought likely to back Muzorewa. In 1975 the breakdown of the détente exercise led to an increasingly bitter rift between ZANU militants and Muzorewa. Thousands of young men and women flooded into Mozambique to be trained as guerrillas; Mugabe and Edgar Tekere went into Mozambique also and ultimately gained control over these forces. But this development of radicalism did not at this stage involve an attack on a rural petty-bourgeoisie. In 1975 businessmen and yeoman farmers with cars or trucks played an important part in ferrying young volunteers to the Mozambique border. And Tekere himself, in an illuminating letter from Mozambique in July 1975, reveals the particular atmosphere of ZANU radicalism at that time:

Since Robert Mugabe and I fled from home on the night of April 3rd and crossed into Mozambique on night of April 5th, we have remained in the country. It is where I am writing from – from a small rural town called Vila Gouveia where we have been temporarily resident in a military barracks since July 12th. We are with a group of 182 of our recent recruits from home . . . There is an endless flow of men from home and those of our home people who fought the war here and others ordinarily settled here in the past are similarly opting to join our army. Right from the time we left detention in December we spared no time at all in going out to the people to speak nothing else but violence and urge people to join our military. We did not mince our words and did not care who listened in house to house meetings right across the country . . . we ignored the whole talk about talks, denounced the whole concept of talks at every platform offered and worked hard to ensure that such talks do not really start because we saw them as nothing else but a trick to defuse our military effort without a ghost of a prospect for *majority rule now* . . . In the meantime Nkomo was getting himself into all sorts of secret deals with the whites and he and Muzorewa were actually sweating to kill the war effort. We ourselves could see that we were making a terrific impact on the minds of the people, especially the younger ones, the tribesmen and the African businessmen. We could also say that the overwhelming majority of the enlightened and thinking fell for us while Nkomo went swimming among his riff-raff . . .

Tekere suggested that correspondence and funds be sent to him via 'a man from home – a very old party member', who had 'a flourishing business back home and is in a flourishing transport business here in Mozambique.' This contact was safe to send money to 'in that he is not himself a man in need. He has in fact spent quite a bit of money on us here already. He is very much in touch with our military in Tete and spends much of his personal money helping us to ease the problems of recruits in transit.'[108] It is still very much the same atmosphere as the early days of ZANU in Zambia where those really behind the party were 'business people, buses, taxis, things like that . . . at that particular time they ran the party', donating transport and funds.[109]

Clearly radicalism and commitment to continued war did not imply a repudiation of businessmen, or of the 'enlightened'. In 1975 it was certainly still possible to analyse the situation in terms of a united countryside, alienated from and standing against the regime. Yet it seems to me that after 1975, as the war hotted up, class differentiation in the rural areas did come to play a particular part in two ways which I have not yet discussed. In the first place, men of particular resources or funds or influence or information, such as salaried teachers or storekeepers, were in a key structural position in the guerrilla war. In the second place, after the Internal Settlement of 1978, the presumed petty-bourgeois supporters of Muzorewa in the rural areas *did* come under attack from the guerrillas, though they did not come under the protection of the new regime.

To illustrate the structural dilemma of men of resources, let me take once again the case of Makoni District and the example of rural businessmen. Guerrillas had a continuous need for cash, food and clothing. By far the readiest way to obtain these necessities was from storekeepers, who might order additional stock and hand it over to guerrillas without such transactions being too obvious. Long before the guerrillas entered Makoni District, indeed, they had made contact with some of the storekeepers there. One of these was Basil Nyabadza, pastor of an independent African church on Makoni Farm, owner of Zonga Purchase Area farm number one, and owner too of a butchery, a grinding mill, a general store, an eating house and a bottle store situated along the Rusape to Inyanga road. I have already quoted his evidence to the Monckton Commission in which he expressed the frustrations of the rural entrepreneur. In 1972 he wrote in similar terms to the Pearce Commission, rejecting the Smith/Home constitutional proposals. Like almost everyone else in Makoni he joined the ANC, donated money to it, and became known as a prominent supporter.[110] This did not mean, however, that he adopted a 'moderate' political position or had reservations about the guerrilla war. Indeed, he became increasingly committed to support of the guerrillas. He made use of gifts of money donated by friends overseas to buy very large stocks of food and clothes which were then transported to guerrilla groups operating in adjacent districts. Early in 1975 Nyabadza's car was used in the movement of volunteers into Mozambique.[111]

When the guerrillas entered Makoni District itself, every storekeeper had to make up his mind whether to cooperate in this way, often at great personal expense, or to seek to gain protection from a police or army guard. Meanwhile, the Security Forces kept a constant watch on storekeepers, and government men disguised as guerrillas were used to try to trick them into betraying their help to the guerrillas. 'As you know,' wrote Patricia Chater from St Francis, Makoni Farm, in August 1976:

there is already immunity from prosecution for anyone in the Security Forces, Police, etc who causes injury or even death to a civilian in 'good faith'. Now they can apparently be even less careful. There have been three shootings in the Makoni T.T.L in the last week and we believe that they have all been killed by the Rhodesian black soldiers . . . The second man was a youngish businessman . . . who lives in the Chiduku. He was visited by the CID, who pretended to be 'terrorists' and demanded food and clothing, which they were given. The next day . . . he was stopped on his way home from Rusape by Security people and shot.[112]

Basil Nyabadza himself was the object of three such attempts to trap him into revealing his aid to the guerrillas. In July 1976 a Selous Scouts group pretending to be guerrillas came to St Francis. His wife Rosemary has described what happened:

These men had AK rifles and they looked like the boys. . . They asked to speak to Baba privately and he went outside with them. One of the group stayed behind in the kitchen . . . He talked to me. 'Your *mudzimu* (spirit) is very strong,' he said, 'and I am made to say this. We are not *wakomana*, we are the Selous Scouts. They want to destroy your business and to kill the father. He will be asked to keep our weapons, and this is a trap. You must tell him to refuse' . . . He told me that we must go to the police and report. . .

Next day she did go to the police. 'They said they were surprised that I had come "because we never thought your husband would report terrorists".' Another such attempt was made just before Christmas 1976 and in 1977 a bogus letter was sent purporting to be from a guerrilla group operating in Inyanga:

They said they had heard that he could help them with clothing, and they asked him to meet them at a certain place near Inyanga. Baba was a bit suspicious and he showed the letter to some of the local guerrillas. 'This is bad,' they said, 'don't go. The people who sent this letter are not ZANLA, they are Selous Scouts. They want to kill you. . . ' So Baba didn't go.[113]

Meanwhile, guerrillas themselves were suspicious of store-owners and believed that some of them had been issued with supplies of poisoned tinned food which the government had ordered them to issue when guerrillas asked for supplies.

The rural businessmen of Makoni tried to negotiate these treacherous currents as well as they could. Some of them survived. One of them was Isidore Nyamusamba who testifies that:

During the war I was forced to close the three stores in the country and I opened one in Rusape . . . I opened this store in 1977. I lost a lot of money during the war, and I supported the guerrillas by giving suits, boots, jackets and food. This is the way I survived the war. One day a whole lorry of beer was taken by the boys and I lost hundreds of dollars due to that. But I can openly say that God really protected me. I never got any bodily injury by the war, but my possessions were decreased considerably.[114]

Other businessmen were not so lucky. At the edge of Makoni TTL, along the Rusape to Inyanga road were three African-owned stores. Basil Nyabadza owned one of these, and on 1 April 1977 he was shot and killed at his church by CID men pretending to be guerrillas.[115] A little later leaflets were dropped over Makoni TTL headed 'Warning To All':

Tigers. Terrorist Informers. Terrorist Agents. Sympathisers and Feeders of Terrorists. Recruiters for Terrorist Training. There are still some people who continue to help the terrorists and few even try to do their evil work for them. These people are counted as terrorists and will be killed by the Security Forces. They have not been forced at gunpoint to help the cowardly terrorist as many people are. They openly support the terrorist.[116]

The second store was owned by a man known to be a business and personal rival of Nyabadza's. It was believed that he had denounced Nyabadza to the police and the guerrillas killed him in revenge for Nyabadza's death.

The third store-owner was Isaac Tsungo who testifies that:

The guerrillas used to send for clothes, jeans, underwear. I got them from whole-salers as if for the store. I think that at the time Basil, myself and the Chief were their main suppliers. 1978 was a very hard year. There were so many demands for clothes and shoes as more and more guerrillas came into the district. Messages and demands were coming in from all sides. I cannot count the money it cost. I have been working to repay it ever since.

When Basil was killed and after him the other storekeeper, I thought 'The third one is me'. So I didn't go to the store, especially at night. In 1979, though, the Security Forces came at night and smashed up the store and took all the goods. The next day they came and told me it was the 'terrorists'. I did not say anything; I was glad to be alive.[117]

Tsungu did not reopen the store. Indeed, all over Makoni stores closed down. In March 1978 Basil Nyabadza's son Francis, who had taken over the church, was summoned to the CID camp in Rusape:

Don't tell me you're not assisting the 'terrs' [he was told] because every single businessman in Makoni without exception is, and you definitely are . . . There is a way you can carry on your business but I want you to let me know whenever the 'terrs' or their helpers come to your store . . . I know your father was supporting the 'terrs'. In fact I saw him one day with a lot of stuff he'd bought in Salisbury. He was delivering to them. I thought his death would have discouraged you from supporting them . . . I'm going to give you two days to decide whether to co-operate with me or not. After that two days, if I haven't heard from you, don't blame me for whatever happens to you or your family.[118]

Francis closed the store and took his immediate family to Salisbury.

A similar account could be written of the dilemma of school-teachers and headmasters, who paid a regular proportion of their salaries over to the guerrillas and who were constantly in danger of denunciation by informers. In short, it is clear that it was especially dangerous to be a businessman or a teacher in the rural areas during the war, but it is far from clear that they were marked out as petty-bourgeois 'class-enemies' by the guerrillas. If they were pre-pared to co-operate with the guerrillas, indeed, they were regarded as invaluable allies. Much the same was true of other 'progressives' in Makoni – purchase farmers, master-farmers in the TTLs, etc. A headmaster told me in 1981 that:

One guerrilla group operating in Tanda were very vicious. The people there who had property and goods wanted to keep them away from the comrades. So the people without property informed on them as 'sell-outs' and many were killed. But where men with property did make contact with the comrades and supply them with food and clothes, they were able to control and influence them. I supplied the guerrillas, through money given by the church, with what they needed. But if one asked for a suit I would say to him 'Are you getting married in the mountains?', or if one asked for too many things I would say 'Do you have a shop in the mountains?'.[119]

The same man wrote to the Dean of Salisbury in November 1979, noting that:

The boys in our area are a little bit under our influence . . . We have converted some hard-core boys into very reasonable beings . . . The boys must feel loved. The number of boys wanting help is increasing daily. Food is becoming scarce because some of the homes where they get food were burnt and crops were destroyed . . . We need food to help the boys.[120]

But the final point I wish to make is that the sort of bargain here described – reasonableness in return for aid – came under very heavy pressure after Muzorewa's participation in the Internal Settlement of 1978. The settlement appeared as a betrayal; those who remained loyal to Muzorewa were seen as class enemies of the peasants. 'It is very surprising,' wrote Moven Mahachi – now Minister of Lands and Resettlement – from prison:

that our two devoted friends, who were in fact the founders of our revolution, can at last buy their way out of the revolution . . . The masses of our people have and will continue to live in permanent poverty . . . The internal leaders are not negotiating for our true freedom but for ever-lasting economic exploitation . . . We have to be very careful for the vultures and their running dogs [who] want to hijack our revolution and to twist it into an instrument of capitalist exploitation.[121]

ZANU/Mugabe's radio, 'Voice of Zimbabwe', declared later in 1978 that 'there is now a crisis among the Zimbabwean black bourgeoisie . . . They know that the Patriotic Front will soon be ruling Zimbabwe and are wondering what may be in store for them.'[122] Really for the first time, the language of internal class war came to be used in Zimbabwe's rural areas. It was in this context, as we have already seen, that the guerrilla assaults on Gandanzara were launched.

Now was the moment, if there was ever to be one, for a Kenya-style cleavage. But there was precious little sign that Muzorewa's government had anything tangible to offer to rural entrepreneurs. So far from using the Protected Village system as a means of handing out the cleared land to 'loyalists', the Muzorewa government closed down most Protected Villages and let everybody back onto their old lands. We have already seen the claim that Muzorewa's Auxiliaries 'freed' the people of Gandanzara, but the

Auxiliaries were a very different body from the Kikuyu Home Guard as described by Lamb. They were not made up of wealthy peasants, but were 'the biggest rabble I've come across', to quote a Rhodesian Intelligence Corps member: 'Undisciplined political thugs . . . Most were shanghaied. The DCs got orders to recruit so many auxiliaries in a month's time, so they went through the TTLs in a truck and if they saw a young guy with no job, up he went in the back of the truck.'[123] Like the Selous Scouts, the Auxiliaries were part of a strategy of 'counter-terror', operating out of forts in the TTLs. Most rural 'progressives' would much have preferred not to have been 'freed' by the Auxiliaries.[124]

Thus in many parts of rural Zimbabwe, businessmen and entrepreneur farmers fell under guerrilla suspicion in this period, but were in no sense protected by or recruited for the Muzorewa regime. Their plight emerges very clearly from two piteous pleas now in the archives of the Catholic Commission for Justice and Peace in Harare. The first is from the African Farmers Union, speaking on behalf of Purchase Area farmers, in February 1979:

The AFU has 9,000 members who have been suffering intimidation from both sides. The situation changed on the 3rd March (1978). The *vakomana* (boys) were not sure of the local attitude to the Agreement and so have hardened towards African farmers. . .

The African Farmers Union saw the local leaders last week and told them that their situation was much worse, as AFU members are victimised by all sides. Sithole and Muzorewa said the auxiliaries were for the protection of the people, but when confronted by evidence of auxiliaries killing farmers, they could not reply.

The *vakomana* are competing with Smith in killing the people. Prominent African farmers are killed simply because they are better off than most of the people.[125]

The second is a plaint by a self-styled 'Middle Class Business Man in a War Zone', also from February 1979:

My experience in a war zone is that the middle class businessman suffered more threat from both the security forces and the boys in the bush as well as the rest of the forces . . . All the grinding mills have been stopped to function just because they [the Security Forces] think they are trying to starve the man with a gun. The ordinary TTL person is more starved . . .The dealer was told not to sell shoes, jeans, shirts . . . trousers . . . mealie meal, beef, tins of fish . . . With such behaviour business became doomed. Finally all shops were closed right through [Buhera] district.

Auxiliary Force . . . are the most brutal gang of people. If you happen to refuse him credit facilities make sure he come and threaten the children being armed so that he will get anything for nothing . . .The first word they ask is where is the Gandangas? You tell him you had never seen such a person then you are severely hit. They will ask for all the young boys and girls to join them whether they like it or not it makes no difference . . .You can see gentlemen that it is a middle class person who suffers from both sides for no cause of his.

The Comrades . . . accept no other man's suggestion. His approach to his parent is superhuman. His demands for money is quite above human dignity. He does not allow anybody to show that whatever one has worked for must be asked for but just takes it unconditionally . . .

The security forces have closed all my sources of income by closing my shop. The terrs have killed many of my relatives and friends . . .Many businessmen has been made refugees for no fault of theirs. These people have suffered more than the man who caused the situation to be like this . . .

If one day I could meet the real man who brought my present situation into being after I had worked so hard for the good of my children and myself, the devil would finally decide for me.[126]

This is the authentic voice of the rural middle class; a man neither a loyalist Home Guard, nor a Kavandame; neither a wealthy ally of government, fighting for increased prosperity, nor a man seeking to shape liberation ideology and failing to do so. By 1979 the rural middle class did not know who 'the real man' was who had brought them into their present situation; by contrast with the clarity of radical peasant ideology, they did not know even what to hope for, except for an end to the war.

NOTES

1 The confidence of this statement may have to be modified. In August 1979, Josiah Tongogara told John Conradie that in some areas of Zimbabwe guerrillas were ploughing and producing their own food and that in 'liberated' areas villagers accepted collective production and distribution. 'If at the end of the revolution they want to change it we will look into that' but 'the protractedness of the revolution really solves some problems that you'd not be able to solve if the revolution was short.' Interview between John Conradie and Josiah Tongogara, Maputo, 20 August 1979.
2 G. Lamb, *Peasant Politics. Conflict and Development in Muranga* (Lewes: 1974), p. 14.
3 ibid., pp. 11–16.
4 E.A. Alpers, 'To seek a better life: the implication of migration from northern Mozambique to colonial and independent Tanzania for class formation and political behaviour in the struggle to liberate Mozambique', unpublished paper presented at Conference on the 'Class Base of Nationalist Movements in Angola, Guinea-Bissau and Mozambique', Minneapolis, May 1983, pp. 23–4.

5   Allen Isaacman, 'The Mozambiquan cotton cooperative: the creation of a grassroots alternative to forced commodity production', paper presented to Conference on Zimbabwean History: Progress and Development, University of Zimbabwe, August 1982, p. 9.
6   Alpers, 'To seek a better life', pp. 27–8.
7   Isaacman, 'The Mozambiquan cotton cooperative', pp.27–8.
8   L.H. Gann and T.H. Henriksen, *The Struggle for Zimbabwe. Battle in the Bush* (New York: 1981), p. 87. Gann and Henriksen, however, think that 'guerrilla war turned into a black civil war' in Zimbabwe, in which 'many more Africans died at the hands of bush fighters than did Europeans.' Standing on the other side to the guerrillas were 'traditional chiefs and headmen . . . an entire army of black functionaries, telegraphists, detectives, court interpreters and policemen . . . African "master farmers", building contractors and transport operators [who] had obtained a modest, and sometimes a considerable degree of prosperity', and who 'distrusted the guerrilla's promises.' p. 90.
9   'Our Path to Liberation. Being Comments at an ANC-ZAPU Consultation and Information Meeting, November 1976, now issued as a Party Document.'
10 J.W. Murisi, 'The history of class consciousness in Zimbabwe', in *Report. Zimbabwe Conference. A Study of the Current Situation and Long-term Development Problems* (The Hague: October 1979).
11 Aquino de Braganca and colleagues, *Zimbabwe. Notes and Reflections on the Rhodesian Question* (University of Eduardo Mondlane, Maputo, Centre of African Studies: July 1977), a translation of *Zimbabwe: Alguns Dados E Reflexoes Sobre A Questao Rodesiana*, October 1976, pp. 19, 20, 32, 37.
12 Native Commissioner, Rusape, to Chief Native Commissioner, 3 April 1937, file S.1542.C6.N – Z, National Archives, Harare (NAH)
13 Minutes of the 69th meeting of the Native Land Board, 12 October 1938, file S.1123. Vol. 3, NAH.
14 Interview with Peter Chawandamira, Manchester, 24 August 1983. Peter Chawandamira tells a delightful story of how his father was converted to Seventh Day Adventism which brings out a good deal about peasant religion: 'My father had a vast, big land. I persuaded Seventh Day Adventists from their mission to go and work on his land for porridge only, no beer. In one day they cleared the whole land. My father said that was a fine religion and began to go to church.'
15 ibid.
16 Abel Muzorewa, *Rise Up and Walk. An Autobiography* (London: 1978), pp. 23–4.
17 ibid., p. 25.
18 For the predicament of the headman Mukuwapasi's people around Zonga see Father Konrad Answenger to Native Commissioner, Makoni, 12 April 1926, file S.138.21. vol. 1, NAH. Tangai was a Sergeant in the Native Affairs Department (Interview with Roland Hatendi, Tandi, 6 February 1981). His application for a farm in Zonga was the very first received for a NPA farm in Makoni district.

(Assistant Director of Native Lands to Chief Native Commissioner, 29 June 1931, file S.138.21. vol. 4, NAH. Native Commissioner, Makoni to Chief Native Commissioner, 19 October 1934, file S.1542.L4, 1933/1935, NAH; Minutes of the seventh meeting of the Native Land Board, 3 November 1931, file S.1123. vol. 1, NAH.) Tangai's farm passed into the possession of Basil Nyabadza, pastor of the St Francis African Church at Makoni Farm. Maurice Nyagumbo remembers that when he used to visit Zonga with Nyabadza in the 1950s 'the people of Mukuwapasi were very hostile. When we used to go out there they wouldn't speak to us'. Interview with Maurice Nyagumbo, Harare, 14 January 1981.

19   The minutes of the Native Land Board in the S.1123 series, NAH, allow us to build up a picture of the settlement of Dowa.
20   Interview with Solomon Chavunduka, Harare, 16 March 1981.
21   Stan Made, *Made in Zimbabwe* (Gwelo: 1980), pp. 10, 11, 15, 37, 38, 39.
22   Muzorewa, *Rise Up and Walk*, pp. 23–4.
23   Made, *Made in Zimbabwe*, p. 20.
24   Interview with Roland Hatendi, Tandi, Chiduku, 6 February 1981.
25   Made, *Made in Zimbabwe*, pp. 26–7.
26   ibid., p. 48.
27   Oliver Pollak, 'Black farmers and white politics in Rhodesia', *African Affairs*, vol 74, no. 296, (July 1975), pp. 270–1.
28   Barry Munslow, 'Zimbabwe's emerging African bourgeoisie', *Review of African Political Economy*, no. 19 (1980), p. 64.
29   Quarterly Reports, Makoni, March 1948, June 1948, September 1951, file S.168. NAH.
30   Quarterly Reports, Makoni, September 1948, June and September 1949, file S.168, NAH. It is plain, however, that even at this point Dowa was still functioning on a relatively small scale. To market 2000 bags of maize did not exceed the performance of the Reserves entrepreneurs of a decade earlier. In 1953 an Extension report on the purchase areas showed that at that time 140 farms in Dowa were occupied; 3000 acres were cultivated; in that year 7200 bags of grain had been produced at an average of only 2.5 bags per acre; there were 2043 head of cattle. In Tanda in 1953 there were only 14 occupied farms and only 224 acres cultivated. In the same year Zivyambe had 219 farms and Msengezi had 339. File S.160.AGR.16/1/54, Chart IX, NAH.
31   Pollak, 'Black farmers and white politics', pp. 272–3.
32   Annual Report, Makoni, 1938, file S.1563, NAH.
33   Annual Report, Wedza, 1946, file S.1563, NAH.
34   Annual Report, Makoni, 1947, file S.1563, NAH.
35   Annual Report, Makoni, 1948, file S.1563, NAH.
36   B.J. Mukonyora to Director, Native Agriculture, 18 March 1948, file S.160.GC1 – GC2, NAH.
37   A.K.H. Weinrich, *Black and White Elites in Rural Rhodesia* (Manchester: 1973), pp. 194, 200, 201, 203.

38 J. Condy, Inspection Report for St Killian's, Makoni, 21 April 1922, file 'Old Forgotten Far Off Things and Battles Long Ago', St Killian's archives.
39 Deed of Gift by Michael Nyamusamba, 27 July 1925, ibid.
40 Interview with Father Peter Turner, Umtali, 14 March 1981. Turner added after describing this gesture, 'admittedly his wealth was now in a chain of stores and trucks'.
41 Interview between Sister Emilia Chiteka and Isidore Nyamusamba, Triashill, 21 February 1981.
42 Interview between P.M. Chakanyuka and Mhondiwa Remus Rungodo, Nedewedzo, 30 January 1981.
43 Maurice Nyagumbo, *With The People. An Autobiography from the Zimbabwe Struggle*, (London: 1980), pp. 87, 94.
44 Entries for 14 September 1960, 24 January 1962, Black Minute Book, Carmelite Diary, Triashill archives.
45 Entry for 13 September 1961, ibid. It should be noted, however, that conditions at Triashill were not quite as placid as this. A letter of October 1st 1962, interleaved with the Carmelite Diary, remarks that 'It has been decided to close the [carpentry] school completely. This course of action has been necessitated not only by the recent burning of school buildings, but also by the cowardly threats which have been directed at the Sisters who have given their service for so many years to the people of the district'.
46 Weinrich, *Black and White Elites*, pp. 202–4.
47 Patricia Chater to Ralph Ibbot, 28 February 1959, Chater Papers, file C. During my field research in Makoni district I stayed at St Francis Church on Makoni Farm, where Patricia Chater was my hostess. She then had in her possession a very large collection of papers relating to the St Faith's co-operative farm, the Makoni Students Association, the African National Congress, and to many other topics. I worked on them at St Francis and my references here are to the file numbers as they then existed. Since then most of these papers have been placed in the National Archives and will no doubt be catalogued and reclassified.
48 Patricia Chater to Peter Kuenstler, 2 March 1959, Chater Papers, file C.
49 Chief Native Commissioner, Annual Report, 1948, file S.1563, NAH.
50 Weinrich, *Black and White Elites*, pp. 166, 171.
51 Report to members of the Makoni Students Association, December 1955, Chater papers, file A.
52 William Chigutsa Rugoyi to Native Commissioner, Makoni, 8 October 1951, file 'Old Papers. Chief Makoni', District Commissioner's office, Rusape (DCOR). Rugoyi was Chief Instructor at the Makoholi Training Centre, having worked as a Demonstrator for many years and claimed to have centralized Zimutu and Mangwende Reserves.
53 J. Makoni, Mrewa to Assistant Native Commissioner, Rusape, n.d., 1951, ibid.

54 Maynard Makoni to District Commissioner, Rusape, 21 October 1971, file 'Makoni', DCOR.
55 T. Gwatidzo to District Commissioner, Rusape, 10 August 1975, file 'Gandanzara. Headman', DCOR.
56 'A letter from the President', MSA News-sheet, No. 1, March 1957, Chater papers file A.
57 Reports to members of the Makoni Students Association, December 1955, Chater papers, file A.
58 Loria S.K. Simbabure, Report on the Chingono Conference, September 1957, Chater papers, file A.
59 Maynard Makoni, 'Shall We Not Participate Also', Makoni Students Association News Sheet No. 3, November 1957, Chater papers, file A.
60 ibid; Agenda. Meeting of the Executive Committee, 9 January 1958, Chater papers, file A.
61 Minute book of St Faith's Discussion Group, 12 April to 29 November 1956, minutes of the meeting of 7 March 1956 by Sarah Chavunduka, Chater papers, file B.
62 Meetings of 4 June, 16 June, 16 July 1955, by F.M. Govera, ibid.
63 Meeting of 18 June 1958, Minute book, 17 March to 28 October 1958, Chater papers, file B.
64 Meeting of 1 August 1958, ibid.
65 Interview with John Mutasa, Makoni, 11 September 1982.
66 Weinrich, *Black and White Elites*, pp. 172–3.
67 Evidence of W.H. Stead to Natural Resources Board Native Enquiry, 16 July 1942, file S.988, NAH.
68 Evidence of Provincial Native Commissioner, Umtali, 22 July 1942, ibid.
69 Assistant Secretary, Purchase Land Authority to Mr Carlisle, 5 April 1977, file 'St Faith's', DCOR.
70 District Commissioner, Makoni to Secretary, Internal Affairs, 5 May 1977, ibid.
71 Chief Native Commissioner's quarterly report, September 1951, file S.1618, NAH.
72 Basil Nyabadza to H.E. Davies, 17 October 1960, Chater papers, file 'St Francis correspondence'. This file is still retained in Patricia Chater's possession. Basil Nyabadza aspired to buy further land to expand his farming and business activity but the only land adjacent to him was land in the 'European' area. His written submission to the Pearce Commission in 1972 reiterated his opposition. 'We do not believe that the Rhodesia Front Government and Party intend to be bound by the promises made in the Settlement Proposals about racial discrimination, land tenure, job opportunity or the release of detainees', since 'they have been moving steadily along the path towards apartheid.' Sanctions should be tightened. 'These proposals fall very far short of African aspirations.' Basil Nyabadza to Secretary, Pearce Commission, 9 February 1972.
73 Evidence of F.A. Marr to the Native Trade and Production

Commission, 13 July 1944, file ZBJ 1/1/2, NAH. Marr wanted to reinvent African communalism. African peasants were 'a lot of little people . . . doing work as individuals' rather than engaging in 'organised production on a communal basis.' He wanted Land Development Officers with directive powers to create peasant farming on combined holdings.

74   Marginal comment on Maynard Makoni to District Commissioner, 21 October 1971, file 'Makoni', DCOR.
75   Provincial Commissioner to District Commissioner, 20 April 1970, file 'Chipunza. Chiduku', DCOR.
76   Native Commissioner, Makoni to Secretary for Native Affairs, 6 May 1957, file 'St Faith's', DCOR.
77   Kate Truscott and N.C. Pambieri, 'Census survey of Chiweshe ward, (Buhera). Preliminary report', (Harare, Agritex: 1983), p. 11.
78   N.E. Thomas, 'Christianity, politics and the Manyika', (Boston University: PhD thesis, 1968), p. 81.
79   ibid, p. 99.
80   ibid, pp. 105–6.
81   ibid, pp. 161, 232, 275.
82   J.C. Kandiero, 'Analysis. Kraal Information for Development Purposes, 28th August 1976 – 21st Ocotber 1976', file 'Weya/Chendambuya', DCOR.
83   File 'Gandanzara', DCOR.
84   File 'Chemere Maparura', DCOR.
85   Kate Truscott and N.C. Pambieri, 'Wedza baseline study. Summary and analysis. Wedza evaluation No. 1', (Harare, Agritex: January 1983), p. 11. It is interesting to compare their findings on Wedza with the indications for Makoni. As in Makoni they find a general distinction between regions, though in this case north Wedza has the advantage over south: 'Farmers in the north tend to be better off in every way, having more land, higher yields, more sales, more livestock and more family members in paid employment . . . They get more extension advice . . . and obtain all the loans that are available in Wedza.' In general they find: 'The wide range among farmers of the volume of maize analysed by yield, sales and retention per household, indicates the existence of at least two socio-economic strata in Wedza: the slightly "better-off" and the rest. Again, the concept of different strata is relative. In terms of income from farming, this difference is in the order of an average annual income (from maize alone) of 320 dollars for the "better-off" and 36 dollars for the sample as a whole . . . In terms of maize retention per household members (mostly for food) the "better-off" retain 2.4 bags while the whole sample retain only 1.2.' The 'better-off' also have access to other sources of income derived from a high proportion of grown-up children employed in the towns. The 'better-off' also own more farm implements and draught animals and hence farm more intensively and obtain better yields. But they find that 'the vast majority of children in Wedza now attend school', a result of the

Zimbabwe government's great expansion of educational facilties and abolition of primary school fees. With this exception their findings probably give a good indication of rural differentiation in an area like Chiduku in the 1970s.

For Wedza see also Gert Van Vulpen, 'The political economy of the African peasant agriculture in Marondera District, 1930–1950', (University of Amsterdam: doctoral thesis, 1983); Diana Callear, *The Social and Cultural Factors Involved in Production by Small Farmers in Wezda Communal Area, Zimbabwe, of Maize and its Marketing*, (Paris: Unesco, December 1982); idem 'Who wants to be a peasant? Food production in a labour-exporting area of Zimbabwe', unpublished paper, May 1983. Callear finds 'three categories' of Wedza 'families [who] fail to make an adequate income' – young families with little land, few or no cattle and few or no implements'; 'widows with children or grandchildren'; 'the families of labour migrants who were providing very little'.

86 'The African National Council Manifesto Under the Banner of Unity', 1972; Michael Mawema to Canon John Collins, 2 August 1972, Clutton-Brock correspondence, 1970–80, file 'ANC'.
87 Guy Clutton-Brock to Cyril Dunn, 6 March 1972, ibid.
88 A.K.H. Weinrich, 'Rhodesia's African National Council', 28 June 1974, Catholic Commission for Justice and Peace (CCJP) Archives, Harare, p. 8.
89 African Farmers' Union of Rhodesia, Evidence to the Pearce Commission and Supplement to the Evidence, 27 January and 11 February 1972, Clutton-Brock correspondence, file 'ANC'.
90 'Research Projects Sub-Committee Enquiry into African National Council', CCJP Archives, Harare, p. 3.
91 A.K.H. Weinrich, 'Rhodesia's African National Council', pp. 9–11.
92 'Three appear in court for possessing firearms', *Moto*, 29 January 1972. The report runs: 'Three tribesmen here [Mtoko] are to appear in court on Thursday for illegal possession of firearms, hunting in a prohibited area and cutting down trees without permission . . . The deputy organizing secretary of the ANC, Mr Arthur Chadzingwa . . . was found by the Mtoko police spending a night with the tribesmen . . . The tribesmen have engaged a Salisbury firm of Attorneys to represent them.'
93 Interview with Amon Shonge, Weya, 25 March 1981.
94 Interview with P.M. Chakanyuka, Harare, 29 March 1981.
95 Interview between P.M. Chakanyuka and Mhondiwa Remus Rungodo, Nedewedzo, 30 January 1981.
96 Interview with John Mutasa, Makoni 11 September 1982.
97 Interview with Columbus Makoni, Harare, 29 January 1981.
98 Interview with George Bhongoghozo, Rusape, 16 February 1981.
99 Interview with Amos Waretsa, Toriro, Chiduku, 24 March 1981.
100 Interview with Langton Charidza, Rusape, 25 February 1981.
101 Interview between P.M. Chakanyuka and Mavengeni Annah, Nedewedzo, 8 February 1981.

102   W.R. Duggan, 'The Native Land Husbandry Act of 1951 and the rural African middle class of Southern Rhodesia', *African Affairs*, vol. 79, no. 315 (April 1980) pp. 238–9.

103   D.B. Scholz, 'Report on the Conducted Tour of the Chiweshe Tribal Trust Land', 10 September 1974, pp. 7–8, file 'Catholic Commission for Justice and Peace', Centre for Southern African Studies Archives, University of York (CSASA).

104   *Rhodesia Herald*, 16 August 1974.

105   'Report on Chiweshe TTL', 26 August 1974, file 'Catholic Commission for Justice and Peace', CSASA.

106   Scholz, 'Report on the Conducted Tour', p. 4. Superintendent Reeves explained that 'within weeks of their first attacks on European farms (in the north-east) the guerrillas had established themselves in the Chiweshe Tribal Trust Land. This area was a crucial importance for their operations. Surrounded by the Umvukwes, Centenary, Mtepatepa and Mazoe European farming areas, it provided nearby operational targets while at the same time serving as a safe retreat. Rocky outcrops, often densely covered with bush, are spread through Chiweshe, making it an ideal territory for guerrilla hide-outs; moreover, the local people willingly offered what support and protection they could.'

107   Duggan suggested that the Protected Villages left 'the reserves vulnerable to a Kenyan solution' should political control pass from the Rhodesia Front to a regime representative of the interests of the African petty-bourgeoisie. (Duggan, 'The Native Land Husbandry Act', p. 239). Muzorewa's government, however, in one of its few widely popular acts, opened up the Protected Villages and allowed everyone back to their old areas.

108   Edgar Tekere to Didymus Mutasa, 22 July 1975, enclosed in Didymus Mutasa to Guy Clutton-Brock, 6 August 1975, Clutton-Brock correspondence, 1970–80 file, 'Correspondents in Mozambique'.

109   Interview between John Conradie and Kumbirai Kangai, Maputo, 21 August 1979. 'These people in Kitwe, Ndola, Lusaka, Livingstone, we'll never forget them,' said Kangai. 'If those people had grown weak I don't think the revolution would have reached where it is today.'

110   Bishop Abel Muzorewa to Patricia Chater, 21 August 1973, Chater correspondence, file 'St Francis' Correspondence.

111   Interview with Maurice Nyagumbo, Harare, 11 April 1981.

112   Patricia Chater to Shelagh Ranger, 1 August 1976, correspondence in author's possession.

113   Patricia Chater, *Caught in the Crossfire*, forthcoming, pp. 83 et seq.

114   Interview between Emilia Chiteka and Isidore Nyamusamba, Triashill, 21 February 1981.

115   The proceedings of the inquest on Basil Nyabadza's death, held in Rusape, 18–20 July 1977, are in Patricia Chater's possession.

116   This and other leaflets dropped over Makoni are in Patricia Chater's possession.

117 Interview with Isaac Tsungo, Mbobo, 14 February 1981.
118 Chater, *Caught in the Crossfire*, pp. 116–7.
119 Interview with Stephen Matewa, Toriro, 23 March 1981. For Matewa's role as a mediator between guerrillas and the peasantry of his
   area, see Terence Ranger, 'Holy men and rural communities in
   Zimbabwe, 1970–1980', in W.J. Sheils (ed.), *The Church and War*,
   (Oxford, Studies in Church History, vol. 20: 1983)
120 Stephen Matewa to Dean of Salisbury, 2 November 1979, Matewa
   correspondence, Toriro, Chiduku.
121 Moven Mahachi to Guy and Molly Clutton-Brock, n.d. 1978,
   Clutton-Brock correspondence, file 'Letters from Prison.'.
122 Voice of Zimbabwe, 13 November 1978, cited in Julie Frederikse,
   None But Ourselves Masses vs. Media in the Making of Zimbabwe
   (Johannesburg: 1982), p. 278.
123 Bob North, Rhodesian Intelligence Corps, quoted in ibid., p. 257.
124 In May 1979 a Community Development and Local Government
   Officer, recently based in Fort Victoria, gave a seminar at the
   University of Manchester. He described how in early 1976 Victoria
   Province was 'more or less at peace'; then 'all of a sudden over Easter
   1976 war came to Victoria Province'. No-one had known until then
   that there were any guerrillas there but inquiries established that they
   had been building up a presence for six months. By the end of 1978
   guerrillas commanded every TTL in an area the size of England. The
   army sought to sweep the area; Protected Villages were set up; but by
   mid 1978 it was realised that 'the Army had lost the province to the
   guerrillas.' So it was decided to launch 'counter-terror'. All officers
   were called to a security briefing by the Head of the Special Branch
   who told them of the intention to set up bands of 'on-side' guerrillas
   and volunteers to get into the TTLs and to contest their possession
   with the guerrillas. This strategy had success in hampering the
   guerrillas but only at the expense of much intensified suffering for the
   people: 'The tribesmen find the Internal Settlement intolerable.'
125 African Farmers Union Report, 13 February 1979, CCJP Archives,
   Harare.
126 Mr Pasipanodya, Buhera, 'A Middle Class Man in a War Zone',
   February 1979, CCJP Archive, Harare.

CONCLUSION:

Peasant consciousness in an independent Zimbabwe

I have sought to build up in my previous chapters a picture of the Zimbabwean peasant experience and of the levels of consciousness to which it gave rise. I have argued that a consistent peasant political ideology and programme developed from the 1940s; that this was not captured or diverted by 'petty-bourgeois' leadership during the period of open mass nationalism; that it was not turned despairingly inward as a result of the failure of the nationalist parties in 1964; and that it contributed powerfully to the ideology and programme of the rural guerrilla war. I have also argued that during the war itself peasant aspirations were focused upon the recovery of the land lost to the whites and upon the exclusion from the communal areas of administrative coercion.

It is true, of course, that peasant resentments were not only directed against the whites. As we have seen, many peasants had been evicted from their land in order that Native Purchase Areas could be created and they had not forgotten. Such resentment had some effect during the war and has had some effect since. In Makoni District, for example, Headman Maparura was killed in November 1976 'by the terrorists while visiting his farm in the Tanda Purchase Land. . . .'[1] This was one Dambaza, appointed as Headman in late 1975 after the death of Chemere Maparura, who had been a ZAPU supporter. Dambaza was appointed precisely in order to hold Tanda for the government. 'Tanda Tribal Trust Land has always been known as an area of disaffection,' wrote the District Commissioner, 'and it is therefore important that an effective Headman be appointed. . . .'[2] Dambaza, who had already held out against local radical nationalism sufficiently to acquire a farm in the hated Purchase Area, seemed an appropriate choice. But, as the same District Commissioner told me in January 1981, the kraals which had been evicted to make way for the Tanda purchase farms had preserved their bitter resentment. Dambaza's death and 'a great deal besides can be traced to their resentment. Everyone in Tanda has blood on his hands.'[3] I found in 1981 that purchase farmers were worried by claims for the restoration of Chief Makoni's original territory which could only be achieved by handing back the purchase areas to communal cultivators.[4] And since the end of the war there have been instances of 'squatter' invasions of purchase areas, and even of 'citizens' arrests' of purchase farmers.[5]

Similarly, a part of the predicament of rural businessmen during the war arose from the readiness of peasants who resented or disliked them to denounce them to the guerrillas or to the Security Forces. After the war peasants took the opportunities offered by government inquiries to articulate their grievances against local store-owners. In Makoni there was a meeting of peasants with some of the Commissioners inquiring into incomes and prices; a large gathering discussed prices at a business centre in Makoni communal area on 21 October 1980. Peasant women in particular complained of the high prices charged by the store-owner while he tried as best he could to defend himself. The Commission's report reflected these lively debates in sober but telling prose:

Two other major problems presented to the Commission by the peasants were the lack of marketing facilities and high transport costs. The further a peasant community is from a major town or city, the more difficult it is for the people to sell their crops at the prices fixed by Government, and the more the middlemen exploit the small producers . . . Since official marketing depots are out of the reach of most peasants, those who have a surplus over consumption needs sell their produce to local shop owners who frequently write off peasant crops against credit already advanced . . . These informal channels have the advantage over formal ones in that they realize money at once. Where peasants are paid by cross cheques from the GMB they have the additional difficulty of cashing such cheques . . . As a result many farmers take their cheques to local storekeepers who sometimes demand that a proportion of the value of the cheques be used to purchase goods from their store . . . Other instances of shopkeepers taking advantage of peasant farmers were brought to the attention of the Commission. In Makoni, for example, it was reported that storekeepers buy maize for 3 dollars a bucket from peasants in the marketing season and sell it for 8 dollars when shortages occur. . .

A direct consequence of high transport costs is the high cost of consumer goods for the poorest section of the population . . . In Svosve one bag of fertilizer costs 9.95 dollars; in Makoni it sells at between 13 and 14 dollars; and in Honde Valley at 14.50 dollars . . . Furthermore, in Makoni two kilograms of sugar costs 85 cents; in Svosve 75 cents; and in the towns 56 cents. And a bar of blue soap which in town costs 47 cents sells in Makoni for 78 cents . . . Businessmen claim that high prices in rural areas are inevitable . . . Still 10 per cent (spent on transport) is not 50 per cent or 100 per cent, and these are the prices sometimes charged in village shops.[6]

An Agritex research team which worked in the Chiweshe ward of Buhera district, which borders on Makoni, found in 1983 that 'marketing was seen as the overwhelming problem . . . Cheques must be changed with local businessmen who charge us commission. For example, a storekeeper makes us buy 20 dollars of groceries to change 100 dollars cheque.' The researchers remark that although 'every household is tied to the land in some way', 'judging by the open hostility to 2 of the wealthiest elements in the area – the lorry owners and store-keepers – it would appear that a certain level of socio-economic stratification exists.'[7]

Another expression of peasant hostility during the war has continued into the peace. This was hostility towards migrant workers from Malawi, Zambia or Mozambique who were working on white farms. In Makoni District, as in many other places, there were many guerrilla attacks on farm labour compounds, designed, of course, to cripple white farming. These attacks were often guided by local families who lived on white farmland. As a result such indigenous families were evicted off the commercial farms and into the Tribal Trust Lands, thereby intensifying resentments. Mrs John Mugura, for example, testifies that:

My husband had a job on Tapson's farm . . . My husband looked after cattle. This rancher gave us a place to live on and he also gave us acres of land to grow our crops . . . This place was a fertile area and we only needed to put cattle manure in order to harvest a good crop . . . We sold our surplus maize and beans to the European farmer who in turn gave these to his labourers . . . This was indeed a comfortable life . . . The disturbances came in the 1970s with the dawn of the war. It so happened that the guerrillas came and we gave them food . . . We were sold out to the soldiers and the next thing we got was an ultimatum from the soldiers demanding that we should leave this place . . . Having moved in November 1978 we got a place to build anew, and this is Chitsanza village, Makoni Tribal Trust Land . . . Life here proved very difficult from the start because we had a very small area for a field . . . no place whatsoever to graze . . . We could no more grow crops . . . We sank back to real backwards subsistence farmers who grew what was not even enough for our sustenance.[8]

Since the end of the war peasant desire to return to the lost lands has sometimes resulted in further friction with the Malawian, Zambian and Mozambican farm workers. Some of these workers have become members, for example, of rural co-operatives founded by excombatants and supported by the Zimbabwe government with gifts of land acquired from the commercial sector for resettlement.

The old labour migrants are already on the land and their experience of the agricultural history of these farms in the past has proved very valuable to the younger ex-combatant co-operators. But to neighbouring peasant communities who desired that land for their own expansion, the continued presence of the farm workers on land from which they are still excluded has constituted a profound grievance.[9]

Nevertheless, these tensions have been a minor theme by comparison with peasant participation in the attack on white farm and ranchland during the war, and peasant demand that government allocate that land to them now that the war has ended. The Purchase Areas, after all, represented only a small proportion of the land lost through eviction and were usually ill-placed in relation to communications and markets. As for local businessmen, whatever the resentments against them they were perceived as necessary and when their stores began to reopen after the 1980 election there was often considerable local jubilation. Peasantization was, after all, still the ideal; peasantization on the most favourable terms, of course, with high prices, fair trading, good land, no interference and input from wage labour, but still a peasantization that crucially required buying agencies. But there was no mitigation of the clamour for the return of the lost lands. In 1981 the Commission on Incomes and Prices reported that:

The greatest problem facing the peasantry is land. In practically every peasant area which the Commissioners visited, the first issue raised by the people was land shortage . . . The question of land shortage, together with the related problems of the relationships between peasants and commercial farmers with properties contiguous to peasant areas, were as a rule characterized in evidence sessions with the Commissioners by a very pronounced degree of discontent, frustration and often anger.[10]

This intense focus on the recovery of the lost lands was given every encouragement not only by guerrilla political education but also by the campaigning speeches of ZANU/PF candidates in the 1980 elections. ZANU/PF's printed manifesto in February 1980 might promise 'swift collectivisation of peasant agriculture and establishment of state farms', but at the ground level the candidates spoke to the existing peasant consciousness. 'We went to London and for three months we argued very hard,' Davis Mugabe told his election audience in Gutu:

What were we arguing about? There are five things on which we failed to agree with the Bishop. The first thing is the land. We said if we take the land we want the people to work on the productive areas too. (Roars of approval). Perhaps on Bob Richards' farm. (Another roar of approval). We also want the same productive areas for everybody. (Applause and ululations). And the Bishop said 'No, it's not allowed to take Bob Richards' farm without having to pay compensation. You have to buy it from him.' We said 'What about Bob Richards himself? Who did he buy it from? Where did he get that land from? Did he bring it with him in a plane?' The Bishop said 'No! Not with regards to white-owned farms.' There are unoccupied white-owned farms with many cattle, kudus, buffaloes, and sables. These are the farms we of ZANU say we want to take and resettle people in. (Applause and ululations). But others say these farms must be bought. We have to pay compensation for them. That's one issue we disagree with Muzorewa.[11]

Davis Mugabe also gave encouragement to the other fundamental element in peasant consciousness – the desire to be in charge of their own affairs, no longer to be bossed about. (I was told in April 1982 in Oxford by someone who had spent a year in a TTL in Shabani district that the peasants there had told him what independence meant to them: 'Now no-one will be able to come and tell us how to farm.') 'People's Power! What does it mean?', asked Davis Mugabe in Gutu:

It means that here at Munyikwa we are responsible for decisions on how to run our dipping centres. We, the people, make the decisions. You and me, we are the decision makers. No district commissioner will tell us what fees to pay for dipping cattle, failure of which may result with a jail sentence being passed on you. We discuss among ourselves and agree . . . We want irrigation schemes to make growing of maize possible even in winter. (Roars of approval). So many things have to be done in this country. Such things cannot run on decisions of a man in Salisbury. No! It has to be you who make the decisions. That's what People's Power is all about.[12]

Return of the lost lands and this kind of people's power: these were the promises which carried the Shona-speaking peasant areas overwhelmingly for ZANU/PF in 1980.

In my view this type of peasant consciousness was significant not merely as something to be appealed to by populist politicians. It existed as a real factor in the post-independence situation and even in some questions as a determining factor. Largely because of it neither a Kenyan nor a Mozambican outcome was possible for the peasant areas of Zimbabwe. No matter how committed a politician might be to entrepreneurial capitalism, he could not possibly envisage clearing people off land in the communal areas in order to parcel it out to yeoman farmers. Nor is it possible, even if it were desired, to use the land resettlement schemes in order to produce a class of prosperous land-holding yeomanry; the pressure upon land resettlement of the landless and the poorest is much too great for that. And finally, despite ZANU/PF's formal commitment to the idea of collectivization, it has been manifestly impossible to move towards this goal directly. The Commission on Incomes and Prices concluded in 1981 that:

there was little indication . . . that in-depth discussion of major structural change in the rural economy was taking place . . . Peasants drew the Commission's attention to grievances dating back in history to the 1920s when some of the people were moved to make way for settler farms . . . Most seemed to cling to past notions and to think merely of increasing the size of their small peasant holdings and communal grazing areas. When directly asked their opinion of cooperative and communal farming, the majority of peasants expressed ignorance as to what these organisational forms involved and recommended that new ventures be left to the youth to experiment with, showing great suspicion of such change.[13]

Vincent Tickner, whom I quoted in Chapter 1, declared that Zimbabwean peasants had not attained to a class consciousness, one indication of which was their lack of commitment to 'collective agricultural production systems'. A recent article in *Moto*, while emphasizing that the peasantry 'bore the brunt of the war', goes on to stress that 'the success of the transition must depend on the development of a skilled, educated and knowledgeable working class conscious of its leading role.' Still, 'the peasants must not be forgotten. They remain the under-dogs in every struggle. Although their poverty, lack of education and overall underdevelopment and their limited knowledge of political affairs limit their capacity to lead, they must be regarded, and assisted, as a class on its way to becoming part of the proletariat.'[14] But to my mind the Zimbabwean peasantry cannot be regarded as merely a class in transition to being proletarian. The Zimbabwean peasantry, diversified as it is, must nevertheless be regarded as a class in itself. And the consciousness of a peasant class is hardly ever committed to 'collective agricultural production systems.' In Zimbabwe, after a war fought among the peasantry and an election won on the basis of promises to fulfil the peasant political programme, the new government had to be seen to be trying to do just that.

Hence the Mugabe government made it clear that it did not intend to coerce peasants into collective, or even into cooperative, patterns of settlement and production. Visiting Shanghai in May 1981, Mugabe announced that:

Zimbabwe plans to send some peasants to China to gain experience of collective farming at a commune . . . This was intended to be a prelude to the introduction in Zimbabwe of collective farming in the peasant sector which was prejudiced against the idea . . . Mr Mugabe said that in implementing its policy of collective farming the Government was working against a background of opposition, caused by the propaganda of the former colonial government which regarded communism as anathema. 'We have first to get rid of that opposition by persuasion and education.' Mr Mugabe said the sending of some peasants to China was also intended to help them evaluate the advantages of collective farming and to provide a nucleus of collective farmers for Zimbabwe should they recommend the system.[15]

It is as well to make myself quite clear here. I am *not* saying that the Zimbabwean peasantry emerged from the war in a state of total and unreconstructed individualism. In fact I think that a 1981 Oxfam village development assessment gets the situation right:

Rural people still have a remarkable sense of the revolutionary possibilities of participating in the shaping of their own development. They are working towards a kind of development and training projects that emancipate a whole community and not just a few educated and economically successful individuals . . . They are resistant to any procedures that make them feel as if they could be pushed back into pre-liberation conditions. They no longer want to be passive, isolated and non-participating recipients of prescribed development training and projects.[16]

This enlivened peasantry, which was yet a peasantry rather than a body in transition towards a revolutionary proletariat, possessed a number of advantages unusual to African peasantries in the period after the 1980 election. The new government itself recognized and proclaimed its debt to the peasantry and asserted that its main development priority was the improvement of the rural economy. Articulate and literate men living among the peasantry did not hesitate to remind government of this debt and this priority. In April 1980 Stephen Matewa, headmaster at Toriro school in Chiduku, summed up the effect of the war upon the Makoni peasantry in a letter to Didymus Mutasa, now Speaker of the new Zimbabwean parliament. 'The war has left them poorer materially but richer mentally. They now would like material things to celebrate this gain of self.'[17] Matewa felt:

a strong conviction of the people in the TTL being forgotten . . . They say when war was hot the people in towns left the boys with the tribesmen. When help from the Red Cross came it was mostly in town. The TTL was just described as sensitive. When Christian Care came to help again it helped mostly those in towns . . . Now you come. Don't do the same. Come and help those who were with the fighting boys, the people who helped more, the people who suffered more. They supported you, No, they supported the cause.[18]

Matewa urged the establishment of a Chiduku 'Heroes Acre' so that the rural areas could participate in their own commemoration of their own sufferings; he protested when peasants were prosecuted for going on to white farms to cut grass for thatching; and in October 1980 he called on the Ministry of Lands and Resettlement to honour its obligations:

Chiduku TTL . . . is one of the barest pieces of land – no trees, no grass. Oxen are dying because there is no grass and because they have never been anywhere near a dipping place. Some people lost their cattle during the war. They were killed by soldiers and farmers as a penalty for their stolen cattle. This sounds gloomy. We are positive here. We suggest a number of things to do with your help . . . A farm or farms to be bought so that cattle are taken on to them in order to allow grass to grow . . .We want to be doing something. We cannot wait when we are free. We are free to ACT, to DO, not to receive.[19]

Moreover, the peasantry were unusually capable of speaking and acting for themselves. In the twelve months after the 1980 elections there existed in the rural areas of Zimbabwe a self-conscious and even organized peasantry which confronted an enfeebled, transitional and rudimentary state apparatus. During 1980 throughout the Shona-speaking rural areas there developed a network of village ZANU/PF committees, topped by district committees. These village committees were during this period the effective centres of administration in the communal areas; they heard cases, allocated land, and so on. One might suppose that the development of these party branches brought the peasantry under central party discipline; but this was not the case and for two reasons. The first was that in the year after independence there was hardly any effective link between the central party mechanisms and those at district and village level. The second was that the peasantry used the election of village party committees in order to bring about a conservative revolution. David Lan argues that in the Dande the emergence of the village committees was by far the most profound transformation to be produced by the war; he sees rural power moving from the chiefs through the mediums through the guerrillas to the committees. But at the same time that the committees established peasant power at the village level as it had never been exercised before, they also represented a return to the pre-war situation. Those elected to the village committees were the resident junior elders, the sort of men and women who had been dominant in peasant nationalism before the war but whose influence had had to take second place to that of the guerrillas and their adolescent helpers during the war itself. I found in Makoni in early 1981 that there was a good deal of remembered resentment among elders and parents directed against the power exercised by the *mujibas* during the war. Peter Chakanyuka tells us of Takapera Moda Chakanyuka that 'He is of the opinion that the mujibas did more harm to civilians than the guerrillas. Some were demanding donations in the form of money and fowls for their personal use.' [20] Madironda Beatrice, he tells us:

witnessed punishments administered to the mujibas and chimbwidos who were staying away from home with their boy friends, committing sexual intercourse, coming to parents asking for fowls saying they were sent by guerrillas, yet not. When the guerrillas learnt about this all the youths involved and the parents of the villages supporting the guerrillas were gathered together one night. The case was made known to the parents. The guerrillas told parents plainly that they treat people who misbehave in a war situation by beating. It was a sad moment for most parents but they felt pleased about this correction. Beatrice's daughter was among the chimbwidos who were punished this day by beating.[21]

Mavengeni Annah, he tell us, 'believes that most of the people who are said to have been killed by the guerrillas are the direct victims of the mujibas. These sometimes robbed civilians, abused the populace at beer parties, and in most cases misrepresented the comrades' aims and commitments.'[22] The election of the village committees was an opportunity to put youth in its place. In 1980 there were few guerrillas living and working in the rural areas, though plenty visited them. There were even fewer elected to the village ZANU/ PF committees, and in Makoni District at any rate there were no *mujibas* either. 'Politics,' I was told by the district committee, 'is a business for grown-ups'.[23]

In 1980 this network of committees confronted a 'lame-duck' administration. One can document this out of the one file to have survived an otherwise total clear out of the administrative archives in Rusape. It begins with the minutes of a conference of the District Commissioners of Manicaland on 27 and 28 March 1980 which noted that 'with the abandonment of para-military activities, it is advisable for certain staff members, both black and white, who have been engaged mainly in anti-terrorist duties, to start working in a purely administrative role in a different District where their presence will not be associated with combatant service.' The personal files of such people were to be immediately destroyed. But as the

District Commissioner, Chipinga, pointed out, 'due to his para-military wartime role he is frequently regarded with some suspicion by the people. It is important that local M.P.s or party officials should hold meetings and explain clearly that the District administration is now concerned with implementing the policies of the new Government.'[24]

Such clear explanations were either never given or else not credited by the people. In October 1980 the District Commissioner, Makoni, who had administered the district for a longer continuous period than anyone for fifty years, complained to the Provincial Commissioner that:

there appears to be a campaign organised by the governing Party at this time, to denigrate as well as abuse members of the staff of this Ministry. Enclosed are two reports concerning meetings which were addressed by members of ZANU (P.F.), which are an example of the type of message which is being put across through-out all of the Tribal Trust Lands in this district.

The position of members of the staff of this office is not being assisted by the actions of our own Minister, and whilst not wishing to appear disloyal, I must state that in spite of assurances having been received from Head Office, that the Minister would arrange through Party officials to summon people for a meeting – this did not take place. As a result no-one turned up for the meetings that had been laid on for him to address, and, in fact, it was made quite clear to district assistants that they would not attend any meetings unless they had been called by the Party.[25]

In fact the enclosed reports described meetings held in Tanda and Chikore by members of the Rusape ZANU/PF district committee; meetings which represented more the expression of local peasant consciousness than that of ZANU/PF as a national body. At the Chikore meeting it was declared that:

people should not co-operate with District Assistants, as they were not the Government's representatives, and would only be operating in the Tribal Trust Lands until October. The people should not co-operate with the Z.R. Police. The people should have nothing to do with DEVAG staff, as they were forcing old people to make contour ridges . . . The Extension Assistants were threatening the old people with 50 dollars fine or 6 months imprisonment, if they did not build contours. When one of our District Assistants stated that he must represent the Government as he represented the Hon. Minister Zvogbo, Mr Mugomba said that it was impossible for District Assistants to represent Mr Zvogbo, as Mr Zvogbo was a member of ZANU PF, and District Assistants were not . . . During the meeting, Messrs. Mugomba and Mukaronda shouted slogans such as 'Down with District Assistants', 'Down with Police' and 'Down with Oppressors'. The result of the meeting is that it has alienated the whole of the CHIKORE TRIBAL TRUST LAND against the various Government Agencies operating there.[26]

In Tanda similar points were made and some additional ones were added. 'People,' the report noted 'should not collect the fertilizer, seeds and implements being distributed to refugees at Tanda Administrative Base . . . All the people should get this free, not only the refugees . . . He advised people not to attend the clinic held at Tanda by a member of the District Commissioner's staff.'[27]

The District Commissioner asserted that this meeting had destroyed 'the rapport and spirit of joint co-operation which members of our staff had built up in the Tanda area', but readers of this book will not readily believe that much external influence was required to make peasants in Tanda ready to repudiate or exclude personnel whom they associated with the hated colonial administration.[28] It was the same in Makoni TTL where peasants assaulted and drove out police – 'If they are *our* police now, as they claim,' I was told, 'let them not come in that hated uniform.' Throughout the peasant areas the old administrative structures had almost ceased to function. While I was carrying out research in Makoni in the first months of 1981 I saw a number of patrol reports by African administrative assistants recording their cautious movements in the TTLs. They moved about visiting business centres, headmasters of schools and 'tribal authorities' where these still functioned; they began to sound out mediums and chiefly lineages so that the many chiefs and headmen who were killed in the war might be replaced; they reported gratefully any kindness shown to them. But as they sought to revive the old system their reports gave all too many indications of the new realities. ZANU/PF village committees were distributing food, fertilizer and seed and carrying out a wide range of other administrative functions. 'Going to area thirteen with District Assistant Nyenya,' reported Sergeant Ncube on 5 February 1981:

we first visited ZANU/PF office of Gwidza branch and found Mr Giria who was a vice-chairman recently selected to a chairman's post after J. Tendere was appointed to the district council. Talking with Mr Giria we were told that there are two people in Mutsai kraal who are being sent in the T.T.L. stealing cattle for butchery. Locals in the area do not know that such cases are to be reported to the police. They just inform the branch.[29]

Families were welcoming sons and daughters whom they had not seen since they went over the border into Mozambique during the war. 'I went to a kraal, Chaka's', reported District Assistant Manyela on 14 February 1981, 'and I saw him and talked to him about living in the area and he said he is happy because his son is back from Mozambique so they were dancing and singing at his kraal. That is the very good thing in the life.'[30] Returning guerrillas did not always think African administrative staff a very good thing however. District Assistant Mushanduli reported on 9 February that:

I was with L/Cpl. Murowe and D.A. Chiboora and my mission was to see kraal head Nyandoro [in Chikore]. So on my way to the kraalhead's house I met two former Comrades nearby Samuti's house and they stopped me and one of the two men asked me where are you going? what are you looking for? . . . They have been giving me too many questions . . . and they have been provoking . . . At last one of these men told me to move and I proceeded to the kraalhead's house . . . and I proceed back to the branch chairman and told him the whole story and he told me that this Comrade was from Chitungwiza Salisbury.[31]

Sometimes, indeed, District Assistants were 'provoked' with more than words:

D/A Ngorima reported that he was beaten by . . . four boys. The four boys first wanted to beat D/A Ngorima's young brother as they wanted to know who he was and what he was after in this area. When D/A Ngorima wanted to know what was going on to his brother, he was insulted for being a D/A and he was told that they are not even hesitating to beat him. After he was beaten he ran into Mr Bukuta's shop and still was followed as he was trying to cover himself.[32]

Ngorima reported the assault to the police in Rusape but ruefully recorded two days later that 'the police was delaying to respond to the incident.'[33] Indeed the police were delaying to respond to very many incidents in the TTLs which would once have produced immediate repression. On the day that he was beaten Ngorima recorded that 'all the locals in Chipunza kraal were away. They had gone to Chief Makoni for there are some witches etc in the kraal. They had a Svikiro called to prove so they had proved and had to be justified by the Chief.'[34]

Meanwhile, of course, the Mugabe government was planning and beginning to introduce structures which were intended to replace this discredited administration. In doing so, however, they certainly could not take peasant acquiescence for granted. Peasants were certainly not prepared to accept state directives unquestioningly if these seemed to conflict with the long-held tenets of radical rural nationalism. A central plank of government policy was that elected councils should assume administrative responsibility for the communal areas. This was determined very early on. At the District Commissioner's meeting in Umtali in March 1980 the District Commissioner 'raised the question of the tribal structure and the role of the chiefs. The Minister explained that it is important to retain the social fabric . . . The people will participate in the election of Local Government bodies.'[35] By May 1980 no steps had been taken to replace dead chiefs and headmen but the District Commissioners of Manicaland were told that 'our immediate task is to establish district councils and to try to fit the political elements into recognised statutory bodies. It will be essential to work through the party. Government is being directive in the matter of formation of councils, there is no question of whether or not the people want councils – the Prime Minister has said there WILL be councils.'[36]

But in Manicaland, as elsewhere, 'the people' were in fact very suspicious of the idea of councils. They had, after all, opposed them for years on nationalist grounds, denouncing them as mere covers for administrative authoritarianism or mere devices to throw the cost of rural development on to the peasantry. During the war council buildings had been attacked by guerrillas and often destroyed. In 1980 and 1981 peasants still suspected that the new councils would once again be a device to make them pay for the services provided to them. Moreover, they were happy with the elected village party committees and saw no need to 'fit the political elements into recognised statutory bodies.' The patrol reports for early 1981 make clear both what reservations peasants in Makoni had about councils and also the extent of the promises made to them that the councils would be *their* agents, not the agents of the state. A report of a meeting in Chikore on 7 February 1981, recalls that:

The meeting was held by the Local Government Promotion Officer and Mr Matimba, the Secretary of the Makoni District. They were telling the people how the council works like. The L.G.P. officer was good in talking to the people at the meeting but Mr Matimba was not very good, he saying things are now changing. All the Zimbabwe Republic Police and the District Assistants we shall take off from their jobs and we are going to put in the comrades, and no-one is going to be arrested by the Z.R.P. without the permission from the people.

Nevertheless, 'the people of Chikore T.T.L. argued about the council'.[37] At Rugoyi in Makoni TTL people. 'wanted to know from us how the council was going to be run if it will be there as they are having the information that they will be paying money in order that their area develops.'[38] As an informant from western Chiduku told me in March 1981, 'the council is still a problem in Dewedzo. In 1980 the Minister was told by the people that if you want us to have anything to do with it call it something else. Hardly anyone voted in the election.'[39]

Gradually over the months the new council structure was nevertheless built up. The new system of elected local courts was developed. The authority of Chiefs and headmen was thus replaced, but so also were the administrative powers of the village ZANU/PF committees. In August 1982 I talked with the new African District Administrator of Marondera District. 'The state is now fully in charge of everything', he assured me. In Marondera, as in Makoni, the peasants had initially opposed the idea of a council for the TTLs; now they accepted it as they saw it begin to work. Even so the councils in the communal areas had not yet imposed a rate, which was still 'politically impossible'. Nor had he been able completely to undercut the office of chief, since 'the rural masses are very mystical', and all the more anxious for the appointment of men to chiefly vacancies now that the office was no longer compromised by possessing formal administrative functions.[40]

Government agencies, anxious not to renew their clash with the peasantry, passed their more unpopular functions over to the new councils. Diana Callear carried out research in Wedza Communal Area between June 1981 and July 1982. She found that in Wedza 'Agritex is dissociating itself as far as possible from conservation issues for which the council now has responsibility. This is an attempt to distance the present service from the unpopularity of past measures.'[41] Agricultural advisers had also been relieved of all responsibility for enforcing cattle dipping. Agritex has in general shown itself most anxious to escape the image of the 'demonstrator as policeman . . .' Its Socio-Economic Research Section is engaged in a number of projects to 'strengthen the dialogue between the government extension service and farming communities'. One of these is focused on a ward in Buhera district. Peasants in Buhera shared in the radical nationalism of the neighbouring Makoni District. John Mutasa describes how after the founding of the Rusape and Weya branches of the African National Congress he went into Buhera with George Nyandoro, 'preaching Congress':

We came to a kraal where we were astonished to be greeted with great joy by an old man, who slaughtered two goats for a feast, as though it was his birthday. 'This is wonderful, you young men. It's what I've always wanted.' It was old Masoja Ndlovu who had moved to Buhera when his attempts to prevent the eviction of his people had failed. He became Chairman and was arrested and imprisoned in 1959.[42]

The peasants of Buhera supported the guerrillas strongly.

Conclusion

'Although this is a long-established remote community,' says the
Agritex preliminary report on Chiwesha ward,

with many traditional customs or beliefs still intact it was also deeply
politicised during the war . . . The area seems well organised in terms of
local government and party structures . . . From our meetings, we did
detect a hint of a feeling of having been forgotten by government . . . There
was also a hint of bitterness against Agritex and Extension workers for not
doing enough to improve local agriculture, and extension and extension
workers were still associated in some people's minds with the forced
building of contours under the previous government.

The Agritex team found that 'almost no contours were in good
condition', but they also found that 'the extent of soil erosion did
not seem disastrous.' Their recommendations were that the extension services should concentrate rather upon the people's 'eagerness to learn new skills . . . willingness to change and ability to
organise themselves'. Instead of compulsion there should be 'improved extension . . . based on local enthusiasm and
organisation.'[43]
   Even the Natural Resources officers approached peasants in the
communal areas with a new and marked discretion. Oliver
Chapeyama, Regional Secretary, Natural Resources, Manicaland
wrote in September 1982 that:

Due to the neglect of the communal areas by past regimes, environmental
degradation is at its worst in these areas. Some people might argue that this
degradation was due to the ignorance of the African population about the
value of natural resources, but the truth of the matter is that the masses
were never taught about this value. Instead conservation measures were
introduced with a whip behind which caused resistance to conservation
measures by the masses. The formation of committees made up of popular
community leaders chosen by the people themselves will ensure the success
of the ventures undertaken and the once unpopular mechanical conservation works will be readily accepted in the communal areas . . . The change
of attitude among the people is going to take time before it spreads through
the province but nobody expects this to happen overnight.[44]

As for the new councils, on which so many unpopular responsibili-
ties have now been thrown, they began with similar disclaimers of
compulsion. The chairman of the conservation committee of
Maungwe Council, which is responsible for the communal areas of
Makoni District, is Amon Shonge, whom I quoted in Chapter 4 as
explaining why the peasants of Weya had no alternative but to
oppose agricultural rules. 'We must not return to the bad old days of

coercion,' he says. 'Everything must be done by example and self-help.'[45]

At the end of 1982, then, it seemed as if the peasants of Makoni and elsewhere had had a good deal of success with one part of their programme. In the communal areas external interference in peasant use of labour and choice of crops had indeed been greatly reduced. But what about the other part, the demand for the restoration of the lost lands? Could the peasantry do anything about this for themselves or did they have to wait until government redeemed its election promises?

On this issue there has in fact been a most complex dialectic between peasant action and government response. It naturally took the Mugabe government some time to devise a policy for land resettlement. It was launched in September 1980 with the announced objective of resettling some 18000 families from the communal areas on 1.1 million ha of formerly commercial farming land over a period of three years. Meanwhile a good deal of friction had been generated between peasants, white farmers and District Commissioners. Many peasants expected ZANU/PF's election to be followed by an immediate throwing down of the fences and did not wish to wait for a formal government programme before moving themselves or at least their cattle onto 'the lost lands'. 'There were quite a lot of mixed feelings amongst people,' wrote Shonge in August 1980. 'Some thought life would become easy overnight and yet we have another long way to go to rebuild ZIMBABWE!'[46] For their part the District Commissioners, even if they could not make their authority felt inside the TTLs, were determined not to allow things to become *too* easy and to stop a 'squatter' invasion of the white farms. Almost immediately after the elections, in March 1980, the Manicaland District Commissioners noted that 'a definite policy is required regarding the settlement and development of vacant land, to prevent a state of haphazard and illegal occupation.'[47] In September 1980 District Commissioners throughout the whole country received a circular from the Secretary for District Administration:

Reports from throughout the country indicate that a very serious squatter problem is developing on vacant land, including those areas which have been purchased for resettlement purposes, but which have not yet been settled, on a planned, controlled basis. The Secretary is anxious to apprise the Secretary for Lands, Resettlement and Rural Development of the current situation and trends, in the hope that something can be done to control squatters before the point of no return is reached. To this end District Commissioners are asked to report to their Provincial Commissioners on the squatter situation within their districts . . . Any efforts made to prevent squatting or to move squatters from affected land should be noted . . . It may well be possible to make an assessment . . . by overflying an area.[48]

District Commissioners thereupon took to the skies and made aerial surveys of the squatter frontier. The Makoni report on 'The Squatter Problem' revealed that the District Commissioner had been surprisingly successful in holding back the resentful peasants of Weya and Tanda from the lost lands of Mayo, Inyati Block, Rathcline and the rest. Half a dozen 'tribesmen' from Chikore were spotted engaging in 'stream-bank cultivation' in an area 'which has remained vacant for some 4 years, and was until recently part of the no-go area . . . .' Otherwise, 'on the unoccupied properties in Rathcline and Inyati Block, an attempt was made in March to occupy these properties but was thwarted by prompt action by police, guard force and this office.' While the District Commissioner's attention had been focused on the northern frontier, however, 'approximately 1000 tribesmen from the Buhera District have occupied land' on the Romsley Estate, south of Chiduku, and were reported to be 'denuding the farm of all its natural resources; the timber is being sold in towns. It would appear,' added the District Commissioner, 'that their occupation is with the approval of certain politicians. The people who are involved certainly believe that they have Government's authority to be there.' In addition some 250 peasants from Chiduku had moved on to farms bordering the TTL.[49]

In fact, despite these appearances and indeed realities of confrontation, the squatter movement had hardly got under way in 1980. The first necessity in 1980 was to rescue peasant agriculture from collapse; so devastating were the last months of the war and the attack on peasant food production in 'Operation Turkey' that the historian, T.J.B. Jokonya, was predicting in 1979 'the end of the Tribal Trust Land'. Jokonya quotes a song by Thomas Mapfumo which tells how:

> The Tribal Trust Land has disappeared
> In the death and destruction of the war.
> In the past women used to cook vegetables in the TTL.
> Men carved hoe handles in the TTL . . .
> Nephews looked after cattle.
> People danced 'chikendeya'
> and 'chinhundurwa'.
> War is a sad affair.
> People have lost their legs
> And others have died in the TTL.[50]

The first return made by the Mugabe government for the services of the peasants in the war was a crash programme of emergency relief – the universal distribution of seeds, fertilizers and food through the agency of the ZANU/PF committees. These crucial distributions were made available only to people living in the TTLs and this helped to stem the flow of squatters in 1980. The splendid rains of the 1980/81 season and the record high prices guaranteed by government for the purchase of maize did a good deal to restore a peasant economy and to defuse peasant discontent. Peasants who were in place on their lands in September 1980 certainly wanted to remain there until the end of the 1981 harvest.,

Nevertheless, discontent *was* building up. I found in Makoni District in early 1981 a widespread sense that government was not acting urgently enough and a widespread bitterness at the arrests and prosecutions of peasants who had let their cattle run on white ranches or 'trespassed' to cut grass. Stephen Matewa told me in March 1981 that:

Land is going to be a very big problem. People here in Chiduku do not seem to be considered; no-one seems to be thinking of land for us. The land here is bare; there is no grass for thatching, let alone for grazing. There is no wood. The people at St John's School, Mupanguri, go to steal grass and firewood from a European farm at night. On the white farms that border Chiduku the grass is as high as a man. When I go as auxiliary priest to the church at Mupanguri they confess to me every day. One man was arrested for stealing grass. I went to see the member in charge of the police at Inyazura and told him that in the TTLs there is no grass for thatching and no wood.[51]

'The problem may not be solved by sentences,' Matewa wrote to the officer commanding the police; 'the best way is to go to the root of the matter.'[52]

The veteran nationalist activist in western Chiduku, Mhondiwa Remus Rungodo, told Peter Chakanyuka in January 1981 that he thought the government:

rather too slow in fulfilling their promises of land allocation. He is seeing no change in this direction particularly when people are arrested for settling on undeveloped or deserted farms. He has noted minor changes but wishes to see the land problem settled quicker than is happening at present. He notes that prices are escalating while the masses have no means of making money. It is the quick redistribution of land he thinks will partly solve some of the problems of the rural people most of whom are land hungry.[53]

In March 1981 Amon Shonge described to me the situation which then existed around Weya:

Conclusion

Around Weya Europeans who deserted their farms during the war are putting two or three workers and some cattle on to the land just to re-establish claims. This will bring a row between the Government and the people if the Government does not take action. It should not tolerate absentee landlords. People in Weya have not moved on to these farms yet – they are waiting for the harvest. They are pegging out their claims ready to move so soon as the harvest is in. It will be a fight between the people because some will be greedy and take more than they need. We have been asking time and time again what land the Government plans to buy. Moven Mahachi (then deputy Minister of Lands and Resettlement) says that farms at Mayo have been bought but we don't know the details.[54]

Even the District Commissioner – now very much on the sidelines – criticized the ZANU/PF government for slowness over land redistribution in an ironic reversal of roles. In February 1981, he told me he could not understand:

why more rapid and straightforward action has not been taken. No-one seems to appreciate the power of land hunger. Wait another two years and we'll be back where we were six or seven years ago, on the verge of another guerrilla war. Government thinking is too elaborate and they have various plans for resettlement which will cost too much money and take too much time to implement. After all, look at what happened in the past with all the schemes for moving and resettling people. None of them happened quickly or were ever completed.[55]

And indeed in one area of Chiduku at the time I was there dissident guerrillas from the ZANU/PF assembly point in Buhera were moving among the peasantry telling them that the government had betrayed its promises over land and seeking their support for a return to guerrilla war.[56]

All of this provides a background for the developments of the next few months, in which two things happened. One was that the government's intensive resettlement scheme got under way. This scheme was an impressive achievement in itself, particularly by comparison with the slowness of previous settlement schemes in the colonial period. Bill Kinsey writes:

To March 1982 the Government had acquired some 750,000 ha for its resettlement programmes and of this approximately 520,000 ha had been used to settle about 8600 households. This achievement is the more remarkable by comparison, for in only eighteen months Zimbabwe transferred from white to black control only ten per cent less land than Kenya had transferred under its small-holder resettlement schemes dating from before independence to the middle of 1976 – a period of more than fifteen years. Indeed the three year target of 1.1 million hectares for the intensive resettlement programme alone is only seven per cent less than the total of all land transfers (large and small-scale) achieved in Kenya over fifteen years; and more than half of the Kenyan transfers were made by private sale.[57]

Some observers, persisting with a less cheering Kenyan comparison, feared that resettlement 'on an individual basis will create powerful class interests that will be more difficult to reform in the future than is the conflict between black and white interests at present'.[58] Such a fear was based on the relatively small proportion of families resettled; the amount of money it cost to resettle each family and provide it with minimal services; and the cited average of 60 to 70 ha of land per settled household. It was pointed out that 'Kenya's small-holder programmes created 49,400 holdings, averaging slightly less than 12 ha in size in 582,000 ha of former European land,' so that 'Zimbabwe is redistributing far more land than Kenya did, but the redistribution is creating proportionately far fewer holdings and therefore benefitting fewer would-be settlers.'[59] But in practice implementation of the original intensive resettlement scheme, while undeniably expensive, looked most unlikely to create a privileged rural class. Virtually all resettlement in this period was on the basis of the so-called Model A, that is intensive village settlements with allocations of some five ha of arable land per family and communal grazing. This was much more like an expansion of small peasant production than the creation of a yeomanry. As Kinsey remarks: 'the amount of arable land per settlement holding in Zimbabwe is only five hectares . . . the balance of the average holding size of 60 to 70 ha is accounted for entirely by the grazing land made necessary because the use of animal draft power is assumed.'[60] Indeed the most recent radical critique of resettlement has bemoaned the fact that settled households, having been chosen from among 'only the poorest families', have not received *enough* assistance rather than an excessive or privileged amount.[61] In short, the government was plainly making a real effort to meet peasant demands for an expansion of peasant farming rather than trying either to create a privileged rural class on the one hand or trying to create models of collective production on the other.

But this official and formal resettlement was overshadowed by the great outburst of peasant 'squatting' after the harvest of 1981. When I was in Makoni in March 1981 I could feel this wave gathering itself up in preparation for the surge forward. I could see for myself the white stone markers with which peasants had reserved for themselves the land on to which they planned soon to move: white farmers or their managers would go round moving the

Conclusion

stones away and next morning they would be back again. The District Commissioner predicted that Weya peasants would 'flood' south into the farms from which many of them had been evicted in the 1940s. The old farmer Leonard Ziehl, himself retired from farming land bordering Chiduku, described to me in February 1981 the turning of the tide:

My younger son is very optimistic. Money can be made. Maize is 12 dollars a bag and costs 9 to produce, so tobacco plantings are down and maize up. The farmers are under pressure though. My son-in-law who farms Carolina has found pegs driven in by Africans to mark out their land and has removed them. My son has abandoned a third of Recondite bordering Chiduku and squatters have practically occupied the whole valley. My son says he has enough land left and that if he tries to drive them off he'll have trouble and lose trade and good will. But a lot of people won't allow squatting and they have a lot of trouble. Their fences are always being cut and their stock stolen. The police won't do anything about it. Of course, the land on the investment company estates should have been given to the African years ago. I agree with Mugabe about that. Maybe that would have saved the producing farms. My brother-in-law, Barnes Pope, farmed Reserve land for many years; now the movement is all the other way.[62]

The frail dams erected by the District Commissioners in 1980 were now swept aside, especially in Manicaland. The Commission of Inquiry into Incomes, Prices and Conditions of Service documented in early 1981 both the frustrations of the peasantry and the determination of those in the eastern region of the country to do something about them:

Even with the carving up of grazing land, the majority of married younger people are landless and villagers informed the Commission that older men, with only small family holdings, have to feed the families of their grown-up sons . . . The subdivision of grazing land into arable, initiated in the late 1960s by many chiefs, has caused severe herding problems and many villagers therefore drive their herds surreptitiously onto adjoining commercial farms. If they are detected their cattle are impounded and have to be recovered on payment of fine . . . In Chief Mvutu's area, where very little grazing land is left, people used to drive their herds into a nearby forest area, a practice now forbidden. The people are now desperate. They were moved only 25 years ago from a rich area in the Essexvale district. . .
 On the positive side, the Commissioners noticed in certain areas, especially in Mashonaland East and Manicaland, a dynamic and new spirit among the peasants . . . But these were the exceptions. In most areas . . . frustration about the slowness of change out-weighed positive attitudes.[63]

The 'dynamic and new spirit' of Manicaland peasants found expression very largely in moving out onto white land. On 11 September 1981 the *Umtali Post*, under the heading 'Rusape News', carried a two-page report on a parliamentary debate on a motion deploring 'the illegal occupation and improper use of land by squatters', moved by the white members for Eastern and for Makoni. Des Butler, mover of the motion described it as a:

problem of great immensity. A conservative estimate is that in the eastern part of the country, in Manicaland, there are as many as 70,000 people involved . . . In fact, it is well known that the problem is widespread over the whole of the country . . . It is a form of anarchy, and as such should be and must be dealt with by Government as expeditiously as possible. . .Violence has occurred on farms as a result of squatting and, to say the least, I think that tempers are liable to flare in this regard.[64]

The speech was not well recieved – 'Go to hell', shouted Eddison Zvogbo, Minister of Local Government. 'You have squatted for 90 years and now you want to insult the people.'

Buoyed by this official sympathy, the radical peasants of Weya and Tanda flooded back onto their old lands. In July 1982 the magazine *Moto*, in an article on 'squatting', interviewed 'an old headman, struggling with his family to scratch a living from the arid and stony soils of Weya communal area.' The old man pointed south-west to the commercial farms of Headlands and Umfeseri. 'Until 1946,' he told his interviewer, 'I farmed there, and father before me, and his father before that. Then our land was stolen from us and we were pushed out to this desert. We want to go back, but we will wait for our Government to say when.'[65] Thousands of others were not prepared to wait. By January 1982 some thousand squatters from Weya and Tanda had arrived on the Headlands East farm of Nicholas Oosthuizen, 4000 ha of good land. The squatter movement had thus passed through the more or less abandoned farms to the north and reached profitable commercial farms. In January Oosthuizen applied to the High Court for an eviction order; this was granted and the Court ordered the deputy sheriff of Umtali to evict the squatters.[66] But at this moment such an eviction order was politically impossible to enforce. Government intervened with a compulsory purchase order, which meant that Oosthuizen had to be paid in foreign currency. A BBC television 'Newsnight' programme in March 1982 showed the farm and interviewed the parties. The squatter leader, Lovemore, said that their right to be there stemmed from their occupation of the land until 1945, when they were evicted into Tanda. The BBC reporter remarked that the outcome was the worst of all worlds – the government had had to use scarce foreign exchange; Oosthuizen had not wanted to sell his farm. So far as could be seen on television the squatters looked very happy.[67]

In April 1982 David Caute found in Headlands police station evidence for:

a silent and spontaneous revolution . . . taking place in the Zimbabwean countryside: thousands of landless peasants are invading commercial farms owned by white landlords . . . morally sustained . . . by their own compelling need, by the vast but undefined promise of the Chimurenga, the second Shona war of liberation, and by a burning desire for justice.

In Headlands police station the walls of the Member-in-charge (a black officer, at long last) are covered by large-scale maps depicting squatter concentrations and invasions. The mood is scrupulously neutral: the outraged landowners have the law on their side but the squatters have the party . . .

Caute himself followed up the case of a squatter he calls 'Mishek Katiwa' who 'with ten other families has evacuated the parched and overcrowded Chiduku reserve', moved on to 'Folkestone Farm' owned by 'Leonard Lyle', and 'hacked down the tall elephant grass, ploughed himself an acre with a tool very similar to the ones used by Winstanley's Diggers 300 years ago, cut enough wood to build a round hut – and gone to prison for three months on a charge of trespass.' While the squatters were in prison:

Lyle and his retainers took advantage . . . to pull down all the squatters' huts . . . When Mishek and his comrades came out of prison they re-built their huts; when Lyle came bumping across the dirt tracks, threading his angry path between homesteads burnt down by ZANLA four years ago, Mishek stood his ground. He had paid the price demanded by colonial law; now the land was his. Lyle's logic was different; and since neither the state nor the militia would allow him to resort to violence, to use the guns he still kept locked in his house, he had no alternative but to resume litigation.

At this point the Ministry of Lands intervened sending a team to the farm 'with ZANU (PF) district chairman on hand, and the police too. . . .' The squatters were persuaded to sign a document promising to remove themselves and their cattle 'after their maize was harvested . . . ' But they were still there in June 1981 and 'the cattle were still in the area, hidden beyond the high rock kopje which was once a guerrilla redoubt along ZANLA's main line of communication between the Chiduku and Weya reserves.' Lyle persuaded the police to prosecute:

The Member in Charge explained to him that permission had to be sought not only from the Ministry of Lands but also from the office of the Prime Minister – Mugabe wants to know every time an eviction order is moved against a rural squatter. Permission was granted. On the appointed day Lyle turned up promptly at 9 a.m. at Rusape court. No one was there. Presently the magistrate drifted in; then the prosecutor. Mishek and his comrades had been advised by the local ZANU (PF) political committee to boycott the proceedings. At 11.30 Lyle was casually informed by the police that the summonses had been withdrawn. 'On whose authority?' he yelled. He never found out.[68]

In these doggedly persistent ways the peasant squatters of Makoni and other districts both put pressure on the government and also gave opportunities for those members of it who wished to act more radically on land resettlement. 'What I like about the Makoni people,' Moven Mahachi, then junior Minister for Lands and Resettlement and himself from Nedewedzo in Chiduku, told me in April 1981:

is that they do not just sit idle, saying 'We have won the war, now we can rest'. They take action to solve the land problem for themselves. Makoni district is more infested with squatters than any district in the country and this makes it easier for us: it puts pressures on the Ministry and pressure on the owners. After all, the owners know that whether they sell or not they have lost . . . Mayo, they have lost Inyati Block . . . We are not going to move squatters out though we tell them they must not worry people who are really producing. We also tell them that they are only temporarily allowed where they are and that they will eventually have to move so as to conform to Government farm plans.[69]

In face of peasant squatting the government began to expand its plans for resettlement. The Minister of Lands and Resettlement, Dr Sydney Sekeramayi responded to the debate on squatting in parliament in September 1981 by saying that 'the ministry had formed a structure that would speed up the resettlement programme all over the country. He did not believe that the programme of . . . redistribution should take more than two years, and added "I believe that this next year the squatter problem will be history".'[70] The government's sense of urgency was sharpened when Robert Mugabe visited rural areas throughout the country and heard for himself at first hand the peasant sense of grievance over land. Out of all this there emerged early in 1982 the 'accelerated resettlement programme':

In essence, accelerated resettlement is a 'fire-fighting' or phased version of the intensive programme and is aimed at tackling quickly some of the most serious instances of squatting and some of the severe cases of over-population. The basic objective is to resettle as many people as possible in the shortest period of time by minimising planning, and postponing indefinitely the building of infrastructure . . . The global target figure of 162,000 families over three years (from 1 July 1982) and the figure of 18,000 for the intensive programme alone (for three years from September 1980) imply a target of approximately 102,000 settler households, or some 34,000 a year. Planning procedures are drastically curtailed and consist of little more than interpretation of aerial photography to identify arable land and sites for villages. Settlers are then put on to the land (or their prior presence there is formally recognized) and no facilities or services provided . . . Evidently settlers are being chosen to a considerable extent through a process of self-selection; and sceptics among the technical planners refer to the programme as a 'squatters' licence'.[71]

In June 1982, Moven Mahachi, now Minister of Lands and Resettlement, repudiated the protestations of white farmers and defended the potential of small peasant production:

Mr Mahachi said: 'Commercial farmers are complaining that their land is being taken and production will go down as a result. Yes, we are taking this land and will continue to take especially big farms and give them to the people of Zimbabwe. We think that the life of an African is in the soil and that anyone with soil has wealth. We will continue to take this land until most of the soil is in the hands of the masses.' Analysts had said that people in communal and small-scale farming areas could grow better crops than commercial farmers if given the tools. 'This is what we believe in', he said. 'Our people are not lazy'. The minister said most of the benefits from increased producer prices were going to 6,000 commercial farmers . . . 'We will divide acquired farms and give them to people so that they can earn a good living from it'.[72]

Identification of the government with the radical peasant programme could hardly go further. And there is no doubt that all this had some important effects. When I revisited Makoni District in September 1982 the frustrations of early 1981 had given way to a real sense that a major shift in land occupation was taking place. A resettlement scheme at Mayo was well-established; the Inyati Block was being developed as Chinyika resettlement area; plans were on foot to resettle Rathcline. The huge investment estates from which peasants had been driven in the late 1940s were being reoccupied. There was a sense of movement in Makoni communal area, where I was staying, as some families on Makoni Farm were packing up to go for voluntary resettlement in the Headlands area and as pegging was beginning on recently purchased white farms bordering the communal area for resettlement at twelve acres a family. As well as excluding most interference in their production, peasants in Makoni had gone some way towards 'solving the land problem for themselves.'[73]

And yet it is important not to overstate the extent to which peasants could act for themselves to bring about their political programme. For one thing Makoni District is different in important respects from many others. Historians have argued that the original land settlement of early colonial Rhodesia was shaped by the patterns which emerged out of the 1896 war. Similarly, the patterns of resettlement and squatting in the early 1980s have been shaped by the balance reached between black and white agriculture at the end of the guerrilla war. In Makoni, as we have seen, the combined assault of peasants and guerrillas had driven many white farmers off their land, which remained empty or nearly so, vulnerable to squatter assault or available for government purchase. In other districts – like Marondera, for example – the assault on white farming had been much less successful; farms remained occupied and in production and there has been much less of either squatting or resettlement. As Mahachi told me, 'Makoni District has more land free than most others because so many farmers were Afrikaners and have gone to South Africa: So much land in northern Makoni is vacant.'[74] Even in Makoni itself the land transfer amounts to much less than a revolution. What was being regained was essentially the marginal zone which has always been in dispute between blacks and whites – the land which early Native Commissioners wanted for Reserves but which went to the investment companies instead; the land which the investment companies wanted to sell back to the government in the 1930s for settlement of Africans under Land Apportionment and which local administrators wanted very much to obtain; the land which was briefly farmed successfully by whites in the late 1940s and 1950s but a good deal of which had been almost abandoned even before the war began. Despite the compulsory purchase of Oostuizen's farm in Headlands and Mahachi's brave talk in June 1982, very little really productive commercial farm land had been bought by government or wrested from white control by squatters. Mahachi himself was obliged to reassure white farmers later in June that 'since the resettlement exercise began two years ago, land which is effectively under production has not been affected. That policy has not changed. All farmers who are active on their farms . . . have nothing to fear.'[75] In Makoni the long-established farms with their airstrips and their opulent houses, their graded roads and complex and expensive machinery, flourished as never before on the high support prices which government had offered after independence. As Barry Munslow and Phil O'Keefe write:

The [resettlement] scheme has certainly faced great difficulties, not least because of the entrenched provisions of the Lancaster House agreement, stipulating that land could only be gained on a willing buyer/willing seller basis. A glance at the agro-ecological map showing the country's natural farming regions and the resettlement areas, quickly reveals what has happened. Around 85 per cent of resettlement schemes are on poor or even marginal land with low rainfall. The good quality land in the north-eastern central region remains a white farming preserve, the only exception being those few farms abandoned during the war which the Government is permitted to take over.[76]

Moreover, certain tensions grew up between peasants and government agencies during the working out of the interaction of squatting and resettlement. On their side many peasants have disliked the conditions attached to resettlement on government schemes. Meanwhile many people in government became less certain of the moral right of the squatter movement, less confident of the productivity of small peasant agriculture, and less ready to commit themselves to resettlement on so massive a scale.

I have described the Model A resettlement schemes as essentially an extension of small peasant production. Nevertheless, the schemes involved certain significant modifications of peasant practice as it exists in the communal areas. According to Kinsey, the schemes implied that 'Settlers are expected to live in closer proximity to one another than has been the custom in the communal areas . . . Each settler is allocated a residential plot within a planned village . . . All land is occupied and used initially on the basis of a number of temporary permits (covering occupancy, cultivation and depasturing of livestock) which spell out the conditions of occupancy.' Among these conditions was an obligation to work within the farm plan laid down by the extension services. Such a pattern gave rise to serious peasant anxieties since the 'ultimate nature of . . . tenure is unresolved . . . The permits are the equivalent of neither leases nor title deeds . . . and any permit may be revoked for a wide variety of reasons on the sole discretion of the Minister of Lands.' It is not surprising that many settlers have been unwilling to make the required surrender of all land claims in the communal areas in order to obtain such uncertain titles. Moreover, in entering such a scheme the peasant found himself once again in the world of direction and agricultural rules from which the communal area had largely escaped. 'Very little stress is given to consultation with the settlers during the course of implementation.' Finally, those who accepted land on Model A schemes were supposed to undertake a commitment to full-time cultivation and to give up paid employment in the towns. Since the peasant option had become viable almost everywhere only on the basis of male family members having access to extra-agricultural wages, this too was a very difficult condition to meet.[77]

It is not surprising, then, that peasants in Makoni as elsewhere often showed their dislike of the settlement scheme conditions. The first settlement scheme in Makoni was on the old Mayo investment estate, which lies between Tanda and Weya, where government had bought out twenty-two commercial farms. In September 1982, Amon Shonge told me that:

Much land has become available for resettlement. One big area is Mayo, into which many families have gone but where there is still room. I have heard complaints from people about the scheme. One is that people don't like to have to settle in villages and say they are far from their lands. For this reason some people have left the land allocated to them on Mayo and have moved south to 'squat' on land in Headlands. People out of Mtoko district have also moved south into Makoni. Many of them are now in Mayo and some have gone past it as squatters.[78]

In July 1982 *Moto* reported on what its reporters found on a visit to Mayo:

In Mayo, where the government has bought up 22 commercial farms for the largest single resettlement scheme so far, a despairing development officer was trying to persuade hundreds of unauthorised settlers – in other words, squatters – from felling trees and planting crops on river banks. He was told, by men pointing at one of the few remaining msasa trees: 'Go away, or we will hang you from that tree'. And when local ZANU (PF) officials explained that resettlement must be carried out in a planned and supervised way so as not to turn Mayo's rich soil into a wasteland, the response was: 'Do you want us to vote for the Bishop next time?'[79]

Where more effective control *had* been established, many settlers had left to go on to farm land as squatters where they were for the moment, at least, free of supervision.

For their part, many government officials increasingly pointed to the inegalitarian character of much of the squatting movement. The journal *Commerce* was quick to pick up a *Sunday Mail* report of Chiduku 'businessman', Benedict Tokoyo, who 'with his three wives and 24 children . . . had become the self-styled "king" of the squatters in the Inyati Block commercial farming area north of Headlands.' *Commerce* drew its own conclusions:

Conclusion

All hearts bleed for the landless but it is patently obvious by now that not all squatters are landless. In fact, many are get-rich-quick capitalists riding on the land bandwagon and this was admitted by Dr Sidney Sekeremayi when he was a Minister of Lands, Resettlement and Rural Development. Farmers, economists, investors and long-term planners believe that the wheat and the chaff of the squatting world should be sorted out . . . and fast before it is too late.[80]

Moto accepted the findings of an inquiry by that less than disinterested party, the Commercial Farmers Union, that:

less than half the squatters were driven by genuine need. Many squatters, the survey found, lived and worked in the towns and cities, and wanted a plot in the country either to grow crops for profit or to escape urban rents and rates. Still others, as MOTO observed in Mayo, were interested only in felling trees and selling them for timber or firewood while keeping their homes in the towns or communal lands. Others are prosperous businessmen who simply take over an area and divide it into plots, selling or renting them to people, frequently poorer relatives, they have trucked in from over-crowded areas. Some go further and set up stores selling over-priced goods to the squatters they have brought in. A district development officer in Makoni observed bitterly: 'They call themselves the "squatter kings". They are nothing but scoundrels'.[81]

Anyone familiar with the colonial history of rural Zimbabwe has every reason to be suspicious of such charges. As we have seen, the idiom of conservation has all too often been employed to put the blame on African cultivators for problems really created by unjust land division so that charges of total destruction of timber or of 'soil-mining' made by commercial farmers can hardly be taken at immediate face value. Equally, we have seen the ways in which African rural entrepreneurs were constantly cut down under colonialism and it rings a little oddly when a journal representing the interests of white business enterprise accuses many squatters of being 'get-rich-quick capitalists'. On the other hand, there is little doubt that however much we may see squatting as action taken by the 'people' in their own interests it has been, nevertheless, an untidy and ambiguous business. Before the great squatter explosion took over in Makoni, Amon Shonge, predicting it, also predicted that it would 'be a fight between the people because some will be greedy and take more than they need.' When I went back to Makoni in September 1982 and had another chance to talk with Shonge he told me that in the Romsley Estate area south of Chiduku, hundreds of squatters out of Chiduku met along an uneasy frontier with hundreds from Buhera, among them many 'front-men' sent in to stake out claims for land – and to timber – on behalf of businessmen

312

resident in Harare. He also told me that action had had to be taken against the 'squatter kings' and that Benedict Tokoyo had been evicted from the Inyati Block. I also found that the same 'powerful official trouble-shooter', whom Caute had seen defending squatters against prosecution and eviction at the beginning of the year was now cast in the role of 'the hammer of the squatters', or at least of those who would not heed official instruction.

Meanwhile a wider disenchantment began to be shown in relation to productive performance in the resettlement areas. There was an obvious tension here between the social purposes of resettlement and the ambition for 'improved' farming. Many of the 'poorest families' who were given priority as settlers did not possess cattle for ploughing and in accelerated resettlement areas they were given little of no assistance. Many had hitherto been landless and had little farming experience. Together with the drought, this resulted in low levels of production. By September 1982 Moven Mahachi was appealing to the master farmers, gathered together at their National Farmers' Association meeting:

The Government appealed to members to co-operate in the resettlement areas because most resettled people do not know how to farm . . . Previously his ministry sent out forms to screen potential settlers and the policy was to take on people without land. But yesterday Cde Mahachi said: 'In resettlement we have given land to 15,000 people but most of them do not know how to farm. We want . . . to give land that will be acquired this year to members of your association. We know that many of you are champion farmers with fine holdings and nice homes. Some of you may not want to leave your homes and go to resettlement schemes, but we know that with your knowledge and ambition to farm, you will do a good job.[82]

By the end of 1982 it was clear that government tolerance of the squatter flood had come to an end. When Mahachi had told me in April 1981 that the Makoni squatters were playing a useful role in putting pressure on landowners to sell, he also told me that 'they are only temporarily allowed where they are and that they will eventually have to move so as to conform to Government farm plans'. Government felt that the accelerated resettlement scheme, with all its financial and administrative and even political costs, was an earnest show of their intention to fulfill their debt to the peasantry, and they were understandably impatient with those who preferred to squat rather then to move onto official schemes. Controlled settlement schemes, it was felt, would ultimately be more productive, better conserve the land, and more effectively prevent inequality and exploitation. In December 1982 the deputy Minister for

Lands, Mark Dube, announced that all squatters must vacate the land on which they were living and declared 25 January 1983 as a deadline for such evacuation. He declared an 'all-out war' on squatters and embarked on a tour of that great region of squatting, Manicaland. On 16 December he ordered squatters on farms around Headlands to move within three days to neighbouring resettlement schemes. At the end of his Manicaland tour he announced that the squatter problem would soon be under control and that many squatters had already obeyed his commands.

Plainly, two different concepts of peasant interest are here at stake – the concept that rural 'people' can best define and act towards their own good as against the concept that this good can only be achieved through controlled planning by the representatives of the people. There is much to be said in favour of central planning, if only because peasants cannot themselves command the resources needed for development. But there are at least three reasons why peasants may not be convinced by the superior efficacy of planning or content with a ban on squatting. One is that some of the conditions of resettlement are difficult for peasants to fulfil, as we have seen. Another is that all centrally devised plans in the past have worked out to the disadvantage of the peasantry. A third is that however imperfect, messy and even destructive a process squatting might have been, at least it had served as a way of putting pressure upon government for more extensive land redistribution. It is plain that the 25 January 1983 deadline was not observed by all squatters. The *Herald* reported on 28 January that many squatters in Matabeleland had ignored the deadline, and I should be very surprised if all squatters in Makoni observed it. But certainly the squatting tide had been contained sufficiently for a good deal of this pressure to have been lifted. In 1983 the Zimbabwe economy experienced a serious depression. The budget made considerable cuts in the government expenditure, and among these were cuts in the money available for land resettlement. In a situation of very real economic stringency there is no reason to suppose that the Zimbabwean government positively wished to curtail the resettlement programme. But the point is that at one time a curtailment of land redistribution would have been politically impossible.

Some observers predicted that the result would be a revival of independent peasant action. Munslow and O'Keefe write:

Robert Mugabe's ZANU (PF) party swept to victory in the independence elections because the electorate trusted that his party would get back the land. Hence last year, when the new Government announced its intention of settling 162,000 families on the former white land over a three year period, it appeared the people's hopes were finally to be fulfilled. It came as a shock to many, therefore, when the announcement was recently made that no new land would be purchased for resettlement over the coming year . . . The 1982/3 budget provided for nearly £27 million to be spent on new resettlement . . .This year nothing is to be spent on further expansion . . . The Government is cutting the scheme, for a year only, it says, because of severe financial constraints. Zimbabwe's economy is facing negative growth . . .

But for many Zimbabweans, freezing the resettlement scheme cannot be easily justified. Restoring land to the people remains the central issue, and no official freeze will prevent the process continuing. Squatting will increase massively in the coming year as the dual crises of land hunger and drought force people to take the matter into their own hands. Fear of scaring the European farmers and reducing their production is used as an argument for halting resettlement. But only a small proportion of the commercial land is actually being utilised. That which remains unused could be put to good effect by massively increasing the resettlement programme. If the Government does not do it, the people will.[83]

It remained to be seen whether the 'people' could once again surge out in a yet greater squatter movement, powerful enough to carry the well-defended fortifications of the commercial sector in the face of official disfavour. It remained to be seen also whether the government could either respond to or forestall such a movement by breaking through the financial log-jam and compulsorily acquiring unutilized land.

Meanwhile, the Transitional National Development Plan, published in November 1982, envisaged for its own reasons a heightened peasant consciousness:

In its main thrust, the Plan will seek to correct the existing imbalance between the depressed rural communal sector and the developed sectors of the economy by injecting adequate factor inputs into the former sector as well as by the vigorous involvement of the peasantry in the production processes envisaged under the Plan programmes. It will be necessary to organise the peasants into Peasant Associations as an important means of creating in them a greater consciousness of their productive role and of facilitating their co-operation and stimulating the collective spirit.[84]

And it is precisely in the matter of how the communal areas themselves can be developed that we are most clearly up against the limitations on peasant agency. Peasants have proved capable up to this point of repudiating authoritarian interference in production in the communal areas; they have been able to put pressure on government for land resettlement. But can they act positively for the improvement of the areas in which they live? Or must we conclude that peasant consciousness took on in the colonial period an essentially negative, defensive character which makes it incapable of participation in constructive development?

It is important for a moment to return to the past. Of course, peasant action against the colonial regime *did* involve filling dip tanks with stones, breaking down contour ridges, and other actions which it was easy enough for the administration to characterize as reactionary and self-injurious. But peasant spokesmen always drew a clear distinction between what they would refuse to do when forced and what they were prepared and wanted to do freely. I described earlier in this book how the people of Matobo and Gwanda organized themselves to oppose administrative authoritarianism in the late 1940s. In July 1949 they listed the sequence of their confrontations to that date:

In the year 1946 our Native Commissioner . . . told the people of Wenlock to move to Dibulashaba giving reasons that the Rhodesia Co-operation Farm did not want the people to remain there any longer. We humbly but strongly refused to go and leave our original country, giving, of course, many various reasons on this point.

In the following year our Native Commissioner called for destocking and culling of our livestock which was done to a very high percentage. We consented against our wishes after which we found we had lost a great number of beasts in one year.

In 1948 we refused destocking continuing because we felt it was not necessary giving our reasons that our Native Commissioner must know that livestock is a blackman's bank . . .

It was in 1947 when Forced Labour came in operation. People worked against their wishes on a fixed wage. Sir, as far as we are concerned we hate everything in force. We appreciate with pleasure everything free will.[85]

Two years later those bodies which spoke more for Reserves 'progressives' nevertheless made much the same point. In 1951 a Congress memorandum against Land Husbandry noted that:

Taking careful observations on the work that is being done by Africans concerning agriculture, it is found that Africans have, within a short time responded satisfactorily to the teaching of the Native Agriculture Department, because yearly their products have gone up appreciably; even in bad years they have done well, therefore, they should not be taken as people who have failed to respond to the teachings of Government, who require measures to force them to learn the new methods.[86]

A protest by the Southern Rhodesian African Association noted that:

If the Select Committee could see into the minds of the Native people they would see that many are afraid that a measure of this kind . . . may be intended to bring all natives under a more autocratic authority and reduce all their holdings to an equal minimum . . . They also fear that the intention may be to abandon the idea behind the demonstrator system – of improving farming by education, example and persuasion – and to substitute a system of punishments . . . We fear that there is a real danger of the growth of antagonism between Natives and European 'authority'.[87]

And when that antagonism had reached its peak, readers may remember Amon Shonge's account of the feelings of the radical peasants of Tanda:

People were anxious to pick up new things but the way they were introduced did not give the people any choice. It was without any good introduction. And also threatening people, fining them, punishing them. This made people very angry. Definitely if there had been a proper agricultural education scheme people would have wanted new things. But when it was forced they would not have it. Since the enemy were using these things the people thought that the only thing to do first was to destroy and then build later.[88]

We have seen already how peasants have brought about a repudiation of force and a return to 'education, example and persuasion' on the part of the extension services since the election of 1980. But what do they want of their 'free will'? It is clear that they do not want to retreat into a 'traditional' isolation but that they have a very clear sense of their development priorities and that they make urgent requests for official assistance to realize them. 'From our meeting,' write the Agritex researchers on Chiweshe ward, Buhera:

we did detect a hint of a feeling of having been forgotten by government. It was said that we were the first people to have shown any real interest in them since Independence. There was also a hint of bitterness against Agritex and Extension Workers for not doing enough to improve local agriculture, and extension and extension workers were still associated in some people's minds with forced building of contours . . .However we feel that this was not a major factor at the meetings. Much more important was the very strong feelings and ideas expressed about what could be done in a real practical way, and the apparent strength and cohesion of the farmers as a group and the womens club as a group.

The researchers invited peasants 'to freely express their views about farming in the area', promising to report these to the Manicaland office. What was asked for was aid to make the peasant option viable.

'Marketing was seen as the overwhelming problem'; peasants demanded local delivery depots so as to cut out transportation costs; a local market for vegetables; 'a local farmers co-op run by the goverment which includes a local depot for selling and co-ordination for in-puts and out-puts (fertilizers, seeds, cheques, credits, etc).' Overcrowding would have to be remedied: 'The government must come and say that certain kraals should go for resettlement. But it must be *voluntary*, no one must be forced to go.' They needed help to break out of the 'vicious circle' of inadequate grazing and dependence on cattle traction. Peasants were expressing a need for 'proper grazing areas. At the moment, cattle are wandering on to other peoples' land who charge us for trespassing! Our cattle are in poor condition, they are thin and can't plough big fields. There is a vicious circle. Poor ploughing or late ploughing means poor crops. Cattle are thin and some die. We need tractors to break this circle.' And they demanded *more* Extension Workers; 'proper training'; 'advice on fertiliser'; 'advice on growing traditional crops. We only get advice on maize and cotton, but we also want advise on mhunga, rukweza, nyimo, sweet potatoes and pumpkins.' Impressed by 'the eagerness of local people to learn new skills and to improve their techniques', the researchers concluded that 'with careful planning of new resources, improved extension and based on local enthusiasm and organisation, the area has great potential for improvement.'[89]

Diana Callear records for Wedza 'the rise in expectations about the role of "the people's government" in rural areas . . .' Her peasant respondents asked for credit facilities; that ZANU/PF or the local council should provide tractors and cheap or free fertilizer; that a local grain buying depot be set up. 'Farmers firmly expect help to raise their productivity and returns.' Callear comments that such expectations. 'show ignorance of the evidence that greater government intrusion and control in agriculture in other countries throughout tropical Africa has nearly always had exactly the opposite effects. Perhaps this shows how easily governments can move into a predatory role.'[90] In fact it seems unlikely that the peasants of Wedza, whose experience of colonialism was not very different from that of Makoni, could really be ignorant of the dangers of government intrusion and control, from which they had suffered for decades. Very possibly they are now unrealistic to imagine that they can obtain a great deal of government assistance without intrusion or control, but they and peasants elsewhere ask it for two reasons. One is that they feel they deserve it because of their part in the war. The other is that they see no alternative source of inputs. Peasants are aware of the fragility of their political muscle; but they are even more aware of rural poverty. As a peasant farmer in Buhera put it:

A migrant worker can build a beautiful house and asbestos roofing, but I must depend on my son for such things. It's very discouraging. The government is more afraid of workers in town, because they can go on strike. But we cannot go on strike. (The thought of farmers going on strike had the whole meeting in laughter). We fed the freedom fighters during the war, but now we feel forgotten.[91]

This mixture of attitudes determined peasant attitudes towards the new councils – a combination of scepticism that these bodies can or will adequately represent them and of hope that they may be a conduit of assistance. In 1982 scepticism seemed well-founded, for in the composition of the councils resided another crucial limitation of the wartime victory of black over white agriculture. In Makoni, for example, the commercial farming areas remained under the old white-dominated Makoni Rural Council, which was allowed to choose whether it continued to operate separately or amalgamate with the new Maungwe Council in the communal areas. Needless to say, the Makoni Rural Council opted for separation, thereby ensuring that it could continue to expend the substantial revenue it derived from rates on the fat farmlands exclusively for services within the commercial area. The Maungwe Council, though currently receiving government subsidy, was expected to be self-financing within five years and would have to depend thereafter on the rates and taxes it could raise locally. Callear remarks that in Wedza 'the Council's main problem is to finance any activities it wishes to pursue'; she also remarks that 'given wide differences in income and experience in the area in it will be extremely surprising if the council is not run by, and on behalf of, an emerging rural elite of businessmen and more favoured male farmers.' Whether or not this prediction is realized, it is clear that local government bodies will not dispose of the resources effectively to develop the communal areas unless there is integration of local government throughout districts as a whole. It is clear, also, that as the new administrative system stabilizes and as the negative peasant achievement of ending agrarian coercion and the positive peasant achievement of exerting pressure for land redistribution come to their natural term, the unusual advantageous position of Zimbabwean peasants vis-à-vis the state will give way to quite another balance of power. Whether or not Callear's gloomy expectation that the Zimbabwean state will become a predator in relation to the Zimbabwean peasantry is realized, depends upon the prospects for the kind of rural development envisaged in the Buhera survey – development based on the assumption that rural 'problems must be solved from the bottom up, not the top down', development which begins with 'an understanding of the conditions in which people live and their potential for change', and continues with provision of 'new resources'. In attaining such ideal development both the Zimbabwean government and the Zimbabwean peasantry are cripplingly handicapped by the lasting effects of the colonial agrarian history which this book has described and from which it will take a very long time to escape. But so far as the 'potential for change' of the Zimbabwean peasantry is concerned – so far, that is, as their capacity to play their part in bottom-up development is concerned – my feeling in general is the same as that of the Buhera researchers, who noted of that particular case that it 'might be well to remember here that although this is a long-established community with many traditional customs or beliefs still intact it was also deeply politicised during the war. . . This is an important social factor which indicates . . . peoples willingness to change and their ability to organise themselves.'[92] In this way the peasant consciousness which I have shown developing in this book, and which reached its fullest expression in the guerrilla war, *is* relevant to rural development.

A conjunction of peasant aspiration and of government thinking might conceivably take place in the form of rural producer cooperatives. The government has made increasingly explicit that this is the form it wishes rural socialism to assume. In November 1982 Robert Mugabe told a ZANU (PF) seminar that 'members who scorn the concept of co-operatives are at variance with the party's policies and principles . . . We want people to form co-operatives voluntarily; they should be educated so that they understand that by working together they can succeed . . . People should understand that what they produced would be theirs and the government would take nothing.' Cde Mugabe added: 'The government will not interfere; it is there to help co-operatives succeed.'[93] The Three Year Plan asserts that 'some of the experience in mass organisation during the liberation war will be exploited to advance the co-operative movement. . .'[94]

I have said little in this book about the historical antecedents of commitment to rural cooperative production because such a commitment has not been a major theme of peasant consciousness. Neither communal tenure nor the institution of the harvesting work-party did anything to modify the autonomy of the individual peasant household; both were rather stimulants to than constraints upon entrepreneurial accumulation. On the other hand, one cannot end a book which has drawn so heavily on the experience on Makoni District without noting that there *have* developed some peasant foundations for cooperative production.

I have shown that the communal farm experiment at St Faith's was important to the development of nationalism in Makoni District. With its mixture of grass-roots initiative and internally administered discipline, it also embodied an alternative way to good farming which was attractive to farmers confronted with administrative autocracy. At a very early stage of the St Faith's experiment Guy Clutton-Brock defined the difference between his approach and that of the administration:

I am not primarily interested in contour ridge making but only in so far as it is a part of good farming. We do not want to become a contour ridge factory, any more than a tobacco factory . . . It can only be done by education of the people . . . Just policemen can never make good farmers. When the conservation officer talks about putting the thumb-screw on, it is only any good if people know for what they are having their thumbs screwed . . . If one is to farm well one cannot depend too much upon central office direction, a system which I understand has been tried in Russia with only limited success.[95]

This repudiation of authoritarianism and the emergence of the village committee as the decision-making and disciplinary body was attractive to many both inside and outside Makoni District. In March 1954, for example, a peasant farmer from Marandellas asked Clutton-Brock if he might visit St Faith's to see for himself what could be done. 'Our position as African farmers is a deplorable one,' he wrote, 'We are poor imitation of the white in Southern Rhodesia. We tried to work hard sometimes. Still we reverse. We have demonstrators with us, but they become only Native Constables prosecuting people of some offences of National Resources Board Act. They had failed to lead us.'[96]

The St Faith's experiment collapsed in the face of administrative hostility and ecclesiastical suspicion. But its influence continues in Makoni District, most strikingly at Mukute in Weya. Here, right in the heart of the arid sand soils of Weya and right at the heart of radical peasant repudiation of agrarian rules, Amon and Elizabeth Shonge founded in 1971 a rural cooperative still 'unique in that it is situated on communal land. . ..'[97] The Shonges had been members of the Cold Comfort Farm cooperative and after its suppression had decided to take the cooperative ideal back to their home area. Shonge says that:

I decided to come home with my wife. I went to all the local political leaders and to the headmen to ask for land where I could start a cooperative. None of them agreed because they did not understand the idea. So I took my father's land because he was getting too old to use it. Only 9 arable acres at first though since then people have given land so we now have 36 acres. My wife and I were alone for the first year. Then my nephew came and a few other young people not related to us.[98]

It was a difficult business getting the surrounding peasants to understand the cooperative principle. 'We were very disturbed in April this year,' runs the Mukute Farm Society newsletter in October 1975:

when two of our members . . . left. . . Since it is a free community we let them go, but we were very unhappy about their decision. We think it is likely that pressure was put on them by relatives and friends, because people tend to think that a man must work for a boss and a wage, or else for his own family. Our way of working with no wage and no boss and sharing what we get from our work is difficult to understand . . .It is our belief that the work we are trying to do here may be of benefit to our people and our country in the future. No doubt some people think Mukute Farm is an individual enterprise, and we are sorry for those who think so. It is probably the disease that is in many people's minds, created by those who think in an individualistic way . . . It is our duty to produce more out of a small piece of land and to show the way of working and living together in a good spirit.[99]

When the guerrillas entered Weya in 1976 some peasants told them that Shonge was an 'exploiter' and he had to explain to each successive band what Mukute was seeking to do. Moreover, Mukute had to operate very unobtrusively:

We here had hid ourselves from the authorities. We did not want our Cold Comfort associations to be known nor to be called 'communists' for living in community. Now in the war there was the danger that the police or army would think these young men were all comrades. But people were so wonderful during the war. They were very, very sensitive to danger. So we usually had notice and the brothers (members of the cooperative) dispersed.[100]

But Mukute survived and gradually improved its soil and its output per acre. In fact, it passed the hardest test that any cooperative could face since its survival really depended on its capacity to feed not only its own members but also guerrillas and the neighbouring impoverished. 'Life is getting harder,' wrote Shonge to Clutton Brock in March 1978, 'But we are still carrying on despite the difficulties. The Salisbury agreement [Internal Settlement] is not acceptable and for that reason the other side is intensifying the war. Now the man who suffers more is the unarmed one! More and more deaths are taking place day after day . . . We are expecting quite good yields in the fields. That means we can suffer but we will be able to have some food to eat.'[101] The guerrillas began to understand what was happening at Mukute – 'The comrades have taken a great interest in what we are doing at Mukute', Shonge was able to report after the war, 'and have said "You are doing the things and living the kind of life we are fighting for." We feel we are beginning to have some influence in the district.'[102]

And the peasantry began to be impressed by the visible increases in productivity. In May 1977 the cooperators reported:

We have improved our soil considerably. Our soil was known previously to be a useless white sandy one by the local people, but now many people are turning up to admire how fertile it is. We have been keeping compost from the poultry and cattle and have been turning this on to the land ever since we started in 1971. Many friends and villagers have since copied our ideas. This encourages us very much because it shows that the 'seeds' we are sowing are germinating.[103]

The Mukute community had to survive particularly intensive pressure from the Security Forces in 1979 as Shonge worked in his role of member of the committee set up by the guerrillas. But once the war was over, the cooperative was ready to emerge into a much more public role. In May 1980 Shonge wrote to the Ministry of Lands and Resettlement that:

We are a community of 17 people, plus 4 children. We are situated in the North of Weya Reserve, where we have a piece of land in common and are doing our farming in common. Our aim is to become self-supporting . . . We have been here since 1971. During the war we suffered with all the toiling masses around us badly from Imperialist oppression. Miraculously we remained not very badly hurt by the war. Since our existence we have and are still doing all our best to share with others who may be in need for help. Our help included food, clothing and medicines to people in the villages and our 'heroes' the ZANLA forces. We wish to come open now since we are free and self determination nation . . . All along we have been doing this under or behind the 'curtains' for security reasons. As we lived communal life, it was also obvious that we could be labelled Communists . . . Now we would like to continue and even improve and extend our community Development ideas.[104]

And this has happened. Weinrich in her forthcoming book on the cooperative movement, describes the great tenth anniversary rally on 1 August 1981 for which 'civil authorities from Manicaland and beyond visited the farm.' She also described the five local Batani clubs, formed of local peasants who 'grouped themselves together after the war to cultivate some of their land in common and to imitate the agricultural techniques of the Mukute Brothers', an outcome which she rightly regards as 'an extraordinary success . . . for in so poor a communal land as Weya, people are little inclined to risk something new unless they are well assured of success.'[105] In July 1981 the Weya Community Training Centre was established, largely at the initiative of Mukute, in order 'to promote the development of the Communal Areas in order for people to achieve self-reliance: staying on the land and pursuing a productive life, instead of moving off to the cities.'[106] Largely as a result of all this Weya and Tanda peasants, for so long known for their relentless opposition to agrarian coercion, now became known as exceptionally open to ideas of communal production. In September 1982 the *Herald* reported that:

Fears among some people that they would lose by joining co-operatives were allayed yesterday by the Deputy Minister of Lands, Resettlement and Rural development, Cde Mark Dube. Officially opening a Macheke workshop on promoting self-reliance and co-operative effort . . . Cde Dube praised the Tanda and Chiendambuya (Weya) communal farmers for responding positively to the Government's call for co-operative and group effort. The area had last year nine groups with 390 members, but now there were 14 groups with 510 members.[107]

Weinrich is right to say that Mukute has 'opened Weya up for a more open attitude towards the Government's policy of communal farming . . . .'[108]

There are thus some valuable links in Makoni between the peasant experience of guerrilla war and the cooperative idea. The foundations for communal production have been laid slowly and thoroughly and with a repudiation of all compulsion. It remains to be seen whether such slow and voluntary growth will prove enough to meet government's expectations of cooperative growth or whether in Zimbabwe, as elsewhere in Africa, recourse will be had to more rapid and coercive measures.

The time has come to return to the comparisons made with Kenya and Mozambique which I have left implicit in this chapter while setting out the current state of Zimbabwean peasant consciousness and its interaction with the Zimbabwean state. In a television programme modestly entitled 'Mazrui's Zimbabwe', Professor Ali Mazrui is 'shown interviewing Robert Mugabe. Will Zimbabwe become, he asks, another Kenya or another Mozambique? Neither, Mugabe, replies. It will be a Zimbabwe. I suppose that is what I too have been saying in this book though at very much greater length. But of course what it means for the future to say this is as yet undetermined. If the character of peasant experience and consciousness in Zimbabwe has made African rural capitalism impossible to obtain *on the Kenyan model*, it does not necessarily follow that another sort of African rural capitalism will not develop in Zimbabwe. If rural socialism on the Mozambique model also looks currently improbable, that is not to say, of course, that the Zimbabwean state will not inevitably become stronger in its relation to the peasantry and more and more able to insist upon its own version of rural socialism. There is even a prospect, however utopian it may sound, that a fruitful interaction between peasant consciousness and official inputs may be achieved. Whichever of these outcomes eventuates it will start from a different place and follow different trajectories than have Kenya and Mozambican developments. I hope that peasants in Zimbabwe will themselves be able to play a more direct part in determining the shape of their own future than has been possible for peasants either in Kenya or in Mozambique, because it seems to me that they have earnt the right to do so. But nothing in the rural history of Zimbabwe allows me to predict whether that will happen. Majority rule opens up so many new possibilities even if it cannot change some of the profound formations inherited from colonialism. This book has to end with a question rather then with an answer.

It will end it by borrowing a question from one of the protagonists in the contestation over the future or rural Zimbabwe. A rural bourgeoisie has not been able to establish itself in the communal areas or on the resettlement schemes. But there has emerged an as yet small class of Africans who have bought land in the commercial area from whites. There has not been a great deal of room for them yet in between peasant squatting and white prosperity at the commercial core. In Makoni their geographical position is appropriately and symbolically marginal. Whites sell land to government or to black purchasers in the area bordering on the communal areas and then reinvest in land at the commercial core. The new black purchasers are left to deal with the cattle driven across their boundary lines from the communal areas and with the raids on their wood and grass supplies; at least one of the new black landowners in Makoni has taken to patrolling his boundaries with a shotgun just as his white predecessor used to do. The drought has made it very difficult for them to keep up their repayments of the loans from the Agricultural Development Bank which made their purchase of the land possible. It may be that they are doomed to inhabit an odd black parody of Doris Lessing-land, that territory of indebtedness and failure. It may be, on the other hand, that they represent the beginnings of a dominant rural bourgeoisie. At any rate I end with the questions posed by a member of this amiguous class:

Conclusion

Does Zimbabwe mean you can take someone's property and tell him to keep quiet? People are taking advantage of the independence of Zimbabwe. A lot of evil is happening because they claim they took part in the armed struggle. Who didn't?

My father recently bought a farm in the Rusape area. The problem he faces is that of squatters. These people do whatever they wish on the property. Is this what we looked forward to? If so then all his years of hard work mean nothing. You work to improve yourself and the country, but not for every Jack and Jill . . . There seems to be no understanding in the people. Finally my father has been asked to come before the 'jury' (chiefs and elders of that area). What for? Is this not our property?

One begins to wonder what kind of life lies ahead in this country.[109]

Even after this long historical survey, one does indeed.

NOTES

1 District Commissioner to Provincial Commissioner, 16 December 1976, file 'Headman Maparura', District Commissioner's office, Rusape (DCOR)
2 District Commissioner to Provincial Commissioner, 22 August 1975, ibid.
3 Interviews with District Commissioner I.S.L. Bickersteth, Rusape, 22 January and 6 February 1981, and with Roland Hatendi, Tandi, 6 February 1981.
4 Interviews with Chief Muzanenamo Makoni and his councillors, Makoni, 8 February 1981; Isaac Tsungo, Mbobo purchase area, 14 February 1981.
5 The *Herald* of 28 May 1983 reported that 'squatters in the Sanyatwe commercial farming area near Inyanga last week "arrested" registered farmers and some government officials in the course of a dispute over land ownership'. Summarized in *Zimbabwe Project News Bulletin*, (*ZPNB*) no. 27, May 1983, p. 8.
6 *Zimbabwe. Report of the Commission of Inquiry into Incomes, Prices and Conditions of Service* (Harare: Government Printer, June 1981), pp. 35–6; 40.
7 Kate Truscott and N.C. Pambieri, 'Census survey of Chiweshe ward (Buhera). Preliminary report', (Harare, Agritex: 1983)
8 Interview between Sister Emilia Chiteka and Mrs John Mugura, Chitsanza, 28 January 1981.
9 Interview with Caston Makoni, Shandisai Pfungwa Cooperative, Marondera, 28 August 1982. Caston Makoni told me that there were strained relations between the peasants of Svosve and the members of the co-operative, which is on a farm bordering the communal area. The peasants claimed that they had been promised the land by government officials in 1980 and they particularly resented the fact that old farm workers from Malawi, Mozambique and Zambia were still on the land. None of the co-operators came from Svosve. The

peasants trespassed on the land to cut wood and drove their cattle on
to it.

10   *Zimbabwe. Report of the Commission of Inquiry into Incomes, Prices
     and Conditions·of Service,* p. 34.
11   Election speech by Davis Mugabe, Munyikwa TTL, Gutu, recorded
     by Kees Maxey, translated by Eustacius Valisai.
12   ibid.
13   *Zimbabwe. Report of the Commission of Inquiry into Incomes, Prices
     and Conditions of Service,* p. 34.
14   This article in *Moto* for November 1982 is summarized and quoted in
     ZPNB, no. 26, April 1983, pp. 17–18.
15   *Sunday Mail,* 17 May 1981. Mr Mugabe said that 'Zimbabwe would
     begin as China had, by introducing cooperatives and after gaining
     experience communes would be introduced'.
16   Unpublished Oxfam report, 1980.
17   Stephen Matewa to Didymus Mutasa, 10 April 1980, Matewa papers,
     Toriro.
18   Stephen Matewa to 'dear Madibura', 15 April 1980, ibid.
19   Stephen Matewa to Moven Mahachi, 24 October 1980, ibid.
20   Interview between Peter Chakanyuka and Takapera Moda Chakany-
     uka, Nedewedzo, 16 January 1981.
21   Interview between Peter Chananyuka and Mandironda Beatrice, 1
     February 1981.
22   Interview between Peter Chakanyuka and Mavengeni Annah, 8
     February 1981.
23   Interview with ZANU/PF Makoni District Committee, Rusape, 22
     February 1981. The extent to which officers of the District Commit-
     tee represented the archetypal experience of rural Makoni rather
     than long-standing commitment to ZANU emerges from the biog-
     raphies of the Chairman and Secretary. The Chairman, S. Nengo-
     masha, was a teacher until 1964 and thereafter a builder. He did not
     belong to the nationalist parties of the early 1960s. He lived in
     Mutunungore village at the foot of Chinyamambara mountain. In
     1978 the guerrillas asked the people of the village to select a man who
     could be responsible for them in their dealings with the guerrillas.
     They selected him and he became responsible for the collection of
     food, clothes and money. The guerrillas made him a member of one
     of the wartime committees and 'I became a member of ZANU/PF in
     my heart'. In 1979 the Security Forces arrested him along with many
     other men and women and took them first to Inyazura and then to
     Senga farm, where they were told they would be shot if they tried to
     escape. He was held for a week, the police 'questioning us and
     beating us', some men being beaten with axe handles, some girls
     being given electric torture.
        The Secretary, P. Matimba, had been a policeman. He was posted
     to the Hondi valley where he made contact with guerrillas and
     FRELIMO men on the frontier. He told them that he wanted to leave
     the police and assist the war so they 'abducted' him into Mozambi-

que. When he was released, he returned to Rusape and put in his resignation from the police but it was refused and he was put in the cells under suspicion of collusion with the guerrillas. Eventually he was released and went home to his village in Bvekera in Chiduku. He made contact with the guerrillas and told them his story which they believed because his 'abductors' had made a report on him. So he was appointed to a committee by the guerrillas. In December 1979 the Security Forces captured a document which contained his name and began to search for him everywhere. He went to the guerrillas who told him to remain in hiding and to move among the people preparing them for the election. The police arrested his wife, who was nine months pregnant, and held her for three weeks in Rusape. She gave birth somewhere along the road as she was walking home from prison.

In general the District Committee told me that they did not think any of its members had been ZANU since 1963/1964. 'ZAPU was very strong in those days. People began to turn to ZANU when the comrades came into the country.' When the guerrillas came in they began by selecting one man in a village with whom to do business; thereafter they appointed committees. Only after the 1980 elections were ZANU/PF committees elected in the villages. By the time of the 1980 elections 'it was already a one-party state' in Makoni. The new elected 'village' committees in fact represented clusters of twenty to thirty homesteads or 'kraals', smaller than the old Headmen's areas but bigger than those of kraalheads. By February 1981 some seventy committees had been elected in Makoni. The membership of forty-three of these was listed on the wall of the District Committee office. Women members were notably very much in the minority though there were some women chairmen and political commissars. The District Committee itself was elected in September 1980 by representatives of the village committees which were then in existence.

24 Minutes of District Commissioners' Conference, Manicaland, Umtali, 27 and 28 March 1980, file 'Confidential', DCOR. In September 1982 I visited the office of the new District Administrator in the hope of being able to see the military and political files which had not been open to me in 1981. The District Administrator kindly accompanied me on a search of the buildings: this file was the only one surviving.

25 District Commissioner, Makoni to Provincial Commissioner, 1 October 1980, ibid.

26 'Report on Meeting held in Chikore T.T.L. on 19th September 1980', 24 September 1980, ibid.

27 'Report on Meeting held at St Michael's School Tanda T.T.L. on 20/9/80', 24 September 1980, ibid.

28 Columbus Makoni, one of the ZANU/PF Manicaland members of parliament, in an interview on 29 January 1981 told me that 'the people of Tanda and Weya had not allowed the District Commissioner or his assistants or the demonstrators to enter those areas since the end of the war. In December 1980 I went there with my wife and the

District Commissioner and his wife, travelling by helicopter. It was the first ZANU/PF rally. I told them that the District Commissioner and his men were now servants of the people and should be allowed in.'

29 Sergeant Ncube's log, Rugoyi base, Makoni, 5 February 1981 DCOR.
30 District Assistant Manyela's log, Rugoyi base, 4 February 1981, ibid.
31 District Assistant Mashanduli's log, Chikore base, 9 February 1981, ibid.
32 Sergeant Ncube's log, 31 January 1981, ibid.
33 District Assistant Ngorima's log, Rugoyi base, 2 February 1981, ibid.
34 District Assistant Ngorima's log, 31 January 1981, ibid.
35 Minutes of District Commissioners' Conference, Manicaland, Umtali, 27 and 28 March 1980, file 'Confidential', DCOR.
36 Minutes of District Commissioners' Conference, Manicaland, Umtali, 6 and 7 May 1980, ibid.
37 District Assistant's log, Chikore base, 7 February 1981, DCOR. The signature on this report is not decipherable.
38 Sergeant Ncube's log, Rugoyi, 6 February 1981, ibid.
39 Interview with P.M. Chakanyuka, Harare, 29 March 1981.
40 Interview with District Administrator, Rusape, 28 August 1982.
41 Diana Callear, *The Social and Cultural Factors Involved in Production by Small Farmers in Wedza Communal Area, Zimbabwe, of Maize and its Marketing*, (Paris: Unesco December 1982), p. D.43.
42 Interview with John Mutasa, Makoni, 11 September 1982.
43 Truscott and Pambieri, 'Census Survey of Chiweshe Ward', pp. 5, 7, 13.
44 Oliver Chapeyama, 'Everybody's responsibility to conserve resources', *Manica Post Show Supplement*, 10 September 1982, p. 11.
45 Interview with Amon Shonge, St Francis, Makoni, 11 September 1982.
46 Amon Shonge to Sally Roschnick, 22 August 1980, Shonge letter-book, Mukute, Weya.
47 Minutes of District Commissioners' Conference, Manicaland, Umtali, 27 and 28 March 1980, file 'Confidential', DCOR.
48 Secretary for Administration, Confidential Circular to all Provincial Commissioners and District Commissioners, 10 September 1980, ibid.
49 District Commissioner, Makoni to Provincial Commissioner, 23 September 1980, ibid.
50 T.J.B. Jokonya, 'End of the Tribal Trust Land. The effects of war on the rural population of Zimbabwe Rhodesia', University of Zimbabwe, History seminar, 1979. Mapfumo's *Chirizevha Chapere* is given in translation on page 15.
51 Interview with Stephen Matewa, Toriro, 25 March 1981.
52 Stephen Matewa to Officer Commanding, British South Africa Police, Inyazura, 19 June 1980, Matewa letter-book, Toriro.
53 Interview between Peter Chakanyuka and Mhondiwa Remus Rungo-

do, Nedewedzo, 30 January 1981.

54 Interview with Amon Shonge, Weya, 25 March 1981.

55 Interview with District Commissioner I.S.L. Bickersteth, Rusape, 6 February 1981.

56 Interview with Needmore Ndhlovu, 'Comrade Believe', Old Umtali, 9 March 1981. Needmore Ndhlovu had walked all the way from Bulawayo to Mozambique with a band of ZANLA guerrillas in 1976; thereafter she had worked in the Social and Cultural division inside Mozambique. After the war she became a teacher and was sent to teach in St Agatha's school, Bvereka, in Chiduku, ten km from St Theresa's Catholic mission. When I met and talked with her in March 1981 she had left the area because her school and others, including St Theresa's, had been closed down. Prior to that she had had to give a month's wages to dissidents. Three hundred men of the National Army and sixty police were now based at St Theresa's and patrolling the area. I did not depend on 'Comrade Believe' for my knowledge of these events – the District Committee itself had asked me not to enter that part of Chiduku. But she was able to add insights into a situation which is eloquent of the upheavals which the war had created and which still affected events more than a year after it had ended. According to her, discontent in the area did not only arise from land shortage but also from intense competition between denominations and conflict over schools. In an effort to reestablish and enlarge educational provision, ZANU/PF had encouraged the reopening of mission schools and had also begun to put pressure on parents to send their children to school. In this part of Chiduku there were many Vapostori who did not wish to send their children to school and especially not to schools run by other denominations; many of the younger Vapostori had been *mujibas* during the war and were now acting in this role for the dissidents. Moreover, during the war St Theresa's had been closed and much of the property from the mission and school had been taken by local people. ZANU/PF had ordered that it be returned but people were reluctant to do so. Finally, people in the area had come to dislike the churches and to support mediums during the war: at St Agatha's itself people were refusing to attend services in the church, claiming that it was haunted and that the preacher was a witch. The returned priests and nuns at St Theresa's had received threats and been told to go away again. While most of the local mediums were loyal to ZANU/PF at least one female *svikiro* was working with the dissidents and predicting that ZANU/PF would split between those 'not fighting for freedom but for their own profit' and those who wished to go on fighting. The party had backed the churches and in December 1981 had had leaflets dropped from a plane telling people that 'there is nothing wrong with the Church.' This account indicates both how some danger existed of the revival of the practical and ideological alliance of peasants and guerrillas which had characterized the guerrilla war, and also the paradoxical ways in which rural religious developments continued to work themselves

out. Things had happened very differently in centres of 'folk Christianity' where Christian leaders had acted as intermediaries between their congregations and the guerrillas during the war. At places like St Killian's in Makoni TTL or Triashill and St Barbara's, or at Toriro in Chiduku, church schools and other plant had remained untouched during the war and were reopening and expanding in early 1981 with full local support.

57 B.H. Kinsey, 'Forever gained: resettlement and land policy in the context of national development in Zimbabwe' in J.D.Y. Peel and T.O. Ranger (eds.), *Past and Present in Zimbabwe* (Manchester: 1983), p. 102,
58 ibid., p. 93.
59 ibid., p. 102.
60 ibid., p. 103
61 Barry Munslow and Phil O'Keefe, 'Hopes buried in the land slide', *The Guardian*, 16 September 1983.
62 Interview with Leonard Ziehl, Rusape, 19 February 1981.
63 *Zimbabwe. Report of the Commission of Inquiry into Incomes, Prices and Conditions of Service*, pp. 34–5.
64 'Manicaland MPs called for "Positive Statement" on Squatter Situation', *Umtali Post*, 11 September 1981.
65 'Squatters: "Our land was stolen from us",' *Moto*, July 1982, p. 6.
66 'Farm Squatter Headache', *Commerce*, vol. 16, April 1982, p. 17.
67 BBC TV 'Newsnight', 11 March 1982.
68 David Caute, 'The politics of rough justice', *New Statesman*, 16 April 1982, pp. 12–13.
69 Interview with Moven Mahachi, Harare, 7 April 1981
70 *ZPNB*, no. 10, August/September 1981, p. 4, citing *Herald*, 10 September 1981.
71 Kinsey, 'Forever gained', p. 101.
72 *ZPNB*, no. 16/17, April–June 1982, P. 22, citing the *Herald*, 11 June 1982.
73 Interview with Amon Shonge and with Emmanuel Nyabadza, Makoni Farm, 11 September 1982.
74 Interview with Moven Mahachi, Harare, 7 April 1981.
75 *ZPNB* no. 16/17, April/June 1982, p. 23, citing the *Herald*, 23 June 1982.
76 Munslow and O'Keefe, 'Hopes buried in the land slide'.
77 Kinsey, 'Forever gained', pp. 98–9, 108. Callear emphasizes that in Wedza all peasant families regard the advantages of labour migration as 'overwhelming'. 'I heard the greatest complaints about the difficulties of making a living from agriculture from families on the most favoured soils with the largest holdings and highest productivity and returns.' (*Social and Cultural Factors Involved in Production*, p. E 10). In a paper given in May 1983 she explored the apparent contrast between my own emphasis on demand for land and her own findings in Wedza that almost nobody gave shortage of land as a major constraint on production. 'When asked what limited the area put to

maize they answered, in order, labour constraints, then lack of draught power, third, lack of cash or credit to buy inputs, and then, fourthly, shortage of land.' She concludes that 'many families do not look to agriculture now or in the future to provide the major part of income but do wish both to continue and to improve their agricultural production.' I suspect that northern Wedza is unusual in that it does not suffer intense land shortage and that, moreover, Callear's respondents were thinking of land acquisition in the context of official resettlement schemes which would indeed not have advantaged them. But her general point that wage inputs are regarded as essential is very widely applicable. As she says 'The "peasant option" is becoming more difficult over time for those families with no other income, and this trend will continue even in the unlikely event of a major redistribution of land holdings from the large farm sector.' ('Who Wants To Be A Peasant?' Food Production in a labour exporting area of Zimbabwe', unpublished paper, May 1983, pp. 10 and 13.

78   Interview with Amon Shonge, Makoni Farm, 11 September 1982.
79   'Squatters: "Our land was stolen from us"', *Moto*, July 1982, p. 6.
80   'Farm Squatter Headache', *Commerce*, vol. 16, April 1982, p. 17.
81   'Squatters: "Our land was stolen from us" ', *Moto*, July 1982, p. 7.
82   'New Land Open to Master Farmers', *Herald*, 7 September 1982.
83   Munslow and O'Keefe, 'Hopes buried in the land slide'. See also 'Settling debts before peasants', *Moto*, September 1983.
84   *ZPNB*, no. 22, November/December 1982, p. 13.
85   'The People of Wenlock Block, Gwanda District and Some People of the Matopo National Park. Ngabe Xosa, Chairman' to Chief Native Commissioner, 23 July 1949, file S.1542.C6, 1940–1952, National Archives, Harare (NAH)
86   Southern Rhodesian African National Congress, Memorandum on Native Land Husbandry Bill, 1951, file MC 104/1/51, NAH.
87   This memorandum is cited in the manuscript autobiography of H.H.C. Holderness.
88   Interview with Amon Shonge, Weya, 25 March 1981.
89   Truscott and Pambieri, 'Census Survey of Chiweshe ward', pp. 2–9.
90   Callear, *The Social and Cultural Factors Involved in Production*, p. E.13.
91   Truscott and Pambieri, 'Census Survey', p. 9.
92   ibid., pp. 12–13.
93   *Herald*, 15 November 1982.
94   *ZPNB*, no. 27, May 1983, pp. 9 et seq.
95   Guy Clutton Brock to St John Evans, 3 August 1950, Chater papers, file K, 'Miscellaneous Correspondence'.
96   G. Paddington Gargwe to Guy Clutton-Brock, 13 March 1954, ibid.
97   'A report on an informal gathering of Producer Co-operatives initiated by Zimbabwe Project at Cold Comfort Farm', 23 January 1982, p. 3. I am grateful to John Conradie for showing me this.
98   Interview with Amon Shonge, Weya, 25 March 1981.

Conclusion

99   Mukute Farm Society, Report, October 1975.
100 Interview with Amon Shonge, Weya, 25 March 1981.
101 Amon Shonge to Guy Clutton-Brock, 28 March 1978, Clutton-Brock correspondence, 1970–80, file 'Correspondence with Amon Shonge'.
102 Mukute Farm Society, Report, August 1980.
103 Mukute Farm Society, Report, May 1977.
104 Amon Shonge to Secretary, Ministry of Lands, Resettlement and Rural Development, 31 May 1980, Shonge letter-book, Mukute.
105 A.K.H. Weinrich, *Struggle for the Land. A History of Co-operatives in Zimbabwe* (Harare: forthcoming), p. 119.
106 Gerulf Augustin, 'Weya Community Training Centre', August 1982.
107 'Fears over setting up co-operatives are irrational', *Herald*, 11 September 1982.
108 Weinrich *Struggle for the Land*, p. 120.
109 'We fought as hard as the squatters in the war', *Herald*, 9 September 1980. A correspondent in *Moto* in September 1983 thought that 'a growing and powerful body determined to curtail any further resettlement' had emerged consisting of 'commercial farmers and of the emergent black landowners'; this alliance had 'finally found receptive ears within government circles where it is increasingly held that the only way to protect Zimbabwe's land. . .is to strengthen the commercial farmers whilst at the same time ensuring that retiring white commercial farmers are replaced by emergent black commercial farmers. . . It is held that peasant farmers will only destroy the land's potential.' *Moto* no. 16, September 1983, p. 16.

APPENDIX 1:

Matabeleland since the end of the war

I am aware that since the end of Chaper 4 of this book I have not dealt with events in rural Matabeleland. This is essentially because I have little or no primary evidence to enable me to do so. On the other hand it seems vitally necessary that the experience of Matabeleland be integrated into the history of Zimbabwe as a whole, particularly into a 'people's history'. I venture some tentative remarks, therefore, based entirely on the reports published in the Zimbabwean press. What has struck me in reading these reports is the remarkable extent to which the contemporary situation in Matabeleland is still shaped by the colonial legacy of expropriation and eviction. Once the commercial farming and ranching region had been firmly established in Matabeleland and had become prosperous, and once the evictions of Africans from that region had been largely completed, it became notoriously difficult in colonial times and remains difficult now to find any viable land upon which to resettle Africans – even more difficult, that is, than was the case in Mashonaland and Manicaland. Colonial administrators themselves admitted frankly that both the Reserves and the Native Purchase Areas set aside in Matabeleland were arid and infertile. The movement of thousands of African families into these lands, which so greatly accelerated in the late 1940s and early 1950s, underlies most of the really severe problems of rural Matabeleland today. The 1981 Commission on Incomes and Prices, for example, found that 'In Chief Mvutu's area, where very little grazing land is left, people used to drive their herds into a nearby forest area, a practice now forbidden. The people are now desperate. They were moved only 25 years ago from a rich area in the Essexvale district.'[1] Moreover, as I remarked above, the possibilities both for squatting and for official resettlement since the end of war vary from district to district depending upon the success of the attack on white farming during the war. In Matabeleland, where the guerrilla war was fought less intensely by ZIPRA, fewer whites abandoned their land and less land became available for voluntary purchase. There are some senses in which dissident attacks on white farms and ranches in the last two years arise out of the failure to mount a true guerrilla war in the 1970s. There are some senses, too, in which the disorder created by dissidents in Matabeleland has given an opportunity for peasants to express in a particularly violent way the resentments built up by Matabeleland's agrarian history. Two incidents reported in October 1982, for example, seem to fall into this category:

The *Herald* carries the story of an 83-year-old farmer in the Tuli commercial farming area, Cde William Sibanda, who was stabbed to death by 5 men who demanded to know where he obtained the money to buy the farm and why he charged communal area farmers for grazing . . . The president of the Matabeleland Commercial Farmers Union says farmers who round up communal area cattle (that peasants have put to graze on their land because of the critical grazing situation) have been threatened with death.[2]

This is a situation in which it is extremely difficult for the new Zimbabwe government to implement a resettlement programme which can meet the needs of Matabeleland peasants – and which would have been extremely difficult for *any* government of Zimbabwe no matter of what political complexion. For one thing, many peasants in Matabeleland remember all too clearly the arbitrary and dislocating removals of the past and are wary of new resettlements:

When the Prime Minister, Mr Mugabe [in October 1981] stood in front of more than 3000 people on a sandy football field and under the blazing sun in Binga his message was simple, reassuring and to the point: 'We are coming to Binga to see how you are living. Although my party won the elections we are united with ZAPU in the Government. We are a government of national unity. Your grievances are of a concern to us all regardless of tribal, racial or political affiliations . . .' According to one council official, land or lack of it, was still a burning issue. It was at Jambezi that Mr Mugabe appealed to the people to fill resettlement forms. The Prime Minister noted that some people had refused to give their names because they were afraid if they did they would 'be taken to some other far away place. I assure you we will not put you where you don't want. We will agree where you can stay.'[3]

For another thing, in the crisis of drought and collapse of grazing in 1982 and 1983 many peasants in Matabeleland reacted to the idea of resettlement in much the same ways as their predecessors of the 1930s. They still looked to chiefs and 'big men' to act as leaders and spokesmen, and they still demanded additional land for grazing

rather than for agrarian resettlement. 'The resettlement programme ran into a different sort of problem in the Western Province,'
noted the Zimbabwe Project bulletin in December 1981:

from where it was reported that only 2.7% of the 88,000 people circularised
with resettlement application forms had responded. . . There was a desire
by some people 'to move as a village group together with their chief. This
was in direct conflict with the Government policy which was not aimed at
creating extension of chiefs' families in newly resettled areas' . . . Another
reason cited for the poor response was that 'the Matabeleland people did
not agree that the resettlement scheme worked out by the Government
would redress their problems, mainly in grazing . . . The Government was
having a second look [because] the agriculture orientated scheme, while
suitable to regions in Mashonaland, might not be entirely satisfactory in the
stock-oriented Matabeleland.[4]

In June 1982 the Deputy Minister of Lands and Resettlement, Mark
Dube, made a tour of Matabeleland resettlement schemes. He
remarked that 'some people were demanding that land be made
available solely for grazing', but declared that the government's
intention was 'to buy property and settle the people. We cannot say
people should move their cattle into the properties we bought
without making arrangements for proper resettlement . . . Making
land available for grazing would benefit people with cattle at the
expense of the landless without cattle.'[5]
    Dube's two meetings in Gwanda read like a heightened version of
Native Board meetings in the 1930s:

One district councillor after another rose to demand that the resettlement
priorities be reversed to give priority to grazing land. 'Cattle raising is our
lifeblood. We would rather stay crowded in the communal areas and let the
purchased farms be used for grazing', said one councillor . . . The deputy
minister said Government was aware of the stock-oriented nature of the
economy of the region. . . Mr Dube challenged some councillors who said
they did not want to move from places where 'our ancestors are buried'.
'What the Government is saying is: Look for a better place to live rather
than the place of your ancestors. You can imagine how much movement
throughout the country there would be if everybody decided they wanted to
live where their ancestors lie buried'.

Later Dube met about a hundred peasants at Sitezi business centre
in Gwanda and ran into very articulate opposition:

Peasants rose one after another to demand that the resettlement schemes
be solely for grazing purposes. 'We are happy where we are. We only need
grazing land for our starving cattle', was a typical comment. But Mr Dube

repeated that Government policy was that people should be given priority over animals. In a voice that occasionally rose with impatience he stressed that the Government was not minimising the importance of cattle. It was eager to ensure that people in resettlement areas entered into modern and productive methods of stockbreeding. It was for this reason that before land could be opened, resettlement and Agritex officials had to prepare it and teach people better methods of breeding stock. Mr Dube was interrupted again by one peasant who said he had not come to be taught cattle breeding. Another said: 'The intimidation of the resettlement officers is not our responsibility until we get grazing land for our cattle. Don't talk to us about policing this area. We will do so as soon as we have been given more land for grazing.'[6]

In July 1982 at a meeting of peasant farmers and resettlement officers at Ntabazinduna, Chief Ndiweni characterized official resettlement policies as 'un-African and against the wishes of the people . . . All they want is an extension of the communal lands'.[7]

The government has interpreted such objections in class terms and in terms of political manipulation. Early in July 1982 Dube himself 'described the few who has resisted the Government resettlement policy during the meetings as a few petty bourgeois who have a few hundred cattle and were more concerned with their cattle. "They forget the majority of the people who are poor". Their resistance would be short-lived as the poor and landless masses would battle against their bourgeois mentality.' A *Herald* editorial had remarked earlier that 'For almost two decades a political party which always claimed to be the natural party for the Ndebele-speaking people had been claiming, dangerously, that unless it is in power, the Ndebele people will always be at the bottom of the rung of the economic ladder. The poor response to resettlement and other development schemes in certain parts of Matabeleland is a case in point.'[8] And there is no doubt that resettlement schemes have been made the object of attack by dissidents. Thus in June and July 1983 three resettlement villages in Dombodema and Lupane were destroyed by armed dissidents who accused settlers of 'selling out' by participating.[9]

In the context of the whole historical record of the twentieth century, I would guess that the fundamental socio-economic problems of rural Matabeleland allow politicians and 'big men' to manipulate peasant feeling, but that if the government is going to succeed in separating the 'poor and landless masses' from chiefs and large cattle owners and dissidents it can only do so by finding ways of resolving these problems. I would guess that it is around these issues rather than around the question of ethnic rivalry, which has so obsessed the overseas press, that the contemporary history of

Matabeleland revolves. In 1983 as well as the much publicized military and police actions against dissidents there were signs of a real attempt to recast policy so as to meet the needs of the peasants. 'A new resettlement model for dry areas is being planned'.[10] ZANU/PF 'men of the people', like Maurice Nyagumbo, have been campaigning in rural Matabeleland, holding week-end 'seminars' with peasants. More land in the commercial farming area has become available for purchase. And it seems to me that historians could help in the resolution of peasant problems in Matabeleland by tracing very much more effectively than I have done the particular agrarian history of that province.

NOTES

1   *Zimbabwe. Report of the Commission of Inquiry into Incomes, Prices and Conditions of Service* (Harare; Government Printer: June 1981), p. 35
2   *Zimbabwe Project News Bulletin* (*ZPNB*), no. 21, October 1982, pp. 3–4, noting news items carried in the *Herald* on 12 and 14 October.
3   *ZPNB*, no. 11, October 1981, p. 5.
4   *ZPNB*, no. 12, November/December 1981, p. 4 citing *Herald*, 22 October 1981, the quotations being from a Ministry of Lands and Resettlement spokesman.
5   *ZPNB*, no. 16/17, April/June 1982, p. 24.
6   ibid., pp. 24–25, citing the *Herald* of 5 and 29 June 1982.
7   *ZPNB*, no. 19, August 1982, p. 9, citing the *Herald*, 27 July 1982.
8   ibid., p. 7; *ZPNB*, no. 14, February/March 1982, p. 19.
9   *The Guardian*, 18 June and 8 July 1983.
10 *ZPNB*, no. 23, January 1983, p. 6.

APPENDIX 2:

Peasant religion in contemporary Zimbabwe

Although I have written at some length about the role of religious belief in peasant consciousness in earlier chapters, I had no space to discuss its contemporary significance in my Conclusion. A few words are perhaps necessary to carry all the themes of this book through to the present.

In general one should perhaps make the point that the religious atmosphere of contemporary Zimbabwe is very different from that of post-independence Kenya or post-independence Mozambique. In Mozambique the Catholic church, with its long history of collaboration with the Salazar regime, is viewed with a fully understandable suspicion and hostility: in Zimbabwe, or at least in certain areas of Zimbabwe, Catholic priests worked closely with the guerrillas, and Catholic educational institutions have been encouraged to reopen and expand. In Mozambique, manifestations of 'traditional' religious ideas are judged to be 'obscurantist', even when connected to popular traditions of anti-colonial resistance. In Zimbabwe, on the other hand, cabinet ministers have attributed their victory in the war and the elections to the power of the ancestral spirits. As for Kenya, while there has been an ebullient expansion of Christianity since independence, 'traditional' religious ideas have been officially condemned as 'unprogressive', and there is little evidence that 'seers' have continued to be influential in Kikuyu country since the end of Mau Mau. Spirit mediums, however, continue to be influential in Zimbabwe, not only at the level of cultural nationalist rhetoric, but in the rural areas.

They have continued to be influential because they are still playing the combination of roles which made them so important during the war. Their endorsement, which gave legitimacy to the guerrillas, now gives legitimacy to village committees. They can still speak in the voice of the ancestors in order to articulate the peasant political programme. And they remain relevant to rural production. In the Dande, writes David Lan, 'the chiefs have gone, but the spirit mediums remain.' At the time Lan was working in the Dande the political functions of the chiefs had been taken over by the village ZANU/PF committees, which administered law, allocated land and settled disputes. The elected members of these committees visited the local spirit medium soon after their election to seek 'his approval and advice'; at the beginning of every meeting of the village committees in Dande the intermediary of the local *mhondoro* spirit asked 'his approval of the business of the day.' The medium who worked most closely with the guerrillas during the war has announced while in trance the abrogation of the ritual prohibitions which reserved certain foods for chiefs alone–the people through their elected representatives, are the chiefs now. Yet the same medium has also articulated peasant political grievances 'at the slow rate of progress achieved by the government in fulfilling their promises of economic aid to the Dande region.'[1]

The mediums, moreover, have taken up a series of explicit positions on the character of the rural economy in the new Zimbabwe. Some have argued that the avoidance of white technology which was necessary while political power rested with aliens is now no longer appropriate: so long as the *chisi* days are observed and due veneration paid to the ancestors, peasants should use fertilizers and seek the advice of extension workers. Others have continued to be suspicious of 'modernizing' techniques. Yet others have endorsed cooperative forms of production. In the Dande, Lan tells us, the 'medium of Chiodzamamera combines his reputation as rainbringer and hero of the resistance with his position as elected chairman of a small cooperative farming group.'[2] The members of Mukute cooperative in Weya affirm their belief in the protection of the spirits – 'during the difficulites we were totally relying on God and on our spirit mediums', Amon Shonge told A.K.H. Weinrich, 'who really were our saviours throughout the war. If it had not been for them we would all have died'. Meanwhile, as Weinrich writes, at the long-established cooperative at Nyafaru, on the Inyanga border with Mozambique:

traditional African religion constantly grew in importance. The spirit medium directed the lives of the Tangwena people and the members of Nyafaru also listened to the medium and carried out its orders. As soon as Nyafaru was reorganised under completely African leadership, the whole way of life became much more focussed on traditional values than had ever been the case at Cold Comfort Farm, where Europeans actively shared in the lives of the youths.

Tinaani, now leader at Nyafaru, told her:

The spirit medium has always been important to us and is so even today. We always follow its advice because it helped us much during the war. During the war, of course, we could not observe the appropriate ritual because we had no opportunity to brew beer and beat drums to cause the medium to become possessed. Now we can make up for this . . . These days the medium is telling us to grow more maize and millet and that we shall have a good future. It also says that many people are looking to us for help, and that we should work together cooperatively to improve the future for all people.[3]

In July 1983 a panel on religion and resistance in Africa took place in London during the course of a History Workshop conference on Religion and Society. I gave a paper describing the combined ideology of peasants and guerrillas during the Zimbabwean war in much the same terms as I have in this book. Basil Davidson was in the chair. In the revised version of my paper I sought to summarize the concluding differences between us on the topic of religion and transformation in Zimbabwe:

[Basil Davidson's] comment was that he thought we were arguing at two different levels. He did not dispute that peasants could be mobilised in the way I have described. But unless there developed within the liberation movement as a whole a more effective 'modern' ideology there could not after the war be an effective transformation of colonial society nor could the needs of peasants be met. The regular appeal to the memory of the great mediums by ZANU/PF politicians, which was one legacy of the role of religion in the war, did not seem to bode well for the emergence of an effective modernising ideology. And as for the peasants, they were certainly able to participate very effectively in the war, at each local level, by drawing on the sort of ideologies I have been describing. But these did not allow them to demand and to produce the sort of state which could or would bring about a profound revolution in the rural economy. I think that maybe we are still arguing about something substantive. To my mind it is everywhere almost impossible for peasants, no matter how ideologically sophisticated, to be able to create for themselves a state which will act in their interests. There is an inevitable tension between peasantries and states, even revolutionary and liberationary states. To my mind, if peasant programmes are to be achieved, this has to be done by means of constant peasant pressures upon the state. In Zimbabwe there has been, since the war, very effective peasant pressure, especially in the form of peasant 'squatting', the mass invasion of the lost lands. Peasants have continued to demand more land and less interference. And this demand is certainly still powered by religious ideologies, as spirit mediums continue to claim the land of the ancestors and as local folk Christian communities continue to exercise the autonomy from hierarchies which they won during the war.[4]

The conclusion of this citation reminds us that even during the war the religious elements in radical peasant consciousness were by no means exclusively provided by the spirit mediums. Since the end of the war, as rural solidarities have necessarily given way to social, generational and ideological divisions, rural Christianity has become more important. The government and party, emphasizing educational expansion, have encouraged the churches to reopen and enlarge their schools. The old connection in the mind of the peasantry between education and Christianity persists, even if many primary schools are now run by elected councils and not by any church. In this way, the administrative structures of the churches have resumed importance. But at the same time the local, organic Christian communities, which survived the war on their own, hold on to their new powers of initiative. 'Since the 4th April 1966 when the first guns were fired at Sinoia', Reverend N.P. Mudzvovera told the Anglican Synod in July 1980:

Christians in Tribal Trust Lands became open to war propaganda. This propaganda has shaped the thinking and life of these Christians to such an extent that some of these Christians are now different Christians from the Christians they were before the war started. Their thinking has been very much coloured by the events of the war . . . In what direction is the Anglican church in Zimbabwe going?[5]

'Methods and ideas which were effective in previous years no longer had the same impact,' reported the travelling liason officer of the Buriro/Esizeni Reflection Centre in July 1982, 'since the liberation war had changed congregations from unquestioning, passive recipients of the word coming from authority into challenging, analytical thinkers who recognise that degree of authority which is in themselves.'[6] The Buriro/Esizeni centre itself exists to give articulation to rural religious initiatives and to transform ecclesiastical institutions from within by 'guerrilla warfare tactics: working on specific targets bit by bit until the whole fabric of the institution is changed'. 'It was found that often outside of formal church programmes the people of Zimbabwe were reflecting critically on the meaning of their Christian faith in the context of the liberation war, the developing national socialist character, and their traditional roots. Buriro/Esizeni seeks to encourage and bring into the open this reflection.'[7]

Meanwhile out in the rural areas religious ceremonial has succeeded in dramatizing and commemorating the suffering of the rural population during the war. I have written above, for instance, of the killing of Basil Nyabadza, storeowner and priest, during the

Appendix 2

war in Makoni District. Since his death the African Sisters, novices and other members of St Francis African Church have commemorated their slain pastor in a ceremony on the anniversary of his death, 1 April. Nyabadza has been buried by the side of his father, Francis, founder of the church; a shrine has been erected at the spot in the church courtyard where he was killed; together with the church itself, this grave and this shrine constitute a formidable concentration of spiritual power on the edge of Makoni communal area. Every year the various religious traditions of the district come together to commemorate Nyabadza's death – on the evening before, ex-*mujibas* come to dance and sing the *chimurenga* songs to the ancestral spirits; on the day of the annual commemoration African priests and catechists of the mission churches come to receive communion from the hands of Basil's son, Francis, now pastor of this little independent church. Old Chief Makoni attends, and the members of the ZANU/PF district committee, and ZANU/PF members of parliament and cabinet ministers. On 1 April 1983 Robert Mugabe himself attended the commemoration and spoke both of Nyabadza's own role in the war and of the way in which his death was a reminder of the general rural suffering:

Cde Nyabadza continued, especially after Zanla had opened the eastern military front . . . to supply, as best he could, the needs of the 'boys'. It was for that reason that the Smith regime's soldiers killed him in 1977. The death of Basil Nyabadza robbed his family and St. Francis of Assisi of their beloved father in both the physical and spiritual sense. It also robbed the people of Makoni of a great man they always regarded as father of the poor (Baba vevarombo) . . . To my party, Zanu, and the people of Zimbabwe generally, his cruel death deprived us of a stalwart freedom fighter . . . As we remember Basil Nyabadza today, let us not forget that the freedom we the survivors now enjoy could never have been achieved without the degree of extreme sacrifice which entailed the death and suffering of people like him.[8]

It seems clear, in short, that the long history of peasant religious consciousness has still a great deal of life left in it.

NOTES

1 David Lan, 'Making History. Spirit mediums and the guerrilla war in the Dande area of Zimbabwe' (London School of Economics: PhD thesis, 1983), pp. 304, 305, 310. Lan writes: 'His warning was perfectly clear. it was, he said, the *mhondoro* who had enabled the present

government to come to power. If they failed the people, and therefore failed the ancestors, the *mhondoro* would transfer their moral authority elsewhere.'
2 ibid., p. 316.
3 A.K.H. Weinrich, *Struggle for the Land. A History of Co-operatives in Zimbabwe* (Harare: forthcoming), pp. 115, 273, 239.
4 Terence Ranger, 'Religion in the Zimbabwe guerrilla war', History Workshop, London, July 1983, p. 18.
5 'Hopes and aspirations of the black Anglican Christians in the independent Zimbabwe', 9 July 1980, Matewa Papers, Toriro.
6 *Buriro*/Esizeni Reflection Centre seminar, 26 and 27 September 1981.
7 *Buriro/Esizeni Threshing Floor*, vol. 1, no. 2, (June/July 1983). p. 1.
8 'Mugabe Pays Tribute to Slain Priest', *Sunday Mail*, 3 April 1983.

SOURCES
AND SELECT
BIBLIOGRAPHY

PRIMARY SOURCES

Native Department, Makoni District; National Archives of Zimbabwe, Harare (NAZ)

Files N 3/1/10 and N 3/1/11, Native Commissioner, Makoni, correspondence.

Files NUA 1/1/1, NUA 1/1/2, NUA 1/2/1, NUA 2/1/1 to NUA 2/1/12, NUA 3/1/1 to NUA 3/1/3, NUA 3/2/1 and 3/23/2, Superintendent of Natives, Umtali, correspondence.

Files NUD 2/1/1 and NUD 2/1/2, Civil Cases, Rusape District Court.

Files D 3/33/1 to D 3/33/5 and D 4/40/1, Criminal Cases, Rusape District Court.

Files S.289, S.2173/1, S.377 (five volumes), S.1382, S.538, S.1695 (five volumes), S.2172 (two volumes), S.1695 (11 volumes), Criminal Cases, Rusape Court.

Monthly reports for Makoni and other Districts (NAZ)

Files N 9/4/1 to N 9/4/45, monthly reports, 1899 to 1923.

Files NUA 6/2/1 to NUA 6/2/3, monthly reports, Manicaland, 1909 to 1913; 1917 to 1923. File S.235/519 to S.235/539, monthly reports, 1923 to 1937.

Files S.1619/1937 to S.1619/1947, monthly reports, 1937 to 1947.

File N 3/33/12, vols. 1 and 2, Chief Native Commissioner's correspondence on matters arising from monthly reports.

Quarterly reports for Makoni and other Districts (NAZ)

File LO 5/4/1, folio 448, quarterly report, Umtali, 11 January 1897.

File LO 5/4/6, folio 124, half yearly report, Makoni, 30 June 1987.

File N 3/1/10, quarterly report, Makoni, October 1898.

File Series 1618, Chief Native Commissioner's summaries of quarterly reports, 1927-36; 1938-47; District quarterly reports, 1946-52.

Annual reports for Makoni and other Districts (NAZ)

File series N 9/1/1 to N 9/1/26, annual reports, 1897-1923.

File series S.235/500, annual reports from 1923.

File series S.1563, annual reports, 1938-48.

Native Department/Internal Affairs, Makoni District

Files consulted in the District Commissioner's office, Rusape, since sent to the Ministry of Local Government, Harare;

File series on Chiefs and Headmen

'Old papers on Chief Makoni', 1921–52.
'Makoni', 1916–75.
'Chief Chipunza. Chiduku', 1966–78.
'Chief Tandi. Chiduku', 1938–76.
'Chief Chiduku. Chiduku', 1937–79.
'Headman Nedewedzo. Chiduku', 1944–79.
'Headman Bvekerwa. Chiduku', 1959–76.
'Headman Rukweza. Chiduku', 1958–78.
'Headman Dzwairo. Chiduku', 1963–79.
'Headman Masvosva. Chiduku', 1957–77.
'Headman Nyangombe. Chiduku', 1968–79.
'Headman Mudzimikunze. Chiduku', 1964–77.
'Headman Madziwa. Makoni', 1958–77.
'Headman Rugoyi. Makoni', 1966–78.
'Headman Ngirazi. Makoni', 1975.
'Headman Changadzo. Makoni', 1968–73.
'Headman Nyamende Ngorima, Makoni', 1958–73
'Headman Gandanzara. Makoni', 1958–78.
'Headman Makumbe. Tanda', 1966–78.
'Headman Maparura. Tanda', 1960–75.
'Chief Chendambuya, Weya', 1934–76.
'Headman Mwendaziuya. Weya'.
'Chief Chikore. Chikore', 1940–76.

File series on kraals

'Kraal information. Gandanzara'.
'Kraal History. Headman Maparura'.
'Kraal Analysis. Chemere Maparura'.

Other files

'Weya. Spirit Mediums', 1975.
'Schools', 1974–6.
'St Faith's', 1957–77.
File GN 202/45, land allocation in Tanda.
Police and Administrative Assistant's reports, January/February 1981.
Memorandum by District Criminal Investigation Officer, Rusape, 3 March 1981.
'Confidential Correspondence. District Commissioners', March to December 1980.

Rhodesia Intelligence Corps Mapping and Research Unit, set of maps
produced in 1978 showing abandoned farms, spirit medium headquarters, guerrilla bases, etc, in Makoni Distric.

Native Department, General Correspondence (NAZ)

Chiefs and Headmen

A 3/18/18/2, A 11/2/12/11, A 11/2/12/12.
N 3/4/1 to N 3/4/5.
N 3/31/5 Murder of Native Messenger Rudzidzo. Inquiries into role of
Chief Makoni.
N 3/33/8.
N 9/5/3.
NUA 2/1/12.
S.628/1227, Preliminary examination. Criminal Sessions, Umtali, Rud-
zidzo case, 1919–20.
S.1561/10 to S.1561/17, Chiefs and Headmen, 1916–34.
S.1542.C6, many volumes, alphabetically indexed, 1935–52.

'Delineation of Communities. Makoni District', November/December
1965.

Reserves and Land Apportionment

A 3/18/39/10, Chiduku Reserve, 1911–20.
AT 1/2/11/8.
L. 2/2/117/31.
N. 3/24/16.
S. 138/21, five volumes, land correspondence, 1926–32.
S. 138/197, Centralisation and Land Apportionment, 1925.
S. 235/370.
S. 924/G1/5; S.924/G6/2.
S.988. Native Affairs. Oral Evidence. Natural Resources Board Native
Enquiry, 1942.
S.1123, seven volumes, Minutes of Native Land Board, 1930–6.
S.1542.L4, three volumes, 1933–9.
S.1542. F2, 1935–9.
S.160.LS/3A/50, to S.160.LS/3C/50.
S.160.LS/100/1/50 to S.160.LS/106/1/50.
S.160.LS/101/3/50, LS/103/1/50, to LS/103/4/50, LS 104/1/50.
S.160.DMN/2/12/51, Native Land Board minutes, 1949 to 1952.
S.160.DMN/33/55, Native Affairs Advisory Board, 1953 to 1956. S.1619.
ZAD 3/1/1 and ZAD 3/2/, Reserves Commission evidence, 1915.

African agriculture

S.138/206, Demonstrators and African agriculture, 1924–7.

S.138/72, two files, 1927–33.

S.1542.A4, six files, 1933–9.

S.1542.M2, Maize Control Correspondence, 1933–6.

S.160.ACC/14/133/53, Monthly reports of Provincial Agriculturalist, N.Mashonaland, 1953 to 1954; annual reports of Provincial Agriculturalists, 1952–5.

S.160.AGR/4/6/51, monthly reports, Land Development Officers, Manicaland, 1951–3.

S.160.AGR/4/3/51 to AGR/7/51, monthly reports, other Provinces.

S.160.AGR/5/25/55, Natural Resources Board, 1954–6.

S.160.AGR/16/1/54, Centralisation and Native Purchase, 1953–4.

S.160.CG/102/2/50, Groundnuts, 1947.

S.160.CM/100/50, Maize, 1946–50.

S.160.GC1 and GC2, General correspondence, African agriculture, 1945–50.

S.160.MC/103/2/50, African Voice Association protest meetings, 1951.

S.1611, Agricultural statistics, 1948.

ZBJ 1/1/2 and 1/2/2, evidence and working papers, Native Trade and Production Commission, 1944.

Farms and farmers

A 3/9/8.

A 3/18/8.

DT 6/1/1.

E 2/11/51/1 to E 2/11/51/5, Farm schools, 1914–20.

E 5/3/27/1, Farm schools, 1917–23.

L 2/3/45, L 4/4/16.

M 3/10/123, Makoni Farmers Association, 1915–23.

M 3/10/211 to M 3/10/215, Rural roads.

S 231, S.246.55, S.1215/1207/1, S.1232.3882, Barnes Pope.

Health

H 2/4/19, District Surgeon, 1913–22.

H 2/10/6, African Dispensaries, 1912–14.

Various administrative correspondence

A 3/18/33/1 and A 3/18/33/2, labour crisis of 1911 and Makoni inquiry.

MC 103/2/51, British African Voice Association, 1951.

MC 104/1/51, Debate on Land Husbandry Act, 1951.

N 3/28/2, Labour crisis of 1911.

S.138.10, five files, 'African Advancement', 1923–33.

S.138.22, seven files, General correspondence, 1923–33.

S.138.260, Native Affairs Act, 1926–8.

S.1542.A6, file series, Associations, 1933–40.

S.1542.N2, Native Boards, Matabeleland, 1931–9.
S.1542.S12, file series, African development, 1835–9.
S.4813.2/43, Land Husbandry, 1951.

Material on African religion

Administrative files on missions and independent churches (NAZ)

A 3/6/1 to A 3/6/10, file series on missions and independent churches, to early 1920s.
A 3/18/3 and A 3/18/11.
L 2/1/236, Triashill, 1901–9.
N 3/5/1/1 to N 3/5/1/8, file series, missions and schools, 1901–22.
N 3/5/2 to N 3/5/8, file series, independent churches.
NUC 1/3/1, Triashill, 1915–7.
S.138.17, four files, missions and churches, 1924-33.
S.138.226, series of files, independent churches.
S.138.48, Apostolic Faith Church.
S.158.143, missions and schools, 1923.
S.840/1/3 to S.840/5/3, government grants to missions, 1920s.
S.840/1/18 to S.840/3/18, government grants to missions, 1920s.
S.1542.M8, three files, missions and churches, 1933-9.
S.1542.M8B, Apostolic Faith Mission, two files, 1924-39.
S.1542.P10, 'Pseudo-religious', 1934-6.
S.1542.R10, African nuns, 1930s.
S.2014/6/27, Triashill hospital, 1928-38.

Mission files; Roman Catholic

In the Jesuit Archives, Mount Pleasant, Harare:

Box 139, Correspondence on Triashill.
Box 146, Correspondence relating to Monte Cassino.
Box 163, Correspondence relating to St Benedict's Weya.
Box 195, Correspondence relating to Triashill.
Box 196, drafts by Hylda Richards towards a history of Triashill.
Box 209, Father Brosig's letters, Triashill, 1930s.
Box 260, Correspondence on language.
Box 300, Correspondence on African nuns.

At Triashill church, Manyika:

'Chronicle of Triashill', 1895-1947.
File 'Old letters', 1946-62.
Minute book of the Catholic Association, 1960s and 1970s.
Box 'District Commissioner and Government Correspondence', 1977.
Box 'Newspaper cuttings'.
File '1963 -1979. Papers relating to Triashill Farm'.

Sources and select bibliography

Black Minute-book, Carmelite Diary, 1955-68, with letters interleaved.
P.D. Chiwara, 'Sister Ida Mwatse', record of an interview, September 1973.

At St Killian's church, Makoni:

Historia Domus, 1951-60.
File 'Old Forgotten Far Off Things and Battles long ago', 1922-64.

At St Barbara's church, Manyika:

Journal, 1933-68, interleaved.

Mission files; Anglican

In the National Archives of Zimbabwe: Harare personal deposits:

CR 4/1/1 and CR 5/1/6, Arthur Shearly Cripps correspondence, 1920-54.
LL 1/1/1 to LL 1/1/3, Edgar Lloyd correspondence, 1916-34.
PA 7/1/2, Paget collection, St Faith's farm, 1971.
PE 3/1/1 and 3/1/3, Douglas Pelly correspondence, 1892-7.

In NAZ, deposits by the Anglican church:

ANG 1/1/7, correspondence between Lloyd and Paget, 1927.
ANG 1/1/15, Paget out-letters, 1929-33.
ANG 16/1/1/1. St Faith's Executive Committee, 1952.
ANG 16/1/8, St Faith's farm, 1940s and 1950s.
ANG 16/1/10, St Faith's, Epiphany and out-stations, 1930s and 1940s.
ANG 16/4/1, Case book of Executive Committee, St Faith's, 1950s.
ANG 16/6/9/1, St Faith's Hospital log, 1945-55.
ANG 16/7/5, St Faith's farm, 1953 and 1954.
ANG 16/11/1, Circular letters from Olive Lloyd, 1933 and 1934.
ANG 16/17/1/1 to ANG 16/17/1/4, Materials relating to St Faith's.
ANG 16/17/7, 'Notes of a Journey'.

In the United Society for the Propagation of the Gospel archives, Westminister:

SPG Annual Reports, 1920-39.
Missionary correspondence, 1920-39.

Mission files; American Methodists

In the archives of the Old Umtali mission:

Letter-books of R. Wodehouse, April 1902 to March 1906.
Box-file series:
'J.R. Gates'

'Wodehouse'
'Coffin'
'Baba Greeley'
'Finance Committee Notes, 1913 to 1921'
'District Misc. D.S's office, Mtasa. Makoni', 1964-9.
Note-book 'Out-stations', 1916.
Black ledger, 'Record of Out-stations'.
Black ledger, 'Record of Pastor-Teachers'.
Brown folders, 'Teachers and Workers up to 1928'.

Capital red box-files:
'Miscellaneous correspondence'
'African sermons noted by H.N. Howard'

Green Files: 'Early District Conference'
'Early Christians'
'E.L. Sells'
'Sells letters'
'Archives'
'Christian Conference'
'Conference Reports. Nyadiri', 1959.
'Language Policy'.
'Agriculture'.
'Old Umtali Executive Committee'.

Buff files complied by Shepherd Machuma:
'Revival'.
'1918 Revival and Chibvuwi'.
'Healing of Dorcas Muredzwa'.
'Mtasa'.
'Evangelism'.
'Out-stations'.
'Persons'.
'Women'.
'Agriculture'.
'Makoni'.

Independent church files: Church of God Temple Beth-El.

In the possession of A. Mukuwaza, Tandi: letter from A. Mukuwaza to Meir
     Kagirer, Bar-Ilan University, Israel, 16 May 1978.

The African Church of St Francis

'A brief summary for the African Church History'.
Sekuru Nyanpfene,' 'Baba Tafatiresu Nyabadza', 1981.

Sources and select bibliography

Material in archives other than NAZ or missions

Archives of the Catholic Commission of Justice and Peace, Harare.

Files and packets:

'Counter-terrorism', 1973.
'Maurice Nyagumbo and Phillip Foya', 1975.
'Miscellaneous Papers', 1976.
'Reverend Kuwana and Wife murdered', 1976.
'Murder. Mr Nyaume', 1976.
'Selous Scouts', 1976 and 1977.
'Civilian Deaths', 1977.
'Guerrilla Reports', 1977.
'Collective Punishment', 1977.
'Isidore Katsere', 1977.
'Guerrilla Reports', 1978.
'Security Force Reports', 1979.
'Particular incidents: Auxiliaries', 1980.

Mr Pasipanodya, 'A Middle Class Business Man in a War Zone', February 1979.
African Farmers Union report, February 1979.

Archives of the Makoni Rural District Council, Rusape

A.5 'Vengere'.
A.6. Headlands'.
A.12 'Sansaguru'.
C.1 'Civil Defence', 1977-9.
G.3 'General Correspondence'.
L.7 'Land Tenure'.
R.3 'Reports'.

Collection of *Makoni Clarion*, February 1977 to November 1980.

Archives of the Centre for Southern African Studies, University of York

Justice and Peace Commission, Harare, file 1, Chiweshe reports, 1974.

Material in Private hands

Patricia Chater papers

Deposited in NAZ, but listed here in the original file sequence in which they were consulted at St Francis, Makoni:

File A, 'Makoni Students Association', 1954-8; 'Letters to parents', 1952; 'Materials on the African National Congress', 1957-9.
File B, 'St Faith's Discussion Group', 1956-9; five note-books of the Discussion Group's meetings, 1956-60.
File C, 'Correspondence with African Development Trust', 1958-60; 'Correspondence on the case of Edwin Mutasa'; 'Correspondence with Bishop Paget', 1956.
File D, 'Future of St Faith's, Diocese, etc', 1957-60.
File E, 'Correspondence', 1960.
File F, 'Correspondence', 1961.
File G, 'Press Cuttings'.
File H, 'Duplicates'.
File I, 'Letters to Donors', 1958-61.
File J, 'Co-operative', 1954-6.
File K, 'Miscellaneous Correspondence'.
File L, 'Drafts. Reports'.
File M, 'Adult Education'.
File N, 'Co-operative Society'.

Two sets of note-books, 'Headman's Meeting. Minutes' and 'Meetings. Notes'. 1949-55.

Retained at St Francis:
'Miscellanous Correspondence', 1977.
'St Francis. Miscellanous', 1960-73.
'Miscellaneous Correspondence', 1975-7, including Inquest Proceedings on the death of Basil Nyabadza, 18-20 July 1977.

Guy Clutton-Brock correspondence files

Now in the care of the author.
'Letters from Patricia Chater', 1971-80.
'Letters from Arthur Chazingwa', 1971-80.
'Letters from Didymus Mutasa', three files, 1972-80.
'Letters from Moven Mahachi', 1970s.
'Letters from Stephen Matewa', 1971-80.
'Letters from Amon Shonge', 1977-81.
'Letters from Edgar Tekere, Sally Mugabe, etc', 1974-8.

Packets of documents relating to ZAPU, ZANU, FROLIZI, PF, UANC.
Packets of correspondence with detainees, prisoners and others.

Jack Grant papers

Now in NAZ, but consulted in Cambridge.
Circular letters from Epworth, January 1976 to May 1976.
'Mission Farms. St Faith's and Hlekweni, December 1975/January 1976'.

Patrick Kwesha materials

In the care of Augustine Kwesha, Manyika.
'Memorandum Book: Will – To Renew The Face of the World'.
Note-book, 'The Habit'.
Red note-book, 'Wrote 1943. Johannesburg'.

Stephen Matewa materials

In possession of Stephen Matewa, Toriro, Chiduku.
Correspondence files, 1976-7.
Two copy books of correspondence, 1978-80.

Amon Shonge materials

In Amon Shonge's possession, Mukute, Weya.
Letter-book, Mukute, 1980.
Constitution of Mukute Farm Society, January 1981.
Circular letters, M.F.S., October 1975, May 1977, September 1978, August 1980.
'Weya Community Training Centre', August 1982.

Oral Interviews

From the Oral History collection at NAZ

Between Dawson Munjeri and Amon Alwen Nengomasha, 17 February and 3 March 1977, AOH/4.
Between Dawson Munjeri and Aaron Mutambirwa Makoni, 10 and 17 May 1979, AOH/54.
Between Dawson Munjeri and Sylvester Mushauripo, 14 February 1980, AOH/65.

Interviews carried out by John Conradie, Maputo, August 1979

With Tongogara, Kangai, Samuel Mamutsi Mrimbo, Simon Muzenda, Didymus Mutasa, Edgar Tekere.

Interviews carried out by Terence Ranger

With Maurice Nyagumbo, Harare, 14 January 1981.
With Columbus Makoni, Harare, 29 January 1981.
With Bishop Peter Hatendi, Harare, 29 January 1981.
With District Commissioner, Rusape, 2 February 1981.
With Archdeacon Alban Makoni, Rusape, 2 February 1981.
With Secretary, Makoni Rural District Council, 2 February 1981.

With Father G. Gwatidzo, St Faith's, 3 February 1981.
With Father Michael, Triashill, 4 February 1981.
With Father Isaiah Gosho, St Faith's, 5 February 1981.
With District Commissioner, Rusape, 6 February 1981.
With Roland Hatendi, Tandi, 7 February 1981.
With Ambrose Joash Mukuwaza, Elder Madziwandzira, Deacon Solomon Mukamba, Church of God, Tandi, 7 February 1981.
With Chief Makoni Muzananemo and councillors, Makoni, 8 February 1981.
With the ZANU/PF Village Committee, Zumbani, Makoni, 9 and 10 February 1981.
With Eric Mugadza, Makoni, 10 February 1981.
With Father Vernon, St Killian's, Makoni, 10 February 1981.
With Comrades Tangwena and Trigger, Rusape, 13 February 1981.
With Isaac Tsungo, Mbobo, 14 February 1981.
With Father Vernon, St Killian's Makoni, 15 February 1981.
With George Bhongoghozo, Rusape, 16 February 1981.
With Lameck Madzwendira (Comrade Mutsawareyi), Makoni, 16 February 1981.
With Columbus Makoni, Rusape, 18 February 1981.
With Leonard Ziehl, Rusape, 19 February 1981.
With Ambrose Mukuwaza and Roland Hatendi, 21 February 1981.
With Comrade Kisswell, north Makoni, 22 February 1981.
With Donnie Chimhowa (Comrade Chaminuka), Makoni, 23 February 1981.
With S. Nengomasha, Chairman; W. Mauye, Vice-Chairman; P. Matimba, Secretary of the Makoni District Committee of ZANU/PF, Rusape, 24 February 1981.
With Langton Charidza, Rusape, 25 February 1981.
With Father Michael Kenny, St Barbara's, 26 February 1981.
With Philip Van Heerden, Rusape, 27 February 1981.
With S.D. Madziwandzira, Tandi, 27 February 1981.
With Robert Tinarwo, medium of Akuchwa, Tandi, 27 February 1981.
With Chief Tandi, Tandi, 27 February 1981.
With African ex-Selous Scout, Rusape, 27 February 1981.
With Augustine Kwesha, St Xavier's, Manyika, 28 February 1981.
With Erita Karimupfumbi and Rafael Hakutangwi, Manyika, 28 February 1981.
With Iona Margaret Glover, Rusape, 2 March 1981.
With Maynard Makoni, Makoni, 2 March 1981.
With Sister Clara (Phillida Madani), 6 March 1981.
With James Makoni, 8 March 1981.
With Miss Needmore Ndhlovu (Comrade Believe), Old Umtali, 9 March 1981.
With Father Peter Turner, Umtali, 14 March 1981.
With Solomon Chavunduka, Harare, 16 March 1981.
With Maurice Nyagumbo, Harare, 17 March 1981.
With Father Conrad Answenger, Macheke, 17 March 1981.

With Sylvester Zwidzidzayi Mudzimuremba, Rugoyi, 22 March 1981.
With Amos Waretsa, Toriro, 23 March 1981.
With Stephen Matewa, Toriro, 23 March 1981.
With Malachia Chapurendima, Toriro, 24 March 1981.
With Headman Gova Mpambawhale, Toriro, 24 March 1981.
With Amon Shonge, Weya, 25 March 1981.
With Samson Mukambachaza, Katsanzira, Makoni, 28 March 1981.
With P.M. Chakanyuka, Harare, 29 March 1981.
With Chad Chipunza, Harare, 2 April 1981.
With Moven Mahachi, Harare, 7 April 1981.
With Maurice Nyagumbo, Harare, 11 April 1981.
With Happiness Chawandamira, Harare, 19 August 1982.
With Didymus Mutasa, Harare, 20 August 1982.
With District Administrator, Marondera, 28 August 1982.
With Caston Makoni (Comrade Revenge), Shandisai Pfungwa, 28 August 1982.
With Maurice Nyagumbo, Harare, 11 September 1982.
With Peter Chadwandamira, Manchester, 24 August 1983.

Interviews carried out by Peter Moda Chakanyuka

With Manyukire Gorembeu, Nedewedzo, 4 January 1981.
With Mapani Magadza Rinah Gertrude, Nedewedzo, 9 January 1981.
With Takapera Moda Chakanyuka, Nedewedzo, 16 January 1981.
With Mbidzeni Luciah, 18 January 1981.
With Mandironda Beatrice, Nedewedzo, 1 February 1981.
With Mavengeni Annah, Nedewedzo, 8 February 1981.
With Mhondiwa Remus Rungodo, Nedewedzo, 30 January 1981.

Interviews carried out by Sister Emilia Chiteka

With Bepas Manyoka Chiro, Chewa Village, 4 January 1981.
With Denis Tahusarira Name, Mawango village, 11 January 1981.
With Mrs John Mugura, Chitsanza village, 23 January 1981.
With Laura Mandienga Manjoro, Manjoro kraal, 25 January 1981.
With Rosemary Uraryayi Raza, Triashill clinic, 30 January 1981.
With Maria Rosa Gumisai Chimbandidza, Mawango village, 12 February 1981.
With Andreas Makandiona Manjoro, Triashill Farm, 14 February 1981.
With Ermentia Majakira, Madziva village, 19 February 1981.
With Bruno Zvekutamba Nyamutswa, Madziva village, 20 February 1981.
With Isidore Nyamusamba, Rusape, 21 February 1981.
With Agnes Manhide, Triashill Farm, 25 February 1981.

Speech recorded by Kees Maxey

Campaign speech for ZANU/PF by Davis Mugabe in Munyikwa TTL, Gutu, during the 1980 election campaign, recorded by Kees Maxey, translated by Eustacius Valisai.

SECONDARY SOURCES

BOOKS, REPORTS, OFFICIAL PUBLICATIONS, ETC.

Abrams, P.D., *Kenya's Land Resettlement Story* (Nairobi: Challenge Publishers, 1979).

Atieno-Odhiambo, E.S., *The Paradox of Collaboration and Other Essays* (Nairobi: East African Literature Bureau, 1974).

Bak, Janos and Benecke, Gerhard (eds), *Religion and Rural Revolt* 'Manchester: Manchester University Press, 1984).

Barnett, D.L., *Peasant Types and Revolutionary Potential in Colonial Africa* (Richmond: Liberation Support Movement, 1973).

Barnett, D.L. and Njama, K., *Mau Mau from within: Autobiography and Analysis on Kenya's Peasant Revolt* (New York: Monthly Review Press, 1966).

Bhebe, N., *Christianity and Traditional Religion in Western Zimbabwe, 1859-1923* (London: Longman, 1979).

Bhila, H.H.K., *Trade and Politics in a Shona Kingdom. The Manyika and their Portuguese and African Neighbours*, 1575-1902 (London: Longman, 1982).

Buijtenhuijs, Robert, *Le Mouvement 'Mau Mau'* (The Hague: Mouton, 1971).

Buijtenhuis, Robert, *Mau Mau Twenty Years After* (The Hague: Mouton, 1971).

Buijtenhuijs, Robert, *Essays on Mau Mau* (Leiden: African Studies Centre, Research Report No. 17, 1982).

Callear, Diana, *The Social and Cultural Factors Involved in Production by Small Farmers in Wedza Communal Area, Zimbabwe, of Maize and its Marketing* (Paris: UNESCO, 1982).

Caute, David, *Under the Skin. The Death of White Rhodesia* (London: Allen Lane, 1983.)

Chater, Patricia, *Grass Roots. The Story of St Faith's Farm* (London: Hodder & Stoughton, 1962).

Chater Patricia, *Caught in the Cross-fire* (Harare: Zimbabwe Publishing House, 1984).

Clayton, A., *Counter Insurgency in Kenya, 1952-1960* (Nairobi: Transafrica, 1975).

Cornwall, Barbara, *The Bush Rebels. A Personal Account of Black Revolt in Africa* (London: Deutsch, 1972).

Davidson, Basil, *Africa in Modern History. The Search for a New Society* (London: Longman, 1978).

Davidson, Basil, *The People's Cause. A History of Guerrillas in Africa* (London: Longman, 1981).

de Braganca, Aquino and others, *Zimbabwe. Notes and Reflections on the Rhodesia Question* (Maputo: University of Eduardo Mondlane, July 1977).

Dickinson, H. (ed.), *Mozambique* (Edinburgh: University of Edinburgh, Centre of African Studies, 1979).

Dillon-Malone, C.M., *The Korsten Basket Makers. A study of the Masowe Apostles, an Indigenous African Religious Movement* (Manchester: Manchester University Press, 1978).

Dumbutshena, Enoch, *Zimbabwe Tragedy* (Nairobi: East Africa Publishing House, 1975).

Dunlop, H., *The Development of European Agriculture in Rhodesia, 1945-1965* (Salisbury: University of Rhodesia, 1971).

First, Ruth et al., *The Mozambiquan Miner. A Study in the Export of Labour* (Maputo: IICM, 1977).

Frederikse, Julie, *None But Ourselves. Masses vs. Media in the Making of Zimbabwe* (Johannesburg: Ravan, 1982; Harare: Zimbabwe Publishing House, 1983; London: Heinemann, 1984).

Fry, Peter, *Spirits of Protest. Spirit-mediums and the Articulation of Consensus amongst the Zezuru of Southern Rhodesia (Zimbabwe)* (Cambridge: Cambridge University Press, 1976).

Gann, L.H., and Henriksen, T.H., *The Struggle for Zimbabwe. Battle in the Bush* (New York: Praeger, 1981).

Gelfand, Michael, *The Spiritual Beliefs of the Shona* (Gwelo: Mambo, 1977).

Gjerstad, Ole, *The Organizer. Story of Temba Moyo* (Richmond: LSM, 1974).

Geschiere, Peter, *Village Communities and the State. Changing Relations among the Maka of Southeastern Cameroon since the Colonial Conquest* (London: Kegan Paul International, 1982).

Hodder-Williams, Richard, *White Farmers in Rhodesia, 1890-1965. A History of the Marandellas District* (London: Macmillan, 1983).

Isaacman Allen, *The Tradition of Resistance in Mozambique, 1850-1921* (London: Heinemann, 1976).

Kadhani, M. and Zimunya, M., *And Now the Poets Speak* (Gwelo: Mambo, 1981).

Keyter, C.F., *Maize Control in Southern Rhodesia, 1931 — 1941. The African contribution to white survival* (Salisbury: Historical Association, 1978).

Kitching, Gavin, *Class and Economic Change in Kenya. The Making of an African Petite-Bourgeoisie* (New Haven and London: Yale University Press, 1980).

Klein, M.A., (ed.), *Peasants in Africa. Historical and Contemporary Perspectives* (London: Sage, 1980).

Lamb, G., *Peasant Politics. Conflict and Development in Muranga* (Lewes: Julian Friedman, 1974).

Linden, I, *The Catholic Church and the struggle for Zimbabwe* (London: Longman, 1980).

Made, Stan, *Made in Zimbabwe* (Gwelo: Mambo, 1980).

Martin, David and Johnson, Phyllis, *The Struggle for Zimbabwe. The Chimurenga War* (London: Faber, 1981).

Mondlane, E., *The Struggle for Mozambique* (London: Penguin, 1969).

Munslow, B., *Mozambique: the Revolution and its Origins* (London: Longman, 1983).

Muzorewa, Bishop Abel, *Rise Up and Walk. An Autobiography* (London: Evans Bros, 1978).

Newman, J.R., *The Ukamba Members Association* (Nairobi: Transafrica, 1974).

Nyagumbo, Maurice, *With the People. An Autobiography from the Zimbabwe Struggle* (London: Allison & Busby, 1980).

N'yongo'o, P.A. (ed.), *Kenya. The Agrarian Question (Special Issue, Review of African Political Economy*, 20, January/April 1981).

Ochieng, W.R. and Janmohammed, K.K., (eds), *Some Perspectives on the Mau Mau Movement* (Nairobi, Kenya Literature Bureau, 1977).

Palmer, R. and Parsons, N. (eds), *The Roots of Rural Poverty in Central and Southern Africa* (London: Heinemann, 1977).

Palmer, R., *Land and Racial Discrimination in Rhodesia* (London: Heinemann, 1977).

Past and Present Society, *Agrarian Unrest in British and French Africa, British India and French Indo-China* (Oxford: Past and Present, 1982).

Peel, J.D.Y. and Ranger, T.O. (eds), *Past and Present in Zimbabwe* (Manchester: Manchester University Press, 1983).

Raeburn, Michael, *Black Fire. Accounts of the Guerrilla War in Rhodesia* (London: Julian Friedmann, 1978).

Ranger, Terence, *The African Voice in Southern Rhodesia 1898 – 1930* (London: Heinemann, 1970).

Ranger, Terence and Weller, John, *Themes in the Christian History of Central Africa* (London: Heinemann, 1975).

Rosberg, Carl G. and Callaghy, Thomas M. (eds), *Socialism in Sub-Saharan Africa. A New Assessment* (Berkeley: University of California Press, 1978).

Saul, John, *The State and Revolution in Eastern Africa* (London: Heinemann, 1979).

Schofeleers, Matthew and van Binsbergen, Wim (eds), *The Social Science of African Religion* (London: Routledge & Kegan Paul, forthcoming).

Shamuyaria, N. (ed.), *Essays on the liberation of Southern Africa* (Dar es Salaam: Tanzania Publishing House, 1972).

Sheils, W.J. (ed.), *The Church and War* (Oxford: Blackwell, studies in Church History, vol. 20, 1983).

Sorrenson, M.P.K., *Land Reform in the Kikuyu Country: A Study in Government Policy* (London: Oxford University Press, 1967).

Stichter, Sharon, *Migrant Labour in Kenya. Capitalism and African Response, 1895 – 1975* (London: Longman, 1982).

Stoneman, Colin (ed.), *Zimbabwe's Inheritance* (London: Macmillan, 1981).

Vail, L. and White, L., *Capitalism and Colonialism in Mozambique. A Study of Quelimane District* (London: Heinemann, 1980).

Vambe, Lawrence, *From Rhodesia to Zimbabwe* (London: Heinemann, 1976).

van Onselen, Charles, *Chibaro. African Mine Labour in Southern Rhodesia* (London: Pluto Press, 1976).

Wasserman, G., *Politics of Decolonisation. Kenya Europeans and the Land*

Issue, 1960 – 1965 (Cambridge: Cambridge University Press, 1976).

Weinrich, A.K.H., *Black and White Elites in Rural Rhodesia* (Manchester: Manchester University Press, 1973).

Weinrich, A.K.H., *African Farmers in Rhodesia. Old and New Peasant Communities in Karangaland* (London: Oxford University Press, 1975).

Weinrich, A.K.H., *Struggle for the Land. A History of Co-operatives in Zimbabwe* (Harare: Zimbabwe Publishing House, forthcoming).

Wiley, David and Isaacman, Allen (eds), *Southern Africa: Society, Economy and Liberation* (East Lansing: Michigan State, 1981).

Zachrisson, Per, *An African Area in Change. Belingwe 1894-1946* (Gothenburg: University of Gothenburg, 1978).

Zimbabwe, *Report of the Commission of Inquiry into Incomes, Prices and Conditions of Service* (Harare: Government Printer, 1981).

Zimbabwe Project, *Stories and Poems from the Struggle* (Harare: Zimbabwe Project, 1982).

ARTICLES AND CHAPTERS IN BOOKS

Alpers, E.A., 'Ethnicity, Politics and History in Mozambique', *Africa Today*, vol. 21, no. 4 (fall 1974), pp. 39–52.

Alpers, E.A., 'The struggle for socialism in Mozambique, 1960-1972', in Carl G. Rosberg and Thomas M. Callaghy (eds), *Socialism in Sub-Saharan Africa. A New Assessment* (Berkeley; University of California Press, 1978), pp. 267-95.

Anon, 'Southern Africa: a smuggled account from a guerrilla fighter', *Ramparts*, vol. 8, no. 4 (October 1969), pp. 8-18.

Aylen, Douglas, 'Conserving soil in the native reserve', *Rhodesian Agricultural Journal*, vol. 39 (May/June 1942), pp. 152–60.

Beinart, W., 'Conflict in Qumbu: Rural Consciousness, Ethnicity and Violence', *Journal of Southern African Studies*, vol. 8, no. 1 (October 1981), pp. 94-122.

Beinart, W. and Bundy, Colin, 'Rural Political Movements in South Africa', in Past and Present Society, *Agrarian Unrest* (Oxford: Past and Present, 1982), pp. 1-24.

Bratton, Michael, 'Settler State, Guerrilla War and Rural Underdevelopment in Rhodesia', *Rural Africana*, nos. 4/5 (spring/fall 1979), pp. 115-29.

Bratton, Michael, 'Structural transformation in Zimbabwe: some comparative notes from the neo-colonization in Kenya', in David Wiley and Allen Isaacman (eds), *Southern Africa: Society, Economy and Liberation* (East Lansing: Michigan State, 1981), pp. 83–102.

Caute, David, 'The politics of rough justice', *New Statesman*, 16 April 1982, pp. 12-13.

Cliffe, Lionel, Mpofu, Joshua and Munslow, Barry, 'Nationalist politics in Zimbabwe: the 1980 elections and beyond', *Review of African Political Economy*, no. 18, (May/August 1980), pp. 44-67.

Coquery-Vidrovitch, Catherine, 'Peasant unrest in Black Africa', in Past and Present Society, *Agrarian Unrest* (Oxford: Past and Present, 1982), pp. 1-36.

Cooper, F., 'Peasants, Capitalists and Historians: Review Article', *Journal of Southern African Studies*, vol. 7, no. 2 (April 1981), pp. 284-314.

Duggan, William, 'The Native Land Husbandry Act of 1951 and the rural African middle class of Southern Rhodesia', *African Affairs,* vol. 79, no. 315 (April 1980), pp. 227-39.

Furedi, F., 'The Social Composition of the Mau Mau Movement in the White Highlands', *Journal of Peasant Studies*, vol. 1, no. 4, (July 1974), pp. 486-505.

Greenfield Richard, 'No Mau Mau in Rhodesia', *Legon Observer*, vol. 2, nos 12 and 13 (June/July 1967), not paginated.

Isaacman, Allen, 'Social Banditry in Zimbabwe (Rhodesia) and Mozambique, 1894-1907: An Expression of Early Peasant Protest', *Journal of Southern African Studies*, vol. 4, no. 1 (October 1977), pp. 1–30.

Isaacman, Allen, 'Transforming Mozambique's Rural Economy', *Issue*, vol. 8, no. 1. (1978), pp. 17–24.

Isaacman, Allen, Stephen, Michael, Adam Yussuf, Homem, Maria Joao, Macamo, Eugenio and Pililao, Augustine, ' "Cotton is the mother of poverty": peasant resistance to forced cotton production in Mozambique, 1938 – 1961', *International Journal of African Historical Studies* vol. 13, no. 4 (1980), pp. 581–615.

Keller, E., 'A Twentieth Century Model: the Mau Mau Transformation from Social Banditry to Social Rebellion', *Kenya Historical Review*, vol. 1, no. 2 (1973), pp. 189–206.

Kinsey, B.H., 'Forever gained: resettlement and land policy in the context of national development in Zimbabwe', in J.D.Y. Peel and Terence Ranger (eds), *Past and Present in Zimbabwe* (Manchester: Manchester University Press, 1983), pp. 92–113.

Kitching, Gavin, 'Capitalism and Colonialism in Mozambique: Review Article', *Journal of Southern African Studies,* vol. 9, no. 2 (April 1983), pp. 258–63.

Lonsdale, J.M., 'A state of agrarian unrest: colonial Kenya', in Past and Present Society, *Agrarian Unrest* (Oxford: Past and Present, 1982), pp. 1–8.

Liberation Support Movement, *Zimbabwe. The Final Advance. Documents on the Zimbabwe Liberation Movements* (Oakland: LSM, 1978).

McCracken, J., 'Planters, Peasants and the Colonial State', *Journal of Southern African Studies*, vol, 9, no. 2 (April 1983), pp. 172–92.

Madziyire, S.K., 'Heathen practices in the urban and rural parts of Marandellas area and their effects upon Christianity', in Terence Ranger and John Weller (eds), *Themes in the Christian History of Central Africa* (London: Heinemann, 1975), pp. 76–82.

Mashingaidze, E., 'Christianity and the Mhondoro Cult', *Mohlomi*, vol. 1 (1976), pp. 71–87.

Meyns, P., 'Liberation Ideology and National Development Strategy in Mozambique', *Review of African Political Economy*, no. 21 (May/ September 1981), pp. 42–64.

Mosley, Paul, 'Kenya in the 1970s', *African Affairs*, vol. 81, no. 323 (April 1982) pp. 271–7.

Mosley, Paul, 'Agricultural development and government policy in settler economies: the case of Kenya and Southern Rhodesia, 1900–1960', *Economic History Review*, vol. 35, no. 3 (August 1982), pp. 390–408.

Munslow, Barry, 'Zimbabwe's emerging African Bourgeoisie', *Review of African Political Economy*, no. 19 (Sept/December 1980), pp. 63–9.

Murisi, J.W., 'The history of class consciousness in Zimbabwe', in *Report. Zimbabwe Conference. A Study of the Current Situation and Long-term Development Problems* (The Hague: October 1979), pp. 23–6.

Murray, Martin, 'Agrarian Social Stratification and Rural Class Relations', *Rural Africana*, nos. 4/5 (Spring/Fall 1979), pp. 83–96.

Museveni, Y.T., 'Fanon's theory of violence: its verification in liberated Mozambique', in N. Shamuyarira (ed.), *Essays on the Liberation of Southern Africa* (Dar es Salaam: Tanzania Publishing House, 1972), pp. 1–24.

Ogot, B.A., 'Revolt of the Elders: An anatomy of the Loyalist Crowd in the Mau Mau Uprising, 1952–1956', *Hadith, 4. Politics and Nationalism in Colonial Kenya* (Nairobi: East African Publishing House, 1972), pp. 134–48.

Palmer, Robin, 'The agricultural history of Rhodesia', in Robin Palmer and Neil Parsons (eds), *The Roots of Rural Poverty in Central and Southern Africa* (London: Heinemann, 1977), pp. 221–53.

Phimister, Ian, 'Peasant Production and Under-development in Southern Rhodesia', *African Affairs,* 13 (1974), pp. 217–25.

'Pasi ne class struggle? The new history for schools in Zimbabwe', *History in Africa* (forthcoming).

Pollak, Oliver, 'Black farmers and white politics in Rhodesia', *African Affairs* vol. 74, no. 296 (July 1975), pp. 263–277.

Ranger, Terence, 'The People in African Resistance: a review', *Journal of Southern African Studies*, vol. 4, no. 1 (October 1977), pp. 125–146.

Ranger, Terence, 'Guerrilla War and Peasant Violence: Makoni District, Zimbabwe', *Political Violence*, Institute of Commonwealth Studies, London, Collected Seminar Papers, no. 30 (1982), pp. 100–123.

Ranger, Terence, 'Growing from the roots: reflections on peasant research in Central and Southern Africa', *Journal of Southern African Studies*, vol. 5, no. 1 (October 1978), pp. 99–133.

Ranger, Terence, 'The death of Chaminuka: spirit mediums, nationalism and the guerrilla war in Zimbabwe', *African Affairs*, vol. 81, no. 324 (July 1982), pp. 349–369.

Ranger, Terence, 'Literature and political economy: Arthur Shearly Cripps and the Makoni labour crisis of 1911', *Journal of Southern African Studies,* vol. 9, no. 1 (October 1982), pp. 33–53.

Ranger, Terence, 'Tradition and Travesty: chiefs and the administration in Makoni District, Zimbabwe, 1960–1980', *Africa*, vol. 52 no. 3 (1982), pp. 20–41.

Ranger, Terence, 'Revolutions in the wheel of Zimbabwean history', *Moto*, vol. 1, no. 8 (December 1982).

Ranger, Terence, 'Holy men and rural communities in Zimbabwe, 1970–

1980', in W.J. Sheils (ed.), *The Church and War* (Oxford: Blackwell, 1983), pp. 443–61.

Ranger, Terence, 'Religions and rural protest: Makoni District, Zimbabwe, 1900 to 1980', in Janos Bak and Gerhard Benecke (eds), *Religion and Rural Revolt* (Manchester: Manchester University Press, 1984).

Ranger, Terence, 'Religious studies and political economy: the Mwari cult and the peasant experience in Southern Rhodesia', in Matthew Schoffeleers and Wim van Binsbergen (eds), *The Social Science of African Religion* (London: Routledge & Kegan Paul, forthcoming).

Rennie, K., 'White Farmers, Black Tenants and Landlord Legislation: Southern Rhodesia, 1890–1930', *Journal of Southern African Studies,* vol. 5, no. 1 (October 1978), pp. 86–98.

Riddell, R., 'Prospects for Land Reform in Zimbabwe', *Rural Africana,* nos. 4/5 (Spring/Fall 1979), pp. 17–32.

Saul, J.S., 'Transforming the struggle in Zimbabwe', in John Saul, *The State and Revolution in Eastern Africa* (London: Heinemann, 1979), pp. 107–122.

Truscott, Kate and Pambieri, N.C., 'Census Survey of Chiweshe ward (Buhera). Preliminary report' (Harare: Agritex, 1983).

Truscott, Kate and Pambieri, N.C. 'Wedza baseline study. Summary and analysis. Wedza evaluation No. 1' (Harare: Agritex, January 1983).

Tsomondo, M.S., 'The Zionist and the Apostolic Prophetic Churches in Zimbabwe. A critical conceptualization of Cultural Nationalism', *Ufahamu,* vol. 6, no. 3 (1973), pp. 3–29.

Vail, L. and White, L., 'Plantation Protest: the History of a Mozambiquan Song', *Journal of Southern African Studies,* vol. 5, no. 1 (October 1978), pp. 1–25.

Vail, L and White, L., 'Tawane Machambero: Forced Rice and Cotton Cultivation on the lower Zambezi', *Journal of African History,* vol. 19, no. 2, (1978), pp. 293–63.

Vail, L, and White, L. 'The Art of Being Ruled: Ndebele Praise Poetry, 1835–1971', in T. Couzens and L. White (eds), *Literature and Society in Southern Africa* (London: Longman, forthcoming).

van Onselen, Charles, 'Worker consciousness in black miners: Southern Rhodesia, 1900–1920', *Journal of African History,* vol. 14, no. 2 (1973), pp. 237–55.

van Onselen, Charles and Phimister, I., 'The political economy of tribal animosity: a case study of the 1929 Bulawayo Location "faction fight" ', *Journal of Southern African Studies,* vol. 6, no. 1 (October 1979), pp. 1–43.

Wasserman, G., 'The economic transition to Zimbabwe', *Africa Report* (November/December 1978), pp. 39–45.

Weinrich, A.K.H., 'Strategic Resettlement in Rhodesia', *Journal of Southern African Studies,* vol. 3, no. 2 (April 1977), pp. 207–229.

Wield, David, 'Mine labour and peasant production in southern Mozambique', in H. Dickinson (ed.), *Mozambique* (Edinburgh: University of Edinburgh, Centre of African Studies, 1979), pp. 78–85.

Williams, Gavin, 'Equity, growth and the state', in J.D.Y. Peel and Terence Ranger (eds), *Past and Present in Zimbabwe* (Manchester: Manchester University Press, 1983), pp. 114–120.
Yates, Peter, 'The prospects for a socialist transition in Zimbabwe', *Review of African Political Economy*, no. 18 (May/August 1980), pp. 68–88.

SEMINAR PAPERS, THESES AND UNPUBLISHED MANUSCRIPTS

Alpers, E.A., 'To seek a better life: the implications of migration from Northern Mozambique to colonial and independent Tanzania for class formation and political behaviour in the struggle to liberate Mozambique', paper presented at Conference on 'The Class Base of Nationalist Movements in Angola, Guinea- Bissau and Mozambique', Minneapolis, May 1983.
Alvord, E.D., 'Development of native agriculture and land tenure in Southern Rhodesia', unpublished ms., 1958.
Anon, 'Chiendambuya – East Mupuru: experiences of the guerrilla war', unpublished ms., in possession of the author, 1981.
Beinart, W., 'Soil erosion, Conservationism and Ideas about Development; a Southern African Exploration', unpublished ms., 1984.
Brown, Sarah, 'The Ndebele, 1897–1912; aspects of religious, economic and political life in the early colonial era' (Manchester University: BA Honours thesis, 1983)
Callear, Diana, 'Who wants to be a peasant? Food production in a labour-exporting area of Zimbabwe', unpublished ms., May 1983.
Cliffe, L., 'Towards an evaluation of the Zimbabwe national movement', paper presented at Political Studies Association of the United Kingdom conference, Exter, March/April 1980.
Cliffe, L. and Munslow, B., 'The 1980 Elections in Victoria Province, Zimbabwe: An interim report', paper presented to the conference on Zimbabwe, Leeds, 1980.
Edwards, J.A., 'Southern Rhodesia, the response to adversity, 1935–1936' (University of London: PhD thesis, 1978).
England, K., 'A political economy of Black Female Labour in Zimbabwe, 1900–1980' (Manchester University: BA Honours thesis, 1982)
Isaacman, Allen, 'The Mozambiquan cotton co-operative: the creation of a grassroots alternative to forced commodity production', paper presented to the conference on Zimbabwean History: Progress and Development, University of Zimbabwe, August 1982.
Jokonya, T.J.B., 'End of the Tribal Trust Land. The effects of war on the rural population of Zimbabwe Rhodesia', University of Zimbabwe, Department of History seminar paper, 1979.
Hastings, Adrian, 'Mediums, Martyrs and Morals', Inaugural lecture, University of Zimbabwe, June 1983.
Kosmin, B.A., 'Ethnic and Commercial Relations in Southern Rhodesia. A socio-historical study of the Asian, Hellene and Jewish Populations,

1898–1943' (University of Rhodesia: PhD thesis, 1974)

Lan, David, 'Spirit mediums and the authority to resist in the struggle for Zimbabwe', paper for the Southern African seminar, Institute of Commonwealth Studies, London, 14 January 1983.

Lan, David, 'Making History. Spirit Mediums and the Guerrilla War in the Dande area of Zimbabwe' (London School of Economics: PhD thesis, 1983).

Lawson, Rosemary, 'Protest or participation? A study of Wesleyan Methodist African agents in Southern Rhodesia during the 1930s' (Manchester University: BA Honours thesis, 1982).

Lonsdale, J.M., 'How the People of Kenya Spoke for themselves, 1895–1923', paper presented to the American African Studies Association, 1976.

Lonsdale, J.M., 'The growth and transformation of the colonial state in Kenya, 1929–1952', seminar paper, Institute of Commonwealth Studies, London, 1980.

Lonsdale, J.M., 'Unhappy Valley: state and class formation in colonial Kenya' unpublished ms., February 1982.

Lonsdale, J.M., 'African elites and social classes in colonial Kenya', paper presented to the Round Table on Elites and Colonisation, Paris, July 1982.

Lunn, Jon, 'The political economy of protest: the strikes and unrest of 1948 in Southern Rhodesia' (Manchester University: BA Honours thesis, 1982).

Mandala, E.C., 'Capitalism, Ecology and Society: the Lower Tchiri Valley of Malawi, 1860–1960' (University of Minnesota: PhD., 1983).

Mashingaidze, E., 'Christian Missions in Mashonaland, Southern Rhodesia, 1890–1930' (York University: PhD thesis, 1973)

Mashingaidze, V., 'The Development of Settler Capitalist Agriculture in Southern Rhodesia, 1903–1963' (University of London: PhD thesis, 1980)

Mosley, Paul., 'The settler economies: studies in the economic history of Kenya and Southern Rhodesia, 1900–1963' (University of Cambridge: PhD., 1980)

Mpofu, J.M.M., 'The February 1980 Elections. The Matabeleland North and South Provinces', paper presented to the conference on Zimbabwe, Leeds, 1980.

Mtetwa, Richard, 'The political and economic history of the Duma people of south-eastern Rhodesia' (University of Rhodesia: PhD thesis, 1976)

Muntemba, M., 'An Economic History of Kabwe Rural District' (University of California, Los Angeles: PhD., 1977)

Munslow, Barry, 'Peasants, politics and production. The case of Mozambique', paper presented at Political Studies Association of the United Kingdom conference, Exeter, 1980.

Njonjo, A.L., 'The Africanisation of the "White Highlands": a study in agrarian class struggles in Kenya, 1950–1974' (Princeton University: PhD, 1977).

Phimister, Ian, 'Reconstruction and the rise of domestic capital, 1903–1922', and 'Compromise of the Settler State, 1923–1929', chapters in an unpublished ms., 1983.

Ranger, Terence, 'Poverty and prophetism: religious movements in the Makoni District', seminar paper, School of Oriental and African Studies, October 1981.

Ranger, Terence, 'Survival, revival and disaster: Shona traditional elites under colonialism', paper presented to the Round Table on Elites and Colonisation, Paris, July 1982.

Ranger, Terence, 'Missionaries, migrants and the Manyika: the invention of ethnicity in Zimbabwe', paper presented to the International conference on the history of ethnic awareness in Southern Africa, Charlottesville, April 1973.

Ranger, Terence, 'Religion in the Zimbabwean guerrilla war', paper presented to the History Workshop conference on Religion and Society, London, July 1983.

Rifkind, Malcolm, 'The politics of land in Rhodesia' (University of Edinburgh: MSC thesis, 1968)

Robertshaw, P., 'Irrigation in Melsetter and Chipinga: a case study in the transfer of agriculture hegemony', unpublished ms., Manchester, 1983.

Robertshaw, P., 'Introduction: The Rural Background and European occupation', unpublished paper, Manchester, 1984.

Steele, M.C., 'The challenge of Rhodesia to European Liberal thought, 1893–1953' (University of Edinburgh: M.Litt thesis, 1968)

Taylor, J.J., 'The Emergence and Development of the Native Department in Southern Rhodesia, 1894–1914' (University of London: PhD, 1974)

Thomas, N.E., 'Christianity, politics and the Manyika' (University of Boston: PhD, 1968)

Throup, D.W., 'The origins of Mau Mau', seminar paper, Institute of Commonwealth studies, London, October 1982.

Tickner, Vincent, 'Class struggles and the food supply sector in Zimbabwe', paper presented to the conference on Zimbabwe, Leeds, 1980.

Van Vulpen, Gert, 'The political economy of the African peasant agriculture in Marondera District, 1930–1950' (University of Amsterdam: doctoral thesis, 1983)

Weinrich, A.K.H., 'Agricultural Reconstruction in Zimbabwe', unpublished ms., 1977.

Woods, Roger, 'The dynamics of land settlement. Pointers from a Rhodesian land settlement scheme', unpublished paper, Dar es Salaam, December 1966.

Young, S.Y., 'Change in Diet and Production in Southern Mozambique, 1855–1960', paper presented to the African Studies of the United Kingdom conference, Durham, 1976.

INDEX
OF THEMES

Index of Themes

Railways, 29–30, 32–4, 37–8, 41, 59, 65, 95, 101, 118, 140, 231, 234

Resettlement, 3–6, 9–11, 15, 132, 227, 289, 299, 302, 307–11, 313–14, 316, 318, 332, 335–7

Self-Peasantisation, 15, 21, 26–9, 31–2, 34, 37, 40, 46–7, 92, 185

Squatters, 13, 31–3, 70, 80, 100–3, 107–9, 118, 128–9, 141, 146, 158, 198, 231, 233, 238, 285, 299–301. 303–15, 325–6, 335

Social differentiation, 4–6, 11, 13–15, 25–6, 45, 57–65, 68–72, 74–81, 83–4, 91–4, 100–2, 116, 122–3, 130, 196, Chapter 6 (especially 224, 230–1, 236, 254–8, 276, 280–1), 286, 303, 312, 319, 325–6, 333, 336–7
see also Businessmen, Christianity, Education, Native Purchase, Ploughs and ploughmen, and Stores

Spirit mediums and 'traditional religion', 14, 44–5, 90, 173, 183, 185–206, 208–15, 218–23, 292, 294–5, 331, 339–42

Stores and traders
  white traders, 27–8, 34–40, 46, 52, 54, 61, 63–4, 67, 84–5, 88–9, 94, 120, 140, 231, 250
  Indian traders, 34–5, 38–9, 250
  African traders, 15, 100, 120, 162, 196, 208, 213, 225–6, 229, 239–43, 249–51, 254, 260, 269–72, 274–5, 285–7, 295, 343

Traders *see* Stores
Tradition *see* Custom
Traditional religion *see* Spirit mediums

Urban political associations other than nationalist parties, 80–3, 101–2, 110, 112, 117–18, 120–1, 123–8, 130–1, 133–4, 316–17

Women, African, rural, 28–30, 36–7, 41, 44–6, 52, 71, 78, 91, 94–5, 143, 145–7, 163–4, 193, 206–7, 212, 214, 232, 234–6, 257–8, 263, 265, 281, 285, 292, 328, 330

Worker consciousness, 26–7, 31, 82–3, 99–101, 123, 131
  see also Migrant labour

INDEX
OF NAMES
AND PLACES

Index of Names and Places

Mosley, Paul, African agricultural prosperity, 67–8; land policies, 58; Maize Control, 62, 67; Rhodesian agricultural economy, 59; Rhodesian entrepreneurs, 70

Moyo, Shoniwa Masedza Tandi, 89–90

Mozambique, Catholic church, 339; comparison with Zimbabwe, 47; cotton, 24, 55–6, 224–6; FRELIMO, 21, 24, 223; guerrillas, 6–8 *passim*, 178, 204, 207, 262, 264, 268; intellectuals, 179; local petty bourgeouisie, 226; migrant workers from, 286, 287; nationalism, 2; peasantry of central and southern, 25; peasantry of northern, 21–5, 184; reactions to forced cultivation of cotton, 78–9; rural entrepreneurs and guerrilla war, 227; spirit mediums, 223; ZANU radicalism, 268–9

Mpofu, Joshua, ZANLA guerrillas, 216

Mrewa District, ANC, 261; evicted Manyika in, 141, 232; under young chief, 245

Muchetera, spirit medium, 201

Mudzvovera, N.P., 342

Mugabe, Davis, ancestral spirits, 213–14; People's Power, 288; resettlement of white-owned farms, 288

Mugabe, Robert (*see also next entry*), 325; eviction orders, 307; guerrilla war, 180; Makoni peasants transfer allegiance to, 207; in Mozambique, 268; Nyabadza commemoration, 343; resettlement of Matabeleland, 335; support for, 137, 146; 'Voice of Zimbabwe', 273; ZANU/PF, 182; Wasserman on ZANU and, 9–10

Mugabe, Robert, government under: emergency relief, 300; farming, 290, 320; land resettlement, 299–301, 302, 305–8 *passim*, 311, 313–14, 315; new council structure, 295–7; Transitional National Development Plan, 315

Mugura, Mrs John, 286

Mukute, 321–4, 340

Munslow, Barry, African farmer employers, 237; bourgeoisie, 5–6; land resettlement, 310, 315; Mozambique cotton economy, 56; ZANLA guerrillas, 216

Murango, 65

Murisi, J.W., Zimbabwean class/ national struggle, 228–9

Museveni, Yoweri, cleansing effect of revolution, 184

Mushonga, Paul, 248

Mutasa, Didymus, 246, 290

Mutasa, John, ANC, 154, 248, 253, 297–8; detained, 243; importance of educated Africans, 248; Makoni Students Association, 246; militancy at Tanda, 157; Muzorewa, 263; nationalism in Makoni, 155; peasant discontent, 156; ZANU and ZAPU, 160

Muzorewa, Abel, 236; ANC, 258, 260–65 *passim*; Auxiliaries, 273–4; Brock on, 259; Davis Mugabe on, 214; decolonization, 3; education, 235; eviction of his family, 64–5; future of Zimbabwe, 9; government under, 273, 274; Internal Settlement of 1978, 273; supporters of, 215; Tekere on, 268; ZANU, 268

Muzorewa, Haadi Philemon, history, 65, 233; achievements in face of white domination, 259

Name, Denis Tahusarira, influence of spirit mediums, 193

Ndebele people, agriculture, 45–6; agricultural economy, 55, 56; plight of, 337; raids by, 31; support for guerrillas, 137; support Nkomo, 216

Nedewedzo, peasant radicalism, 249; political transitions, 262–3; spirit mediums, 202; ZAPU detainees, 161, 242

Nengomasha, Amon, on Johana Masowe, 89

Nehanda, Mbuya, 204–5

Newman, J.R., Kamba protest movement and its consequences, 79–80

Njelele, 216

Nkomo, Joshua, 160; and future of Zimbabwe, 9, 10; Ndebele support, 216; Tekere on, 268, 269

Nyabadza, Basil, aids guerrillas, 269–70; commemorated, 343; death of, 270; Native Department, 251

Nyabadza, Francis junior, 343

Nyabadza, Francis senior, 272, 343

Nyabadza, Rosemary, 270–71

Nyagumbo, Maurice, peasant

discount, 156; radical nationalism, 242; shopkeeper, 241–2; 'trained boys with weapons', 211; ZANU, 160, 242–3
Nyahwa, 66
Nyamusamba, Michael Jack, history, 240–241; prestige, 242, 243
Nyamusamba, Isidore, and guerrillas, 242, 271; history, 241, 242
Nyanza, 57
Nyasaland, 24

O'Hea, Father Jerome, native cowardice, 209; unrest among Manyikas, 82
O'Keefe, Phil, land resettlement, 310, 315
Old Umtali, 65
Onselen, Charles van, 'worker consciousness', 26
Oosthuizen, Nicholas, 305–6

Palmer, Robin, 58; agricultural economy by end of 1930s, 54–5
Phayre, Native Commissioner, centralization, 72, 73, 78; contour ridging, 86–7; peasant resistance to Land Apportionment, 87; uneasiness in Makoni, 78
Phimister, Ian, proletarianization, 54; struggle against capital and state, 48
Pollack, Oliver, AFU, 238; Native Purchase Area scheme, 76, 77, 237
Pope, H. Barnes, 304; peasant strategies of land settlement, 33–4; remembered, 48, 198; undercutting of peasant production, 234

Rathcline, 141, 300, 308
Rhodesia, attitude to African entrepreneurs, 68; 1930s, 80–81; peasant consciousness matures, 84; settler control of, 66–8; White Rhodesians and the Depression, 66
Robertshaw, Philip, rural change, 76
Rukadza, Diki, 191
Rungodo, Mhondiwa Remus, businessman, 241; land problem, 301; national activist, 157–8, 242; political transitions in Newedzo, 262–3
Rusape, administrative archives, 292–3; agriculture, 144; ANC, 155, 248; CID camp, 272; evictions, 169; maze

production, 64; squatters, 326; trade, 37, 65, 234, 237, ZANU, 160, 293

St Faith's, co-operative farm, 154, 250, 321; detainees taken, 243; Discussion Group, 247–8, 252; guerrilla stronghold, 215; influence of, 321
St Francis, 207; Selous Scouts, 270; Nyabadza commemorated, 343
Salazar, Antonio de Oliviera, 55–6
Salisbury, 82, 207
Saul, John, 10; Zimbabwean guerrilla and nationalist movements, 7–8, 11
Seke Reserve, 61
Sekeramayi, Sydney, squatters, 307, 312
Shona people, agricultural economy, 55, 56; 'collective farming', 267; conformists, 65; mutual aid, 191; political ideals, 137–8; spirit mediums, 188–9
Shonge, Amon, anti-guerrilla operations, 181; causes of peasant disaffection, 154, 317; communal farming, 178; conservation committee chairman, 298–9; encourages subversion, 163–4; guerrilla war, 182; guerrillas in Weya, 168, 322; land, 302; Mukute rural cooperative, 322–4; political transitions, 262; spirit mediums, 212, 340; squatters, 311, 312, 313; ZAPU, 160, 163
Shonge, Elizabeth, 322
Sirewu, Makoni entrepreneur, 63
Smith, Ian, Brock on, 259
Stead, W.H., fears for future, 146; Native Purchase scheme, 249; prosecution of entrepreneurs, 74; soil conservation, 142
Stichter, Sharon, 'worker consciousness', 26–7

Tadokera, Abel, appeal by, 165–6
Tanda, ANC, 157; businessmen, 250; clashes with government, 157; communal production, 324; conservation enforcement frustrated, 168; disaffection, 150, 152–5 *passim*, 159, 284–5, 294; ecological threat, 152; evictions, 285, 306; guerrilla war, 171, 181, 182; land, 305; Land Apportionment Act, 141, 146–50, 233; National Democratic Party, 157; peasant radicalism, 189, 249;